Be Fruitful and Multiply

Be Fruitful and Multiply

A Crux of Thematic Repetition in Genesis 1–11

ANDREW J. SCHMUTZER

WIPF & STOCK · Eugene, Oregon

BE FRUITFUL AND MULTIPLY
A Crux of Thematic Repetition in Genesis 1–11

Copyright © 2009 Andrew J. Schmutzer. All rights reserved. Except for brief quotations in critical publications or reviews, no part of this book may be reproduced in any manner without prior written permission from the publisher. Write: Permissions, Wipf and Stock Publishers, 199 W. 8th Ave., Suite 3, Eugene, OR 97401.

Wipf & Stock
An imprint of Wipf and Stock Publishers
199 W. 8th Ave., Suite 3
Eugene, OR 97401

www.wipfandstock.com

ISBN 13: 978-1-60608-440-3

Manufactured in the U.S.A.

Dedicated to:

Ashley ~
Thank you for believing in me,
even when I didn't.

Zöe ~
Your love of language
helped bring this revision to life.
Write on, read on.

Cody ~
Your timely assistance
was invaluable.

Contents

List of Figures / ix

List of Abbreviations / xi

1. Introduction / 1
2. Approaches to Genesis 1–11 / 23
3. Semantic and Literary Analysis of Mandate Terms / 61
4. Exegetical Analysis of the Mandate in Genesis 1–11 / 89
5. Themes, Image of God, and Gender in Genesis 1–11 / 159
6. Key Currents in the History of Interpretation / 205
7. Conclusion / 226

   Appendix A: The Rhetorical Structure of Genesis 1:1—2:3 / 231

   Bibliography / 233

Figures

Figure 1: Genesis 1:22 / 90

Figure 2: Genesis 1:28 / 95

Figure 3: Shared Structure in 1:22 and 1:28 / 97

Figure 4: Genesis 8:17 / 126

Figure 5: Genesis 9:1 / 140

Figure 6: Genesis 9:7 / 151

Figure 7: Genesis 1:26–28 / 180

Abbreviations

AB	Anchor Bible
ABD	Anchor Bible Dictionary
Akk	Akkadian
AnBib	Analecta Biblica
ANE	Ancient Near East(ern)
Aq	Aquila's Greek translation of the Old Testament
Arab	Arabic
Aram	Aramaic
ATSDS	Adventist Theological Society Dissertation Series
AUSS	*Andrews University Seminary Studies*
BA	*Biblical Archaeologist*
BDF	Blass-Debrunner-Funk
BETL	Bibliotheca Ephemeridum Theologicarum Lovaniensium
BBR	*Bulletin for Biblical Research*
BDB	Brown, F., S. R. Driver, and C. A. Briggs. *A Hebrew and English Lexicon of the Old Testament.*
Berkeley	The Holy Bible: The New Berkeley Version in Modern English
BHK	*Biblia Hebraica.* Ed. R. Kittel Stuttgartiae.
BHS	*Biblica Hebraica Stutgartensia.* Ed. K. Elliger and W. Rudolf.
BHQ	*Biblica Hebraica Quinta.* Fascicle 18: General Introduction and Megilloth
Bib	*Biblica*
BibInt	*Biblical Interpretation*

Abbreviations

BR	Biblical Research
BSac	*Bibliotheca Sacra*
BZAW	*Beihefte zur Zeitschrift für die alttestamentliche Wissenschaft*
C	Cairo Geniza (Fragments)
CBQ	Catholic Biblical Quarterly
CC	Continental Commentary
cf.	*confer*, compare
ch(s)	chapter(s)
Col	column
consec.	Consecutive
const.	Construct
Contra	in contrast to; against
COS	*The Context of Scripture*
Crux	*Crux*
CSR	*Christian Scholar's Review*
CTQ	*Condordia Theological Quarterly*
DCH	*Dictionary of Classical Hebrew*. Ed. D. J. A. Clines.
diss.	Dissertation
DOTP	*Dictionary of the Old Testament: Pentateuch*. Ed. T. D. Alexander and D. W. Baker.
DSS	Dead Sea Scrolls
EBC	Encountering Biblical Studies
EBS	The Expositor's Bible Commentary
ECDSS	Eerdmans Commentaries on the Dead Sea Scrolls
ed(s)	editor(s), edited by
edn.	Edition
e.g.	*exempli gratia*, for example
E-H	Epigenetic-Historical
ERT	*Evangelical Review of Theology*
ESV	English Standard Version

Abbreviations

et. al.	*et alii*, and others
Even-Shoshan	Even-Shoshan, A. (ed.). *A New Concordance of the Bible*.
EvQ	*Evangelical Quarterly*
ExAud	*Ex auditu*
FCB	Feminist Companion to the Bible
f./fem.	Feminine
FOTL	Forms of the Old Testament Literature
Frg. Tg.	*Fragmentary Targum*
FRLANT	Forschungen zur Religion und Literatur des Alten und Neuen Testaments
GBS	Guides to Biblical Scholarship
GBHS	*A Guide to Biblical Hebrew Syntax*
GELS	*Greek-English Lexicon of the Septuagint: Chiefly of the Pentateuch and the Twelve Prophets*
Gib	Gibson, J. C. L., *Davidson's Introductory Hebrew Grammar: Syntax*
Gk	Greek
GKC	Gesenius' Hebrew Grammar. Ed. E. Kautzsch. Trans. A. E. Cowley. 2nd ed.
HALOT	Koehler, L., W. Baumgartner, and J. J. Stamm, *The Hebrew and Aramaic Lexicon of the Old Testament*. Trans. and ed. M. E. J. Richardson.
HBT	*Horizons in Biblical Theology*
HCOT	Historical Commentary on the Old Testament
HCSB	Holman Christian Standard Bible
Holladay	Holladay, W. L. (ed.). *A Concise Hebrew and Aramaic Lexicon of the Old Testament*.
HSM	Harvard Semitic Monographs
HSS	Harvard Semitic Studies
HTR	*Harvard Theological Review*

Abbreviations

IBHS	*An Introduction to Biblical Hebrew Syntax*. B. K. Waltke and M. O'Connor
Ibid.	*ibidem*, in the same place
IBT	Interpreting Biblical Texts
Idem.	the same
i.e.	*id est*, that is
imperf.	Imperfect
impv.	Imperative
inf.	Infinitive
Int	*Interpretation*
JANES	*Journal of the Ancient Near Eastern Society*
JATS	*Journal of the Adventist Theological Society*
JB	Jerusalem Bible
JBL	*Journal of Biblical Literature*
JBTh	Jahrbuch für Biblische Theologie
JETS	*Journal of the Evangelical Theological Society*
JFSR	*Journal of Feminist Studies in Religion*
JNES	*Journal of Near Eastern Studies*
JNSL	*Journal of Northwest Semitic Languages*
JOTT	*Journal of Translation and Textlinguistics*
Joüon	Joüon, P. *A Grammar of Biblical Hebrew*. Trans. and rev. T. Muraoka.
JPS	Jewish Publication Society
JQR	*Jewish Quarterly Review*
JSOT	*Journal for the Study of the Old Testament*
JSOTSup	Supplement to *Journal for the Study of the Old Testament*
JTS	*Journal of Theological Studies*
juss.	Jussive
KBL	Koehler, L., and W. Baumgartner. *Lexicon in Veteris Testamenti Libros.*
KJV	King James Version

Abbreviations

Lat	Latin
LBI	Library of Biblical Interpretation
LEH	J. Lust, E. Eynikel, and K. Hauspie. *Greek-English Lexicon of the Septuagint*. Rev. Ed.
L-I	Literary-Ideological
LXX	Septuagint
m./masc.	Masculine
MSJ	The Master's Seminary Journal
MT	Masoretic Text
n.	number
NAB	New American Bible
NAC	New American Commentary
NASB	New American Standard Bible
NEB	New English Bible
NET	New English Translation
NIBCOT	New International Biblical Commentary on the Old Testament
NICOT	New International Commentary on the Old Testament
NIDOTTE	*New International Dictionary of Old Testament Theology and Exegesis*
NIV	New International Version
NIVAC	New International Version Application Commentary
NKJV	New King James Version
NLT	New Living Translation
NLT²	New Living Translation, 2nd Ed.
NRSV	New Revised Standard Version
NSBT	New Studies in Biblical Theology
NT	New Testament
OBT	Overtures to Biblical Theology
orig.	originally
OT	Old Testament

Abbreviations

OTG	Old Testament Guides
OTL	Old Testament Library
OTS	Old Testament Studies
perf.	Perfect
pl.	Plural
Presby	*Presbyterion*
Proof	*Prooftexts: A Journal of Jewish Literary History*
PRSt	*Perspectives in Religious Studies*
PTMS	*Pittsburgh Theological Monograph Series*
PWCJS	*Proceedings of the Ninth World Congress of Jewish Studies*
QD	*Quaestiones Disputatae*
RB	*Revue Biblique*
REB	Revised English Bible
repr.	reprinted, reprinted in
rev.	revised (by)
RSV	Revised Standard Version
S	Syriac
Sam. Tg.	*Samaritan Targum*
SBL	Society of Biblical Literature
SBLDS	Society of Biblical Literature Dissertation
SBT	Studies in Biblical Theology
SBTS	Sources for Biblical and Theological Study
SCS	Septuagint and Cognate Studies
Semeia	*Semeia*
SemiaSt	*Semeia Studies*
sg.	singular
SIL	Summer Institute of Linguistics
SJOT	*Scandinavian Journal of the Old Testament*
SJT	*Scottish Journal of Theology*
SOBLSS	Society of Biblical Literature Symposium Series

Abbreviations

SP	Samaritan Pentateuch
SSN	Studia Semitica Neerlandica
SSS	Semitic Study Series
StudBib	*Studia Biblica*
Sym	Symmachus' Greek Translation of the Old Testament
TBS	Today's Biblical Studies
TDOT	*Theological Dictionary of the Old Testament*. Ed. G J. Botterweck and H. Ringgren. Trans. J. T. Willis, G. W. Bromiley, and D. E. Green.
TDNT	*Theological Dictionary of the New Testament*. Ed. G. Kittle and G. Friedrich. Tran. J. T. Willis, G. W. Bromiley, and D. E. Green.
Theod	Theodotion's Greek translation of the Old Testament
Tg. Neb.	Targum of the Prophets
Tg. Neof.	Targum Neofiti
Tg. Onq.	Targum Onqelos
Tg. Ps.-J.	Targum Pseudo-Jonathan
Them	*Themelios*
Theod	Theodotian
THS	Theological and Hermeneutical Studies
TLOT	*Theological Lexicon of the Old Testament*. Ed. E. Jenni and C. Westermann. Trans. M. E. Biddle.
TNIV	Today's New International Version
trans.	translated by
TS	*Theological Studies*
TSFBul	*Theological Student's Fellowship Bulletin*
T-T	Thematic-Theological
TWOT	*Theological Wordbook of the Old Testament*. Ed. R. L. Harris and G. L. Archer Jr.
TynBul	*Tyndale Bulletin*
V	Vulgate

van der Merwe	van der Merwe, C. H. J., J. A. Naudé, and J. H. Kroeze. *A Biblical Hebrew Reference Grammar.*
vol(s).	volume(s)
V-S-O	Verb, Subject, Object
O-V-S	Object, Verb, Subject
VT	*Vetus Testamentum*
*VT*Sup	Supplements to *Vetus Testamentum*
WBC	Word Biblical Commentary
WHS	*William's Hebrew Syntax: An Outline.* 2nd Ed.
WTJ	*Westminster Theological Journal*
WUNT	Wissenschaftliche Untersuchungen zum Neuen Testament
ZAW	*Zeitschrift für die Alttestamentliche Wissenschaft*

1

Introduction

PROBLEMS AND APPROACHES TO GENESIS 1–11

As with few other biblical texts, Genesis 1–11 has served as a testing ground for various methods and approaches of biblical interpretation. Since the onset of Enlightenment rationalism, Genesis in general, and 1–11 in particular, has been a microcosm for various critical approaches. Not surprisingly, there is a pervading bias in much contemporary interpretation to view source-critical or literary-critical readings as the most viable means of approaching the biblical text.[1] Yet the history of interpretation did not begin with the source criticism of J. Astruc[2] or De Wette.[3] To better understand the contemporary state of Pentateuchal

---

1. See, for example, E. Nicholson, *The Pentateuch in the Twentieth Century: The Legacy of Julius Wellhausen* (Oxford: Clarendon, 1998). Covering the last two centuries, his two-fold goal is essentially to defend the historical-critical method by addressing the inadequacies of the newer (synchronic) approaches. The work is flawed by Nicholson's exclusive focus on Wellhausen, his omission of Jewish scholars in Pentateuchal criticism, and his omission of the ground-breaking works of M. Fishbane, M. Weiss, J. Levenson, and R. Alter.

For another substantive discussion and defense of the historical-critical method, see A. Rofé, *Introduction to the Composition of the Pentateuch* (Sheffield: Sheffield Academic Press, 1999). He offers fourteen cases of "contradictions" he sees in the narrative and five problematic issues from legal portions.

2. At this time, Astruc himself was not disputing Mosaic authorship per se, but wanted to investigate the various sources Moses might have used in the composition. See G. Wenham et al., ed., *New Bible Commentary: 21st Century Edition* (Downers Grove: InterVarsity, 1994), 48.

3. De Wette took Pentateuchal study in a new direction when he applied a retrojection of cultic issues described in Chronicles to the Hellenistic times, dating the ritual legislation of the Pentateuch to a time after the monarchy. This approach is exemplified by the claim he popularized that Josiah's reform (2 Kgs 22–23) was stimulated by an early edition of Deuteronomy. Among other things, this means that the early texts of the

studies in general, and the unique issues surrounding Genesis 1–11, it is helpful to overview some key periods and their literature leading up to deconstruction and contemporary postmodern approaches.

Until the modern critical period there was a near-consensus that Genesis was a coherent and unified work that essentially came from Moses. But the absentee God of eighteenth-century deism[4] coupled with the nineteenth century Hegelian philosophy of history gave rise to radical skepticism, and historical-critical methods took root. In addition, it was believed that "there was no longer any need for the Christian church to burden itself with the Jewish Scriptures.[5] The effect was an ousting of the centuries-long agreement of an essentially homogeneous Genesis text. Assuming a rationalistic worldview, a new paradigm arose built on naturalism,[6] developmental presuppositions, and a romanticizing of the past. A composite text resulted, a text constructed by many hands that spanned many centuries. As Wenham assesses,

> Hitherto the main purpose of study had been to understand the text as it stood and to apply its teaching. Now the main purpose of study was to understand how the text came into existence and the historical circumstances of its composition … The assumption was that the scholar's duty is to recover the earliest form of a narrative,

---

Pentateuch cannot be used as source material for history, but instead represent Israel's unique mythology of her origins and outcome (R. H. Pfeiffer, *Introduction to the Old Testament* [New York: Harper and Brothers, 1941], 52, 137).

4. Deism propounded a "natural religion," so that that which could be known about God and the moral way of life through nature and reason was viewed as the highest form of religion. Given this philosophical worldview, Christianity cannot be unique, and the degree that it differs from natural religion is the degree to which it has become hobbled by superstition. Therefore, the following beliefs: that reason is contrary to prophecy and miracles, that reason is a sure source of certitude, and that the Bible is an unsure source of certitude, captures the premises and impact of Deism in Pentateuchal studies of the time.

5. J. Blenkinsopp, *The Pentateuch: An Introduction to the First Five Books of the Pentateuch* (New York: Doubleday, 1992), 7.

6. By the early 1700s, English Deism was having an effect on dogmatic German theology which had an aversion to reason separated from revelation. Particularly, it was the Socinian Doctrine of Accommodation that had such great impact. This view saw the biblical writers "accommodating" their teaching to the erroneous cosmologies and prejudices of the culture receiving the revelation. As such, those outside a particular culture and purview needed to strain out everything untrue to find the essential kernel. This seems to be one of the key elements fueling the rise of higher critical thought.

Introduction

law or other tradition; the canonical text, since it was produced quite late, is of little interest.[7]

By the end of the nineteenth century this source-critical approach enshrouded Old Testament scholarship, reaching a status akin to "orthodoxy." No writer was more influential in codifying this methodology than Julius Wellhausen.[8] Considered a methodological break-through, Wellhausen found a way to wed a source-critical approach with a developmental view of Israelite religion. Only ten years after his *Introduction to the History of Israel* was published, "Wellhausen's reconstruction of Israel's religious history captured the academic chairs of all British and European Old Testament scholarship."[9] This new *Zeitgeist* was more a product of "academic nomination" rather than validation of the data. Nonetheless, it constituted a powerful consensus because it represented an all-encompassing epistemology that gathered together key aspects of modernist thought operating through the lens of German rationalism. Though emphasizing "OT religion," Wellhausen was later criticized for minimizing the deeper connections between Israel's religion and the surrounding nations.[10]

Some of the ideologies of the rationalism that sustained this approach can be summarized as: preoccupation with the past, commitment to the development of ideas, an overriding anthropocentric sociology, and a sequential ordering of source material. These elements, among others, crystallized into a distinct diachronic analysis of the biblical text that became characteristic of the modernist era of Genesis study.

Now, over a century removed from the historical positivism and developmentalism of Wellhausen, hindsight reveals that horrific wars along with cultural degeneration at large have shaken key historiographical,

---

7. G. Wenham, "Pentateuchal Studies Today," *Them* 22 (1996), 3. His later essay, "Pondering the Pentateuch: The Search for a New Paradigm," in *The Face of Old Testament Studies: A Survey of Contemporary Approaches*, ed. D. W. Baker and B. T. Arnold (Grand Rapids: Baker, 1999), 116–44, is a helpful expansion of many issues he has discussed elsewhere.

8. His most important works were *The Composition of the Hexateuch and the Historical Books of the Old Testament*, 3rd ed. (Berlin: Georg Reimer, 1899), and *Introduction to the History of Israel* (1878; reprinted *Prolegomena to the History of Ancient Israel* [Eugene: Wipf & Stock, 2003]).

9. K. Mathews, *Genesis 1—11:26*, NAC (Nashville: Broadman and Holman, 1996), 71.

10. J. H. Hayes and F. Prussner, *Old Testament Theology: Its History and Development* (Atlanta: John Knox, 1985), 132.

linguistic, and sociological assumptions of source-critical methodology causing it to slide from the status it once held. Even the constant modifications within source criticism itself have revealed a core epistemology now under suspicion by many. Hindsight has also shown that the attention once devoted to dating and describing the "behind-the-scenes" texts was a truncated endeavor. Blenkinsopp explains:

> Much less attention was paid to the editorial process by means of which these sources were incorporated into one comprehensive narrative structure. Questions that may seem obvious to us were rarely asked: Why were contradictions and inconsistencies between one source and another not resolved in the editorial process? Why were earlier versions of events, re-narrated in later sources, not simply omitted?[11]

It was so easy to affirm a diversity of sources through genre or content that the possibility of an editor or author who saw them as interconnected was essentially dismissed.[12]

Four decades ago, however, this orthodox consensus began breaking up, and now, as never before, historical-critical methods are at a crossroads.[13] The old historical-critical method has not died, but has been severely eroded as the respected starting point for scholarly inquiry into Israelite religion and the text of Genesis. Many monographs written against newer approaches are, in reality, a desperate attempt to salvage a legacy and finally address the issue of validity.[14] Today, one can neither presume that

---

11. J. Blenkinsopp, *The Pentateuch*, 7.

12. G. Wenham, "Pondering the Pentateuch," 120–21.

13. The 1996 release of David M. Carr's 388-page book, *Reading the Fractures of Genesis: Historical and Literary Approaches* (Louisville: Westminster/John Knox), is clear evidence that the overt diachronic or atomistic approach is still alive. Carr's book is essentially a detailed study of the formation of Genesis and an argument for the ongoing relevance of such diachronic analysis in the academy.

14. D. L. Petersen, "The Formation of the Pentateuch," in *Old Testament Interpretation: Past, Present, and Future: Essays in Honor of Gene M. Tucker*, ed. J. L. Mays, D. L. Peterson, and K. H. Richards (Nashville: Abingdon, 1995), 31–45. See also the analyses of R. de Vaux, "Reflections on the Present State of Pentateuchal Criticism," in *The Bible and the Ancient Near East* (New York: Doubleday, 1966), 31–48; W. O. Fitch, "Dr. R. H. Kennett and the Sources of the Pentateuch," *StudBib* 1978, ed. E. A. Livingston (Sheffield: JSOT Press, 1979), 145–48; T. Frymer-Kensky, "The Sage in the Pentateuch: Soundings," in *The Sage in Israel and the Ancient Near East*, ed. L. G. Perdue (Winona Lake: Eisenbrauns, 1990), 275–88; D. A. Knight, "The Pentateuch," in *The Old Testament and Modern Study*, ed. D. A. Knight and G. M. Tucker (Chicago: Scholars, 1985), 263–96; and S. J. Schultz,

Introduction

"P" is universally defined or even employed in another scholar's method. The deposing of this monolithic approach leads Wenham to observe,

> In the 1970s this cozy consensus began to be disturbed. The dating of the sources was questioned, the historicity of the narratives was disputed, even the principles underlying source division were challenged. This debate has been in full swing now for twenty years and shows no signs of subsiding. Much of the argument is convoluted and depends on assumptions that are not universally shared.[15]

Today, even within critical circles, there is deep disagreement concerning the date of the sources, the extent to which they can be reconstructed, and even the nature of the sources themselves.[16] This has left the modern reader with many rival theories, increasingly complex ideas, and monographs that are exploring other methodological options.

If "another approach" akin to source-criticism is necessary to capture the academy in order to declare a paradigm shift, such a shift will not occur. What can be classified as a paradigm shift, however, is the pluralism in approaches that exists in the postmodern academy, as evidenced in the dizzying variety of conclusions present in Pentateuchal studies. In this shift, however, "there is a regrettable tendency for each approach to be practiced in isolation from the others."[17] A state in the academy that causes Wenham to conclude:

> Thus the debate about the Pentateuch continues. In the present situation of the scholarly polarization, sometimes the polemic is becoming so strident that the different sides in the debate are in danger of neglecting valid criticisms of their own position. There is certainly as yet no consensus on a new paradigm ...[18]

Before proceeding to the onset of synchronic approaches in the last few decades over against the diachronic, it is appropriate to summarize

---

"Interpreting the Pentateuch," in *The Literature and Meaning of Scripture*, ed. M. A. Inch and C. H. Bullock (Grand Rapids: Baker, 1981), 21–38.

15. G. Wenham, "Pentateuchal Studies Today," 3, 4.

16. Still under discussion is whether "sources" constitute supplements, redactional layers, or discrete entities. It could be argued that the "jagged edges" between sources reflect the author's respect for sources used rather than haphazard editing per se.

17. R. Hendel, "Genesis, Book of," *ABD* 2:933–41.

18. G. Wenham, "Pondering the Pentateuch," 145. He draws similar conclusions in another critique, "Method in Pentateuchal Source Criticism," *VT* 41 (1991): 84–109.

some key reasons why the historical-critical method has seen so many defectors and subsequently lost its place of dominance.

First, the application of historical-criticism as applied to the Pentateuch and Genesis was symptomatic of naïve and reductionistic notions of socio-religious development, often exacerbated by definitions from an "outside" or antagonistically non-semitic perspective. This approach did not survive the scrutiny of more sophisticated historical, sociological, archaeological, and cognate disciplines. The growth of knowledge in ANE cultures and cognate languages should serve as a caution to many older simplistic views that applied modern categories of literature to ancient texts.[19] In addition, the overly realist epistemology was dismantled by the more subjective and existentialist interpretative models of the postmodern era.

Second, the historical-critical approach was not designed to critique questions of an increasingly theological nature applied to both the text of the Pentateuch and its process of composition. Rendtorff passionately argues:

> The dilemma of the recent phase in Pentateuchal criticism lies in the fact that an attempt is being made to answer the newly emerged question about the *theological* intentions of the collection and edition of the old traditions, by a method that was developed to answer entirely different kinds of questions and which therefore proves to be totally unsuitable. If the question about theological intentions is to be put seriously, it must be freed from these traditional methods, and new, adequate methods must be developed.[20]

Because redemptive history had been collapsed to a timeline of social causation, the historical-critical method is profoundly inadequate

---

19. P. A. Viviano, "Source Criticism," in *To Each Its Own Meaning: Biblical Criticisms and Their Application*, ed. S. L. McKenzie and S. R. Haynes, rev. ed., (Louisville: Westminster/John Knox, 1999), 50.

20. R. Rendtorff, "The 'Yahwist' as Theologian? The Dilemma of Pentateuchal Criticism," in *The Pentateuch*, ed. J. W. Rogerson, TBS 39 (Sheffield: Sheffield Academic Press, 1996), 23. Emphasis original. See also H. H. Schmid, "In Search of New Approaches in Pentateuchal Research," 24–32 in the same book. For fuller treatments of these issues by Rendtorff, see *The Problem of the Process of Transmission in the Pentateuch*, trans. J. J. Scullion, JSOTSup 89 (Sheffield: Sheffield Academic Press, 1990); and "The Paradigm Is Changing: Hopes and Fears," *BibInt* 1 (1993): 34–53. For a critique of Rendtorff's traditio-historical arguments against source-criticism, vis-à-vis Blum and Noth, see D. J. Wynn-Williams, *The State of the Pentateuch: A Comparison of the Approaches of M. Noth and E. Blum*, BZAW 249 (Berlin/New York: de Gruyter, 1997).

Introduction

for a theological contribution; both for the academy and the church. Acknowledging this dearth, Blenkinsopp laments:

> It is unfortunate that during the heyday of historical-critical study, throughout the nineteenth and early twentieth centuries, theological interpretation lagged behind the critical analysis of texts, and the gap appears to have widened with the collapse of the Biblical Theology Movement.[21]

James Barr is more pointed, claiming that historical-criticism "did not even *try* to determine meaning. It stopped short of doing that."[22]

Third, the primary concern of historical-criticism in its history and sociology was an abstract excavative[23] function that pillaged the text for reconstructive data and, in turn, failed to give adequate account for the final form of the text. The hypothesis driving historical-criticism could not compete with the final form of the text, which was a *reality*.[24] In part, the Form Criticism of H. Gunkel[25] was an attempt to remedy the problems that surfaced through an era of "atomistic study." Anticipating key concerns of more synchronic methods, Form Criticism identified and classified the smaller compositional units of biblical texts, trying to discover the social setting within which units of these types or literary genres were originally used.[26]

Ironically, it was the synchronic approaches, beginning in the 1970s, that offered breakthroughs if not better answers altogether to "problems" raised by older diachronic methods.[27] The essential point to be made, and

---

21. J. Blenkinsopp, *The Pentateuch*, ix.

22. "Remembrances of 'Historical Criticism': Speiser's Genesis Commentary and Its History of Reception," in *God Who Creates: Essays in Honor of W. Sibley Towner*, ed. W. P. Brown and S. D. McBride Jr. (Grand Rapids: Eerdmans, 2000), 71. Emphasis original.

23. R. Alter, *The Art of Biblical Narrative* (New York: Basic Books, 1981), 13.

24. J. Rogerson, *Genesis 1–11*, OTG, ed. N. R. Whybray (Sheffield: Sheffield Academic Press, 1991), 26.

25. H. Gunkel, *Genesis: The Legends of Genesis* (New York, 1964).

26. J. Barton, "Form Criticism (OT)," *ABD* 2:838–41.

27. Suffice to say that key points of data need to be acknowledged in the present discussion of Genesis as cogent literature within a canonical context: How does one account for issues of 1st-hand knowledge in the text? How does one account for the use of "historical present" or "to this day" language? Why does the New Testament cite the Genesis text using the 2nd person? How does one give account for theological comment and reflection on the part of the author/editor of Genesis? What is the significance of Jesus' own statement that Moses *wrote* of me (John 5:46)? What is the significance of the

one that is at the heart of these recent synchronic approaches, is that the essential object of biblical study is the "seen text" in its final form rather than the hypothetically reconstructed stages of an earlier formation.[28] This was a shift in emphasis to "product" over against "process," particularly that resulting from various theories of reconstruction.

One of the most influential voices for change to a more synchronic hermeneutic was R. N. Whybray. Since the release of his book[29] this continental scholar has become one of the most articulate spokespersons calling for reassessment of the traditional historical-critical methods. He writes against the documentary hypothesis on two fronts. First, that it is illogical and self-contradictory, failing to adequately explain what it professes to demonstrate.

> Thus the hypothesis can only be maintained on the assumption that, while consistency was the hallmark of the various documents, *in*consistency was the hallmark of the redactors.[30]

Secondly, that the phenomena of repetition and stylistic variation, which the hypothesis alleges to explain regarding Genesis, may, in fact, be argued quite differently.[31] Whybray finds reason for a single ancient historian who wrote of the beginnings of the world and the nation of Israel. This historian used "recent" sources that he reworked according to the dictates of the historiography of his time. Yet, Whybray reserves his harshest criticisms for the tradito-historical approach. He argues that the

---

references to Moses' own writing for the historiography of the Pentateuch? (cf. Exod 24:4; Num 33:2; Deut 31:9,24). For recent discussion, see J. C. Geoghegan, "'Until This Day' and the Preexilic Redaction of the Deuteronomistic History," *JBL* 122 (2003): 201–27.

28. See B. Childs' development argument in *Introduction to the Old Testament as Scripture* (Philadelphia: Westminster, 1979).

29. *The Making of the Pentateuch: A Methodological Study*, JSOTSup 53 (Sheffield: Sheffield Academic Press, 1987). For other critiques of source-critical analysis, see J. Blenkinsopp, "The Documentary Hypothesis in Trouble," *BR* (Winter 1985); E. W. Nicholson, "The Pentateuch in Recent Research: A Time for Caution," in *Congress Volume Leuven 1989*, ed. J. A. Emerton, VTSup 43 (Netherlands: E. J. Brill, 1991), 10–21; J. Van Seters, *Abraham in History and Tradition* (New Haven: Yale University Press, 1990).

30. Ibid., 49.

31. See G. Wenham's critique of Radday's statistical analysis of Genesis (Y. T. Radday et al., *Genesis: An Authorship Study in Computer Assisted Statistical Linguistics*, AnBib 103 [Rome: Biblical Institute Press, 1985]) that does make a contribution to the composition of Genesis 1–11, but also repeats key issues observed by critical methods ("Genesis: An Authorship Study and Current Pentateuchal Criticism," *JSOT* 42 [1988]: 3–18).

Introduction

task of tradition critics, for example, is even more difficult than that of their older source analysts. The latter, at least, are working with partially extant documents, but the former are working from their hypothetical reconstructions, for which there is no tangible evidence.

In his most recent book,[32] Whybray develops this stance and method: a belief that the entire Pentateuch was written by the hand of one late writer, and a method that approaches the Pentateuch as a "consistent whole with an overriding theme."[33] Noting the truncated results of source-critical practice, Polzin echoes the same desire for a more synchronic approach, if for no other reason to arrive at a valid *meaning* of the text:

> Traditional biblical scholarship has spent most of its efforts in dissembling the works of a complicated watch before our amazed eyes without apparently realizing that similar efforts by and large have not succeeded in putting the parts back together again in a significant or meaningful way.[34]

It is scholars such as Whybray, then, who have set a new benchmark in their call to read Genesis and the Pentateuchal literature in a more holistic manner, acknowledging the extant text and searching for its unifying "themes." In the concluding chapter of his more recent book, "Reading the Pentateuch," Whybray highlights his approach to the literature as essentially *synchronic*, stating:

> [an important aspect of reading these books is] the intention and meaning of the Pentateuch in its final form in the minds of those who were responsible for its composition ... This approach ... is known as "synchronic." That is the Pentateuch in its final form is treated as a "book" which exists in its own right as an artifact with a theme and message. This approach is distinct from the "diachronic," which may (or may not) have extended over a long period ... The advantage of using the synchronic approach is that in this way one is dealing with something concrete that actually exists, the text of the Pentateuch which lies before us.[35]

With the writings of scholars like Whybray calling for the overturning of source-critical methodologies, the newer synchronic approaches

---

32. R. N. Whybray, *Introduction to the Pentateuch* (Grand Rapids: Eerdmans, 1995).
33. Ibid., 136.
34. R. Polzin, "'The Ancestress of Israel in Danger,'" *Semeia* 3 (1975): 82–83.
35. *Introduction*, 134, 135.

amount to revolutions and counter-revolutions on the landscape of Genesis studies. The synchronic approaches at heart do not deny source-criticism per se, as much as they move beyond it or ignore it altogether.[36]

For some scholars, however, source-critical analysis has emerged from the scrutiny of two centuries essentially unharmed. As Friedman claims, "The Documentary Hypothesis has remained intact in its essentials, and a substantial body of evidence has been added in support of it . . ."[37] For scholars of this persuasion, like Friedman, there can be no alternative, only *complementary* evidence.[38] With this view, Friedman represents the new "guarded," if not desperate, consensus when he concludes:

> [The Torah is] not the work of any one person, it reflects a rare event in literary history, a literary partnership in which the works of many individuals were brought together into a meaningful whole that is more than the sum of its parts. The Torah is quintessentially a work of combination. It is a single work, a collection of five books and an editorially brilliant merging of sources.[39]

Yet, the pursuit of synchronic or text-compiled approaches leads to innumerable thematic connections, developing characters, merging-motifs, lexical resumption, reiteration, and the sustaining of an on-going

---

36. It is arguable that the last bastion of scholars collectively defending source-critical methodology through ideological commitment, are modern Jewish scholars. While accepting Wellhausen's over-arching scheme, they reject his dating. In a similar vein, Jewish scholarship has tended to operate methodologically around scribal revision and supplementation. The history of exegesis and "inter-textual" readings has been most important for them to retain, making a somewhat amorphous line between "lower criticism" and "higher criticism." One could list personalities like: U. Cassuto, M. Weiss, M. Fishbane, R. Alter, E. Greenstein, A. Rofé, J. Milgrom, J. Tigay, N. Sarna, J. Levenson, M. Haran, and S. Sandmel.

37. R. E. Friedman, "Torah (Pentateuch)," *ABD* 6:605–22.

38. Postmodernism values dialogue or perpetual dialectic over legal constructs and is philosophically antagonistic to the dogmatism of higher-critical methodology of the last two hundred years. As a stepchild of Enlightenment realism, critical approaches to the Pentateuch were born in an environment of historical romanticism that helped make it monolithic. For this reason, among others, there will never be a "replacement" for the documentary hypothesis since no approach today boasts an epistemology that is all encompassing.

39. R. E. Friedman, "Torah (Pentateuch)," *ABD* 6:621.

Introduction

message.[40] Other scholars have come to a more mediating position.[41] Blenkinsopp, for example, closes his discussion of the last two hundred years of Pentateuchal research by stating,

> It is true that the documentary hypothesis has increasingly been shown to be flawed, and will survive, if at all, only in a greatly modified form...[42]

A prime example of philosophical commitment to source-criticism, yet one that manifests itself in literary and thematic concerns, is T. W. Mann's, *The Book of the Torah: The Narrative Integrity of the Pentateuch*.[43] While maintaining the "composite genetics" of Genesis (and the Pentateuch), Mann adeptly focuses on the canonical and literary dimensions of the text, surfacing a theological synthesis that is engaging. For Mann, the three themes of order, human responsibility, and divine blessing "stitch" the Pentateuch together (cf. Gen 12:1–3) into an overt unity which finds its beginning in Genesis 1–2.[44]

Another key scholar whose work has greatly shaped more synchronic approaches to Genesis is D. J. A. Clines. His influential book, *The Theme of the Pentateuch*, has helped establish the viability of overt thematic analysis of the biblical text. Clines' main thesis is that:

> The theme of the Pentateuch is the partial fulfillment... of the promise to or blessing of the patriarchs. The promise or blessing is both the divine initiative in a world where human initiatives always led to disaster and a re-affirmation of the primal divine intentions for man.[45]

---

40. See J. S. Kselman, "The Book of Genesis: A Decade of Scholarly Research," *Int* 45 (1991): 380–92.

41. See, for example, J. van Seters who argues that compositional history is the starting point for Pentateuchal interpretation. Moreover, there really is no "final form" of the Pentateuch since the end of Deuteronomy was not based on literary issues (*The Pentateuch: A Social Science Commentary*, Trajectories 1 [Sheffield: Sheffield Academic Press, 1999]).

42. J. Blenkinsopp, *The Pentateuch*, 28.

43. (Atlanta: John Knox, 1988). Also emphasizing the narrative integrity of the Pentateuch is an article of R. Rendtorff, "Covenant as a Structuring Concept in Genesis and Exodus," *JBL* 108 (1989): 385–93.

44. T. W. Mann's analysis is an impressive literary and theological achievement representing this move from analysis to synthesis while hanging on to historical-critical presuppositions that represent the identity of the academy that forged their thinking.

45. D. J. A. Clines, *The Theme of the Pentateuch*, JSOTSup 10 (Sheffield: Sheffield Academic Press, 1978), 29.

For Clines, the promise comprises a three-pronged blessing of posterity, divine-human relationship, and land.[46] Each respective element, according to Clines, is developed in the rest of the Pentateuch with Genesis focusing on the theme of "posterity."[47]

According to Clines, Genesis 1–11 and 12–50 are separate entities with clear thematic distinction. Whereas Genesis 1–11 addresses "universal history," 12–50 concerns itself with "salvation history"—the former leading to judgment and the latter to a "narrowing of vision to Abraham [that] opens the way for an era of blessing, that is, for salvation history."[48]

Twenty years later, Clines released a second edition of his book, but with some key "updating."[49] Philosophically, the changes to Clines' work represent deep espousal of deconstructionist leanings already held, and these are elucidated in an "afterward"[50] to explain where he has moved, and how he would have written the book differently now as a postmodernist:

> A key difference between the *Theme of the Pentateuch* and any book I would write on the Pentateuch now can be described as the difference between the modern and the postmodern ... Nowadays I tend rather to believe that texts do not have meaning in them-

---

46. See T. D. Alexander, *From Paradise to the Promised Land: An Introduction to the Pentateuch*, rev. ed., (Grand Rapids: Baker, 2002), where he focuses entirely on the coalescence of the Pentateuchal books around the themes of seed, blessing, and land. Alexander's is possibly the latest example of this pursuit of themes as the *modus operandi*. Moreover, Alexander is interested in the New Testament's use of these themes initiated in Genesis, and the Pentateuch at large. This overt concern for themes is taken up by K. A. Mathews, "Genesis," in *New Dictionary of Biblical Theology*, ed. T. D. Alexander and Brian S. Rosner (Downers Grove: InterVarsity, 2000), 140–46.

47. Ibid. While Clines acknowledges the "sin—speech—mitigation—punishment" scheme, he ultimately rejects it because it cannot include the creation or genealogies. He does, however, accept that this is a recurrent motif (76). Regardless, this "thematic scheme" can now be found in various forms of expression. There are numerous schematic structures which have been proposed to show the basic repetition of man's sin and punishment in Genesis 1–11 (see M. Bratcher's synthesis [utilizing the work of Clines and Westermann] of six elements present in the Primeval sins of the Garden, Cain, Flood, and the Tower: (1) temptation, (2) sin, (3) discovery, (4) judgment speech, (5) mitigation, and (6) execution ("The Pattern of Sin and Judgment in Genesis 1–11" [PhD diss., Southern Baptist Theological Seminary, 1984], 228).

48. Clines, *The Theme*, 77.

49. *The Theme of the Pentateuch*, 2nd ed. JSOTSup 10 (Sheffield: Sheffield Academic Press, 1997).

50. Ibid., 127–41.

Introduction

selves, and that what we call meaning is something that comes into being at the meeting point of the text and the reader ... since there is no determinate reader any more than there is a determinate text ... the text is relative to the readers themselves and is in a way created and recreated in the process of their reading of it ... if readers are making meaning from the texts they encounter, the idea of responsibility to the author, who is in many cases unknown or even unknowable, and to that author's intention, of which perhaps the author personally had only a vague knowledge, fades away.[51]

Having moved from a more "determinate text" in his second edition, it seems Wenham has overstated his case in seeing Clines' method as one that "holds that the proper subject for literary study is the text itself, not the author."[52] Clines' statements are indicative of crucial shifts in the hermeneutics of postmodern approaches. The move from a "text-dominant" to "reader-dominant" focus signals a severing of connection with history—the author has been struck down. Little wonder historical criticism has diminished along with source criticism.

With deconstruction, the focus has become that of text-product and its rhetorical expression, but this change has also become *non-referential*.[53] For historical-criticism, meaning was *genetic* to the *ANE* historical and cultural environment. With minimal uniqueness, then, the biblical text was merely a "vendor" of its *ANE* context. Deconstruction, on the other hand, has moved the meaning of the text to a product of linguistic function and literary argument.[54] The "death of God" in the 1960s has fueled the "death of the author" for the new millennium of scholarship. This break with the

---

51. Ibid., 130–33. I am perplexed as to how a biblical "text does not have a determinate meaning" (132) yet "afterwards" in re-released monographs do. If there is no determinate meaning, what is the credibility for a book claiming "the theme" of the Pentateuch?

52. "Pentateuchal Studies," 9.

53. Using Exodus 14 as an illustration, D. B. Mathewson argues that the typical binary distinction between source criticism and deconstructive methodology is a false one. His arguments seem correct in what they affirm, but unconvincing in what he denies ("A Critical Binarism: Source Criticism and Deconstructive Criticism," *JSOT* 98 [2002]: 3–28). The two "criticisms" may emerge as philosophically genetic, but were each prompted by a different *Zeitgeist*.

54. The criticisms represented here could be: narrative, canon, Russian formalism, rhetorical, semiotics, French structuralism, literary, and discourse analysis, inasmuch as these approaches are text-dominant and down-play history and authorial determinancy by their very ethos.

historical and philological emerged in the 1920s and 1930s, and became generally known as the New Criticism.[55] Again, Blenkinsopp explains:

> The New Criticism operated on the assumption that the text is a closed system, and as such should be interpreted apart from either the historical or other realia to which it refers or the circumstances of its production and reception. In other words, the text has a life of its own independent of its origins and even of its author's intention, assuming it could be known.[56]

Allied with the earlier concerns of Clines, other studies that emphasize the final form of the text tend to do so with shorter sections.[57] Scholars like J. P. Fokkelman, M. Fishbane, and I. M. Kikawada and A. Quinn have analyzed Genesis 1–11[58] and 25–35. Innumerable other studies of parts of

---

55. See, for example, I. A. Richards, *The Philosophy of Rhetoric* (New York: Oxford University Press, 1936).

56. *The Pentateuch*, 27. This attitude in the academy has produced what is now called the "intentional fallacy." Yet the author's prompting and product are two different things.

57. See, for example, J. P. Fokkelman, *Narrative Art in Genesis* (Amsterdam: van Gorcum, 1975); M. Fishbane, *Text and Texture: Close Readings of Selected Biblical Texts* (New York: Schocken, 1979); and I. M. Kikawada and A. Quinn, *Before Abraham Was: The Unity of Genesis 1-11* (Nashville: Abingdon, 1985). The last book was formulated by two professors of Near Eastern Studies and rhetoric, respectively, to constitute a formal "attack" on the documentary hypothesis at its strongest point, its defining analysis of Genesis 1–11. The authors first examine the alleged evidences for diversity in the Genesis 1–11, then compare the Flood pericope with other ancient flood accounts, concluding that viewed apart from the rationalistic presuppositions of German criticism, but empathetically from the standpoint of ancient listeners and readers, Genesis 1–11 exhibits a coherent narrative rather than a careless hodgepodge: "The evidence commonly used to show that Genesis 1–11 is a literary patchwork does in our opinion—when closely examined and put in its proper context—support the view that Genesis 1–11 is a literary masterpiece by an author of extraordinary skill and subtlety" (83). Other scholars who have reached similar conclusions are F. I. Anderson, R. Longacre, and M. H. Segal.

58. See P. D. Miller, *Genesis 1-11: Studies in Structure and Theme*, JSOTSup 8 (Sheffield: Sheffield Academic Press, 1978); T. E. Fretheim, *Creation, Fall and Flood: Studies in Genesis 1-11* (Minneapolis: Augsburg, 1969); R. Rogerson, *Genesis 1-11*; B. W. Anderson, "From Analysis to Synthesis: The Interpretation of Genesis 1–11," *JBL* 97 (1978): 23–39; R. E. Averbeck, "The Sumerian Historiographic Tradition and Its Implications for Genesis 1–11," in *Faith, Tradition, and History: Old Testament Historiography in Its Near Eastern Context*, ed. A. R. Millard, J. K. Hoffmeier, and D. W. Baker (Winona Lake: Eisenbrauns, 1994), 79–102; S. Gelander, *The Good Creator: Literature and Theology in Genesis 1-11*, ed. J. Neusner, South Florida Studies in the History of Judaism (Atlanta: Scholars Press, 1997), 47; D. J. A. Clines, "The Significance of the 'Sons of God' Episode (Genesis 6.1–4) in the Context of the 'Primeval History' (Genesis 1–11)," in *The Pentateuch: A Sheffield Reader*, ed. J. W. Rogerson (Sheffield: Sheffield Academic Press, 1996), 75–88; idem, "Theme in

Introduction

Genesis have been written,[59] some of the more significant by J. Licht,[60] R. Alter,[61] and M. Sternberg.[62]

A significant volume edited by Richard S. Hess and David T. Tsumura focuses specifically on the text of Genesis 1-11.[63] It is a distillation of some of the best literature on Genesis 1-11. Spanning a wide variety of secondary literature, the articles cover the last 30 years of writing. Acknowledging both older and more recent trends, the book is divided into two main sections: Ancient Near Eastern and Comparative Approaches, and Literary and Linguistic Approaches.[64] In their articles, B. W. Anderson and G. J. Wenham emphasize the literary unity of the Genesis record. Richard S. Hess has collected, evaluated, and integrated the massive literature on Genesis 1-11 generated since 1850. Looking at comparative, linguistic, and literary phases, Hess concludes by claiming that no one method has

---

Genesis 1-11," in *CBQ* 38 (1976): 499-502; D. T. Tsumura, "Genesis and Ancient Near Eastern Stories of Creation and Flood: An Introduction," in *"I Studied Inscriptions from Before the Flood": Ancient Near Eastern, Literary, and Linguistic Approaches to Genesis 1-11*, ed. R. S. Hess and D. T. Tsumura (Winona Lake: Eisenbrauns, 1994), 27-57; P. Gooder, *The Pentateuch: A Story of Beginnings*, Continuum Biblical Studies Series (London: Continuum, 2000); B. K. Gardner, *The Genesis Calendar: The Synchronistic Tradition in Genesis 1-11* (New York/Oxford: University Press of America, 2001); and J. T. K. Lim, *Grace in the Midst of Judgment: Grappling with Genesis 1-11* (Berlin: de Gruyter, 2002).

59. More recent studies include: W. Groß, "Gen 1.26,27; 9,6: Statue oder Ebenbild Gottes? Aufgabe und Würde des Menschen nach dem hebräischen und griechischen Wortlaut," *JBTh* 15 (2000), 11-38; W. J. Dumbrell, "Genesis 2:1-3: Biblical Theology of Creation Covenant," *ERT* 25 (2001), 219-30; and K. Mulzac, "Genesis 9:1-7: Its Theological Connections with the Creation Motif," *JATS* 12 (2001): 65-77.

60. *Storytelling in the Bible* (Jerusalem: Magnus Press, 1978).

61. *The Art of Biblical Narrative* (1981). See his more recent work: *The Five Books of Moses: A Translation with Commentary* (New York: W. W. Norton & Company, 2004).

62. *The Poetics of Biblical Narrative: Ideological Literature and the Drama of Reading* (Bloomington: Indiana University Press, 1985), probably the most important and thorough treatment of Old Testament narrative writing. For more recent essays focusing on topics and themes in Genesis, see David M. Gunn and Dana Nolan Fewell, *Narrative in the Hebrew Bible*, OBS (Oxford: Oxford University Press, 1993) and the helpful bibliography, 206-52; and W. P. Brown and S. D. McBride Jr., *God Who Creates: Essays in Honor of W. Sibley Towner* (Grand Rapids: Eerdmans, 2000).

63. R. S. Hess and D. T. Tsumura, eds., *"I Studied Inscriptions from Before the Flood": Ancient Near Eastern, Literary, and Linguistic Approaches to Genesis 1-11*, SBTS, vol. 4 (Winona Lake: Eisenbrauns, 1994).

64. The contributors include W. G. Lambert, A. R. Millard, E. A. Speiser, D. J. Wiseman, S. N. Kramer, P. Bird, G. J. Wenham, and J. M. Sasson.

fully displaced any other, rather utilization of various methods and cross-disciplinary studies line the road of future work. Hess writes,

> The literary study of the Bible is enhanced by the comparative method, not diminished. If we are to understand the biblical text in terms of its own message, the comparative approach is necessary to show parallels and points of incongruence. But the literary approaches, with their concern for context and/or contextualization, are also valuable as means by which the full implications of the text are made known within and in contrast to its Near Eastern environment.[65]

The mounting literature of postmodern literary approaches shows that scholars are increasingly interpreting the text from their own situation and context.[66] A century ago Genesis 1–11 was viewed in light of science for the benefit of orthodox faith. Later, 1–11 was read in light of ANE literature to ascertain, how Israel employed surrounding cultural traditions to express her own distinctive faith. Most recently, Genesis 1–11 is analyzed amid an expanding pluralism of methods[67] that have served to renew interest in the ethical authority,[68] and literary coherence of 1–11.[69]

Thus, two basic characteristics have emerged in the modern study of Genesis 1–11: (1) an "explosion" in the number of methods, (2) and an emphasis on the *contemporary* relevance of Genesis 1–11 for social equality, gender ideologies, and ecology. It is in this latter emphasis that aggressive socio-political and advocacy criticisms have taken hold.[70]

---

65. "One Hundred Fifty Years of Comparative Studies on Genesis 1–11," in "*I Studied*," 24.

66. A helpful series of essays addressing fourteen different critical approaches is *To Each Its Own Meaning: An Introduction to Biblical Criticisms and Their Application*, rev. and ed. S. L. McKenzie and S. R. Haynes (Louisville: Westminster/John Knox, 1999). Essays addressing portions of Genesis 1–11 include: "Rhetorical Criticism and Intertextuality" (P. K. Tull, 156–80) and "Reading the Bible Ideologically: Feminist Criticism" (D. N. Fewell, 268–82).

67. Socio-pragmatic, semiotics, structuralism, and rhetorical criticism could be included.

68. There is biting irony for much of postmodern concern with social ethics, the same system that "emasculates the voice of the author" (K. Vanhoozer, *First Theology: God, Scripture and Hermeneutics* [Downers Grove: InterVarsity, 2002], 36).

69. General literary studies are represented by H. C. White, *Narration and Discourse in the Book of Genesis* (Cambridge: Cambridge University Press, 1991).

70. Examples of liberationist readings would include: J. R. Levison and P. Pope-Levison, eds., *Return to Babel: Global Perspectives on the Bible* (Louisville: Westminster/

Introduction

These represent a search for "power structures" fueled by an aversion to determinate meaning that, among other things, typifies deconstructionist readings. Critiquing such postmodern hermeneutics, Vanhoozer writes:

> What is happening in the postmodern toolshed is that things are not being put together but *taken apart*. In particular, belief systems are being deconstructed. The deconstructor, like an inquisitive boy who disassembles things to see how they work, pries apart worldviews in order to expose their inner workings and their rhetorical ploys. What the postmodern discovers behind various worldviews are political interests and power levers. For these postmodern disbelievers in knowledge, philosophy is not about truth but about power, rhetoric and ideology.[71]

Public readings span to include hermeneutics of personal-existential relevance and moral conversation, also championed by deconstructive

---

John Knox, 1999); and L. E. Vaage, ed., *Subversive Scriptures: Revolutionary Readings of the Christian Bible in Latin America* (Valley Forge: Trinity Press, 1997).

Feminist readings would include: P. A. Bird, *Missing Persons and Mistaken Identities: Women and Gender in Ancient Israel*, OBT (Minneapolis: Fortress, 1997); P. Trible, *Texts of Terror: Literary-Feminist Readings of Biblical Narratives*, OBT (Minneapolis: Fortress, 1984); and B. J. Stratton, *Out of Eden: A Feminist, Theological Study of Reading, Rhetoric, and Ideology in Genesis 2-3*, JSOTSup 208 (Sheffield: Sheffield Academic Press, 1995). For a helpful review of recent feminist literature, see E. A. Johnson, S. A. Ross, and M. C. Hilkert, "Current Theology, Feminist Theology: A Review of Literature," *TS* 56 (1995): 327-51.

Sociological readings would include: J. Pixley, *Biblical Israel: A People's History* (Minneapolis: Fortress, 1992) and R. S. Sugirtharajah, ed., *Voices from the Margin: Interpreting the Bible in the Third World*, 2nd ed. (Maryknoll: Orbis, 1995). An African (American) reading would include: C. H. Felder, ed., *Stony the Road We Trod: African American Biblical Interpretation* (Minneapolis: Fortress, 1991); G. O. West and M. W. Dube, eds., *The Bible in Africa: Transactions, Trajectories and Trends* (Leiden: Brill, 2001); G. A. Yee, "Gender, Class, and the Social-Scientific Study of Genesis 2-3," in *The Social World of the Hebrew Bible: Twenty-Five Years of the Social Sciences in the Academy*, ed. R. A. Simkins and S. L. Cook, *Semeia* 87 (Atlanta: SBL, 1999), 177-92; J. M. Kennedy, "Peasants in Revolt: Political Allegory in Genesis 2-3," *JSOT* 47 (1990): 3-14; H. Knut, "The Serpent in Eden as a Symbol of Israel's Political Enemies: A Yahwistic Criticism of the Solomonic Foreign Policy?" *SJOT* 1 (1990): 106-12; and H. Räisäanen, E. Schüssler Fiorenza, R. S. Sugirtharajah, K. Stendahl, and J. Barr, *Reading the Bible in the Global Village: Helsinki* (Atlanta: SBL, 2000).

Ecological readings would include: C. Park, *Caring for Creation: A Christian Way Forward* (London: Marshall Pickering, 1992); S. McFague, *Models of God: Theology for an Ecological, Nuclear Age* (Philadelphia: Fortress, 1987); N. C. Habel and S. Wurst, eds., *The Earth Story in Genesis*, The Earth Bible 2 (Sheffield: Sheffield Academic Press, 2001).

71. *First Theology*, 19. Emphasis original.

hermeneutics.[72] Within this deconstructive framework, meaning is "created" or "willed" by the interaction between the narrative world and the reader's own imagination. This has spawned the complex and varied interpretations now strewn across the present-day hermeneutical landscape, the "methodology" of which is unrepeatable from reader to reader with little group consensus. Consensus is achieved through shared ideologies.

Within academic circles, it has amounted to a paradigm shift: "... not simply a new chapter in the hermeneutics of suspicion but a radically new suspicion of hermeneutics itself."[73] Vanhoozer claims:

> This sea-change has affected the academy too. For postmodern biblical critics, the historical-critical approach that has dominated biblical studies for much of modernity is as ideological as any other method. Postmoderns turn a deaf ear to modern appeals to method, science and objectivity; these appeals are merely special pleadings on the part of special interest groups, especially white educated males. Consequently interpretation, of the Bible and of other texts, has in our time become a species of ideological warfare. We are, all of us, stuck in the trenches of language, where exegetical armies clash by night.[74]

While historical criticism is still used it has had to make room alongside many methods now applied to Genesis 1–11.[75] In 1966, von Rad him-

---

72. Methods represented here would include womanist, advocacy criticism, actualization exegesis, and ideological criticism. Regarding such methods, Vanhoozer observes:

> The postmodern ethical response to the notion that texts and their interpretations are governed by some ideology or other is to resist. For if reading is ultimately a political affair, a power struggle, then the ethical response is to champion the otherness of the text and to undermine interpretations that, having become too powerful, threaten to engulf it ... This means acknowledging that there is no interest-free interpretation and committing oneself to protect the 'otherness' of biblical texts that resist being subsumed by grand interpretative schemes. (Ibid., 24, summarizing some ideas of W. Brueggemann, *Texts Under Negotiation: The Bible and Postmodern Imagination* [Minneapolis: Fortress, 1997], 61–114.)

73. Ibid., 23.

74. Ibid., 24.

75. The work of Ellen van Wolde is a good example of a semiotic approach used amid methodological pluralism. See, for example, *Words Became Worlds: Semantic Studies of Genesis 1–11*, Biblical Interpretations Series 6 (Leiden: Brill, 1994); "A Reader-Oriented Exegesis Illustrated by A Study of the Serpent in Genesis 2–3," in *Pentateuchal and Deuteronomistic Studies*, ed. C. Brekelmans and J. Lust, BETL 96 (Leuven: Peeters, 1990), 11–21; "The Trees and YHWH Elohim in Genesis 2–3," in *A Semiotic Analysis of Genesis 2–3*, SSN 25 (Assen: Van Gorcum, 1989), 189–205; "The Study of Cain and Abel: A Narrative Study," *JSOT* 52 (1991): 25–41.

Introduction

self declared, "So far as the analysis of source documents is concerned, there are signs that the road has come to a dead end."[76] In the twentieth century historical criticism was eclipsed and fell from prominence, in large part because it never developed an adequate theoretical justification for itself.[77] From hindsight it becomes clear that the historical sense of the text was guaranteed in the method itself,[78] yet, paradoxically, it imprisoned that text in the past without furnishing adequate tools to uncover that past.[79]

It may be fanciful to expect consensus on some points, but the observations of various approaches must be seriously considered even if the conclusions, in the final analysis, cannot be. The essential contribution of historical criticism lies in its preparatory role of surfacing differences within texts in the interpretative process.[80] What historical criticism has taught us is the appreciation of theological diversity within certain texts. It is likely that both the "liberal" and "conservative" alike have overstated their cases of single or multiple authors. Both parties need to acknowledge their presuppositions and admit that "proper" writing and actual historical convention are often two different things.[81] While it cannot be used for biblical theology or reconstructing Israel's history, historical criticism has relieved us of "the notion that the Bible is through and through literal history."[82] Here is where its contributions end and other methods must carry the interpretive load.

---

76. *The Problem of the Hexateuch and Other Essays*, trans. E. W. Trueman Dicken (New York: McGraw and Hill, 1966), 1.

77. J. Barr, "Remembrances," 60.

78. B. Peckham, "Writing and Editing," in *Fortunate the Eyes That See: Essays in Honor of David Noel Freedman in Celebration of His Seventieth Birthday*, ed. A. B. Beck, A. H. Bartlet, P. R. Raabe, and C. A. Franke (Grand Rapids: Eerdmans, 1995), 364.

79. G. A. Klingbeil, "Historical Criticism," in *DOTP*, 401–20.

80. C. R. Seitz, "Biblical Authority in the Late Twentieth Century," in *Word Without End: The Old Testament as Abiding Theological Witness* (Grand Rapids: Eerdmans, 1998), 99.

81. C. C. Broyles, "Interpreting the Old Testament: Principles and Steps," in *Interpreting the Old Testament: A Guide for Exegesis*, ed. C. C. Broyles (Grand Rapids: Baker, 2001), 55 n.36.

82. D. McCarthy, "Twenty-Five Years of Pentateuch Study," in *The Biblical Heritage in Modern Catholic Scholarship*, ed. J. J. Collins and J. D. Crossan (Wilmington: Michael Glazier, 1986), 39.

GOALS OF THE STUDY

The first and primary goal of this study is an exegetical demonstration of the Creation Mandate as a crucial thematic bridge tying together the two major sections (1ff. and 9ff.) of Genesis 1–11. In addition to analyzing the thematic and rhetorical force of the mandate, we want to investigate the theological implications of the Mandate present in Genesis 1–11.

Secondly, we will identify the semantic pool of terms unique to the Mandate in the context of Genesis 1–11 (e.g., פָּרָה ["fruitful"], רָבָה ["multiply"], מָלֵא ["fill"], כָּבַשׁ ["subdue"], רָדָה ["have dominion"], שָׁרַץ ["swarm"]). Our inquiry will also investigate the terms "image" and "likeness" as they pertain to the Creation Mandate and also the male/female language rooted in Genesis 1:26-28. Exactly how these terms are used and developed in the major text plots (e.g., 1:22, 28; 8:17; 9:1, 7) will constitute the critical mass of our study. The assessment of these terms in the Mandate and their use in other texts of Genesis 1–11 will be crucial in determining their significance within Universal History (Genesis 1–11) and the Old Testament at large.

Thirdly, we will investigate the history of interpretation surrounding the Creation Mandate through an analysis of the LXX and Targumic literature. This investigation will also include ANE literature and rabbinics insofar as they have bearing on the Creation Mandate. Crucial to a balanced exegetical process is, we believe, the depth of insight and perspective gained through an appraisal of key streams in historical interpretation of the OT.

Fourthly, is our desire to contribute to the ongoing dialogue that demonstrates the nature of Genesis 1–11 to be most fruitfully read in its *final form*. While the literary nature of Genesis 1–11 makes its context a challenge to grasp, we prefer to see an essential cohesion with "rough edges" rather than "rough edges" devoid of literary logic.

METHODOLOGY

Concerning the theme of the Creation Mandate, it is crucial in our analysis that we strive to understand the text as it would have been read and understood by the ancient community. This will be attempted by focusing on the literary, historical, and theological aspects of the text. The literary will encompass the semantics, genre, and rhetorical logic of the text. The historical will be sensitive to the customs, people, and socio-religious con-

Introduction

text of the text. The study assumes "essential" Mosaic authorship with the historical setting for Genesis 1–11 initiated at the Sinai event. The theological involves specific parameters of God's working in a unique manner for a specific time and subject. These three circles operate on a progressive scheme that discloses God's acts over time.

We believe it is crucial that we approach our interpretation of the texts with the acknowledgement of this progressive flow of chapters 1–11, and not in spite of it. While it creates tension in the theological context, progressive reading understands that development often occurs through repetition—a repetition that is itself built on prior events. Therefore, emphasis will be placed on the "native text" that serves to highlight successive developments.

Importantly, it is this incremental nature of the Mandate texts (1:22, 28; 8:17; 9:1, 7) that will dictate our use of diachronic analysis, on the one hand, and rhetorical force and semantic analysis on the other. Methodologically, then, our study will not confine itself to one exegetical approach, but will seek the integrated strength of appropriate methods throughout the stages of our study. Thus, at the *macro* level, our method embraces a holistic and synchronic reading of Genesis 1–11, and a semantic analysis of specific words at the *micro* level.

Our study of the Mandate will assume the authority of the Masoretic Text (MT), as our base text, and the historicity of the narratives. Nevertheless, writers not committed to these presuppositions will not hinder our use of their analyses where they have bearing on our study.

DELIMITATIONS

Although some restrictions are built in (i.e., Genesis 1–11), other important ones need to be mentioned. There will be no reconstruction of a history of Israel's religion, preferring instead to "substantiate" biblical history.

No single method will command this study, though a text-dominant or "close reading," with an eye to rhetorical coherence, might be most evident. The textuality and human drama of the passages will remain paramount in our analysis. That said, our study will essentially be an *exegetical theology* focused on the Creation Mandate within Genesis 1–11. As much literature as possible will be addressed that pertains to the Mandate, regardless of its approach.

There will be no disposition to emend the MT aside from clear evidence requiring it. Similarly, a prescriptive search for redactional "layers" in Genesis 1–11 will not be pursued, choosing instead to focus on the literary logic of the various texts in their present canonical shape.

Best described as "believing criticism," we will appropriate all necessary critical tools, but without compromising a belief in the divine origin, authorial intent, and orthodox appreciation of the Bible as normative Scripture. This commitment will lead us to ultimately read texts within the context of the whole of Scripture.

THESIS

"Be fruitful and multiply . . ." (1:28; 9:1, 7) functions as a bridging theme issued and reissued in Genesis 1–11, tying together both the first (i.e., Adam) and second (i.e., Noah) Creation Mandates (1:28; 9:1, 7). These ultimately have their focus on humankind as God's royal *vice-regent* (cf. co-texts 1:26, 27; 5:3; 9:2, 6), clearly established in their role as the image-bearer within the created order, serving to bring about the fulfillment of God's blessing.

2

Approaches to Genesis 1–11

INTRODUCTION

THE GOAL OF THIS chapter is to assess fundamental approaches that have been used in analysis of Genesis 1–11. To do this, we will examine their hermeneutical schemes, contributions, and weaknesses. In the previous chapter, we observed the shifting philosophical presuppositions that have been brought to bear on the early chapters of Genesis, noting key literature germane to the various positions. This chapter will flesh out strategic trends,[1] focusing on three broad methodological approaches under the headings: *Epigenetic-historical* (E-H), *Thematic-theological* (T-T), and *Linguistic-ideological* (L-I).[2] Following a critique of each approach, we will conclude with a description and rationale for the approach we will use.

It is not surprising that the unique literature of Genesis 1–11,[3] its long history of analysis,[4] coupled with differing interpretative schools, has

---

1. Some of the key scholars noted in the first chapter will find further assessment in the second for substantive examples of their exegetical method as it pertains to essential lexemes.

2. The article by V. J. Steiner is worth noting since he employs several of the same terms and categories this study had already drawn up to describe the three broad approaches (cf. esp. 546–49), though our study has Genesis 1–11 in mind ("Literary Structure of the Pentateuch," in *DOTP*, 544–56).

3. G. Osborne describes Genesis 1–11 as "a kaleidoscopic dash through a bewildering sequence of events," *The Hermeneutical Spiral: A Comprehensive Introduction to Biblical Interpretation* (Downers Grove: InterVarsity, 1991), 158.

4. As a classic expression of the form-critical approach, C. Westermann's 606 pages devoted to *Genesis 1–11* is possibly the most exhaustive treatment to date, acknowledging the vast amount of literature in the bibliographical material preceding each unit (Neukirchener Verlag, 1974; repr. *Genesis 1–11: A Commentary*, Trans. J. J. Scullion [Minneapolis: Augsburg, 1984]).

spawned various approaches.[5] At issue is *how* these approaches represent the textual data of Genesis 1–11 through their analysis. For our purposes, the disposition of each approach will be illustrated in the context of Gen 3:16, the woman's oracle regarding offspring, and against the backdrop of the Creation Mandate (1:28) to "be fruitful" and "multiply," etc. In this way Gen 3:16 will serve as a prism to showcase these various analyses. In addition, how each method *incorporates* such lexemes as "curse" (אָרַר), "bless" (בָּרַךְ), and "multiply" (רָבָה) within the larger discourse (3:14–19) as they relate to the Creation Mandate will reveal the contribution, emphasis, and points of weakness within each approach.

INTERPRETATIVE SCHOOLS AND THEIR ASSUMPTIONS

Epigenetic-Historical Approach

The E-H approach views the Old Testament Scriptures as essentially a transmitter of ancient Near East culture and religion. It emphasizes topics of *universal* concern in the intellectual and cosmological environment of Israel (i.e., *horizontal axis*) rather than those subjects unique to Israel's culture and theology (i.e., *vertical axis*).

While proving a fruitful study, cuneiform texts, among others (e.g., Eridu Genesis, Gilgamesh Epic) were initially compared to Genesis 1–11 with a brutish optimism.[6] Fourteenth-century Ugaritic tablets and other epigraphic discoveries clearly placed biblical Israel within a surrounding Canaanite context. Not surprisingly, as early as the post-Enlightenment work of de Wette, the longstanding goal of this approach was to discover the "core reality" of the biblical record through a comparative analysis that was *historically* dominant.

Essential to this kind of "historical" approach was a stripping away of the indigenous superstitions and submitting "the text to a radical histori-

---

5. Evidence of this can be seen in R. S. Hess, "The Genealogies of Genesis 1–11 and Comparative Literature," *Bib* 70 (1989): 241–54; F. F. Batto, *Slaying the Dragon: Mythmaking in the Biblical Tradition* (Louisville: Westminster/John Knox, 1992); W. P. Brown, *Structure, Role, and Ideology in the Hebrew and Greek Texts of Genesis 1:1—2:3*, SBL 132 (Atlanta: Scholars Press, 1993); R. S. Hendel, *The Text of Genesis 1–11: Textual Studies and Critical Edition* (Oxford: Oxford University Press, 1998).

6. See R. S. Hess, "One Hundred Fifty Years," 3–26. Noting the increasing sophistication of analysis, he breaks down his coverage into pre-war, post, and modern studies, observing how comparative studies have been pursued in these stages.

cal reconstruction..."⁷ The biblical text served as a socio-religious "lens" (i.e., the "husk") that required some degree of dismantling in order to ascertain Israel's "true history" (i.e., the "kernel") as it actually interfaced with her Mesopotamian neighbors. Under this scheme it took some time for Israelite history to be viewed on its own terms, and the genetic "connectedness" to be tamed as ancient cultures, sociology,⁸ and comparative linguistics came into their own.

This tendency to "fill in the gaps" of the biblical record would give way to a heightened understanding of "shared origins."⁹ This analysis increasingly merged historical and philological elements in textual study that gave rise to more integrative and "thematic" investigations within the *ANE* context.¹⁰ But these relatively recent transitions occurred against the precedent of "cognate parallels"¹¹ and a method that preserved them by its very presuppositions. Observing the "apparent contradiction,"¹² for example, between YHWH's intention to destroy *all humans,* yet save Noah's family (Gen 6:7, 13; cf. 6:8, 14), Hendel claims that it:

---

7. B. S. Childs, *Biblical Theology of the Old and New Testaments: Theological Reflection on the Christian Bible* (Minneapolis: Fortress, 1992), 198. Against an exilic or post-exilic composition of the Pentateuch is new evidence from silver amulets found at Ketef Hinnom, dated between 725 and 650 BC. Combining both Num 6:24–26 and Deut 7:9, Erik Waaler argues that the texts were conjoined prior to the reform of Josiah from a source earlier still ("A Revised Date for Pentateuchal Texts? Evidence from Ketef Hinnom," *TynBul* 53 [2002]: 29–55; see also Wilfried Warning, "Terminological Patterns and the First Word of the Bible: בְּרֵאשִׁית) '(In The) Beginning,'" *TynBul* 52 [2001]: 267–74).

8. See for example S. Niditch, *Ancient Israelite Religion* (Oxford/New York: Oxford University Press, 1997). While discussing a variety of biblical texts considered in the Albright tradition (e.g., Gen 16, 25, 28; Judg 13; Exod 4, 19; Isa 6; 1 Sam 28), essential evidence in the Bronze and Iron Ages is ignored. For an older treatment comparing creation myths, see J. O'Brien and W. Major, *In the Beginning: Creation Myths from Ancient Mesopotamia, Israel and Greece,* ed. C. Hardwick (Chico: Scholars Press, 1982).

9. Ibid., 11.

10. A helpful study is P. D. Miller, *The Religion of Ancient Israel,* Library of Ancient Israel (Louisville: Westminster/John Knox, 2000). While YHWH is defined through his "southern" desert origins as the deity of the seminomadic tribes, Miller resists following a comprehensive developmental view of history and endorses specific pre-exilic cultic practices for Israel. Working within the Iron Age, Miller's discussion is a startling counter to much of the current debate that has run for more than a century on post-exilic premises.

11. Hendel, "Genesis," *ABD,* 2:939.

12. Ibid., 939.

is clarified by the Mesopotamian tradition where there are two major gods in opposition, one of whom (Enlil) decides to destroy all humans, and another god (Enki) decides to save the flood hero and his family. In the Israelite tradition a single god has taken on both divine roles—destroyer and savior—thus creating an inner tension in his character and a deep ambiguity in the story.[13]

Thus, for Hendel, the biblical text preserves a *conflation* of extant traditions primary to the *ANE* context that are then commandeered by secondary biblical writers with varying degrees of specificity; a spectrum he defines with "cognate parallels" on the one end and "typological parallels" on the other.[14]

The E-H approach can be demonstrated using the text of Genesis 3:16 and its surrounding lexemes: "curse," "bless," and "multiply." Tied to modernist presuppositions, the E-H approach is cognizant of the various strata and redactive "stations" in the growth of the biblical text. This unevenness is addressed by looking "behind" the text, and, as much as possible, reconstructing its unequivocal meaning.[15]

J. M. Husser

For Husser, mythological material has combined with wisdom elements in the narrative of Genesis 2-3.[16] According to Husser's reconstruction,

---

13. Ibid. Such argument of "genetic splicing" in OT stories is common of Hendel's writings and of the method it supports. See, for example, R. S. Hendel, "Of Demigods and the Deluge: Toward an Interpretation of Genesis 6:1-4," *JBL* 106 (1987): 13-26; *The Text of Genesis 1-11*, 3-15, 61-80, 93-105.

14. "Cognate parallels" Hendel defines as "sufficiently precise to indicate a genetic or historical relationship between the stories" ("Genesis," *ABD*, 2:938), and "typological parallels" he defines as "attributed to general habits of thought or universal story telling techniques" (938), admitting that "it is difficult to distinguish between these two classes of parallels" (ibid). Methodologically, how does this "cognate" emphasis address Noah's God who does not "eat" his sacrifice, but only "smells" it (Gen 8:21); or a creation cosmology where both female consort and divine sexuality are conspicuously absent (Gen 1:1—2:3)? Hendel's method requires modification.

15. Whereas midrashic interpretation *builds upon* textual "gaps," modern interpretation has held that any "gap" is reason to *dismantle* the text (e.g., Genesis 1-2), since only an understanding of constituent parts can shed light on meaning once present. See E. Levinas, in "On the Jewish Reading of Scriptures," Levinas and Biblical Studies, ed. T. C. Eskenazi, G. A. Phillips, and D. Jobling, *SemeiaSt* 43 (Atlanta: SBL, 2003), 17-31; M. Greenberg, "Exegesis," in *Studies in The Bible and Jewish Thought*, JPS Scholar of Distinction Series (Philadelphia: JPS, 1995), 361-68.

16. J. M. Husser, "Entre Mythe et Philosophie La Relecture Sapientielle de Genèse 2-3," *RB* 107 (2000): 232-59.

the issues of *knowledge* and *nudity* are the latest accretion in a 3-stage redactional process. These themes in this 3rd stage have brought about a historical and anthropological *re*-reading of the Genesis 2–3 complex—a departure from its initial compositional form(s). This final stage moved Genesis 2–3 away from a theological to a philosophical import. Explaining the recapitulation of the couple's curses (Gen 3:16–19) in the argument(s) of the deuteronomic historian, Husser writes:

> La conclusion du récit qui peut paraître redondante après les malédictions formulées à l'encontre des acteurs du drame (3,14–19) est in réalité tout à fait conforme au schema de l'historiographie deutéronomiste. De *Juges* à 2R 24, la déportation apparaît comme l'ultime punition après un série de malheurs sanctions, conformément à l'énumération des maledictions en Dt 28,15–64 (dtr): la dispersion n'intervient qu'en dernier lieu, après la stérilité des champs, la pauvreté, les maladies et l'opression des ennemis (vv. 36–37.64–65). Il ne s'agit donc pas d'une double conclusion en Gn 3, mais bien de l'evocation proleptique du schema transgression—sanction qui, selon les historiens deutéronomistes, conduit toute l'histoire subséquente.[17]

According to Husser, the garden story, God's prohibition (Gen 2:17), and the ensuing disobedience constitute a "core narrative," functioning as a generic event-type in the argument of the deuteronomic historian. It is this narrative that is employed and embellished by the historian as a foreshadowing of the national exile of Israel for the readers of his time. Israel's national infidelity to the commandments of God's covenant is an existential reliving of the "original" curses (Gen 3:14–19).

Husser continues, arguing that "semantic associations" in Genesis 2–3 reveal the historian's denunciation of Canaanite cultic practices operating in Israel. It is this kind of reading, according to Husser, that accounts for:

> la figure du serpent comme une allégorie dénonçant les cultes cananéens. Ce motif jouait un role non négligeable dans les cultes et les mythologies ouest-sémitiques et était de ce fait emblématique pour un auteur polémiste.[18]

---

17. Ibid., 244–45.

18. Ibid., 245. Here Husser also makes reference to K. Jaroš, ("Die Motive der Heiligen Bäum und der Schlang in Gen 2–3," *ZAW* 92 [1980]: 204–15), noting that the serpent is associated with sexuality, prostitution, female deities, foreign cults, medicinal powers, magic, and forbidden occult rites (245).

Thus, the serpent of the "garden" not only anticipates the Canaanite practices to which Israel would succumb, but also the contemporary women, following "Eve," who would bring idolatry into Israelite religious life. Husser writes:

> Le fait que le séducter s'adresse en premier à la femme reflète bein le jugement porté contre elle par l'ecole deutéronomiste: ce sont bien les femmes qui sont tenues pour responsables de l'infiltration des cultes étrangers et de l'infidélité d'Israël aux commandments. (Ex 34,16 [dtr]; 1R 11)[19]

Thus, in Husser's scheme, this deuteronomic material creates an "exemplar" of Israel's future infidelity.[20] However, he acknowledges that arguing for a "wisdom" accretion in Genesis 2–3 has its limits. The creation and garden context contains difficult lexemes (i.e., אֵד [1:6], נֶחְמָד [3:6], תָּפַר [3:7], תְּשׁוּקָה [3:16b], etc.) that make dating the text or finding its ideological origin "hardly pertinent."[21]

C. Meyers

Carol Meyers' investigation of the historical background "isolates" the central meaning of Genesis 3:16 in the *social* context of the ancient Israelite. For Meyers, the social backdrop for the Eden story (Genesis 2–3) is specifically the premonarchial agrarian society of the Mediterranean highlands.[22] Eden of Genesis 2–3 is indeed "paradise," deriving its identity in stark contrast to the toilsome life of the Israelite family. According to Meyers, these farmers reveal Genesis 3 to be addressing issues of survival and sustenance (i.e., Genesis 3: "food," "eat,"[23] etc.), and is in no way a story of "the fall," that never mentions "sin."[24]

19. Ibid., 245.

20. Ibid.

21. Ibid., 247.

22. C. Meyers, *Discovering Eve: Ancient Israelite Women in Context* (New York: Oxford University Press, 1988), 95–121.

23. Meyers interprets the woman's giving the man the fruit (3:6) as mere social convention surrounding "food"; C. Meyers, "Eve," in *Women in Scripture: A Dictionary of Named and Unnamed Women in the Hebrew Bible, the Apocryphal/ Deuterocanonical Books, and the New Testament*, ed. C. Meyers, T. Craven, and R. S. Kramer (Grand Rapids: Eerdmans, 2000), 79–82.

24. Yet the LORD's question, "Did you eat from the tree about which I *commanded you* 'You shall not eat from it'?" (Gen 3:10) does argue for *rebellion*. Exactly how Meyers construes this "eating" under social food convention, when it is pointedly raised again as breech of *apodictic law* in the man's adjacent oracle (3:17), escapes me.

Within Gen 3:16, she locates three basic genres: (1) a *myth* regarding existential conditions to be applied universally, (2) an *etiology* revealing the status quo, and (3) a *wisdom* tale informing the Israelites in the initial stages of agricultural life about its difficult realities. More specifically, Meyer's argument hangs on a reconstruction of the woman's oracle that she renders:

> I will greatly increase your toil and your pregnancies;
> [along] with travail shall you beget children.
> For to your man is your desire,
> And he shall predominate over you.[25]

For Meyers, this retranslation reflects a dual concern, namely, the judgment of the woman as inclusive of manual labor in the family's fields, and a disassociation between Gen 3:16 and childbirth.[26] In this way, the woman's plight is not the pain of childbirth, but the laborious task of an agrarian life made even harsher by multiple "pregnancies." Gen 3:16, then, "is a mandate for intense productive and reproductive roles for women; it sanctions what life meant for Israelite women."[27] Any subordination pertains to sexual activity,[28] which is strictly how his "rule" (3:16bβ) and her "desire" (3:16bα) are to be understood.[29]

---

25. Ibid., 118; idem, "Gender Roles and Genesis 3:16 Revisited," in *The Word of the Lord Shall Go Forth: Essays in Honor of David Noel Freedman in Celebration of His Sixtieth Birthday*, ed. C. Meyers and M. O'Connor (Winona Lake: Eisenbrauns, 1983); repr. in *A Feminist Guide to Genesis*, ed. A. Brenner, FCB 2 (Sheffield: Sheffield Academic Press, 1993), 118–41.

26. Meyers argues that עִצָּבוֹן is only addressing physical labor (1st line), but this ignores the *internal parallelism* between the 1st and 2nd lines where "pregnancy" and "labor" are clearly juxtaposed. The nominative form עִצָּבוֹן only occurs 3x, all of which are in Primeval History and in the context of judgment, i.e., pain-filled labor (Gen 3:16, 17; 5:29). In addition, she ignores the 2nd line with its *external parallelism* that associates עֶצֶב with its prior etymological cognate. Rather than Meyer's בְּ of *accompaniment* (i.e., "along with . . .") would be an *explanatory* בְּ ("in/with pain . . ."), *HALOT*, 1:104–5.

27. C. Meyers, "Eve," 81.

28. C. Meyers, *Discovering Eve*, 116.

29. Meyer's view is reiterated by J. H. Walton and V. H. Matthews: "While pregnancy and child care periodically restricted the woman's work in the fields or the shop, a couple's survival was largely based on shared labor and the number of children they produced," *The IVP Bible Background Commentary: Genesis-Deuteronomy* (Downers Grove: InterVarsity Press, 1997), 21; see also R. S. Hess, "The Roles of the Woman and the Man in Genesis 3," *Them* 18 (1993): 15–19. However, מָשַׁל־בְּ ("rule over") is never used as a sexual collocation in the Qal (see J. Schmitt, "Like Eve, Like Adam: *mšl* in Gen 3:16," *Bib* 72 [1991]: 1–22).

By way of critique, several observations can be noted regarding the E-H approach. Positively, its strident analysis of the *historical* is essential to the interpretative process: observing official religious tenants, pervasive ideologies, and vital social behaviors. Identifying origins of beliefs and tracing their subsequent influences for the biblical text is an indispensable step neither exegesis nor biblical theology can ignore.[30]

Second, the E-H approach highlights antecedent traditions and sources utilized within the biblical text but opaque to our eyes since the writer's contemporaries needed little explanation or documentation (e.g., sacred sites, religious rites, "frozen" expressions, etc.). For example, the E-H captures important *material data* through archaeology, reminding the interpreter that the window to the past does not merely consist in studying what was *written*, but also in recovering what was *done*. E-H's use of comparative studies from the material culture yields a "three-dimensional" picture of everyday life both in and around Iron Age Israel. Analysis and discussion focuses on human factors of religion and the human side of history.[31]

Thirdly, E-H regularly searches out the political contours of history within which to read textual evidence, as such "parts" coalesce to form a larger "whole." Here is where both the "similar to" and "different from" can fruitfully emerge.

However, several weakness of the E-H approach can also be observed. First, the E-H tends to overplay the issues "behind" the text—a tolerable practice if inter-textual analyses (i.e., issues "between" texts) were equally sought.[32] A rich symbiosis with other disciplines is both possible and nec-

---

30. G. Fohrer, *History of Israelite Religion* (Nashville: Abingdon, 1972), 22–23.

31. E. A. Martens, "The History of Religion, Biblical Theology, and Exegesis," in *Interpreting the Old Testament: A Guide for Exegesis*, ed. C. C. Broyles (Grand Rapids: Baker, 2001), 178.

32. In an instructive essay R. Averbeck calls for an approach of "complete reading," following Hallo and, in particular, Talmon. Citing Talmon, Averbeck argues, "'The interpretation of biblical features ... with the help of inner-biblical parallels should always precede the comparison with extra-biblical materials'" ("Sumer, The Bible, and Comparative Method," in *Mesopotamia and the Bible: Comparative Explorations*, ed. M. W. Chavalas and K. L. Younger, Jr. [Grand Rapids: Baker, 2002], 95). This essay is invaluable as it charts a balanced methodological course for a new era with more circumspect comparative study. To achieve balance in bridging disciplines, Averbeck lays out what he calls "the four major principles of comparative research ... proximity in time and place, the priority of inner biblical parallels, correspondence of social function, and the holistic approach to texts and comparisons" (121).

essary, giving more attention to Scripture's use of Scripture; unfortunately, few quality examples of such symbiosis have emerged.[33] Whether it is Husser's Deuteronomic historian using the Genesis serpent for polemical purposes against the Canaanite cult; or Meyers' reconstruction of Israelite agrarian society and the woman's concession to "additional labor" of pregnancies—too often the biblical text is relegated to the handmaid of socio-religious reconstruction and not granted its own voice.[34]

Second, the E-H approach advocates a type of historical and religious *continuum* that blurs significant textual variation, due to a hermeneutical fixation with similar phenomena. As a disposition the E-H approach is not adequately sensitive to the "textuality" of the biblical material as a witness itself; the larger context and trajectories tend to overrun the details of any smaller unit. More genre analysis at the textual level would help mitigate so many discussions of concession. Genesis 1–11 is more than a "source" book to be analyzed on the human plane; it also raises complex theological concerns that intentionally "lean" in discernable directions. The ancients themselves viewed the text's "theology" as an essential component of their "history"[35] quite apart from modern commonsense notions. The E-H approach likewise needs to do more in investigating categories unique to the biblical text, such as its theological claims. Noting similarities and differences[36] within a book's argument would function as

---

33. A refreshing address of issues in biblical historiography and historicity from various perspectives (i.e., archaeological, textual, extrabiblical, and methodological), are nine essays that describe and prescribe the current state and propose corrective measures in methodology in *Windows into Old Testament History: Evidence, Argument, and the Crisis of "Biblical Israel,"* ed. V. P. Long, D. W. Baker, and G. J. Wenham (Grand Rapids: Eerdmans, 2002).

34. The point is, are we exegeting the biblical text, often illuminated by the invaluable contributions of historical investigation, or employing (post)modernist presuppositions (i.e., power structures, social dialectics, etc.) in an endless referential reconstruction that denies ancient authors their own arguments and the biblical text its own coherence? If there was less disagreement from scholars on issues of historical reconstruction, their own case might appear more credible.

35. R. Averbeck, "Sumer," 109.

36. This is the clarion call issued by W. W. Hallo, "Compare and Contrast: The Contextual Approach to Biblical Literature," in *The Bible in the Light of Cuneiform Literature: Scripture in Context, III*, Ancient Near Eastern Texts and Studies, ed. W. W. Hallo, B. W. Jones, and G. L. Mattingly (Lewiston: The Edward Mellen Press, 1990), 2–3.

a corrective to overstepping hermeneutical "boundaries," particularly as they relate to *ANE* historiography.[37]

Third, in the E-H approach there is a disturbing collapse of the "proximate" and "remote" contexts: the "history" described in the text, on the one hand, and the author and audience of the composition on the other. Hendel represents this consensus when he writes:

> We would expect most of the historical referents to reflect the times when the stories were told, not the times that they purport to describe.[38]

Thus the stories reveal a political agenda at the time of formation, but not an historical occasion consummate with the events described. We submit that a more "comprehensive reading" requires a hearing of both proximate and remote contexts.[39] The information communicated in the biblical text concerns more than the time of its writing, seen in the fact that authorship for many OT books is not even stipulated. Brueggemann astutely warns against such minimalist notions:

> Such a horizon, however, not only fails to satisfy theologically serious biblical interpreters; it also offers a history that is remote from the testimony of the community whose past we claim to recover. That is, a recovered past without the presence of God in the midst of it is a past that would have been of no interest to those who shaped and preserved the biblical narrative.[40]

---

37. Some helpful studies addressing ANE historiography and the biblical text include: P. Machinist, "The Voice of the Historian in the Ancient Near Eastern and Mediterranean World," *Int* (2003): 117–37; A. M. Rodriguez, "Ancient Near Eastern Parallels to the Bible and the Question of Revelation and Inspiration," *JATS* 12 (2001): 43–64; and D. M., Howard, Jr. and M. A. Grisanti, eds., *Giving the Sense: Understanding and Using Old Testament Historical Texts* (Grand Rapids: Kregel, 2003), esp. D. M. Howard, Jr., "History as History: The Search for Meaning," 25–53; R. B. Chisholm Jr., "History or Story?: The Literary Dimension in Narrative Texts," 54–73; and R. E. Averbeck, "Factors in Reading the Patriarchal Narratives: Literary, Historical, and Theological Dimensions," 115–37.

38. "Genesis, Book of," *ABD*, 2:937 So, for Hendel, the Joseph narrative must represent a time when the tribes of Ephraim and Manasseh were the most dominant within the tribal league, not written earlier "than the early monarchy" (937); see also his "Tangled Plots in Genesis," in *Fortunate the Eyes That See: Essays in Honor of David Noel Freedman in Celebration of His Seventieth Birthday*, ed. A. B. Beck, A. H. Bartlet, P. R. Raabe, and C. A. Franke (Grand Rapids: Eerdmans, 1995), 35–51.

39. See Averbeck's discussion, "Sumer," 114–16.

40. "History," in *Reverberations of Faith: A Theological Handbook of Old Testament Themes* (Louisville/London: Westminster/John Knox, 2002), 97.

Fourth, speculation on the compositional history of a text comes too early and too forceful in the interpretative process.[41] Perceived "incongruities" are increasingly proving to be sophisticated rhetorical devices, creating tension as part of the literary style[42] and mode of history writing.[43] This is a tension that does not need to be neutralized by searching for the best voice among voices or by viewing diversity as unresolved heterodoxy.[44] Here, Averbeck issues a helpful caution,

> One must take the sociological function of a text as it fits into a particular culture seriously, but one also needs to realize that what are being examined in the first place are texts, not cultures or the functions of texts in socio-cultural contexts.[45]

Averbeck's caution points up the danger within the E-H approach that too often reduces causality to materialistic forces and one that privileges archaeological data over textual.

---

41. Methodologically similar to Meyers and Husser are the monographs of T. Hiebert and D. Callender, Jr. (*The Yahwist's Landscape: Nature and Religion in Early Israel* [New York/Oxford: Oxford University Press, 1996]; *Adam in Myth and History: Ancient Israelite Perspectives on the Primal Human*, HSS 49 [Winona Lake: Eisenbrauns, 2000]).

Using anthropological models applied to the "Yahwist," Hiebert examines J's environmental presuppositions, attempting to remove the subordination of nature to history. This results in: the Garden of Eden being the fertile Jordan Valley, the antediluvians are representatives of highland agriculture, "adam" is a farmer rather than a royal figure, nature plays an important role in ancestral religion, and the literature of the ancestral period is not historical. However, a *unitary metaphysic* with "adam" as the land's servant contradicts "P" (Gen 1:26-28).

Callender describes the "primal human" as a cultural symbol whose location in the divine abode places him in potential conflict with deity. Callender sees overt royal imagery in Gen 1:26-28 in light of the *ANE*, and comparisons with the Adapa Myth reveals Adam functioning as a mediator between divine and human realms, ultimately serving as a model for kings, priests, and prophets. B. R. Reichenbach ("Genesis 1 as a Theological-Political Narrative of Kingdom Establishment," *BBR* 13 [2003]: 47-69), overturns Heibert's denial of royal imagery in a forceful discussion of royal land ideology, human stewardship, and a theology of divine kingship in Genesis 1.

42. See, for example, N. M. Sarna, "The Anticipatory Use of Information as a Literary Feature of the Genesis Narratives," in *Studies in Biblical Interpretation* (Philadelphia: JPS, 2000), 211-20.

43. See, for example, Y. Avishur, *Studies in Biblical Narrative: Style, Structure, and the Ancient Near Eastern Literary Background* (Tel-Aviv: Archaeological Center Publication, 1999).

44. S. Hafemann, "Biblical Theology: Retrospect and Prospect," in *Biblical Theology: Retrospect and Prospect*, ed. S. Hafemann (Downers Grove: InterVarsity, 2002), 16.

45. "Sumer," 114.

In short, we submit that the interpreter has not finished the exegetical task until a particular text is "situated" both *historically* and *theologically*.[46] Israel's beliefs have both material and theological structure that must be interpreted within its given genre. We believe it is ultimately the contribution of biblical theology that uniquely presses the arrangement of textual data along the axis of meaning.

Thematic-Theological Approach

As early as J. P. Gabler's inaugural address in 1787,[47] he appealed for a culling out of the "universal notions" of the biblical text that were "pure and unmixed with foreign things."[48] While it was an "idealistic philosophy" designed for a new dogmatic theology,[49] it signaled a move toward "abiding truths." To achieve this Gabler sought to distinguish the "era-restricted" material from the "unrestricted" universal notions using inner-biblical criteria.[50] It is within this framework that the T-T approach finds impetus and definition as another school of approach analyzing Genesis 1–11.

The T-T approach represents a shift toward *synchronic* priorities that view the text as "product," over and against the more *diachronic* reading of the E-H approach driven more by notions of organic "processes." While the E-H sees the biblical text "through time" (i.e., "strata"), the T-T sees the text in temporal "same time" as revealed by the writer's "strategy." Thus, for the T-T approach, the text is essentially sufficient for study as it stands.

D. J. A. Clines

In response to the long-standing atomization of the biblical text, D. J. A. Clines sets out to find the unity of the Pentateuch—a methodological counterpoint to the dominant trend. Clines himself states,

---

46. E. A. Martens, "The History of Religion," 186.

47. J. Sandys-Wunsch and L. Eldredge, *De justo discrimine theologiae biblicae et dogmaticae regundisque recte utriusque finibus* ("On the Proper Distinction Between Biblical and Dogmatic Theology and the Specific Objectives of Each," from "J. P. Gabler and the Distinction between Biblical and Dogmatic Theology: Translation, Commentary, and Discussion of His Originality," *SJT* 33 [1980]: 133–58).

48. Ibid., 36.

49. B. Childs, *Biblical Theology of the Old and New Testaments*, 15.

50. R. Knierim, *The Task of Old Testament Theology: Method and Cases* (Grand Rapids: Eerdmans, 1995), 495–556.

> Two major tendencies in current Old Testament studies are challenged by the method and matter of this book . . . I refer to the tendencies toward *atomism* and toward *geneticism*.⁵¹

Not in abandonment of the diachronic approach, however, Clines' is a more holistic analysis seeking the Pentateuch's theme amid preoccupation with antecedent textual strands and diversion "from the extant text."⁵² For Clines, an adequate "theme" captures a "statement of the context, structure and development of a work."⁵³ When the "extraneous" is removed, Clines sees "promise" rising to the fore as the "nerve center:" "the theme of the Pentateuch is the partial fulfillment . . . of the promise to or blessing of the patriarchs,"⁵⁴ amounting to the addition of *divine promise* (Gen 12:1–3) to an existing *divine command* (Gen 1:28).⁵⁵

Rejecting the synchronic proposals of Westermann and von Rad,⁵⁶ Clines' own "creation-uncreation-recreation"⁵⁷ is intentionally open to the future. It is this promise of posterity in future orientation that controls Genesis. Clines explains:

> No matter how drastic human sin becomes, destroying what God has made good and bringing the world to the brink of uncreation, God's grace never fails to deliver humankind from the consequences of their sin. Even when humanity responds to a fresh start with the old pattern of sin, God's commitment to his world stands firm, and sinful humans experience the favour of God as well as his righteous judgment.⁵⁸

---

51. *The Theme*, 9. Emphasis original.

52. Ibid., 12.

53. Ibid., 69.

54. Ibid., 94, see 30, 37–47. Since, according to Clines, Genesis is concerned with "posterity" and Deuteronomy closes with Moses' death and the Israelites *outside* the land, there is a decidedly *non-fulfillment* tenor struck in the Pentateuch. The final form of the Pentateuch represents the nation's existential identification with fulfillment held in abeyance.

55. Ibid., 86. Clines' three-pronged promise entails descendants (19x in Genesis), relationship (10x in Genesis), and land (13x in Genesis), with allusions to the promise totaling 17x in Genesis (31–47).

56. That is, "sin-speech-mitigation-punishment" and "spread-of-sin, spread-of-grace" themes, respectively.

57. Ibid., 80–82.

58. Ibid., 83.

For Clines, the flood is the final stage of a cosmic disintegration that begins in Genesis 3. Whereas the flood dismantles the ordered patterns of Genesis 1, Genesis 3 reveals a disintegration of elemental unions established in Genesis 2. The emphasis on binary distinctions in Genesis 1 is replaced

> by the forging of bonds: between humans and the soil, humans and the animals, the man and the woman, humanity and God. In ch. 3 the relationship of harmony between each of these pairs is disrupted.[59]

Clines sees this "disruption of bonds" evident in the couple's mutual accusations (Gen 3:12), but he minimizes the significance of מָשַׁל, תְּשׁוּקָה, and other lexemes of Divine address shared between 3:16b and 4:7b,[60] believing: "There is no connection of substance between the content of these passages."[61]

Clines' T-T method exposes themes apparent on the broader surface of the text, particularly by answering the *delimitative* "how" questions through an accounting of the textual units viewed rhetorically in Genesis 1–11. Thus, Genesis 1–11 anticipates God's blessing embodied in the patriarchal stories, and initiated in Gen 12:1–3. He has drawn together themes that can construct a synthesizing principle on the one hand, yet reveal capacity for further development, on the other. Clines' analysis discloses the role Genesis 3 plays within the movement of Genesis 1–11. Without

---

59. Ibid., 81.

60. Shared lexemes between Genesis 3 and 4 include: (1) mention of Adam and Eve (cf. 4:1, 25); (2) practically identical expressions (cf. 3:16b, 4:7b); (3) divine "voice" (קוֹל, 3:8, 10; 4:10); (4) judgments affecting the tiller and the ground (cf. 3:17–18; 4:11–12); (5) hiding from YHWH's face (cf. 3:8; 4:14); and (6) the offender's exile east of Eden (cf. 3:22–24; 4:14–16). Broader themes shared between Genesis 3 and 4 include: (1) ground cultivation (cf. 3:23; 4:2); (2) God's interrogating "where" and "what" questions (cf. 3:9–13; 4:9–10); and (3) Divine verdict of "cursed is" to "cursed from" (3:17; 4:11). For further discussion, see J. T. Walsh, "Gen 2:4b—3:24: A Synchronic Approach," *JBL* 96 (1977): 161–77.

61. Ibid., 150, n.30. Here a major defect in Clines' analysis emerges, namely, his acknowledgement of the thematic connection with אדם and אדמה (material origin of man), but the neglect of the same thematic pattern between אשה and איש (material origin of woman). It is these correspondences that go undeveloped by Clines in 3:14–19. That the latter is an ideological agenda for Clines is confirmed in his statement, "…I deny that in any place אדם means 'a man' in the sense of a male, and affirm that the term is ungendered" (310; "אדם, The Hebrew for 'Human, Humanity': A Response to James Barr," *VT* 53, [2003]: 297–310). However, see R. Hess, "Adam," *DOTP*, 18–21.

Approaches to Genesis 1–11

appealing to sources or integrating historical matters, Clines illustrates how a literary reading addresses problems with an eye to textual strategy, the same textual data used by the E-H approach to detect seams and divergent traditions.[62] Downplaying both historical setting and contemporary concerns,[63] Clines instead focuses on the text's thematic strands. This enables some poignant theological observations from Clines, arguably the fruit of the T-T approach.

While Clines' work showcases key contributions within the T-T approach, a critique of specific elements in his use of it is necessary. First, his category of "divine-human relationship,"[64] as a constituent of Gen 12:1–3, minimizes the importance of Gen 1:28 as the inception of blessing given at creation, and collapses the distinction between promise pertaining to nationhood and international blessing, respectively.[65] While Gen 12:1–2a focuses on Abram as *receptor* of Divine blessing, Gen 12:2b–3 focuses on Abram as *agent* or broader *instrument* of blessing. Exactly how Abram's blessing, mentioned 5x (cf. 12:1–3), counters the effects of prior cursing, also mentioned 5x (cf. chaps. 3–9),[66] is not adequately explored by Clines.

---

62. An excellent illustration is Clines' reading of the Babel story (Genesis 11) with the *mitigation* occurring in Genesis 10 (i.e., Table of Nations). He convincingly argues, I believe, that this intentional dischronologization allows Genesis 10 to be viewed as the fulfillment of renewed blessing (Gen 9:1) that would not otherwise be possible had it followed the judgment of the Babel story (Genesis 11).

63. These Clines expresses in such works as: *What Does Eve Do to Help? And Other Readerly Questions to the Old Testament*, JSOTSup 94 (Sheffield: JSOT, 1990), especially chapter 1; and *The Bible in the Modern World*, The Biblical Seminar 51 (Sheffield: Sheffield Academic Press, 1997); and *On the Way to the Postmodern: Old Testament Essays, 1967–1998*, vol. 1, JSOTSup 292 (Sheffield: Sheffield Academic Press, 1998). In these Clines employs reader-response criticism, advocating an interpretive pluralism. Any notion of biblical authority he believes is best defined in terms of function (i.e., its impact) rather than ontology (i.e., its essence). In the second book listed he surprisingly states that Genesis 37–50 is unrelated to the Exodus narrative (99). As with a reader-response approach, one is left with competing interpretative communities, all foisting their own agenda, but often disallowing others the same right. The latter book describes his personal journey arriving as a staunch defender of postmodern deconstruction that "supplants" rather than "supplements" modernist hermeneutics (pp. 146–57).

64. *The Theme*, 31.

65. P. R. Williamson, "Covenant," *DOTP*, 145; an excellent discussion of Gen 12:1–3 (pp. 143–46).

66. Cf. Gen 3:14, 17; 4:11; 5:29; 9:25. The mention of "curse" in 8:21, it seems, reflects God's *internal monologue*, a pledge that Noah never hears. Here, "in his heart" echoes "grieved to the heart" (cf. 6:6), just as "thoughts and actions" echoes "all their thoughts" (cf. 6:5), but resolve for a new order now replaces grief over the old one. Thus, God's

Such an exploration would only enrich his emphasis on the role of Gen 12:1–3.[67]

Second, Clines' preference for the text read as "story" rather than history is ultimately counterproductive. Those employing his method *de facto*, stand to find a one-dimensional text that ignores the significance of dialogue.[68] As a rational construct, biblical language is inherently *receptor* oriented, so that "ideas are transformed when they are stated as historical events in a historical context."[69] We believe this unnecessarily minimizes the text's connection to history and the presence of discourse functioning within those narratives.[70]

Third, Clines' focus on "theme" functions too independently of the text's structure and genres. Exactly how the internal תוֹלְדֹת of "universal history" (Genesis 1–11)[71] interfaces with "patriarchal history" (Genesis 12ff.)[72] and beyond (Exodus, etc.) is ignored.[73] Gen 12:1–3, so central to Clines' theology of blessing, desperately needs explanation as to why no תוֹלְדֹת exists for Abram,[74] the climactic channel and paragon of blessing.

"personal resolve" corresponds to Noah's "silent sacrifice" (v. 20). As a divine reflective comment, "I will never again curse . . . destroying" (v. 21 a,b) seems to refer first to the "ground" (cf. 3:17), then to the recent flood that destroyed "all things" (cf. 7:23). The old curse is not lifted (cf. 5:29), instead God now promises not to *add* to it, establishing new limits for life in a disordered world (cf. Isa 5:29).

67. Blessing has already been seen five times (cf. 1:22, 28; 2:3; 5:2; 9:1), and this concentration anticipates the catalogue of blessings and curses attached to the Sinai Covenant (cf. Leviticus 26; Deuteronomy 28).

68. Gen 3:1b–5; 9–13; 4:9–15; 5:29; 6:7, 14–21; 7:1–4; [8:21]; 9:1–7, 9–17, 25–27; 11:3a, 6–7; 12:1–3, etc.

69. R. McKeon, *Thought, Action and Passion* (Chicago: University of Chicago, 1954), 17. As articulated in the significance of revelation, see W. Eichrodt, *Theology of the Old Testament*, 2 vols., trans. J. Baker (Philadelphia: Westminster, 1961), 1:37.

70. One is struck by the "cosmic presence" of God clearly evidenced throughout Primeval History (chaps. 1–11), making its low profile felt early on in Patriarchal History (chaps. 12–36), until God's voice falls completely silent without any visions in Joseph's life (see the exception of 46:2–4 with Jacob).

71. Gen 2:4; 5:1; 6:9; 10:1, 32; 11:10; 11:27.

72. Gen 25:12, 13, 19; 26:1, 9; 37:2.

73. See G. Rendsburg, *The Redaction of Genesis* (Winona Lake: Eisenbrauns, 1986), 8–25.

74. The following reasons are suggested: (1) his association with Terah identifies the pagan nations from which Abraham must emerge (cf. Exod 4:22). Terah is the link to the "old world," Abraham the blessing for the "new." (2) The absence of a *section heading* boldly illustrates the author's initial point—Sarai is barren (Gen 11:30). The convention

The discourse directed at the serpent and couple (Gen 3:14–19) impinges on the essence of promissory blessing in 1:28, sharpening prior statements and initiating thematic shifts. An overt correspondence exists between the offense and judgment of the couple (cf. Gen 4:11–13) and the source of origin and future orientation of each party.[75] Clines overlooks the fact that the woman (אשה) was extracted from the man (איש, 2:21–23) and subsequently must pursue her fertility amid relational antagonism (3:16b). Likewise, extracted from the soil (אדמה, 2:7), the man must pursue the soil's fertility amid its antagonism (3:17–19). For each party, their point of reference no longer provides intended security, fulfillment, or stands for cosmic harmony (cf. 2:7, 23–24).[76] Against this backdrop, then, God's constructive "I will" speech to Abram (12:1–3)[77] initiates eschatological relief to the destructive "I will" speech levied against the first couple (cf. 3:14–19).[78]

Thus, the boundaries produced by literary and genre categories need further development in Clines' analysis.[79] Within the first תּוֹלְדֹת (Gen 2:4—4:26) lie the Divine interrogation, dialogue, judgment, mitigation, and exile of both Adam and Cain as "workers of the soil" (cf. 2:5; 3:23; 4:4, 11–12). On what grounds, then, can Clines say: "There is no connection of substance" between these two texts when the structure of the text itself

---

of *section headings* is to list the father's sons (cf. 6:9–10; 11:27), but the promised son will not arrive until chapter 21 (cf. 16:15; 25:19). The absence of Abraham's *section heading* increases the struggle for progeny (cf. 12:2). (3) The author's use of 10 generations from Noah to Abraham is the reader's confirmation of another "global deliverer," even if oddly introduced (cf. 5:1ff.; 6:10; 10:1ff.). A barren wife and the lack of a formal *heading* means Abraham's hope of a "nation" (12:2) is beyond biology, requiring another divine act of creation.

75. Among other things, it shows that: (1) God is not capricious, (2) judgment follows violation of a known law, and (3) judgment provides security since it is limited to the nature of the crime (cf. 4:11–12; 9:6, 25–27; 27:29, 40; 49:3–4, 8, 10, 14–15, 26, etc.).

76. See R. A. Simkins, *Creator and Creation: Nature in the Worldview of Ancient Israel* (Peabody: Hendrickson, 1994), 82–120; idem, "Worldview," in *Eerdmans Dictionary of the Bible*, ed. D. N. Freedman (Grand Rapids: Eerdmans, 2000), 1387–89.

77. Regarding Abram: אַרְאֶךָּ (12:1b), אֶעֶשְׂךָ (12:2a), אֲבָרֶכְךָ (12:2aα), אֲבָרְכָה (12:3a), אָאֹר (12:3aα).

78. Regarding Adam and his wife: אָשִׁית (3:15a), אַרְבֶּה (3:16a); see B. K. Waltke, *Genesis: A Commentary* (Grand Rapids: Zondervan, 2002), 206.

79. As the proposals of von Rad and Westermann did not adequately address the Genesis genealogies, similar oversight is seen in Clines' lack of address of issues of law (cf. Exod 20:30; Deut 12–25) and the role of the key Pentateuchal texts within Judaism.

is construing history as a series of *reoccurrences*, showing that Cain did not learn from his father's error?[80] Throughout Genesis 1–11, rebellion and sin are consistently situated within a relational dynamic of "real time" consequences to a current family (cf. 3:8, 16; 4:9–16, 25; 6:9–11; 9:20–27, etc.). Sin is certainly not an abstract notion confined to the mind.[81]

Rooted in the "seen text," the T-T approach draws the reader back to an encounter with the text itself, as it plays out the unique environment and conventions of that text.[82] This emphasis of T-T approach on the "seen text" is also the driving force for a "canonical" emphasis. Childs has lamented that a fundamental breakdown in the biblical theology movement was "its failure to take the biblical text seriously in its canonical form."[83]

Methodologically, "canonical" is broad, encompassing different points of emphasis. From his analysis Schultz has collated the shared elements between key canonical methods as: (1) a focus on the final form of the text regardless of compositional history, (2) canonical presentation of Israel's history regardless of conformity to historical reality, (3) theological normativity for present-day audience regardless of belief in divine origin of the text, (4) accenting the unifying features of the text while minimizing theological discontinuities, and (5) a respect for the unique OT witness regardless of the writer's adoption of the broader claims of Christian belief.[84] Of course, whether the emphasis is placed on a historical author or final editor reflects differing presuppositions with related implications.

---

80. The exact repetition of Hebrew accents applied to the judgments of 3:16b and 4:7b also reveals a Masoretic interpretative tradition that emphasizes their congruity.

81. The first occurrence of "sin" (חטא) finds Cain: (1) responsible, (2) exiled, and (3) a recipient of God's grace, themes repeated from his own father (cf. Gen 3:17ff; A. Luc, "חָטָא," *NIDOTTE*, 2:89). The use of חטא in 4:7 informs the larger unit of Gen 2:4—4:26, and develops the theme of Adam's rebellion (3:17). Both father and son fall prey to disobedience in the context of an animal, personified or otherwise.

82. D. L. Hawk, "Literary/Narrative Criticism," *DOTP*, 536–44.

83. *Biblical Theology in Crisis* (Philadelphia: Westminster, 1970), 52, 102, 122. For a helpful discussion of canon, biblical theology, and the contribution of Childs, see L. G. Perdue's *The Collapse of History: Reconstructing Old Testament Theology* (Minneapolis: Fortress Press, 1994), especially his chapter, "From History to Scripture: Canon and Community," 153–96.

84. "What Is 'Canonical' About a Canonical Biblical Theology," in *Biblical Theology: Retrospect and Prospect*, ed. S. Hafemann (Downers Grove: InterVarsity, 2002), 83–99.

Approaches to Genesis 1–11

J. Sailhamer

Wading into the pool of canonical methods, Sailhamer seeks "to demonstrate the nature of an OT theology based on the approach of *compositional criticism*."[85] This approach tracks "compositional seams," which he believes are used by biblical writers to "knit together" various units of the biblical text,[86] constructing "the messianic thrust of the OT ... the *whole* reason the books of the Hebrew Bible were written."[87] For Sailhamer, overt unity between the New and Old Testaments is crucial since many NT theological themes are anticipated in the "last stages of the composition of the OT."[88] As he explains,

> the later stages in the formation of the Hebrew Bible treat the earlier stages much like the NT treats the OT. They build on and develop the messianic vision that is already present in the earlier texts.[89]

At the level of the entire Pentateuch, Sailhamer's approach assumes continuing textual development of an earlier Mosaic corpus until the period of the Babylonian captivity.[90] Rather than speaking of a "process of canonization," Sailhamer prefers to see a "process of development" that is "punctuated" with moments of formation. This formation is both creative, producing "equilibrium," and instigated by individuals, defined by their

---

85. J. H. Sailhamer, *An Introduction to Old Testament Theology: A Canonical Approach* (Grand Rapids: Zondervan, 1995), 98, emphasis added; see also "The Canonical Approach to the Old Testament: Its Effect on Understanding Prophecy," *JETS* 30 (1987): 307–15.

86. Key texts that reoccur in Sailhamer's writings include: Gen 2:23; 3:14–19; 4:23; 26:5; 48:15–16, 20; 49:10; Num 20:12; Hos 11:1, etc.

87. "The Messiah and the Hebrew Bible," *JETS* 44 (2001), 23. Emphasis original.

88. *An Introduction*, 216; idem, "Hosea 11:1 and Matthew 2:15," *WTJ* 63 (2001): 87–96. This is similar to Childs' *Biblical Theology of the Old and New Testaments*, which develops a Christian canonical strategy that opens up the OT texts to overt influence by reading NT texts back into them; an inappropriate effect for its lack of controls.

89. "The Messiah and the Hebrew Bible," 22.

90. More recently Sailhamer speaks of *composition* and *canonization* as the work of individuals, while the crucial third element of *consolidation* is the work of a community's beliefs ("Biblical Theology and the Composition of the Hebrew Bible," in *Biblical Theology: Retrospect and Prospect*, ed. S. Hafemann [Downers Grove: InterVarsity, 2002], 31).

community,[91] though Sailhamer limits active community involvement for the role of textual *consolidation*.[92]

It is this final textual deposit that crystallized the messianic thrust, the fundamental issue for Sailhamer, "written . . . as the expression of the deep-seated messianic hope of a small group of faithful prophets and their followers."[93] This approach is driven by a "full-human intent" hermeneutic, or *sensus literalis* rather than a typological reading of OT texts (i.e., *sensus plenior*).[94] This leads Sailhamer to conclude a discussion stating:

> The OT is the *light* that points the way to the NT. The NT is not only to cast its light back on the Old, but more importantly, the light of the OT is to be cast on the New.[95]

This can be done, according to Sailhamer, because the OT is merely inserting its organic theme(s) into the message of the NT. Since the "canonical" or authoritative message of the Pentateuch is derived from its intertextual reconfiguration vis-à-vis poetic "connections," then the Pentateuch as it stands is essentially an exilic or post-exilic adaptation of residual Mosaic materials rhetorically edited to communicate an unqualified messianic theology for the final "canonizer's" period.

It is this larger hermeneutical schema of Sailhamer that also determines the thrust of Genesis 1–11. He views the initial chapters of 1–11 as drawn into the framework of Israel's "prophetic eschatology."[96] Particularly,

---

91. Ibid., 30–31. One must ask how any believing community found hope in a text that was ostensibly embryonic or in constant flux. If they did, Sailhamer's hermeneutic proposes such "major shifts" (31) as to render one community's basis of hope unrecognizable to subsequent communities further down the formational stream.

92. Ibid., 31.

93. "The Messiah and the Hebrew Bible," 23.

94. See Sailhamer's concluding remarks in "Hosea 11:1 and Mathew 2:15," 96; see also D. Bock, "Evangelicals and the Use of the Old Testament in the New," *BSac* 142 (1985): 209–23, 306–19; D. Moo, "The Problem of Sensus Plenior" in *Hermeneutics, Authority, and Canon*, ed. D. Carson and J. Woodbridge (Grand Rapids: Zondervan, 1986), 175–212; M. Silva, "The New Testament Use of the Old Testament: Text, Form, and Authority," in *Scripture and Truth*, ed. D. Carson and J. Woodbridge (Grand Rapids: Zondervan, 1992), 147–72; C. Broyles, "Traditions, Intertextuality, and Canon," in *Interpreting the Old Testament: A Guide for Exegesis*, ed. C. C. Broyles (Grand Rapids: Baker, 2001), 157–75; J. Walton, "Inspired Subjectivity and Hermeneutical Objectivity," *MSJ* (2002): 65–77; R. Thomas, "The New Testament Use of the Old Testament," *MSJ* (2002): 79–98.

95. "The Messiah and the Hebrew Bible," 23. Emphasis original.

96. "Creation, Genesis 1–11, and the Canon," *BBR* 10 (2000): 89–106.

these chapters contribute to the "land promise" yet to be played out in Israel's history.⁹⁷ Sailhamer defends his rationale by claiming that Genesis 1–11 is a kind of "prophecy turned backwards."⁹⁸ This, in turn, enables him to employ his well-used citations (i.e., Gen 49:10; Num 24, Deut 32:3, Ezek 38:16, etc.), claiming, "This allowed the extended meaning of one text to serve as the development and explanation of another."⁹⁹ He concludes by stating,

> What I think our exegesis suggests is that the canonical Pentateuch already appears to be in "the unique spiritual realm of the NT ..."¹⁰⁰

In keeping with the more synchronic interests of the T-T approach Sailhamer notes that the woman's oracle (Gen 3:16) is situated within a single syntactical unit where only the initial speech is in the narrative sequence: וַיֹּאמֶר יהוה אֱלֹהִים ("And the LORD God said," v. 14), followed by uptake with the next two parties: אֶל־הָאִשָּׁה אָמַר ("To the woman [for her part] he said," v. 16), concluding with: וּלְאָדָם אָמַר ("and to Adam [for his part] he said," v. 17).¹⁰¹ With only the 2nd and 3rd oracles disrupting the

---

97. Ibid., 106. On Sailhamer's "narrative typology" and the use of "land," see *The Pentateuch as Narrative* (Grand Rapids: Zondervan, 1992), 37–44, 84–89; "The Land and the Blessing," in *Genesis Unbound: A Provocative New Look at the Creation Account* (Sisters: Multnomah Books, 1996), 87–96. For a related emphasis, but with YHWH as cosmic "landlord" who leases his land, see "Genesis 1 as a Theological-Political Narrative of the Kingdom Establishment," *BBR* (2003): 47–69.

98. Ibid., 91.

99. Ibid., 105.

100. Ibid.

101. *Genesis*, EBC, ed. F. E. Gaebelein (Grand Rapids: Zondervan, 1990), 57. Others developing this syntactical relationship, in varying linguistic depth, includes: A. Niccacci, "Analysis of Biblical Narrative" and "On the Hebrew Verbal System" in *Biblical Hebrew and Discourse Linguistics*, ed. R. D. Bergan, SIL (Winona Lake: Eisenbrauns, 1994), 1175–97, 117–37. The essay by F. I. Andersen in the same volume ("Salience, Implicature, Ambiguity, and Redundancy in Clause-Clause Relationships in Biblical Hebrew," 99–116) is also insightful and builds upon his previous ground-breaking monograph, *The Sentence in Biblical Hebrew* (New York: Mouton, 1974). Also approaching Gen 3:14–19 linguistically are R. E. Longacre, "Discourse Perspective on the Hebrew Verb: Affirmation and Restatement," in *Linguistics and Biblical Hebrew*, ed. W. R. Bodine (Winona Lake: Eisenbrauns, 1992), 77–89; N. Levine, "The Curse and the Blessing: Narrative Discourse Syntax and Literary Form," *JSOT* 27 (2002): 189–99.

narrative sequence the narrator "*avoids* implying that the three speeches are successive, and thereby gives them a timeless quality."[102]

For Sailhamer, the language of a blessed fertility (Gen 1:28) and marital harmony (2:18, 21–25) are affected by the LORD's judgments (3:14–19); a countering of the woman's role established prior in Genesis 1–2. For Sailhamer, the woman's judgment directly corresponds to these two elements, namely, children (i.e., fertility, 3:16a) and husband (i.e., marriage, 3:16b). Describing the impact of her judgment, Sailhamer states,

> In those moments of life's greatest blessing, children and marriage, the woman would now sense most clearly the painful consequences of her rebellion from God.[103]

For Sailhamer it is "childbirth" that connects God's words to the woman (v. 16) and the promise stated just prior (v. 15) that:

> the final victory was to be through the 'seed' of the woman . . . the means through which the snake would be defeated and the blessing restored.[104]

Yet, if the "restoration of blessing" is tied to the "defeat of the snake," what is the nature of life to be like *outside* of Eden,[105] and how is the woman's oracle addressing that? In the phrase: וְאֶל־אִישֵׁךְ תְּשׁוּקָתֵךְ וְהוּא יִמְשָׁל־בָּךְ ("And to your husband will be your desire, but he will rule over

---

102. J. T. Walsh, *Style and Structure in Biblical Hebrew Narrative* (Collegeville: The Liturgical Press, 2001), 159. Emphasis original.

103. *The Pentateuch as Narrative*, 108.

104. Ibid., 108. However, Sailhamer's rush to "the final victory" should be tempered by several observations: (1) the LORD's oracle is specifically directed to the serpent, not the woman, (2) the *ANE* notion of *corporate solidarity* allows this dual reference between the collective singular "offspring" (זַרְעֵךְ) and the serpent ("you," זַרְעֲךָ) who, as addressee, is himself viewed as attacking the woman's "offspring" (זַרְעָהּ); the singular pronoun (אַתָּה) is thus in concord with the collective singular "offspring" (cf. Gen 16:10; 22:17; 24:60; 28:14), (3) שׁוּף ("crush, strike") is used for the actions of *both* parties, arguably from the same root (so LXX: τηρήσεις, cf. HALOT 4:1446); Spurrell calls this "a kind of *zeugma . . .* to express the mutual nature of the enmity" (*Notes on the Text of Genesis*, 2nd ed. [Oxford: Clarendon, 1895], 43), (4) the serpent's head is "crushed" first *then* the heel is "struck" (acc. of limitation, Joüon, §126g), startling if "victory" is the point, finally, (5) the imperfect tenses (תְּשׁוּפֶנּוּ, יְשׁוּפְךָ) function *iteratively*, and, coupled with subj. pronoun + verb constructions can also indicate *synchronic* action (cf. Judg 15:14), implying reciprocal and enduring hostility more than predicting a triumphant victor. Better is to see enmity described in metaphorical language that allows for singular development in the progress of redemptive history (cf. Rom 4:13, 16–18; 16:20; Gal 4:4).

105. See Sailhamer, *Genesis*, 56.

you," v. 16b), Sailhamer again reveals his synchronic hermeneutics by taking the woman's "desire" (תְּשׁוּקָתֵךְ) as a foreshadowing of the LORD's words to Cain:[106] וְאֵלֶיךָ תְּשׁוּקָתוֹ וְאַתָּה תִּמְשָׁל־בּוֹ ("and for you is its desire, but you must master it"), a desire to "gain the upper hand."[107] This overt repetition, according to Sailhamer, "suggests that the author intended the two passages to be read together."[108]

Thus, for Sailhamer, Gen 3:16 falls within the context of a curse,[109] one affecting not only birth,[110] but also the relationship of the man and his wife as evidenced in the statement of "ruling over" (יִמְשָׁל־בָּךְ), which upends the "one flesh" (2:24) and "corresponding-companion" (2:18) language.

Through its synchronic breadth, theological unity of the biblical canon, and thematic articulation, Sailhamer's method is a good example of the T-T approach, possibly representing the most successful attempt to wed internal literary consistency with NT interpretation, a kind of canonical theology. In addition, his method is commendable for not becoming embroiled with what are often distracting issues: historical-critical tenants, science, or sociology. Sailhamer's work is refreshingly *textual*. By way of critique, however, several points must be noted.

The first difficulty lies in Sailhamer's overemphasis on the "canonicler" shaping the biblical literature, resulting in the text as the locus of

---

106. Ibid., 58.

107. Ibid.

108. Ibid. That is, two key statements by God only 15 verses apart.

109. Ibid.

110. Sailhamer pursues the theme of "childbirth" because it allows him to emphasize "seed," and funds a "deliverance theology" heavily organic to his reading of the NT. That structure-for-deliverance drives his interest can be substantiated by observing lexemes that are not only more inherent to the Gen 3:16 pericope but ties the *interrogation* (vv. 8–13) and the *judgment* together (vv. 14–15, 16, 17–19) more than he notes. "The man" (vv. 9–12) implicates "the woman" (v. 12b) who in turn implicates "the serpent" (v. 13b). The oracle to the "serpent" (vv. 14–15) anticipates "her seed" (v. 15), and her oracle (v. 16) in turn anticipates the man: "your husband" (v. 16b), leading to the final oracle (vv. 17–19). Moreover, while plural verb forms had been used in the temptation of woman and man (3:1–7 [12x]), the narrative is eerily singular throughout the following five scenes (cf. vv. 8–24). Rhetorically, the rebellion (3:6) and addresses (3:13, 16) move *through* the woman, the only party mentioned in each oracle (cf. 15 [serpent], 16 [woman], 17a [man]). In fact, it is the 1st and 3rd oracles that are most closely tied: ־כִּי (14a, 17a); אָרוּר (14a, 17b); אֹכַל (14b, 18b); כָּל־יְמֵי חַיֶּיךָ (14b, 17b); עָפָר (14b, 19b); שׁוּף ב/ב. . . שׁוּף ב/ב (15b, 19b), etc. Finally, the opening frame: בַּגָּן ("in the garden," v. 8) resonates with the closing frame: מִגָּן ("from the garden," v. 23).

authority to the exclusion of any author(ship). If Childs emphasized the authority of the text and Sanders that of community,[111] Sailhamer reflects more of the latter emphasis by stressing a "canonicler" or "redactor's hand." He intentionally refrains from stipulating Mosaic authorship:

> we should not lose sight of the fact that the Pentateuch itself comes to us as an anonymous work and was apparently intended to be read as such.[112]

Since Jesus states that, "Moses *wrote* of me,"[113] it would be better to at least speak of the "essential authorship" of Moses.[114] But Sailhamer has made the presence of literary shaping the justification for his canonical reading of Messianic theology. While "final form" concerns are applauded, others have also noted a need for caution:

> But when "final form" or "canonical shape" refers to how a completed book of Scripture was interpreted centuries after its composition, when it was combined with other Scriptures, then we simply have an observation, often rather speculative, from the history of exegesis. More often than not, these interpretations deflect attention from the original intention of the texts. As Metzger helpfully explains, the canon is "a collection of authoritative texts," not an "authoritative collection of (authoritative) texts." ... The most important lesson of a study of canon criticism, therefore, is sometimes a lesson in how *not* to interpret the Scriptures![115]

Sailhamer states, "the locus of God's Bible, including the OT had only one Author—God."[116] However, this is a reductionism.

---

111. J. A. Sanders, *Canon and Community* (Philadelphia: Fortress, 1984).

112. *The Pentateuch as Narrative*, 23. However, this does not even acknowledge the deep-seated tradition of mosaic authorship within Judaism—a Judaism Sailhamer readily appeals to elsewhere in his argumentation.

113. Cf. Mark 10:5; 12:19; Luke 20:28; John 1:45, etc.

114. R. Dillard and T. Longman, "Genesis," in *An Introduction to the Old Testament* (Grand Rapids: Zondervan, 1994), 40. They appropriately state: "This expression vigorously affirms Moses as the author of the Torah, while also leaving open the possibility of later canonical additions," (ibid).

115. W. Klein, C. Blomberg, and R. Hubbard, Jr., *Introduction to Biblical Interpretation* (Dallas: Word, 1993), 68. Authors' emphasis; citing B. Metzger, *The Canon of the New Testament: Its Origin, Development, and Significance* (Oxford: Clarendon, 1987), 282–84.

116. *The Pentateuch as Narrative*, 3. "God-as-Author" not only minimizes the human role in the writing process but discards the crucial function of biblical *genres* and author intentionality. Ironically, this hermeneutic is often demonstrated in an over-emphasis

Approaches to Genesis 1–11

The second key problem is the displacement or submersion of (internal) literary genre to the service of (external) theological theme.[117] In as much as genre functions like a contract with the original audience, Ljungberg reminds us of some significant implications, "Genre is constitutive of meaning: it conditions reader expectations and thus allows our understanding."[118] Yet with Sailhamer emphasizing a "morphology of seams" over words or specific genres, he can speak of the entire Torah as the "embodiment of an author's intention . . . strategy designed to carry out an author's intentions."[119] By this he means looking for God's creative intention in the text, ignoring the original author in favor of a "canonicler"—radically shifting from the authorial context to a different "author'(s)" situational context.

Included in the results is a distancing of the text under consideration from its own historical context in which its genre makes determinative sense and reframing it within a (much) later context that has little or no parallels with that genre. Thus, while Sailhamer may have a canonical approach, this does not constitute a canonical method.[120] Opting for a reading of the "final-form" is ultimately inadequate if its complex com-

---

on the organic (i.e., "fixed") *form* of the text, confusing wording with meaning and the value of the message with that of its medium (M. Silva, *Has the Church Misread the Bible? Foundations of Contemporary Interpretation* [Grand Rapids: Zondervan, 1987; reprint, 1996], 24). In J. Barton's words, "The text is not so much a vehicle of meaning as an object in its own right" (*Holy Writings, Sacred Text: The Canon in Early Christianity* [Louisville: Westminster/John Knox, 1998], 132). For the role of inspiration and genres, see J. S. Feinberg, "Literary Forms and Inspiration," in *Cracking Old Testament Codes: A Guide to Interpreting Literary Genres of the Old Testament*, ed. D. B. Sandy and R. L. Giese (Nashville: Broadman and Holman, 1995), 45–67; see also R. B. Chisholm Jr., "History or Story? The Literary Dimension in Narrative Texts," 54–73; R. Averbeck, "Factors in Reading the Patriarchal Narratives: Literary, Historical, and Theological Dimensions," in *Giving the Sense*, 115–37.

117. H. W. Wolff's warning still applies: "There is always the inherent danger of doing violence to the texts if the wide variety of Old Testament texts is [sic] shoved into the press of some unified question that is foreign to the text" ("The Interpretation of the Old Testament," *Int* 25 [1957–71]: 439–72, 440).

118. Bo-Krister Ljungberg, "Genre and Form Criticism in Old Testament Exegesis," in *Biblical Hebrew and Discourse Linguistics*, ed. R. D. Bergan, Summer Institute of Linguistics (Winona Lake: Eisenbrauns, 1994), 421. J. Barton defines "literary competence . . . principally as *the ability to recognize genre*" (*Reading the Old Testament: Method in Biblical Study* [London: Darton, Longman, and Todd, 1984], 16. Emphasis added).

119. *The Pentateuch as Narrative*, 10.

120. R. L. Schultz, "What Is 'Canonical,'" 96.

positional history[121] is not acknowledged and allowed to reveal its own concentric circles of context. Rather, one should:

> emphasize the significance of its final form in view of its development, since there is clearly a relationship between the form . . . and the purpose.[122]

Therefore, it is better to allow a text or book to make its contribution in its *native context* in which it occurs and as the part of the stage of progressive revelation that they in fact are, than to lose the uniqueness of each text in its own context. Citing Vanhoozer, Schultz states,

> a canonical theology is derived by reading the book holistically, focusing "on the distinctive way in which the Bible's message is mediated by its literary forms."[123]

Related to the former, the third problem is a unique derivative of Sailhamer's method, namely, a "collapsing" of history for a soteriological trajectory. Biblical texts were written to address historical-cultural issues in their context through the use of formal writing techniques that produced literary contours unique to that time. Sailhamer's well-known discussion of "text and event"[124] has arguably committed the fallacy of the *excluded middle*,[125] allowing for no mediating ground. "Divine revelation should be located in both historical events and the interpretative word which mediates these events to us."[126] While the Scripture is literature, it is also historically-*referring*—to people and events. That is, it works both within the conventions of stories and operates referentially on the stage of history.[127] Childs states:

---

121. Ibid.

122. Ibid.

123. Ibid.; K. Vanhoozer, "Language, Literature, Hermeneutics and Biblical Theology," in *A Guide to Old Testament Theology and Exegesis*, ed. W. A. Van Gemeren (Downers Grove: InterVarsity, 2002), 35.

124. See "Revelation in Scripture (Text) and in History (Event)," in *The Pentateuch as Narrative*, 16–22.

125. D. A. Carson, *Exegetical Fallacies*, 2nd ed. (Grand Rapids: Baker/Paternoster, 1996), 90–92.

126. V. P. Long, *Art of Biblical History* (Grand Rapids: Zondervan, 1994), 105–6.

127. C. C. Broyles, "Interpreting the Old Testament," 42.

> The Bible reflects the influences of its environment both in terms of its form and content, and therefore cannot be understood apart from the study of its common Near Eastern background.[128]

It is precisely here, where Sailhamer claims to avoid the excesses of historical-critical methods, that he has forged others.[129] We contend that biblical theology, a primary concern of Sailhamer's, must reflect the history and progressive nature of divine revelation. To properly understand the meaning of a passage, one must view it within its historical and literary context. Broyles articulates this crucial area where Sailhamer's method falls short:

> A passage may have two historical contexts. First is the historical context of the characters in the story or poem, that is, the history described in the text. Second is the historical context of the composition's author and audience, that is, the historical situation addressed by the text ... The principle of "progressive revelation" means not only that God gradually unfolds his self-manifestation, but also that the process itself is revelatory, including each stage and its progression from previous stages.[130]

Instead, what Sailhamer's method represents is "retrospective perception" for messianic eschatology, using static hermeneutical grids that push the culminating human understanding of the text back, from each successive stage, to its earliest possible point. This makes the "final compiler" the *super-intender* of the final meaning. At the interpretative level this causes a "flattening" of redemptive history.[131] In his essay on Israel's understanding of the Messiah, Block summarizes our point:

---

128. *Biblical Theology in Crisis*, 48.

129. Sailhamer's article, "Hosea 11:1 and Matthew 2:15," is also peppered with his critique of Evangelicalism's hermeneutical failings.

130. "Interpreting the Old Testament," 43, 40. Speaking of the interpreter's obligation(s), Wolff states,

> He will seek to learn the occasion and intension which caused the author of the text to speak. He will be concerned to establish exactly the proper message of the text in light of the individual words, and the individual words in the light of its proper message. ("Interpretation of the Old Testament," 443.)

131. Regarding Sailhamer's *sensus literalis* hermeneutic, a jointly authored article by D. McCartney and P. Enns is illuminating for their criticisms. See "Matthew and Hosea: A Response to John Sailhamer," *WTJ* 63 (2001): 97–105.

Be Fruitful and Multiply

because the Old Testament sources span a period of one thousand years, derive from a wide geographic range, and come in a variety of literary forms (e.g., narrative, prophetic oracles, poetic verse), one doubts whether we may even speak of *an* Old Testament messianic vision. Each supposedly messianic text needs to be interpreted within its own historical and cultural context and according to rules appropriate for that genre. . . . the Messiah is indeed *an* extremely important theme of the Old Testament, but we exaggerate Luke's interpretation of the significance of Jesus' speech on two counts if we assume that this is *the* theme of the Bible and look for the Messiah on every page.[132]

Aside from critique already given for each author, the T-T approach seems to suffer under the weight of it own thematic constructs; vigorous systems that tend to "break loose" from the biblical text itself, taking on a life of their own. A fundamental weakness, we believe, is that the T-T approach pays too little attention to the study of the historical hermeneutic(s) that produced the text itself.

Linguistic-Ideological Approach

As a disposition, the last few decades have seen an older partnership of biblical tradition and archaeology replaced by a *synthesis* that employs the findings of archaeology, sociology, anthropology, linguistics, and psychology. The result is an interpretative enterprise that has increasingly sidelined the text of the Old Testament itself.[133]

This latest series of methods can only be described as *eclectic*, minimizing interpretive procedure for "self-conscious reading postures."[134] The profile of these methods has been created through feminist criticism,[135]

---

132. D. I. Block, "My Servant David: Ancient Israel's Vision of the Messiah," in *Israel's Messiah in the Bible and the Dead Sea Scrolls*, ed. R. S. Hess and M. D. Carroll R. (Grand Rapids: Baker, 2003), 19. Emphasis original.

133. J. Bimson, "Old Testament History and Sociology," in *Interpreting the Old Testament: A Guide for Exegesis*, ed. C. C. Broyles (Grand Rapids: Baker, 2001), 129–30.

134. D. L. Hawk, "Literary/Narrative Criticism," 538. These "postures" fund such ideologies as: cosmos-ethics, masculist, animal rights, post-colonial, etc.

135. See, for example, B. J. Stratton, *Out of Eden*; S. E. Shapiro, "'And God created Woman': Reading the Bible Otherwise," *SemeiaSt* 159–95; C. V. Camp, "Metaphor in Feminist Biblical Interpretation: Theoretical Perspectives," *SemeiaSt, Women, War, and Metaphor: Language and Society in the Study of the Hebrew Bible*, ed. C. V. Camp and C. R. Fontaine, 61 (Atlanta: Scholars Press, 1993), 3–36. F. Landy's observations in response ("On Metaphor, Play and Nonsense," 219–37) are biting: "It is not simply that it

reader-response, psychoanalytic reading, Marxist reading, semiotics, and deconstruction.[136] The thread running through these is deconstruction itself, arguing that:

> a text advances perspectives and values by negating their opposites, asserts that meaning is ultimately relational rather than absolute and seeks to dismantle the coherence of a text by identifying its *aporia*, the points at which the text contradicts itself.[137]

Rooted in a spectrum of deconstructive notions; the L-I approach is enlivened by *avant-garde* hermeneutical theories and represents a shift from synchronic values of the text to ideological and existential values of the reader. This approach has multiple characteristics. It is oriented around linguistic theory,[138] has a spirit of "methodological adventurousness,"[139] denies determinate meaning,[140] and places a premium on the reader's

---

derives from the tradition of negative theology, and consequently the philosophical appropriation and neutralization of the Bible" (230). And again, "Thus I am not enamoured of the prospect of changing our metaphors to change our world, if it means losing our sense of the past" (231). For constructive assessment and proposal for methodological stability, see K. Greene-McCreight, "Feminist Theology and a Generous Orthodoxy," *SJT* 57 (2004): 95–108.

136. An insightful analysis is L. Perdue's "From History to Fiction: Biblical Story and Narrative Theology," and "From History to Imagination: Between Memory and Vision," in *The Collapse*, 231–62, 263–98, respectively; also P. Trible's description of deconstruction in *Rhetorical Criticism: Context, Method, and the Book of Jonah*, ed. G. M. Tucker, GBS (Minneapolis: Fortress, 1994), 70–73.

137. D. L. Hawk, "Literary/Narrative Criticism," 538. Emphasis added. While it is common today to disavow as *passé* such methods as rhetorical criticism, structuralism, new criticism, and deconstruction as well, in reality deconstruction arguably remains the driving force, via human sciences, that appears to tie postmodern (i.e., poststructuralist) approaches together. See *The New Literary Criticism and the Hebrew Bible*, ed. C. J. Exum, and D. J. A. Clines, JSOTSup 143 (Sheffield: Sheffield Academic Press, 1993), esp. "The New Literary Criticism," 11–25.

138. See P. R. House, "The Rise and Current Status of Literary Criticism of the Old Testament," in *Beyond Form Criticism: Essays in Old Testament Literary Criticism*, ed. P. R. House, Sources for Biblical and Theological Study, vol. 2 (Winona Lake: Eisenbrauns, 1992), 3–22.

139. D. L. Hawk, "Literary/Narrative Criticism," 13.

140. Ibid., 19. See the essay by D. J. A. Clines, "A World Established on Water (Psalm 24): Reader-Response, Deconstruction and Bespoke Interpretation," in *New Literary Criticism and the Hebrew Bible* (Sheffield: JSOT Press, 1993), 79–90, where Clines argues that in the absence of determinate meaning, one should tailor their interpretations to meet the needs of the community being addressed (i.e., "bespoke interpretation").

imagination to "undermine the conventions of orthodoxy in order to usher into existence a new life-defining and life-orienting reality."[141]

The goal of the L-I approach is "moral conversation," a productive interaction between the text and the reader's imagination. Then, according to Ricoeur:

> the right of the reader and the right of the text converge in an important struggle that generates the whole dynamic of interpretation.[142]

Thus, for the L-I approach, meaning is *produced* and *performed* not "discovered" (contra, E-H) or "reflected" (contra, T-T); the critique itself becoming an original work able to adapt to the particulars of each distinct situation. Thus, historical description is abandoned as irrelevant and inflexible with no analogue to the embodiment of human experience.[143] In this vein, "interpretation" is only successful when the needs of the contemporary culture have fused with the biblical text.[144]

S. Gelander

Within these methods of interpretation, Shamai Gelander[145] represents an ideological approach that combines elements of literary and theological interpretation. For Gelander, at the heart of Genesis 1–11 is the principle of freedom of choice, the highest moral value. According to Gelander, Genesis 1–11 forms "a single linear narrative sequence"[146] wherein the plot is "motivated by a conflict between God's ultimate goodness and His own attitude concerning freedom of choice."[147] This distinctive emphasizes biblical stories in terms of human freedom and the divine response to its misuse rather than traditional notions of transgression or punishment.

---

141. L. Perdue, *The Collapse*, 267.

142. P. Ricoeur, *Interpretation Theory: Discourse and the Surplus of Meaning* (Fort Worth: Texas Christian University Press, 1976), 32. See also the helpful volume by D. R. Stiver, *Theology After Ricoeur: New Directions in Hermeneutical Theology* (Louisville: Westminster/John Knox, 2002).

143. J. Goldingay, "Hermeneutics," *DOTP*, 387–401.

144. L. Perdue, *The Collapse*, 305. See also Hans-Georg Gadamer, *Truth and Method*, 2nd ed. (New York: Crossroad, 2000).

145. *The Good Creator: Literature and Theology in Genesis 1–11*, South Florida Studies in the History of Judaism 147 (Atlanta: Scholars Press, 1997).

146. Ibid., 6.

147. Ibid., 9.

Approaches to Genesis 1–11

In this approach, God's response to sin is to foster guidance that preserves human choice rather than impose His absolute goodness. This Gelander explores in the four stories of Eden, Cain, the Flood, and Babel. Each story extends the conflict to new heights that, in turn, reveals the extent to which God will tolerate human use of free will. We can assess Gelander's approach as illustrated in his analysis of Gen 3:16 and its surrounding discourse.

For Gelander, מָשַׁל and תְּשׁוּקָה represent "contradictory notions."[148] Gelander sees in God's speech to the woman (3:16) a creator's overture to "reconciliation rather than anger or disappointment."[149] Regarding the lexeme of מָשַׁל, he believes the word is employing its wisdom denotation thereby moving beyond punitive notions of "domination" to "domination through understanding."[150] For its part, תְּשׁוּקָה represents the antithesis of מָשַׁל, the notion of being dominated by an uncontrollable desire.[151]

As an example, we submit that this ideological reading is inadequate at several levels. At the level of anthropology, wanting to elevate "knowledge" and notions of personal autonomy, Gelander inappropriately applies modern perceptions of personhood to Eve (and Adam), but his hermeneutic is not defined by any historical constraints. In so doing, accredited lexical definitions are also neglected. מָשַׁל is not being used here with its sense of wisdom genre,[152] and furthermore the construction of מָשַׁל־בְּ in 3:16 reflects a formal collocation for "ruling over."[153] For Gelander, God is merely predicting the shape of the future and, in essence, his words to the man and woman are not retaliatory but represent divine "tuition or guidance."[154] It is only when they "voluntarily surrendered freedom and independence that God undertook to prevent human progress from

---

148. Ibid., 32.

149. Ibid., 30.

150. Ibid., 32.

151. Ibid.

152. Cf. *HALOT* 2:647, 48; moreover, one is hard-pressed to find this use of מָשַׁל espoused within the scholarly literature vis-à-vis Gen 3:16.

153. Ibid., 2:647; cf. Gen 1:18 with 3:16; 4:7; and 24:2, etc. For a seminal study on מָשַׁל, see J. J. Schmitt, "Like Eve." His analysis includes a helpful collection of lexical data, but his conclusion that מָשַׁל here is a homonym meaning "to be like" (i.e., couple's mutual sexual desire) is unconvincing. Among other reasons, the meaning "like" is found in other stems, but not the *Qal*, as in 3:16 (cf. Job 30:19; Ps 143:7; Isa 46:5).

154. *The Good Creator*, 30.

becoming a self-destructive process."[155] In the end, "sin," according to Gelander, is the "misuse of mankind's supreme faculty,"[156] choice.

"Human choice," as the philosophical *crux* of Gelander's exegesis, has overrun the data in his ideological approach. What is the basis for consequence amid endless choice and alternative? Further evidence for this over-reaching can be seen in his interpretation of "thorns and thistles" at the close of the 3:14–19 discourse; for him a reference to a "metonymic representation of the trials and errors through which man would have to pass on his way to his achievements."[157]

W. L. Humphreys

This philosophical emphasis on human autonomy has its parallels with W. L. Humphreys'[158] method and literary hermeneutic, a disposition that further illustrates the commanding and formative role of the reader within the L-I approach. For Humphreys, God is a literary character, one of the *dramatis personae* of Genesis who is "in the process of becoming,"[159] but nonetheless manages to be(come) "the most compelling character of the book."[160] In fact, according to Humphreys:

> God does not exist prior to the text and its creation, and he does not exist beyond it, except as readers of the text continue to remember and ponder him.[161]

Humphreys finds this God to be multi-dimensional. Within Humphrey's interpretative scheme, "we center our attention on the character of God as he emerges from our engagement with the text of Genesis."[162] The result makes God a complex and at times a conflicted character,[163] who, according to Humphreys:

---

155. Ibid., 90.
156. Ibid.
157. Ibid., 32.
158. *The Character of God in the Book of Genesis* (Louisville: Westminster/John Knox, 2001).
159. Ibid., 20.
160. Ibid., 2.
161. Ibid., 6.
162. Ibid., 3.
163. Ibid., 255.

receives recognition of the sovereignty he first demonstrated in creation, but only as he is created in turn by his creations in images that serve their own designs for their own lives.[164]

Humphreys uses a formalist approach that on the one hand, unleashes the reader to roam unhindered; and on the other, constructs a "scale of means." At each polar end is movement from outward to inward presentation of God's character.[165] Lying medially are the "actions and speech" of a character that are of a more revelatory nature.[166] Thus, Humphreys tries to distinguish between the narrator's primary characterization and other agents within the text that communicate secondary characteristics of God. These inner thoughts, along with narrative evaluation, provide needed and developing information for the reader.[167] Thus, according to Humphreys, one can observe within Genesis a God who moves from direct to indirect characterization, so that by the close of the book he is known only through the speeches of Jacob and Joseph.[168]

How Humphreys reads Gen 3:16 within its discourse illustrates his emphasis on "becoming-divinity" amid an "intimidating-humanity." He views the divine oracles of vv. 14–19 as God's reassertion of place amid wayward creatures. This allows Humphreys to claim that, "[God] can reestablish hierarchy" since humans uniquely threaten his hierarchy.[169] In fact,

> when through their initiative they transcend this state, he reclaims his place by taking immortality (the Tree of Life) from them . . . If not "monstrous," Yahweh God seems at least jealous of the human's

---

164. Ibid., 256.

165. Ibid., 8. Not surprisingly, Humphreys' discussion of the character's role within the text reflects the insights of R. Alter, A. Berlin, and D. Gunn; i.e., type to full-fledged character (see pp. 8–14, 241).

166. Ibid., 10.

167. Ibid., 12.

168. Arguably God remains dominant throughout the book, though manifested in different ways. In the episodes of Genesis 1–11 human beings are treated as a collective entity. He is most evident, however, in the early stories of Abraham and Jacob (chs. 12–36). He moves into the background as the Joseph narrative is developed (chs. 37–50), yet it should be recognized that Joseph himself speaks most readily, if not profoundly, of God's hand in human affairs (39:9b; 40:8b; 41:16, 51; 42:18b; 45:5–9; 48:9; 50:19–20, 24–25).

169. Ibid., 50.

new knowledge ... It seems Yahweh God is one more "ambivalent parent."[170]

For Humphreys, Gen 3:16 is an extension of the fertility motif in 1:28[171] and invests creative potency with the woman that threatens to rival God's creative impulse. Nevertheless, her generative power "is necessary for them to be fruitful and many ... Best he not get involved with her!"[172] Humphreys carries over the weight of תְּשׁוּקָה ("desire") in Gen 3:16 to Cain's similar scenario in 4:7, which also reemploys מְשָׁל־בְּ ("rule over"; cf. 3:16b). Dismissing notions of judgment within these similar texts, Humphreys sees YHWH staking "out his right to have his favorites or preferences" that "needs no justification before humans ... all they have left is a choice of responses."[173] God's interaction with the woman was limited to interrogation (3:13) followed by putting her in her place (3:16).[174] Thus for Humphreys, the fertility established in 1:28 and acknowledged in 3:16 is a role the woman assumes in chapter 4.[175]

Several elements of Humphreys' literary approach stand out in critique. Adopting the role of a "first-time reader" has the advantage of sequential discovery; a focus on a specific text untouched by what follows.[176] Negatively, however, this is an interpretative approach that baldly omits the dynamic of history, to say nothing of the history of interpretation, Jewish or early Christian. The reading may be existentially vibrant, but lacks sustaining depth.

Secondly, Humphreys' interpretive method overplays the role of characters to the exclusion of plot development. A greater emphasis on plot and thematic structure would contextualize the characters them-

---

170. Ibid., 51.

171. Ibid., 52.

172. Ibid., 54. This sentiment of Humphreys is accentuated by his sympathies for D. Penchansky's own deconstructive interpretation in "God the Monster: Fantasy in the Garden of Eden," in *The Monstrous and the Unspeakable: The Bible as Fantastic Literature.* ed. A. George and T. Pippin, Playing the Texts 1 (Sheffield: Sheffield Academic Press, 1998), 43–60, see *The Character*, 45–46.

173. Ibid., 57.

174. Ibid., 54.

175. Ibid.

176. Within a literary focus, the first-time reader approach is also adopted by L. A. Turner in *Genesis* (Sheffield: Sheffield Academic Press, 2000); similarly P. Borgman, *Genesis: The Story We Haven't Heard* (Downers Grove: InterVarsity, 2001).

Approaches to Genesis 1–11

selves. Instead, Humphreys takes the human characters at face value but routinely views God's persona with suspicion. In the end, God's character becomes more complicated than the text demands, making the Creator the most "tortured soul."

Regarding the weaknesses of the L-I approach, it becomes obvious that there is a hermeneutical "immanence" that is indicative of key areas of excess. Modern linguistics, for example, has key contributions to make, but dangers are obvious when it commandeers the interpretative approach such that determinant meaning is undermined while the fluidity of lexical practice is upheld. Message through "linguistic isotopes" is an inadequate substitute for message rooted in history. Analogic associations of linguistic "signs" tend to state differently what is already resident in the denotative meaning.

Similarly, when "intertextuality" becomes the *modus operandi*, texts no longer speak for a given world, but tend to be harnessed primarily as advocates for oppressed worlds. There is then, with the L-I approach a priority of the relational over the legal. How do the marginalized seize the ideological high ground from the power holders without becoming oppressors themselves or undermining their very reading strategy? We believe this "shift to 'I'" leaves the reader without necessary moorings, an interpretative scheme without adequate "checks," producing results that can even be counter-productive.

CONCLUSION

The distinctives of our approach can now be more clearly observed, vis-à-vis those discussed above. Our reading posture is: literarily sensitive and ethically oriented. We will not only analyze words, but also the author's message via the rhetorical strategy and structure of larger units. We concur with Dorsey's contention:

> Certainly it is time for surface-structure analysis to take its place among the important disciplines within biblical studies. Old Testament authors communicated their message through the *arrangement* of their compositions as well as through *verbal content*. Modern commentators devote much effort to clarifying the verbal content of passages of scripture but give relatively little attention to the arrangement of this content. If we are to understand more fully the books of the Hebrew Bible, we must pay greater attention

to their structures and to what those structures reveal about their meaning.[177]

Our approach attempts to reclaim an "ethical reading;" that is, an interpretative posture which views a life-dynamic in the occasion of writing as much as the current reading of it.[178] We maintain that the claim of methodological objectivity is not adequately evidenced by scholars who are gazing into the well of the text and merely recognizing their own reflections at the bottom.[179] Instead, when the historical author is granted a voice, we find more than history in description, we engage a textual deposit dynamic with an ethical argument that spans time. K. A. Deurloo comments:

> ancient Israelite narrators were to a much greater extent than modern authors deeply involved in traditional data and patterns; and furthermore that they did not create narrative art for the sake of entertainment or general education but told their stories for the purpose of "torah," kerygmatic teaching.[180]

That said, there are strands within new literary criticism that are ethically conscious, but a historically determined ethic proves to be a different matter. We believe that within the text, meaning involves the story's didactic function within Scripture's scheme of sacred history and not just its narrative mechanisms.[181]

Methodological emphases have created trends within Genesis 1–11 studies. Critiquing major methodological trends, we believe that the historical must be read within the textual, the ethical must be rooted in the historical, the literary must be cognizant of genre and socio-religious function, and the theological theme must acknowledge textual develop-

---

177. *The Literary Structure of the Old Testament: A Commentary on Genesis-Malachi* (Grand Rapids: Baker, 1999), 327–28. Emphasis original.

178. See A. C. Thiselton's discussion of literary-critical readings in *New Horizons in Hermeneutics* (London: Harper and Row, 1992), 471–514.

179. See, for example, the critique of G. J. Wenham, "The Face at the Bottom of the Well: Hidden Agendas of the Pentateuchal Commentator," in *He Swore an Oath: Biblical Themes from Genesis 12–50*, ed. R. S. Hess, P. E. Satterthwaite, and G. J. Wenham (Cambridge: Tyndale House, 1993), 185–209.

180. "Narrative Geography in the Abraham Cycle," in *In Quest of the Past: Studies on Israelite Religion, Literature and Prophetism*, ed. A. S. Van der Woude (The Netherlands: Brill, 1990), 61–62.

181. A. Mintz, "On the Tel Aviv School of Poetics," *Proof* 4 (1984), 232.

Approaches to Genesis 1–11

ment and revelatory "stations" within the canon. Our approach will operate based on these methodological convictions.

We find our approach is similar to such scholars as G. J. Wenham, M. Sternberg, and C. C. Broyles. Sternberg's assumptions, for example, we find quite helpful: the precise use of words that communicate emphasis by their nuances and unique syntactical constructions.[182] Moreover, we shall emphasize the unity of the biblical books in as much as one text may shed light on another that came from the same author or editor.[183] While the final form may not be the only valid approach per se, we believe that in an increasingly ideological environment,[184] it is a valid approach that has been wrongly sidelined.[185]

Finally, we maintain that the moral viewpoints of the biblical writers are not only showcased within the ethical statements of the Pentateuch, but the stories themselves regularly *anticipate* an ethical and legal outlook that reverberates beyond any given pericope.[186] In other words we

---

182. *The Poetics*, 456, 454, 460.

183. Ibid., see 462–63.

184. In their book, *Narrative in the Hebrew Bible*, D. M. Gunn and D. N. Fewell conclude with a chapter entitled "Readers and Responsibility" (189–205). Discussing ideology and how it must be reconstructed, they state, "Ideology designates a rich 'system of representations,' worked up in specific material practices, which helps form individuals into social subjects who 'freely' internalize . . ." (190, see 193). Furthermore, they state, "The western intellectual tradition has been preoccupied with the pursuit of truth, *the* truth, as though it were somehow definable . . ." (191, authors' emphasis). They conclude that: "Genesis 2–3 is essentially male mythology" (197), and advocate "reading against the grain" (203). Their application of this ideology comes to the fore when they state:

> . . . certain characteristics of God, established in Genesis 1 and transferred to the humans who were created in the divine image, keep the text from completely succeeding in shifting the blame of the fall on to [sic] the woman and the serpent. God's desire for domination (evident in such language as 'rule' [1:16], 'subjugate' [1:26], and 'subdue' [1:28]), for dividing and naming, for creating self-likeness, and or discovery, colour both God and humans with a mixture of control and freedom. Domination, categorization, labeling, and ensuring sameness or conformity are all manifestations of the need to control . . . Reading against the grain is a call to responsibility. It is a call to see how texts and their interpretations oppress people—and sometimes even creation itself—physically, emotionally, economically, theologically. It is a call to expose domination in order to bring about change. (203, 204)

185. N. Whybray, *The Good Life in the Old Testament* (London: T & T Clark, 2002), 2.

186. Gunn and Fewell illustrate these principles through the story of Dinah (*Narrative in the Hebrew Bible*; Genesis 34; 445–75). See also N. Sarna, "The Anticipatory Use," 211–20; T. L. Brodie, *Genesis as Dialogue: A Literary, Historical, and Theological*

believe, and will attempt to prove, that the pericopies of Genesis 1–11 were written in such a manner as to anticipate or be harbingers of later texts and theological concepts in Genesis 12–15 and into the balance of the Pentateuch.

Genesis adds, as it were, "Elohim-as-Creator" to the nation's recent experience of "YHWH-as-Deliverer" (Gen 2:3; Exod 14:30). In this way, themes such as world creation (1:1—2:25) anticipate Israel's national creation (Exodus 1–18). We believe Genesis 1–11 is an *outward-looking* text, leaning into the rest of the Pentateuch (and Old Testament). While the scenes of Genesis 12–50 are always laden with what's preceded, they also anticipate development in the rest of the Pentateuch. The garden narrative (2–3) and the lives of the patriarchs (12–50) cast long shadows toward the Sinai Covenant through: divine blessings (1:28; cf. 27:27–29), law (2:16–17; 9:6; cf. 26:5), temple imagery (2:9–17; cf. 28:12, 22), curses (3:14–19; cf. 49:7), exiles (3:23; cf. 28:20–21), religious codes (9:2–6; cf. 24:2–4), moral assessments (9:20–27; cf. 15:16), and even plagues (12:17; cf. 20:17–18).

Commentary (Oxford: Oxford University Press, 2001), 1–118; idem, *The Crucial Bridge: The Elijah-Elisha Narrative as an Interpretive Synthesis of Genesis-Kings and a Literary Model for the Gospels* (Collegeville: Michael Glazier, 1999), esp. 32–44.

3

Semantic and Literary Analysis of Mandate Terms

INTRODUCTION

THE GOAL OF THIS chapter is to collect and assess the exegetical data of key lexemes in the Creation Mandate necessary to better understand the central texts of Gen 1:22, 28; 8:17; 9:1, and 9:7. These specific texts will then be explored more fully in chapter four where we will analyze the structure and contextual function of each passage within the literary flow of Genesis 1–11.

In chapter two we explored various methodological approaches applied to Genesis 1–11. Three overarching methods were isolated which we identified as: Epigenetic-Historical (E-H), Thematic-Theological (T-T), and Linguistic-Ideological (L-I). We concluded by noting that, in contradistinction to the core emphases of these three methods, our approach will be typified by ethical and literary sensitivity. An ethical interpretation in which the textual reading not only preserves the historical, but the literary and theological are integrally tied to the biblical genre. These texts in turn can be observed through textual "stations" within the canon as themes are developed and a narrator's hand works to shape the larger plot. We contend that stories within Genesis 1–11 regularly anticipate later narratives, and these advance and even parody earlier content. Thus, our text-dominant approach is also defined by a reading that follows the literary logic of the passage as crucial to theme and theology.

In chapter three we will analyze the constituent terms that comprise the Creation Mandate, assessing them in three clusters: (1) וַיְבָרֶךְ...אֱלֹהִים ("[and] God ... blessed [them]"), (2) פְּרוּ וּרְבוּ ("be fruitful and multiply"), (3) and מָלֵא, שָׁרַץ, כָּבַשׁ, רָדָה ("fill," "bring forth," "subdue," "have dominion"). For each cluster we will pursue a semantic analysis of the word(s), beginning with Genesis 1–11. Establishing usage within Genesis 1–11, we will then broaden our investigation to include the balance of the Old Testament. Following the analysis of each cluster of terms we will summarize our findings.

SEMANTIC ANALYSIS OF וַיְבָרֶךְ ... אֱלֹהִים

Assessing the lexeme ברך, one immediately faces problems in scholarly debate. This debate concerns etymologies, the nature of blessing transfer, and the role and identification of the "blesser" with the person or entity "blessed." Before assessing the usage of ברך, we will consider the significance of these items, first addressing etymology then the transfer and role of the blessing together.

Beginning with BDB, one finds both "kneel" and "bless" under the single root ברך,[1] whereas *HALOT* lists two separate roots: "kneel down" (I) and "blessed" (II).[2] Extending the spectrum, *DCH* lists three roots for ברך: "bless" (I), "be strong" (II), and "kneel" (III),[3] but acknowledges the difficulty surrounding the very existence of root II ("be strong").[4]

Lexica such as BDB reflect certain presuppositions that place kneeling, supplication, and reception of blessing under a single rubric.[5] However, there is a growing consensus that this represents a "popular"

---

1. 138.

2. 1:159; so too M. L. Brown, "ברך," *NIDOTTE*, 1:755–67. "To kneel down" occurs 3x in both Qal (Ps 95:6; 2 Chr 6:13) and Hiph (Gen 24:11). See A. Murtonen, *Hebrew in its West Semitic Setting: A Comparative Survey of Non-Masoretic Hebrew Dialects and Traditions*, Part One, A Comparative Lexicon (Leiden: Brill, 1989), 49–50; and the discussion of "ברך" by E. B. Yehuda in *A Dictionary and Thesaurus of the Hebrew Language* (New York: Sagamore Press, 1960), 1:330–32.

3. *DCH* 2:267–73.

4. *DCH* lists Ps 147:13 and Deut 19:18 [*sic* 29:18] as the only references given for "be strong" (2:271–72). The versions struggle as well. For the form והתברך (Deut 29:18), the LXX employs an aorist middle subjunctive (ἐπιφημίσηται, "congratulate oneself"). The Targums reveal the difficulty, rendering: יחשב (*Tg. Onq.*, "reflect on") and יתפייס (*Tg. Neb.*, "take comfort"). However, C. W. Mitchell argues strongly that texts such as Deut 29:18 are traditionally misapplied (cf. Isa 65:16; Ps 72:17) and have been misconstrued in the methods of Driver, Wehmeier, Scharbert and Keller who inappropriately read reflexive usages back into Gen 22:18 and 26:4, for example (*The Meaning of BRK "To Bless" in the Old Testament*, SBLDS 95 [Atlanta: Scholars Press, 1987], 33, 124, 125, 182).

5. See the extended bibliography from J. Scharbert, "ברך," *TDOT*, 2:279–308, and the smaller listing in *DCH*, 2:613–14.

Semantic and Literary Analysis of Mandate Terms

etymological connection, and one unsubstantiated in Semitic languages.[6] In other words the positivistic assumption of lexical development from "knee" through "kneeling" to reception of "blessing" has largely been laid aside as etymological theorizing that adds little to the significance of ברך.[7] Some would call this the *root* or *etymological fallacy*, believing meaning can be ascertained by isolating origins. J. Barr gives an illustration using לֶחֶם ("bread") and מִלְחָמָה ("war"):

> It must be regarded as doubtful whether the influence of their common root is of any importance semantically in classical Hebrew in the normal usage of the words. And it would be utterly fanciful to connect the two as mutually suggestive or evocative, as if battles were normally for the sake of bread or bread is a necessary provision for battles.[8]

According to Mitchell, ברך "to bless" is not associated with ברך "to kneel" among the biblical writers.[9]

Another debate surrounding ברך concerns the nature of its transfer. Whether it is God or humans issuing the blessing, should blessing be understood in terms of *content* (i.e., fertility and property), *relationship* (i.e., social dynamic of cause), or some combination? Adding to the issue's complexity are various treatments within the literature that resemble description more than explanation.

Using the language of "benediction" and "benefaction," Mitchell describes the blessing of God toward man. For Mitchell, "benediction" is oral and constitutes an *illocutionary* utterance.[10] Within "speech act" theory, performative pertains to the force of an utterance in such cases

---

6. See discussions in C. W. Mitchell, *The Meaning*, 16; and Scharbert, "ברך," *TDOT* 2:284.

7. M. L. Brown, "ברך," *NIDOTTE*, 1:757; Scharbert, "ברך," *TDOT*, 2:303. For an older espousal of this lexical development for ברך, see F. Delitzsch, *A New Commentary on Genesis*, Vol. 1, trans. S. Taylor (Edinburg: T&T Clark, 1888; repr., Eugene: Wipf and Stock Publishers, 2001), 95.

8. *The Semantics of Biblical Language* (Oxford: Oxford University Press, 1961), 102. See also D. Stuart, *Old Testament Exegesis: A Handbook for Students and Pastors*. 3rd ed. (Louisville: Westminster John Knox, 2001), 178.

9. *The Meaning*, 10; cf., 12, 16. "Illocutionary" is Mitchell's term, while "performative" would be mine.

10. Ibid., 62. This is fully addressed in Chapter 3 of Mitchell's book, "God Blessing Man" (29–78). It is this category of "God blessing man" that will comprise the focus of our analysis for Genesis 1–11.

as command, promise, or rebuke.[11] These kinds of "speech acts" achieve something in the very act of doing them;[12] propositional content is not primary here. According to Mitchell "God's benedictions are always illocutionary utterances in which God makes known his feelings toward persons or things."[13] This provides helpful direction for understanding the nature and function of blessing, but further distinction is needed.

The relative power or "efficacy" of blessing has led some to distinguish between magical and religious conceptions.[14] The former attributed an irrevocable and mechanical or self-fulfilling power to words themselves, either in blessing or cursing, while the latter derived the element of efficacy from the collaborative will of the deity(s).[15] More recent consensus of biblical texts, however, reveals a shift away from "magical utterance" to *relational processes*.[16] Blessing is ultimately superintended by God, and results in the strengthened solidarity of individuals and groups in light of their relationship with God.[17] Thus, the primary animating element of blessing derives from the relationship shared between the parties.[18]

---

11. J. W. Voelz, *What Does This Mean? Principles of Biblical Interpretation in the Post-Modern World*, 2nd ed. (St. Louis: Concordia, 1997), 276–77. Voelz's discussion of pragmatics is well-informed (pp. 276–88), even including two addenda to the chapter ("Performative Speech Acts," 289–92; "Genre in Semantic and Pragmatic Perspective," 293–300).

12. Ibid., 289.

13. *The Meaning*, 62.

14. J. Scharbert, "ברך" *TDOT*, 2:303, 304.

15. W. J. Urbrock, "Blessings and Curses," *ABD*, 1:755–61.

16. C. Mitchell asserts, "The statements never effect blessing by the magical power of the spoken word" (*The Meaning*, 62). F. R. Magdalene also senses and agrees with the shift away from the "magical" to a theo-centric origin of blessing ("Bless, Blessing," in *Eerdmans Dictionary of the Bible*, ed. D. N. Freedman (Grand Rapids: Eerdmans, 2000), 192.

17. J. Scharbert, "ברך," *TDOT*, 2:303.

18. K. H. Richards, "Bless/Blessing," *ABD*, 1:753–55. Analyzing performative speech in Ugaritic through theory and philology, S. L. Sanders concludes:

> ... divine language is self-enacting. In the Kothar-wa-Hasis passage ... gods' words are icons of things. Things are endowed with identity by dubbing them with names, but divinely endowed names themselves retain their wordhood in the fullest sense: they are semantically and pragmatically transparent and alive, open to grammatical change that effects physical action. They represent the ideal of "fully productive" pragmatic language. Human language, even magic and ritual language, does not work the same way. Instead of being directly self-enacting, it must work through modeling. God's cannot be invoked directly but must be invoked by narrating the

Semantic and Literary Analysis of Mandate Terms

Operating within a *relational* framework, Mitchell stipulates three elements necessary for blessing to have a "valid" effect: (1) the proper person, (2) the proper form with meaning, and (3) the proper setting.[19] It is through blessing as God's *effective word*[20] that the status of the relationship is affirmed and the recipient becomes aware of the value of their relationship.[21]

Our study of issues surrounding ברך gain clarity from these insights since Genesis 1–11 strictly focuses on God's blessing of (and cursing)[22] human beings. Divine blessing then, carries efficacy because of God's inherent authority and power. This represents movement and endowment from the superior to the inferior party. Except for early Aramaic among non-biblical Semitic languages, the deity remains the one blessing and never the one blessed.[23] God is the *guarantor* of its acquisition; he alone

---

actions of other divine agents invoking them, as in the case of gracious gods, or by drawing on unnamed agents ... ("Performative Utterances and Divine Language in Ugaritic," *JNES* 63 [2004]: 161–81.)

19. *The Meaning*, 173–76.
20. C. A. Keller/G. Wehmeier, "בָּרַךְ," *TLOT*, 1:266–82.
21. K. H. Richards, "Bless/Blessing," 1:754. M. Evans states:

Attention should rather be directed to the single and significant blessing of being in relationship with God and the single curse of being outside God's sphere, no longer in relationship with him. ("Blessing/curse," in *New Dictionary of Biblical Theology*, ed. T. D. Alexander and B. S. Rosner [Downers Grove: InterVarsity, 2000], 397–401, 398.)

22. Comparing performative utterances and the covenant curses of Deuteronomy 28 with magic and ritual in Middle Egyptian, J. Assmann states:

The same potentially performative status applies to our Egyptian images. The execution depicted is not a record of a historical event but a threat that, like the curses written into treaties, will fulfill itself under certain conditions. Therefore we must regard these images as symbolic acts of deterrence, of fending-off by magic, rather than acts of subjugation, which would after all imply a form of inclusion in the Egyptian world. (*The Mind of Egypt: History and Meaning in the Time of the Pharaohs*, trans. A. Jenkins [New York: Metropolitan Books, 1996], 151.)

There are intriguing parallels to God's command against eating from the tree of the knowledge of good and evil (Gen 2:16–17), and the subsequent results. It is significant that "curse" pertains to some *violation* precisely of that relationship with God (V. P. Hamilton, "אָרַר," *TWOT*, 1:75–76).

23. M. L. Brown, "בָּרַךְ," *NIDOTTE*, 1:757. Considering Psalms 103–4 and their use of ברך, H-J. Kraus concurs with Brown that ברך is strictly "blessing" God, per se: "[In] the context of the song of thanksgiving and the song of praise, ברך has the meaning 'to laud,' 'to praise,'" and Kraus translates it as "praise" (*Psalms 60-150*. CC. Tran. H. C. Oswald

sees to the fulfillment of its intent.[24] For this reason, God's blessing exceeds mere wish; it is a bestowal of life-force whereby the power-for-life possessed by God is generously transferred.[25] This kind of blessing "occurs in a world of intense interpersonal relationships [and] is not explainable in any positivistic terms."[26]

Genesis 1–11

We now turn our attention to the particular usage of ברך. Within Genesis 1–11 the verb ברך occurs 6x: 1x in Qal and 5x in the Piel.[27] When one includes Genesis 12–50 with 1–11, ברך occurs 8x in Qal,[28] 3x in Niphal,[29] 2x in Hithpael,[30] and 59x in Piel.[31] The nominal form בְּרָכָה occurs 16x in Genesis.[32] Within the whole of Genesis the root ברך occurs 88x, a quantity exceeding all other Old Testament books,[33] clearly establishing it as a dominant theme. Altogether, the verb ברך and the substantive בְּרָכָה occur 398x in Old Testament.[34]

[Minneapolis: Fortress, 1993], 291; cf. 288–89). J. Scharbert also agrees, taking the *brk* formula as "purely liturgical" ("בּרךְ," *TDOT*, 2:293; so NET, TNIV, HCSB).

24. W. J. Urbrock, "Blessings and Curses," *ABD*, 1:756.

25. W. Brueggemann, *Theology of the Old Testament* (Minneapolis: Fortress, 1997), 165.

26. W. Brueggemann, "Blessing," in *Reverberations of Faith: A Theological Handbook of Old Testament Themes* (Louisville: Westminster John Knox, 2002), 19.

27. Cf. 1:22, 28; 2:3; 5:2; 9:1 (Piel), and 9:26 (Qal passive).

28. Cf. 9:26; 14:19, 20; 24:27, 31; 26:29; 27:29, 33. All these occurrences are Qal passives. The Qal passive occurs 63x elsewhere in the Old Testament, totaling 71x.

29. Cf. 12:3; 18:18; 28:14.

30. Cf. 22:18; 26:4.

31. Cf. 1:22, 28; 2:3; 5:2; 9:1; 12:2, 3[2x]; 14:19; 17:16[2x], 20; 22:17[2x]; 24:1, 35, 48, 60; 25:11; 26:3, 12, 24; 27:4, 7, 10, 19, 23, 25, 27[2x], 29, 30, 31, 33, 34, 38, 41; 28:1, 3, 6[2x]; 30:27, 30; 31:55; 32:1, 26, 27, 29, 30; 35:9; 39:5; 47:7, 10; 48:3, 9, 15, 16, 20[2x]; 49:25, 28[2x].

32. Cf. 12:2; 27:12, 35, 36[2x], 38, 41; 28:4; 33:11; 39:5; 49:25[3x], 26[2x], 28.

33. The book with the 2nd most occurrences of ברך is Psalms (83x) followed by Deuteronomy (51x).

34. See C. A. Keller/G. Wehmeier, "בּרךְ," *TLOT*, 1:267. However, Mitchell's tally totals 403 (cf. *The Meaning*, "Table 1," 185).

Semantic and Literary Analysis of Mandate Terms

With the Piel[35] of ברך occurring 233x[36] in the Old Testament and comprising five of the six occurrences in Genesis 1–11, it is important to consider the particular use of this stem for ברך. However, the Piel stem is so difficult to classify in general, Joüon-Muraoka describe it as "the most elusive of the Hebrew conjugations."[37]

Generally speaking, the Piel can be used to express the *factitive/causative* sense of Qal verbs.[38] More specifically, the Piel denotes cause issuing in a *condition* rather than action. One recent explanation argues:

> the Piel focuses on causation and the outcome of the action, though with a patiency nuance rather than an agency nuance (as in Hiphil). The foregrounded interest is not the event that happens to the subject, but rather the condition attained by it. It is for all practical purposes an adjectival causation predicate ... In the Piel, the object of causation is in a state of suffering the effects of an action and is inherently passive in part.[39]

Thus, the Piel amounts to converting a *telic causative* (i.e., process + built-in goal) that focuses on "accomplishment" into an *atelic* (i.e., no introductory process) use that stresses "achievement." Such *atelic* "achievement" verbs conceal the process behind the result.[40] It appears then, that the Piel use behind the five occurrences of ברך in Genesis 1–11 share elements of both *factitive* (i.e., cause producing a state) and *declarative* usage (i.e., a kind of proclamation or estimative assessment).[41]

Of the 233 occurrences of Piel ברך, 97 pertain to God's blessing achievement.[42] Of those 97 occurrences, a full 87 construe God as the

---

35. Within the Old Testament the Piel stem occurs 6,808x: 2,215x in the Perfect, 2,565x in the Imperfect, 774x in the Participle, 444x in the Imperative, 725x in the Inf. Construct, and 85x in the Inf. Absolute.

36. *HALOT* lists the total for Piel as 235x (1:160).

37. Joüon, 151.

38. C. H. J. van der Merwe, J. A. Naudé, and J. H. Kroeze, *A Biblical Hebrew Reference Grammar*, Hebrew 3 (Sheffield: Sheffield Academic Press, 1999), 80. Building on Jenni, *IBHS* limits "causative" to the Hiphil (see 399–400; §24.1).

39. B. T. Arnold and J. H. Choi, *A Guide to Biblical Hebrew Syntax* (Cambridge: Cambridge University Press, 2003), 43.

40. E. Jenni, SBL Annual Meeting, "Linguistics and Biblical Hebrew Section" (Boston. Nov. 22, 1999).

41. See *GBHS*, 44–45; *IBHS*, §24.2. Keller and Wehmeier agree, assessing the use of the Piel as "primarily factitive and declarative-estimative" ("ברך," *TLOT*, 1:270).

42. Of the 233 occurrences of Piel ברך, 136 pertain to human blessing activity with 87 occurrences construing people as the grammatical subject.

grammatical subject.⁴³ In fact, N.W. Semitic languages outside the Old Testament use the finite verb ברך "almost exclusively with particular deities as the subject."⁴⁴ Within Piel ברך then, five key uses in Genesis 1–11⁴⁵ all have God as the subject.

These five key texts portray divine blessing as equipping or enduing with life-force.⁴⁶ More specifically, within Genesis 1–11 are three texts that stress the power of God's spoken word (אמר) uniquely allied to his creation (Gen 1:22 [לאמר], 28 [ויאמר], and 9:1 [ויאמר]). In these texts, God immediately pronounces blessing following his creation or its restoration to its intended moral state (9:1), soliciting the same creation-like response of blessing.

Furthermore, these initial pronouncements of divine blessing are given to both animal (1:22; cf., Deut 7:13) and human life (1:28).⁴⁷ In addition, the relative "timelessness" of day-seven sets it apart (2:3). As the goal of creation, this day God declares "holy," not merely "good" and it also brings God's blessing (2:3; cf., Exod 20:11).⁴⁸ Like the blessing of the animals (1:22) and humans (1:28), the seventh-day blessing comes from God alone. Oriented to benefit all creation, "such a goal cannot be gained by toil or trial but is given."⁴⁹

---

43. C. A. Keller/G. Wehmeier, "ברך," *TLOT*, 1:270.

44. Ibid.

45. Cf. 1:22, 28; 2:3; 5:2; 9:1.

46. C. A. Keller/G. Wehmeier, "ברך," *TLOT*, 1:270, cf. *HALOT*, 1:160.1.

47. However, God only blesses that which can respond in movement as indicative of "life." Therefore plants are not "blessed" but both animals and humans are called: נֶפֶשׁ חַיָּה ("living being[s]"; cf. Gen 1:20, 24, 30; 2:7, 19).

48. This is the only day not defined with temporal parameters (i.e., "evening and morning," cf. 1:8, 23), but merely announced. Of this W. J. Dumbrell comments:

> It is clear that though the noun *shabbaton* "Sabbath" does not occur, the verb *shabat* is used twice in 2:1–3. It is likely that this creation Sabbath is meant to provide the context in which humankind in Genesis 2 is to operate, since the seventh day, the basis for the latter Sabbath, is presented as unending, with no morning or evening and thus as ongoing throughout human history. (*The Faith of Israel: A Theological Survey of the Old Testament*, 2nd ed. [Grand Rapids: Baker, 2002], 18.)

See also S. E. Balentine, *The Torah's Vision of Worship*, OBT (Minneapolis: Fortress, 1999), 90–95.

49. W. J. Dumbrell, "Creation, Covenant and Work," in *With Heart, Mind and Strength: The Best of Crux 1979–1989*. ed. D. M. Lewis (Langley: Credo, 1990), 151–70, 168.

Semantic and Literary Analysis of Mandate Terms

The significance of the Qal passive בְּרָכָה ("blessing," 9:26) is an indication of the state of possessing divine blessing. בְּרָכָה itself is not the *result* of a prior act of blessing,[50] instead the term identifies the life of one who routinely receives God's benefits.[51] As an example, ויאמר ברוך יהוה אלהי שם ("And he said,[52] 'Blessed be the LORD God of Shem'") recounts Noah's benediction, asking that the LORD be identified as Shem's God and that Shem be allied in partnership with God.

OLD TESTAMENT

Having noted the dominant role of Piel ברך in general, and every occurrence in Genesis 1–11, we can trace key trajectories of God's blessing throughout the Old Testament. At the core of divine blessing stand people in reception.[53] In 80 of the 97 occurrences of Piel ברך with God as subject, the issue concerns divine blessing of people.[54] A distant second is divine blessing of inanimate objects[55] or institutions.[56] However, several other areas should also be noted.

God's blessings are often promises,[57] and are found in: (1) patriarchal narratives,[58] (2) poetic maxims,[59] (3) and prophetic promises.[60] In

---

50. C. A. Keller/G. Wehmeier, "ברך," *TLOT*, 1:268.

51. C. W. Mitchell, *The Meaning*, 51.

52. This blessing is for the LORD, not Shem. If Shem were the recipient of the blessing we would find Piel ברך. Moreover, the narrator rhetorically highlights Shem's oracle through the *double-introductory* ויאמר (vv. 25, 26).

53. Cf. Gen 12:2; 26:12; 32:30; 48:3; Exod 20:24; Num 6:24, 27; 23:20; Deut 1:11; 7:13; 14:24; 16:15; 24:19; 28:8; Josh 24:10; Judg 13:24; 2 Sam 6:11; 7:29; 1 Chron 4:10; 17:27; 1 Chron 31:10; Ruth 2:4; Pss 5:13; 29:11; 67:2, 7, 8; 115:12, 13; 134:3; Prov 3:33; Isa 19:25; 61:9; Jer 31:23, etc.

54. C. A. Keller/G. Wehmeier, "ברך," *TLOT*, 1:272–73.

55. Gen 2:3; 27:27–28; Exod 20:11; 23:25–26; Deut 28:5, 8, 12; 33:13; Job 1:10, etc.

56. Gen 39:5; Deut 7:13; 33:11; Jer 31:23; Pss 65:11; 132:15; Prov 3:33, etc.

57. Th. Hartmann, "רָב," *TLOT*, 3:1194–1201 (cf. Abraham, 22:17; Isaac, 26:3ff., 24; Jacob, 35:11; Joseph, 48:16); C. W. Mitchell, *The Meaning*, 29.

58. Cf., Gen 12:1–3; 17:2–24; 18:18; 22:18; 26:4; 28:14, etc.

59. Cf., Pss 5:13; 24:3–5; 37; 128; Prov 10:22; 22:9; 28:20, etc.

60. Cf., Ezek 34:22, 26; Isa 19:20, 24–25; 51:1–3; Jer 4:1–2; 65:17–18; Hos 2:22; Joel 3:18; Amos 9:13–14; Zech 8:12, etc.

addition, God also displays: (1) oral blessing or material approval,[61] (2) preservation of creation,[62] (3) and fulfillment of patriarchal promises.[63]

On the whole, prophetic books show far less occurrences of blessing since their aim is covenant renewal and often, pending judgment. While it is not surprising to find God's blessing in the patriarchal narratives and historical books, it is startling to note the complete absence of blessing in Esther.[64] Clearly, that which was blessed was assumed to function optimally in accordance with divine design.[65]

SUMMARY

We can now take stock in key points of significance regarding ברך that will affect our study of the Creation Mandate (i.e., 1:22, 28; 8:17; 9:1, 7). First, blessing in the Old Testament is overtly *theo*-centric, which serves to distance the author's notions of God from pagan mantras, ritual, and theogony.[66] God's acts of blessing are not coerced, assisted, or preempted in any way. There is no initial cause or divine obligation requiring God to bless. Particularly in Genesis 1–11, the blessing of God follows creative or

---

61. Cf., Exodus 32; Num 22:12; 1 Sam 9:13; Isa 19:25, etc.
62. Cf., Gen 27:27; Ps 65; Isa 65:8, etc.
63. Cf., Gen 24:1, 35–36; 25:11; 26:12–14, 26–31; 39:2–5, etc.
64. This reflects language of *anti-blessing*, namely divine judgment as estrangement: "Then my anger will be aroused against them in that day, and I will abandon them, and *I will hide my face from them*, and they will be consumed, and many evils and calamities will fall on them. In this way they will say in that day, 'Have not these evils come upon us because our God is not among us?' And *I will surely hide my face* ..." (Deut 31:17–18a; cf. 5:7; 32:20. Emphasis added).

Deut 31:16–18 forms a single unit with the outer frame noting the situation of apostasy (vv. 16b, 18b) and the inner frame delineating YHWH's reaction ("I will hide my face ... in that day" [vv. 17a, 18a]). Consequences lie at the center: "evils and troubles" (v. 17b). Regarding "face," D. L. Christensen states: "The 'face' of God is his attentive presence and favor, his blessing" (*Deuteronomy 21:10—34:12*, WBC [Nashville: Thomas Nelson, 2002], 772).

65. M. L. Brown, "ברך," *NIDOTTE*, 1:759.

66. See C. Westermann's excursus on "blessing" for the theological nature and distinction of ברך in Genesis 1 over against pagan mythological accounts (*Genesis 1–11: A Commentary*, trans. J. J. Scullion [Minneapolis: Augsburg, 1984], 139–41.

Assessing the anthropological and religious use of key pentateuchal texts, see E. T. Mullen, Jr., *Ethnic Myths and Pentateuchal Foundations: A New Approach to the Formation of the Pentateuch* (Atlanta: Scholars Press, 1997), esp. 91–108.

Semantic and Literary Analysis of Mandate Terms

restorative (i.e., re-creative) acts.[67] Following his creation (Genesis 1–2), Genesis 3–11 stresses God's counter-active measures to human hubris.

Secondly, while the reader can hear God pronounce blessings in Genesis 1–11, on the whole the blessing texts are cast *descriptively* by the narrator's hand. However, the trajectory of Divine blessing is essentially forward-looking and as such encompasses a futuristic scope that allowed for eschatological development, primarily of God's covenant people.[68]

Thirdly, neither content nor mechanism is generally cited in blessings since the notion of sufficiency is assumed in the verbal idea.[69] Yet blessing does possess content in that it enables the one blessed.[70] In short, blessing ignites and animates life, giving it direction and purpose. Such a blessing presupposes relationship.[71] God's blessing signals action simultaneous to his verbal pronouncement. "Where modern man talks of success, OT man talked of blessing."[72] A life without God's blessing throws into relief the cosmic strain of pronouncements that curse someone or something, thereby depriving life (Gen 3:14–19; 4:11–12; cf., Deut 28:15ff).

---

67. Leading up to the Mandate itself (1:28) God routinely evaluated his creative work as טוֹב ("good"). However his *seventh* and climatic evaluation (1:31) follows the creation of humankind where we read: וְהִנֵּה־טוֹב מְאֹד ("and look! It was very good"; cf. vv. 4, 10, 12, 18, 21, 25). Here, the use of the particle וְהִנֵּה with the conjunction does not denote "surprise" per se, but serves to "draw attention to the marvelous," especially following verbs of perception (M. Futato, *Beginning Biblical Hebrew* [Winona Lake: Eisenbrauns, 2003], 190). I take "good" to mean his creation completely achieved divine intention and was conducive for life (cf. Ps 104:19–20). Significantly the light rather than the darkness is called "good." In John 1:5, the light does not merely "appear" but victoriously *invades* the realm of darkness (B. F. Westcott, *The Gospel According to St. John: The Authorized Version with Introduction and Notes* [Cambridge, 1881; reprint, Grand Rapids: Eerdmans, 1971], 4). With the mention of light in John 1:5, the author now employs the present tense—an *historical* present with *gnomic* force. One thinks of 1QM, *The War of the Sons of Light with the Sons of Darkness*. John 1:5 reveals this cosmic antithesis highlighted by the antithetical literary structure using an *adversative* καί ("...but the darkness").

68. Similarly, L. Turner states, "These blessings anticipate events beyond the 'creation week'... The fate of the blessings here and on day 6 is one element of interest carried over into the ensuing narrative" (*Genesis*, 23).

69. C. A. Keller/G. Wehmeier, "ברך," *TLOT*, 1:270. Scholarly opinion is still divided as to whether God's blessing reflects "divine approval" (so Mitchell) or "reproductive power" (so Westermann) for a creation made to procreate from the outset (cf., *The Meaning*, 62; *Genesis 1–11*, 140, respectively). Resolution will have to wait for our exegesis of these separate texts in chapter four.

70. M. L. Brown, "ברך," *NIDOTTE*, 1:758.

71. K. Mathews, *Genesis 1—11:26*, 158.

72. G. J. Wenham, *Genesis 1–15*, WBC (Waco: Word Books, 1987), 24.

Be Fruitful and Multiply

SEMANTIC ANALYSIS OF פְּרוּ וּרְבוּ

The second cluster of terms comprising the Creation Mandate are the verbs: פרה and רבה. We will consider whether פְּרוּ וּרְבוּ ("be fruitful and multiply") functions as a hendiadys[73] and to what degree it constitutes a "formula" or formal collocation.[74] Moreover, exactly how the imperatives that comprise these clusters should be understood also needs to be determined (i.e., 1:22, 28; 8:17; 9:1, 7).

GENESIS 1–11

As a verbal lexeme, פרה occurs 29x,[75] 22x in the Qal[76] and 7x in the Hiphil.[77] The Qal means "to bear fruit" and both Qal and Hiphil forms can mean "to multiply" or "make fruitful, numerous."[78] In Genesis 1–11 פרה occurs 5x, with all occurrences in the Qal.[79]

---

73. Some analyses are built on five separate delineated imperatives in texts such as Gen 1:28. However, F. I. Anderson takes the various occurrences of פְּרוּ וּרְבוּ as a hendiadys, stating:

Certain idiomatic sequences of coordinated verbs can amount to a composite description of a single action. Thus $p^e r\bar{u}\ \bar{u}r^e b\bar{u}$, increase and multiply . . . means be abundantly fruitful. (*The Sentence*, 117. Emphasis original.)

74. For a discussion of collocations see S. C. Poole, *An Introduction to Linguistics* (New York: St. Martin's Press), 28, 29.

75. Gen 1:22, 28; 8:17; 9:1, 7; 17:6, 20; 26:2; 28:3; 35:11; 41:52; 47:27; 48:4; 49:22[2x]; Exod 1:7; 23:30; Lev 26:9; Deut 29:18; Pss 105:24; 128:3; Isa 11:1; 17:6; 32:12; 45:8; Jer 3:16; 23:3; Ezek 19:10; 36:11.

76. Gen 1:22, 28; 8:17; 9:1, 7; 26:22; 35:11; 47:27; 49:22; Exod 1:7; 23:30; Deut 29:18; Ps 128:3; Isa 11:1; 17:6; 32:12; 45:8; Jer 3:16; 23:3; Ezek 19:10; 36:11.

77. Only referencing humans: Gen 17:6, 20; 28:3; 41:52; 48:4; Lev 26:9; Ps 105:24. Nominal form: פְּרִי 119x.

78. Cf. BDB, 826; *HALOT*, 3:963–64; Kedar-Kopfstin, "פָּרָה," *TDOT*, 12:81–91.

79. Gen 1:22, 28; 8:17; 9:1, 7.

Semantic and Literary Analysis of Mandate Terms

The verbal lexeme, רבה is more common than פרה, occurring 174x.[80] Within Genesis 1–11, רבה occurs 11x,[81] 9x in Qal[82] and 2x in Hiphil.[83] Within Qal, רבה has a *quantitative* force making it uniquely suited for contexts of blessing that stipulate vast numbers and the actual state of "fruitfulness."[84]

Beyond cognate occurrences of these verbs, our interest lies particularly in the repeated combination פרו ורבו ("be fruitful and multiply"). This tandem use occurs 14x in the Old Testament.[85] In Genesis 1–11 we not only find the verbs פרה and רבה used 5x, but in fact they occur in formal juxtaposition. In other words, פרה is contextually contiguous with רבה and also in combination with other forms.[86]

This contiguous pair is initially used of animals in Gen 1:22. The animals stipulated are aquatic and aerial (1:20, 21). However, unlike the fish and birds of Day Five (1:20–23) the *land animals* receive no such formulaic blessing on Day Six (1:24–31),[87] for they share man's domain

---

80. רבה by cognate encompasses: Gen 26x, Ezek 20x, Deut 19x, Exod 11x, Prov 11x, 1 Chr 9x, Pss 9x, Job 8x, Jer 8x, Isa 7x, Hos 6x, 2 Chr 5x, 1 Sam 4x, Lev, Num, Judg, 2 Sam, Neh, and Eccl all have 3x, Ezra, Lam, Dan all have 2x, with Josh, 1 Kgs, 2 Kgs, Nah, Hab, Zech all having 1x. Within the Pentateuch, רבה occurs 62x with 26 occurrences in Genesis. The related nominal forms of רבה are well attested: רַב ("many, great," 424x); רֹב ("many, great," 151x); רָבָב ("many, numerous," 22x). Even-Shoshan lists a total of 476 occurrences, including Aramaic forms and separate roots of רַב meaning "enough" (13x) and as a political title (35x; 1055).

81. Gen 1:22[2x], 28; 3:16[2x]; 7:17, 18; 8:17; 9:1, 7[2x].

82. Gen 1:22[2x], 28; 7:17, 18; 8:17; 9:1, 7[2x]. The root occurs about 60x in the Qal.

83. Gen 3:16[2x]. The root occurs about 160x in the Hiphil.

84. A. Hill, "רָבָה," *NIDOTTE*, 4:1038.

85. Gen 1:22, 28; 8:17; 9:1, 7; 17:2, 6, 20; 28:3; 35:11; 47:27; 48:4; Exod 1:7; Lev 26:9. Using the Hiphil, emphasizing human objects: Gen 17:20; 28:3; 48:4; Lev 26:9; Jer 23:3.

86. Kedar-Kopfstin, "פָּרָה," *TDOT*, 12:85. These forms being: כָּבַשׁ, שָׁרַץ, מָלֵא, and רָדָה which will be analyzed below.

87. Many commentators note this: T. E. Fretheim calls it "something of a puzzle" ("The Book of Genesis: Introduction, Commentary, and Reflections," in *The New Interpreter's Bible*, Vol. 1 [Nashville: Abingdon, 1994], 345). B. K. Waltke understands the lack of blessing pertaining to man's dominion, and since humans rule the animals it would pose a threat, unlike the fish and birds that inhabit different spheres (cf. Exod 23:29; *Genesis: A Commentary* [Grand Rapids: Zondervan, 2001], 64). V. P. Hamilton proposes that God's blessing demarcates the three "critical junctures": (1) introductory statement [v. 1], (2) creation of organic life [v. 20], (3) and human life [v. 26] (*The Book of Genesis: 1–17*, NICOT [Grand Rapids: Eerdmans, 1990]). Following C. Westermann (*Genesis 1–11*, 141–42), G. Wenham suggests that man's blessing "covered all the works of the sixth day, including animals" (*Genesis 1–15*, 26). J. E. Hartley suggests that the wellbeing of animals

requiring overt measures with significant symbolism to be taken to avoid conflict.[88] As a pair,[89] פרה and רבה occur again regarding animals in 8:17, though this time including land animals. However, this text resembles more of a divine *declaration* than a standard blessing.[90]

Three texts in Genesis 1–11 employ the contiguous formula פרו ורבו ("be fruitful and multiply") for people (Gen 1:28; 9:1, 7). The initial blessing given to Adam (1:28) is reiterated to Noah after the flood (9:1, 7). These verbs constitute a standard expression in the context of divine blessing. In Westermann's words:

> Fertility and increase point to abundance; abundance belongs to blessing; abundance, wealth and plenty are both signs and the effect of blessing.[91]

---

and man are intertwined in his blessing (*Genesis*, NIBCOT, ed. R. L. Hubbard, Jr. and R. K. Johnston [Peabody: Hendrickson, 2000], 50). Cassuto takes it a step further, stipulating that only יִרֶב ("multiply") is used for the aerial creatures (1:22b), revealing a lesser blessing than the aquatic animals (22a) (*A Commentary on the Book of Genesis*, 2 vols., trans. I. Abrahams [Jerusalem: Magnes, 1972], 1:52). Cf. E. Blum, "רָב," *TDOT*, 13:272–93.

The mention of: אֶת־שְׁנֵי הַמְּאֹרֹת הַגְּדֹלִים ("the two great lights") for the sun and moon on Day Four are equally striking since they receive *neither* naming nor blessing (cf. 1:14–19). Additionally, the use of הַתַּנִּינִם הַגְּדֹלִים ("great aquatic denizens") over דָּגִים ("fish," 21) and עוֹף כָּנָף ("flying animals with wings," 21) rather than "birds" reveals an arguable use of polemic (see G. Hasel, "The Polemic Nature of the Genesis Cosmology," *EvQ* 46 [1974]: 81–102).

88. E. Blum, "רָב," *TDOT* 13:282. W. P. Brown agrees with this view (*The Ethos of the Cosmos: The Genesis of Moral Imagination in the Bible* [Grand Rapids: Eerdmans, 1999], 37–38). The narrator's introduction of the "serpent" as a חַיַּת הַשָּׂדֶה ("animal of the field," 3:1) corroborates this, emphasizing the land-based focus of the early chapters (cf. 3:14 with repeated phrases). Aquatic animals and reference to the sea-domain are omitted in Genesis 2 as the emphasis shifts to the function of God's vice-regents in their domain of the garden-sanctuary. Leviticus 11 also lists prohibited animal "kinds" (לְמִינֵהוּ) following the same "domains" initiated in creation, but in reverse order: Earth (Lev 11:2–8) // Heavens (Gen 1:11–14); Water (Lev 11:9–12) // Water (Gen 1:20–23); Heavens (Lev 11:13–25) // Earth (Gen 1:24–31) (See M. Douglas, "The Forbidden Animals in Leviticus," in *The Pentateuch*, ed. J. W. Rogerson, TBS 39 [Sheffield: Sheffield Academic Press, 1996], 255, 242–62).

89. A non-paired expression occurs in Ezek 36:11.

90. This is a scene of disembarking that frames the earlier boarding (Gen 7:7–16). For this reason the imperative mood is found in הַוְצֵא ("bring out") and not with the perfective פָּרוּ וּרְבוּ ("be fruitful and multiply"), elsewhere found in the imperative (cf. Gen 1:22, 28; 9:1, 7, etc. See E. Blum, "רָב," *TDOT* 13:281).

91. *Genesis 1–11*, 141.

Semantic and Literary Analysis of Mandate Terms

OLD TESTAMENT

The use of the contiguous formula פרו ורבו ("be fruitful and multiply") in the balance of the Old Testament reveals an extension or *maturing* of the concept employed earlier in Genesis 1–11. Whereas God is regularly portrayed reacting to human rebellion in Genesis 1–11, Genesis 12–50 appears to minimize judgment in order to accentuate blessing. The formula is concentrated in the lives of the patriarchs that dominate the latter part of Genesis.[92] Here the language of blessing is extended to Abraham,[93] Isaac,[94] and Jacob[95] through the sustained promise of land and descendants. The triad of "Abraham, Isaac, and Jacob" form a stock phrase that uniquely denotes God's land promises.[96]

The formula is strategically used in Gen 17:20 where God ratifies his covenant with Abraham, and Sarah is promised a child (17:15–17). Here it is significant that the promise of progeny is directly linked to the covenant (17:2, 6–7).[97] The contiguous phrase פרו ורבו (28:2–3) is also found in a proverbial form of *farewell blessing*, apparently invoking the fertility of a betrothed couple (cf. 24:60).[98]

---

92. Developing the content of Genesis 1–11, the other crucial texts employing some form of the formula פרו ורבו are: Gen 17:20; 28:3; 35:11; 47:27; 48:4.

93. Cf. 17:2, 6, 8, 16; 22:18, etc.

94. Cf. 26:3–4, 24, etc.

95. Cf. 28:4, 14; 35:12; 48:3, 15–16, etc.

96. Cf. Gen 50:24; Exod 3:6; Lev 26:42; Ps 105:8–11.

97. J. Milgrom, *Leviticus 23–27: A New Translation with Introduction and Commentary*, Vol. AB, 3B (New York: Doubleday, 2001), 2298. With Isaac, there is a unique emphasis on land-fertility (cf. 26:1–13). This serves to heighten Isaac's legal claim to a land; he—among all the patriarchs—will never leave (26:3a). This land-claim is emphasized through Isaac's five named wells and the additional stipulation of his planting (cf. 26:12–16).

98. Kedar-Kopfstein, "פָּרָה," *TDOT*, 12:85. A similar blessing is given to Rebekah when she departs her home to marry Isaac: "Our sister, may you increase (רְבָבָה) to thousands upon thousands; may your offspring possess the gates of their enemies" (Gen 24:60). The notion of blessing entailing *military* endeavor is a reiteration of God's covenant affirmation to Abraham that included a military element for the first time (cf. 22:17). To "possess the gate" was tantamount to conquering the city. Skinner states that the phrase refers to the "capture of the opponent's administrative and military centers" (*Genesis*, 164). Both uses of this conquering-phrase (Gen. 22:17; 24:60) culminate the formal rhetoric of blessing to the core participants (i.e., Abraham, Rebekah), revealing matriarchal participation in the blessing. Like the nation of Israel, both Abraham and Rebekah had to enter the land as aliens destined for land-possession. The language of these blessings is future oriented, verging on the eschatological, constructed for the emerging Israelite community using the collective singular of זרע ("seed"). For the rare use of זרע with a woman as subject, see Gen 3:15; 16:10.

The formula employed for humanity at creation gives way to a successive stewardship of patriarchal blessings[99] that in-turn is enacted in a national story (Exod 1:7). Ironically, it is through God's blessing of the Israelite nation[100] that the world-international will achieve blessing; the role of mediators now becomes crucial. As the blessing *matures* and permeates the world, it is done through the mediatorial function of Noah, Abraham, and David, each initiating a new order of creation patterned on the first Mandate to Adam (פרו ורבו, 1:28). Not surprisingly the language of re-constitution and restoration for an exiled Israel hearkens back to the foundational Mandate of 1:28 (cf. Jer 3:16; 23:3; Ezek 36:11).

SUMMARY

Assessing our analysis of פרו ורבו ("be fruitful and multiply"), several points can be noted. First, the general semantics of פרה and רבה not only reveal a usage in numerous parallels; more specifically they show that פרה and רבה as a pair are essential to communicate the notion of ample progeny;[101] they form the "debut" of creation.[102] According to Milgrom, פרה and רבה denote "fertility yielding an increase ... implying that progeny will survive."[103] It is with the joint lexemes of פרה and רבה that this blessing of increase is articulated.[104]

Secondly, פרו ורבו is more than a lexically contiguous pair; פרו ורבו can be defended as a formal collocation functioning as a hendiadys formula, i.e., "abundantly fruitful."[105] Thus utilizing פרה and רבה, this collocation

---

99. The fulfillment of blessing with its inception in Genesis 1–11 finds key reiteration: Gen 24:1, 35; 25:11; 26:12; 30:27, 30; 32:30; 35:9; 48:3; Deut 2:7; 12:7; 15:6, 14.

100. Cf. Gen 47:27; Exod 1:7; Ps 107:38; Isa 51:2. In a related way, see Jer 3:16; 23:3; Ezek 36:11, etc.

101. J. Milgrom, *Leviticus 23–27*, 2797.

102. E. Blum, "רַב," *TDOT*, 13:281.

103. J. Milgrom, *Leviticus 23–27*, 2797.

104. E. Blum, "רַב," *TDOT*, 13:281.

105. The masoretic tradition of accents supports our contention of a hendiadys for פרו ורבו. In Gen 1:22, the *mûnāḥ* accent initiates the collocation פְּרוּ וּרְבוּ and ends with *rᵉbiaʿ*. The *ʾatnāḥ* precedes the collocation in 1:22. In Gen 8:17 the collocation immediately follows the *zāqēp* with the accents *mêrᵉkā* and *ṭipḥā* setting off the pair (פְּרוּ וּרְבוּ, cf. 9:1). Finally, in Gen 9:7 the pair is combined by the *mûnāḥ* accent on פְּרוּ and the *ʾatnāḥ* closing the clause with וּרְבוּ.

Writing about text division within the masoretic tradition, M. Korpel utilizes J. Oesch, stating:

Semantic and Literary Analysis of Mandate Terms

shares various syntagmatic relations. We agree with Andersen that this contiguous pair forms "a composite description of a single action."[106] This justifies analyzing these two imperatives as a unit though the Creation Mandate includes additional imperatives.

Thirdly, פרה and רבה contribute a highly theological significance to their various texts (i.e., Gen 1:22, 28; 9:1, 7, etc.). Beginning in Gen 1:22 the scope is a cosmic one, not national. In these passages, God initiates magisterial decrees to a designated (inferior) representative (i.e., Adam and Noah) in language that "makes their ongoing existence possible."[107] By this means, the Creator confers on his creation the security of a continued existence.[108] Thus the reality of life, its progress, and flourish are viewed as the very manifestation of God's blessing.

Fourthly, the use of the imperatives in the Creation Mandate arguably goes beyond mere command.[109] The function of accents, genre, divine

---

It seems reasonable to suppose an integral process of writing both the text and its delimitations from the very beginning. It is the only way in which the high degree of correspondence between the different traditions (Hebrew, Samaritan, Greek, Syriac) can be explained... It is far more likely that the author or latest redactor of a work sought to safeguard the correct understanding of the text by dividing it into sense-units. ("Introduction to the Series Pericope," in *Delimitation Criticism: Scripture as Written and Read in Antiquity*, vol. 1, ed. M. Korpel and J. Oesch [The Netherlands: Van Gorcum, 2000], 1–50, 5; see also E. Tov, "The Background of the Sense Divisions in the Biblical Texts" [312–48].).

106. *The Sentence*, 117; so too V. P. Hamilton, *Genesis 1–17*, 131, n. 2; and G. Wenham, *Genesis 1–15*, 4–5. Wrestling with this contiguous form, the English translations variously construe the hendiadys: JPS (1917): "Be fruitful, and multiply"; JPS (1985): "Be fertile and increase"; NASB (1977): "Be fruitful and multiply" (so RSV, ESV, NLT2); NIV (1985): "Be fruitful and increase in number" (similarly NEB); NAB (1970): "Be fertile and multiply"; NET (2003): "Be fruitful and multiply!" [1:28]; HCSB (2004): "Be fruitful, multiply" (so JB); and Berkeley (1959): "Be fruitful; multiply."

107. E. Blum following O. H. Steck (*Der Schöpfungsbericht der Priesterschrift*, FRLANT 116 [1981]: 65, 68–69, 156), "רָבָ," *TDOT* 13: 281.

108. W. Eichrodt, *Theology of the Old Testament*, 2 vols., trans. J. Baker (Philadelphia: Westminster, 1967), 2:350, n. 1.

109. Contra Joüon, (1983), 373. C. M. Kaminski's study of the Creation Mandate texts in Genesis is weakened by her insistence that the five imperatives be read as strict commands requiring human obedience (*From Noah to Israel: Realization of the Primeval Blessing After the Flood*, JSOTSup 413 [London: T&T Clark, 2004]; see "Introduction," 1–9, 115–23, 139–46). Additional weaknesses, we believe, are: her exclusive focus on the initial three imperatives: פרה, רבה, and מלא, ignoring both masoretic accents (which embrace additional imperatives), minimizing Gen 1:22 in the study, applying an overly *realist epistemology* of "filling," and downplaying the significance of "blessing" ברך to the formulary Mandate.

performative speech, and *theo*-centric focus requires us to consider finer nuances for these imperatives.[110] To begin with, Lohfink maintains that "The blessing of fruitfulness ... is a blessing and not a 'commandment.'"[111] For Wenham, פרו ורבו carries an implicit promise of divine enablement for man.[112]

Wenham states:

> The word of blessing, whether pronounced by God or man, guarantees and effects the hoped-for success. So here the words of command "be fruitful and multiply" carry with them the divine promise that they can be carried out.[113]

Other proposals for the imperatives include: *explicative* of conferral,[114] empowerment for a special commission,[115] pronouncement of commission,[116] "vocation,"[117] "creation instruction,"[118] blessing as "power-sharing,"[119] and "blessing ... delineating a privilege."[120]

---

110. "Blessing" and "command" are blurred to some degree in Isaac's farewell to Jacob in Gen 28:1 (cf. 24:60; 27:7). In this text blessing and command merge: וַיְבָרֶךְ אֹתוֹ וַיְצַוֵּהוּ ("And he blessed him, and commanded him"). This example, however, does not exactly replicate the formulaic collocations of the Creation Mandate. Jacob has already been established as the next covenant steward (27:27–29) and 28:1 is Isaac's official recognition of Jacob as the heir of Abraham's blessing. Moreover, this text merely follows a command upon an existing blessing (see N. Stahl, *Law and Liminality in the Bible*, JSOTSup 202 [Sheffield: Sheffield Academic Press, 1995], 31).

111. *The Theology of the Pentateuch: Themes of the Priestly Narrative and Deuteronomy* (Minneapolis: Fortress, 1994), 7.

112. *Genesis 1–15*, 33. Here Wenham follows GKC §110c.

113. Ibid., 24.

114. C. Westermann, *Genesis 1–11*, 140, following GKC §110b; cf. 138–39.

115. B. W. Anderson, *From Creation to New Creation*. Old Testament Perspectives, OBT (Minneapolis: Fortress, 1994), 161.

116. W. P. Brown, *The Ethos*, 37.

117. S. D. McBride, Jr., "Divine Protocol: Genesis 1:1—2:3 as Prologue to the Pentateuch," in *God Who Creates*, 3–41. Elsewhere McBride calls the collocation of פרו ורבו "at once solemn command and blessing," (18), and "benedictory commission" (21).

118. H. A. J. Kruger, "Subscripts to Creation: A Few Exegetical Comments on the Literary Device of Repetition in Genesis 1–11," in *Studies in the Book of Genesis: Literature, Redaction and History*, ed. A. Wénin (Paris: Peters, 2001), 429–45, 436.

119. T. Fretheim, *Genesis*, 346.

120. J. Walton, *Genesis*, NIVAC (Grand Rapids: Zondervan, 2001), 134.

Semantic and Literary Analysis of Mandate Terms

The interpretation of the imperatives in the Creation Mandate has traditionally been taken as the first of the 613 laws in the Rabbinic Codes of the *Mitzvoth* given to humankind. This command was obligatory only for Jewish men, not women.[121] Whereas פרו ורבו in Gen 1:22 was seen as a blessing, its later occurrence in 1:28 was viewed as a commandment reflecting the divine will.[122]

The use of the jussives within the Creation Mandate further illustrates the need to recognize finer distinctions beyond strict command.[123] For example, we find the form יִרֶב in the phrase: וְהָעוֹף יִרֶב בָּאָרֶץ ("and let birds multiply on the earth," 1:22; cf. 1:3). With God as the sovereign Creator issuing a divine pronouncement, we maintain this reflects *divine intention* or *assurance*, since God is the subject in performative speech. Commenting on Gen 1:28, Gesenius states: "the fulfillment of which is altogether out of the power of the one addressed," having the force of "assurance" or "promise."[124] Brown elaborates:

> To cast the divine commands indirectly as jussives, rather than as direct commands, adds to the rhetorical nuance of the commands. The jussive can function as an exhortation, as offering counsel, granting permission, and in the case of a superior addressing an inferior, as a command. Clearly, the series of jussives [1:11, 14, 20a, 20b] function within the context of divine commands, but they also exhibit a nuance that is less intrusive and forward than that of a direct command. In other words, the jussive commands bear an element of exhortation. Thus the use of such indirect commands adds to the rhetoric of divine speech, designed to *enlist* aid from the earth and waters in the cosmogonic process. In short, they are exhorted to perform.[125]

In the case of יִרֶב in Gen 1:22, this jussive functions within the imperatival sequence of decretive collocations already begun with: רבה, פרה, and מלא.[126]

---

121. N. Scherman, *The Chumash: Bereishis* (Brooklyn: Meshrah Publications, 2002), 73.

122. Ibid., 7, 41.

123. See *IBHS*, 564–79; Joüon, 373–79; GKC, 319–26; van der Merwe et al., 150–53.

124. See GKC, 324.

125. *Structure, Role, and Ideology in the Hebrew and Greek Texts of Genesis 1:1—2:3*, SBLDS 132 (Atlanta: Scholars Press, 1993), 122–23.

126. The traditional reading of jussives in Genesis 1 includes: 1:3, 6, 9, 11, 12, 14, 20, 22, 24, 26. The Hebrew forms include: יְהִי (3), יִקָּווּ (9), תַּדְשֵׁא (11), תּוֹצֵא (12), and יִשְׁרְצוּ (20); see D. M. Fouts, "Selected Lexical and Grammatical Studies in Genesis 1," *AUSS* 42 (2004): 79–90, esp. 87–88.

Be Fruitful and Multiply

Semantic Analysis of שָׁרַץ, רָדָה, כָּבַשׁ, מָלֵא

The third and final cluster of terms comprising the Creation Mandate are the verbs: מָלֵא, כָּבַשׁ, רָדָה, שָׁרַץ ("fill," "subdue," "rule," and "swarm"). We will consider each word in succession, noting their use in Genesis 1–11 before considering their subsequent use in the balance of the Old Testament. A final summary and conclusion will explore their implications for the Creation Mandate.

GENESIS 1–11

The verb מלא occurs 246x in the Old Testament.[127] Within Genesis 1–11, מלא occurs 5x,[128] 4x in Qal[129] and 1x in Niphal.[130] The Qal of מלא can be either *transitive* ("to fill") or *intransitive* ("to be full"), which is more common, with the context supplying needed information. The intransitive use employs the accusative object, with or without אֶת.[131] However, וּמִלְאוּ אֶת־הַמַּיִם בַּיַּמִּים, "and fill the water in the seas" (Gen 1:22b) clearly implies "... with aquatic life" (i.e., "fish").[132] The transitive use "frequently assumes a technical, particularly military or cultic significance."[133]

---

127. מלא by cognate encompasses: Ezek 26x, Exod 23x, Isa 22x, Jer 22x, Pss 21x, Job 17x, Gen 16x, 1 Kgs 12x, 2 Chr 11x, 2 Kgs 10, etc. Within the Pentateuch, מלא occurs 58x, with Lev 9x, Num 7x, and Deut 3x. מָלֵא as the noun or substantive ("fullness, full yield") occurs 38x, only 1x in Genesis (48:19). The adjective, מָלֵא occurs 32x as "filled" and 3x in Genesis (23:9; 41:7, 22). There are 31 other uses either traditionally untranslated or occurring once with rare translations. Altogether, the root מלא occurs 383x with two in biblical Aramaic (cf. Dan 2:35; 3:19).

128. Gen 1:22, 28; 6:11, 13; 9:1. Elsewhere, מלא occurs 108x in the Piel, 35x in the Niphal, 1x in Pual (Song 5:14), and 1x in Hithpael (Job 16:10).

129. Gen 1:22, 28; 6:13; 9:1. Altogether, מלא occurs 103x in the Qal.

130. Gen 6:11: ותשחת הארץ לפני האלהים ותמלא הארץ חמס ("Now the earth had become corrupt before God, for the earth was filled with violence"). Gen 6:11–12 forces the reader to view the earth from the perspective of the cosmic Judge. "Corrupt" (שחת, 11a) occurs 7x in this narrative, but juxtaposed with "violence" (חמס, 11b; cf. v. 13) paints a picture of moral degeneration, one we will take up in the context of our analysis of Gen 9:1, 7. Mentioned 9x (cf. vv. 9–22) "earth" (ארץ) is a metonymy for people steeped in cruelty, oppression, and moral perversion. That "violence" rather than people is multiplying is an irony we can note now and develop later (cf. Lev 19:29).

131. M. Delcor, "מָלֵא," *TLOT*, 2:664–66.

132. What something is filled with constructs a double accusative of *substance* (cf. Gen 21:19; Exod 1:7; L. A. Snijders, "מָלֵא," *TDOT*, 8:297–308; *HALOT*, 2:583). However, immaterial things can also be filled (cf. Gen 25:8; 35:29; Deut 34:9).

133. M. Delcor, "מָלֵא," TLOT, 2:665. Cf. Jer 51:11; 2 Sam 23:7; Zech 9:13; 2 Kgs 9:24. This militaristic notion will be explored further in chapter four.

Semantic and Literary Analysis of Mandate Terms

In this way מלא fills something that is empty,[134] and usually what something is filled with directly results from the intentional action of the subject.[135] What is "filled" can have in view literal fish (Gen 1:22) or a figurative use of a land "filled with violence" (Gen 6:13).

The use of מלא in the Creation Mandate texts is essentially *spatial*: וּמִלְאוּ אֶת־הַמַּיִם בַּיַּמִּים ("and fill the *water* in the seas," 1:22); וּמִלְאוּ אֶת־הָאָרֶץ ("and fill the *earth*," 1:28); and וּמִלְאוּ אֶת־הָאָרֶץ ("and fill the *earth*," 9:1). This spatial emphasis of מלא contributes the notions of *abundance* and *profusion* to the divine blessing.

The verb כבש occurs 14x in the Old Testament.[136] כבש occurs 8x in Qal,[137] 5x in Niphal,[138] and 1x in Piel.[139] Used with the accusative, the Qal can mean: "to subjugate." However, S. Wagner claims that: "the meaning can always be rendered by 'subdue.'"[140] כָּבַשׁ in biblical Hebrew is closely related to the Aramaic form כְּבַס, "to suppress, restrain, conquer."[141]

---

134. A. Snijders, "מָלֵא," *TDOT*, 8:298.

135. Ibid.

136. Gen 1:28; Num 32:22, 29; Josh 18:1; 2 Sam 8:11; 1 Chr 22:18; 2 Chr 28:10; Neh 5:5[2x]; Esth 7:8; Jer 34:11; 34:16; Mic 7:19; Zech 9:15.

137. Gen 1:28; 2 Chr 28:10; Neh 5:5a; Esth 7:8; Jer 34:11; 34:16; Mic 7:19; Zech 9:15.

138. Num 32:22, 29; 18:1; 1 Chr 22:18; Neh 5:5b. In the LXX, κατακυριεύω ("dominion") translates MT כָּבַשׁ, with κατακυριεύω occurring 13x. More of this will be developed in chapter four.

Of Num 32:22, J. Wevers states:

> Note the neat word play in which the translator used the verb κατακυριεύω, reminiscent of Gen 1:28 κατακυριεύσατε αὐτῆς "have dominion over it" for כבשה "subdue it," and is then modified by ἔναντι κυρίου. (*Notes on the Greek Text of Numbers*, SCS 46 [Atlanta: Scholars, 1998], 538–39)

139. Cf. 2 Sam 8:11. The Piel form of כָּבַשׁ (perf., 3ms, "had subdued") is noted as a *hapax* in the Masoretic text (*BHS*).

140. M. Wagner, "כָּבַשׁ," *TDOT*, 7:52–57; *HALOT*, 2:460; *BDB* adds, "bring into bondage, dominate," 461. כָּבַשׁ (*kābaš*) seems to lie behind the English idiom, "to put the *kibosh* on" something. English dictionaries surmise an extraction through Yiddish, which L. Rosten leans toward (*The Joys of Yiddish* [New York: McGraw-Hill, 1968], 175). Even Dickens used *kibosh* in 1856 when the word meant "nonsense" or "bosh" (Ibid.). Webster's maintains that the origin is unknown (*Webster's 3rd New International Dictionary* [Springfield: Merriam-Webster, 1993], 1240).

141. M. Jastrow gives the example: שאתה מְכַבֵּשׁ ... בוא וכבוש וכ, "Instead of conquering the barbarians, come and subdue the Jews" (*Dictionary of the Targumim, Talmud Bauli, Talmud Yerushalmi and Midrashic Literature* [HP: Jucaica Treasury, 2004], *Y. Succ.* V, 55ᵇ; 610.6); cf. *HALOT*, 2:460.

Be Fruitful and Multiply

Lexical analysis divides the verb רדה into: רדה I, "rule" (24x), and רדה II, "take, seize" (3x).[142] Our focus lies with רדה I, ("rule").[143] The Qal occurs 22x,[144] with the only exception being a difficult Hiphil form in Isa 41:2.[145] In Genesis 1–11 רדה occurs twice, each time stipulating human rule over aquatic and aerial life with the collocation: רדה ב (1:26 [וְיִרְדּוּ בִדְגַת]; 28 [וּרְדוּ בִדְגַת]).[146]

In Gen 1:26 and 28, the usage is positive and with רדה, as elsewhere, highlighting an action carried out by a human agent.[147] Verse 26 ties רדה to God's image in the intended design of humankind. Verse 28 follows the creation of humankind, stipulating their responsibility within the created order. These two uses of רדה are unique given the largely negative function of רדה in the balance of the Old Testament. The notion of harsh rule with רדה is so evident throughout the Old Testament that *HALOT* describes רדה as having "the associated meaning of oppression."[148]

As a verbal lexeme, שרץ occurs 29x,[149] and all in the Qal. The nominal form (שֶׁרֶץ) occurs 15x,[150] functioning as a *collective* noun (i.e., "swarm"). The verb means "to creep, move, swarm."[151] שרץ as a root is concentrated

---

142. H.-J. Zobel, "רָדָה," *TDOT*, 13:330–36, 330; *HALOT*, 3:1190; cf. *BDB*, 921–22.

143. Together, both roots of רדה (I & II) total 27 uses with the distribution as follows: [רדה I] = Gen (2x), Lev (4x), Num (1x), Deut (1x), 1 Kgs (3x), Isa (3x), Ezk (2x), Joel (1x), Ps (4x), Lam (1x), Neh (1x), 2 Chr (1x), [רדה II] = 1 Kgs (1x), Isa (1x), Ps (1x).

144. Gen 1:26, 28; Lev 25:43, 46, 53; 26:17; Num 24:19; 1 Kgs 4:24; 5:16; 9:23; 2 Chr 8:10; Neh 9:28; Pss 49:14; 68:27; 72:8; 110:2; Isa 14:2, 6; 41:2; Jer 5:31; Ezek 29:15; 34:4; Joel 3:13.

145. "He delivers nations over [to him] and *subdues* kings before him" (Isa 41:2). As a form, the apocopated יְרְדְּ appears to be a *hapax* from רדה. But this makes little sense with "kings" as the object. By *ellipsis*, the object/referent is arguably Cyrus. Qumran (1QIsa^a) and θ read יורד, a Hiphil from ירד. Others propose the Qal form יֵרְדְּ from the root רדד ("he subjugates"; so H.-J. Zobel, "רָדָה," 13:332; *HALOT*, 3:1190; *BDB*, 922).

146. Similarly, וּרְבוּ־בָהּ, "and multiply in it" = בָּאָרֶץ (Gen 9:7b); cf. Lev 25:43, 46; 26:17; 1 Kgs 5:4, 30; 9:23; Isa 14:2; Ezek 29:15; 43:4; Neh 9:28; 2 Chr 8:10. This will be developed in chapter four along with a comparison to collocation משל־ב ("rule over").

147. H.-J. Zobel, "רָדָה," *TDOT*, 13:331.

148. *HALOT*, 3:1190; cf., *BDB*, "dominate," 921; P. J. Nel, "רָדָה," *NIDOTTE*, 3:1055. The Israelites are warned against "dominating" (רדה) their own countrymen (cf. Lev 25:43, 46, 53; Ezek 34:4; ibid.). Whether human "subduing" (כבש) and "rule" (רדה) is intended to be oppressive (Gen 1:28) will be discussed in the following chapters.

149. Gen 1:20, 21; 7:21; 8:17; 9:7; Exod 1:7; 8:3; Lev 11:29, 41, 42, 43, 46; Ps 105:30; Ezek 47:9.

150. Gen 1:20; 7:21; Lev 5:2; 11:10, 20, 21, 32, 29, 31, 41, 42, 43, 44; 22:5; Deut 14:19.

151. *HALOT*, 4:1655; cf., "swarm, teem, be innumerable" (A. E. Hill, "שָׁרַץ," *NIDOTTE*, 4:251; so *BDB*, 1056).

Semantic and Literary Analysis of Mandate Terms

in Genesis and Leviticus, occurring 24x of the total 29.[152] In Genesis the verb שרץ occurs 5x.

The verb is initially used in Gen 1:20 and 21 as an inclusive reference[153] to aquatic life:[154] "Let the waters swarm abundantly (שרץ) with living creatures ([נֶפֶשׁ חַיָּה] שֶׁרֶץ) ... which the waters brought forth ([הַחַיָּה שרץ [נֶפֶשׁ])."[155] Gen 7:21 also addresses animals, but now as land-based: הַשֶּׁרֶץ הַשֹּׁרֵץ עַל־הָאָרֶץ, "the swarm that swarmed on the land."[156] Gen 8:17 is similar to 7:21, with שרץ referring to swarming animals after the flood.[157] שרץ in 9:7 refers neither to aerial nor aquatic life, but to humans: וְאַתֶּם ... שִׁרְצוּ בָאָרֶץ, "you ... *teem* in the earth." While 9:7 uniquely applies שרץ to humans, it is the second text where God speaks of שרץ with the narrator employing the other three uses.[158]

---

152. The verb שרץ in Genesis and Leviticus occurs 10x (Gen 1:20, 21; 7:21; 8:17; 9:7; Lev 11:29, 41, 42, 43, 46). The noun in Genesis and Leviticus occurs 14x (Lev 5:2; 11:10, 20, 21, 32, 29, 31, 41, 42, 43, 44; 22:5). Adding the two verbal occurrences in Exodus (1:7; 8:3) raises the total occurrences of the root שרץ to 26x of a total 29x.

153. *HALOT*, 4:1655. Verse 20 uses a cognate construction, repeating the same root, שרץ. The LXX uses a collective kind of construction: ἐξαγαέτω with a pl. neuter subject. "The Three" employ formal cognate constructions with ἐξερψάτω, "let the water crawl with crawling creatures" (Wevers, *Notes*, 10).

154. According to the LXX, the water produces *both* crawling creatures and birds, construed by the coordinate accusative nouns ἑρπετά and πετεινά. Comparing the MT, the subject of שרץ is not the creatures but the elements native to the creature's life; this aspect is not unique to the MT, however the MT does not suggest the water produces land-based creatures (Wevers, *Notes*, 10; *HALOT*, 4:1656). The substance of origin defines identity and transitive relationships, as man comes from the ground (2:7) but woman from man (2:21; cf. 3:16–19; *GKC* §117z).

155. For נֶפֶשׁ חַיָּה, see Ezek 47:9 for a similar idea and construction (cf. Gen 2:7). נֶפֶשׁ חַיָּה functions *epexegetically* in apposition to שֶׁרֶץ.

156. From birds to humankind, four categories of creation are listed *in the order of their creation*, ending with humankind (7:21; cf. Gen 1:20–27). However, to highlight the "dismantling" of the original creation, 7:23 *reverses* the order of original creation beginning with humankind on day six. Further emphasis comes from "all/every" occurring 6x, two of which construct the compound subject: כל בשר with כל האדם.

157. שרץ as used in 8:17 is unique in that a perfect (וְשָׁרְצוּ) rather than an imperative form is used. This will be developed in chapter four.

158. Cf. Gen 1:20, 21; 7:21.

Be Fruitful and Multiply

OLD TESTAMENT

While מלא also has a *temporal* use,[159] our focus lies with the *spatial* that defines the texts of the Creation Mandate in Genesis 1–11. The balance of the Old Testament merely expands the essential categories of מלא found in Genesis 1–11. Such categories as the abstract use (e.g., guilt, Jer 51:5)[160] and figurative (e.g., "to fill the hand," Num 3:3)[161] become foundational uses.

As כבש is used in the balance of the Old Testament, it shows harsh and even militaristic connotations. From the king's perspective, in Esther, for example, he believes Haman is "assaulting" (כבש) the queen (7:8; cf. Neh 5:5).[162]

Overwhelmingly, כבש pertains to subduing a people group, and by extension their land, especially the Canaanites.[163] As a result of political subjugation, the notion of people in "servitude" is also present.[164] It is significant that the land is "subdued before the LORD"[165] (Num 32:22), possibly implying "on behalf of the LORD,"[166] since every occasion of

---

159. Namely, a period of temporal *dedication* (Num 6:5, 13), Jacob *waiting* for Rachel (Gen 29:21), period of *embalming* (Gen 50:3), and a time of *purification* (Lev 12:4, 6). See also Jer 25:12; 29:10; Dan 9:2; 1 Chr 17:11; Lam 4:18; Esth 1:5; Isa 40:2; Jer 25:34; Ezek 5:2 (M. V. Van Pelt, W. C. Kaiser, Jr., "מָלֵא," *NIDOTTE*, 2:940).

160. Overt theological use occurs when God is portrayed as the unique Deity who "fills the heaven and earth" (Jer 23:24; cf. Num 14:21; Ps 72:19; Isa 6:3), even locally manifesting his theophonic presence (Exod 40:34–35; 1 Kgs 8:10–11; Ezek 10:3).

161. A statement denoting "ordination" (Exod 28:41; cf. Lev 8:42–43; M. V. Van Pelt, W. C. Kaiser, Jr., "מָלֵא," *NIDOTTE*, 2:940). The earth can also be full of "glory," "goodness," and "knowledge of the LORD" (cf. Pss 33:5; 119:64; Isa 11:9; Hab 3:3).

162. Given what Haman is charged with, F. W. Bush believes another term could have been used, but כבש carries the stronger idea of "assault" and "violate" (*Ruth, Esther*, WBC [Dallas: Word, 1996], 430). This is reflected in the NIV's "molest," and the JPS's "ravish."

163. Num 32:22, 29; Josh 18:1, etc.

164. Cf. 2 Chr 28:10; Neh 5:5; Jer 34:11, 16.

165. E.g., ונכבשה הארץ לפני יהוה (cf. Josh 18:1; 1 Chr 22:18, etc.).

166. The phrase: לִפְנֵי יהוה ("before the LORD") occurs 4x in vv. 20–22 with לִפְנֵי, functioning as a "complex/frozen preposition" (see *IBHS* §11.3.1.a). Some translate: "[the land] falls before him" (NEB); "the LORD has conquered [the land]" (NLT²); "[the land] has become subject to Yahweh" (JB). While Gad and Reuben might have marched in front of God's Ark (cf. 10:33), it is likely that לִפְנֵי יהוה addresses more than logistics. The following *adversative* phrase: ליהוה ("against the LORD," v. 23) functions as a contrast with לִפְנֵי יהוה, underscoring their obligation in legal terms prior to release (cf. *WHS* §323). In essence, the land was God's and His gift leased to Israel. By the same token, Israel must take it by military conquest (P. D. Miller, "The Gift of God: The Deuteronomic Theology of the Land," *Int* 23 [1969]: 451–65, 455, quoted in W. Dumbrell, *The Faith*, 64).

force exercised by כבש is ultimately commissioned or permitted by God.[167] Consequently, כבש often assumes that the group "subdued" is a hostile force to the one subduing, which in turn requires some type of force to be employed.[168]

רדה is confined to human rule and is essentially "negative." Therefore, it is significant that the majority of objects receiving this "rule" are human groups and individuals: enemies (Ps 110:2), nations (Isa 45:1), and tribes (Ps 68:28[27]), for example.

In Exod 7:1, שרץ uniquely describes the Hebrews' burgeoning population, a numerical and thus political threat to their Egyptian hosts. The Egyptians themselves experience the "swarming" of frogs in the second plague (8:3[7:28]; cf. Ps 105:30).

It is striking to find the root שרץ 17x in Leviticus and concentrated in chapter 11 (16x).[169] Addressing clean and unclean animals, the comparable term רֶמֶשׂ ("creeping animals") represents an animal taxonomy to be intentionally avoided (cf. Lev 20:25), so רֶמֶשׂ is not used.[170] This served to eliminate the idea of indiscriminate consumption of small "moving things" (i.e., reptiles) over against "swarming animals" (שרץ) such as insects and aquatic life (cf. Gen 9:3).[171]

---

167. M. Wagner, "כָּבַשׁ," *TDOT*, 7:56.

168. J. Oswalt, "כָּבַשׁ," *TWOT*, 1:430. Where intended stewardship ends and rogue-like destruction begins will be addressed in chapters following.

169. The verb: Lev 11:29, 41, 42, 43, 46; the noun: Lev 5:2; 11:10, 20, 21, 32, 29, 31, 41, 42, 43, 44; 22:5.

170. רֶמֶשׂ does occur in Lev 11:44, 45 stressing locomotion (cf. Gen 1:21, 26, 28).

171. A. Hill, "רֶמֶשׂ," *NIDOTTE*, 3:1127. רֶמֶשׂ depicts the locomotion of *ground*-level animals (Gen 1:26, 28, 30; 7:14, 21; 8:17, 19; J. Milgrom, *Leviticus 1–16*, 3:687). Exceptions to the use of רֶמֶשׂ include Ps 104:25 and Hab 1:14 where רֶמֶשׂ refers to sea creatures. Shockingly, even the רֶמֶשׂ of Ps 148:10 are summoned to the cosmic praise of God (cf. Hos 2:18[20]). Discussing dietary distinctions such as this, J. Moskala's dissertation attempts "to discover the purpose of the Mosaic dietary laws as in the composition and structure of various Pentateuchal passages" (161). He is correct to see dietary laws rooted in creation (Genesis 1; see further: R. E. Averbeck, "Clean and Unclean," *NIDOTTE*, 4:477–86, esp. 483–84). Moskala's work is informative, especially the review of dietary laws as understood from the Pseudepigrapha into contemporary interpretation (15–107). Using a Creation—Fall—New Creation paradigm, Moskala believes:

> this terminological, conceptual, structural, and theological study can perceive the universal unifying principle behind the Mosaic dietary laws as the Creation pattern. (345)

BE FRUITFUL AND MULTIPLY

SUMMARY

Within the texts of the Creation Mandate רדה, כבש, מלא, and שרץ communicate the broad notions of *profusion* and *governance*. Statements of principle are couched in specific terminology.[172] The spatial significance of מלא depicts the physical reality of abundance, especially *filling* the domains of land and sea.[173]

While כבש can have an "individual" emphasis, it nonetheless presupposes the subject is the stronger party and the object the weaker. כבש then, can stipulate the "subduing" of a geographical land, even militaristically. However, harnessing the land's potential for general habitation is more arguable in the context of the Creation Mandate. The function of "land" with כבש is, we believe, *graded* from the Creation Mandate (Gen 1:28) issued in Eden, outward. The world at large could become Eden-like.[174]

However, such a statement is indicative of several key errors. Fundamentally misunderstood are the seven "clean animals" of Noah that were arguably intended for sacrifice, not food (Gen 7:1–2); Noah's sacrifice already had precedence (cf. 4:4). Only after the flood was concession given to eat "every living thing that moves" (רֶמֶשׂ, 9:3). The alimentary restriction to "clean" animals only comes with Leviticus 11, however God never stipulated such to Noah. Additionally, the dietary laws are not applicable to aliens (278, 352–53), with the exception of blood and torn animals (Lev 17:10, 13, 15). Moreover, Moskala ignores such directives as Acts 15:20 and the implications of Acts 10, concluding:

> The rationale and theology behind the Pentateuchal dietary laws seem to be valid also in the New Testament economy because the cross of Jesus does not abrogate the theology and rationale behind this specific kind of uncleanness. (*The Laws of Clean and Unclean Animals of Leviticus 11: Their Nature, Theology, and Rationale (An Intertextual Study)*, ATSDS 4 [Berrien Springs: Adventist Theological Society, 2000], 373.)

172. M. Wagner, "כָּבַשׁ," *TDOT*, 7:54.

173. Noting its more eschatological use, Moule, citing J. A. Fitzmyer, asserts:

> Qumran literature lacks both the fulfillment formula found in Matthew and also the "pattern" in the use of the Old Testament ... [found] in the New Testament ... [and] scarcely any examples of the use of *ml'* in a phrase referring to the confirmation or completion of God's promises or plan. (Quoted in M. V. Van Pelt, W. C. Kaiser, Jr., "מָלֵא," *NIDOTTE*, 2:941.)

174. Gen 2:10–14 gives a rather detailed description of the beauty and fecundity of the eastern region around Eden. Standard within *ANE* imagery, this sanctuary-garden of God is portrayed as a cosmic mountain from which rivers flow. The "river" of God's garden-sanctuary had four branches, flowing out to the "four corners" of the world in order to make all lands comparably beautiful (Gen 2:10–14). Material blessings and agricultural fertility are tied to river imagery as a manifestation of God's presence (cf. Ps 46:4; Ezek 47:1–12; Zech 14:8; Rev 22:1–2. See S. Tuell, "The Rivers of Paradise: Ezekiel 47:1–12 and Genesis 2:10–14," in *God Who Creates*, 171–89; W. H. Propp, *Water in the Wilderness*:

Semantic and Literary Analysis of Mandate Terms

In this aggregate of terms, רדה adds the significant notion of *royalty* to the Creation Mandate (Gen 1:28). This means that only humans are granted regal status within God's creation, a gift and responsibility of a "crown" (cf. Ps 8:6[5]). The implications of this for our study are significant, and will be developed later.

The contribution of שרץ is its connotation of "swarming" or "teeming," a heightened significance among an aggregate of terms already used as the substance of divine blessing. The connotation of שרץ differs from רמש in that the former has in mind the "teeming"—multitude (i.e., quantity), whereas the latter has in view the "crawling"—multitude (i.e., movement).[175]

CONCLUSION

In three separate clusters we analyzed the key lexemes with an eye to their usage in the Creation Mandate.[176] On one level these words build a portrait of *abundance*-reality, and on the other, strong ruling imagery.

The inhabited world God created is one that humankind is called to nurture in royal fashion. The exercise of human rule is intended to contribute to the development, benefit, and utilization of God's creation.[177]

These words or syntagms are used with a highly theological emphasis, particularly ברך (1:22, 28; 9:1) that presupposes some kind of relationship between God and what is blessed. Every verse comprising our "Creation Mandate" finds God in some form of speech. While some are traditional "embedded quotes" (1:22), other divine declarations are more sophisticated, adeptly used by the narrator (1:28).

Analyzing the contiguous pair, פרו ורבו, we noted that it functions as a hendiadys. Moreover, this collocation denotes "fertility on the increase" at a level that essentially guarantees survival. These words denote the ongoing wellbeing and security of the blessed entity.

A Biblical Motif and Its Mythological Background, HSM 40 [Atlanta: Scholars, 1987], esp. "Thirst and Creation," 9–15, "Restoration," 95–111).

175. A. Hill, "שָׁרַץ," *NIDOTTE*, 4:251. *Movement* seems determinative among clean and unclean orders of "swarming" animals (cf. Lev 11:20–22, 29, 31). While grasshoppers "swarm," their hopping motion reveals distinct movement as compared with species of ants for example whose crawling reveals little pattern or sense of direction (M. Douglas, *Purity and Danger* [London: Routledge and Kegan Paul, 1966], 56).

176. Cluster 1: (ברך ... אלהים), cluster 2: (פרו ורבו), cluster 3: (מלא, כבש, רדה, שרץ).

177. H.-J. Zobel, "רָדָה," *TDOT*, 13:336.

The four terms (מלא, כבש, רדה, שרץ) that round out the Creation Mandate communicate *abundance* (שרץ, מלא) and *governance* (כבש, רדה), respectively. Ruling comes with notions of royalty and divine representation.

This aggregate of terms carries some technical nuances (i.e., כבש). Moreover, the imperatives arguably function with more than blunt command. Each aspect of creation is defined by the Creator's unique relationship to it, making the imperatives of command more accurately a "blessing of enablement." Various nuances surrounding this divine blessing mean grammar and syntax alone are not determinative here, speech forms also play a key role.

Since these terms define the Creation Mandate and human function within creation, it is not surprising to find substantive distribution on both sides of the flood narrative.[178] While some differences can be found,[179] it is surprising how much of Adam's original Mandate actually extends beyond him.

---

178. ברך (1:22, 28 [FLOOD] 9:1), פרו ורבו (1:22, 28 [FLOOD] 8:17; 9:1, 7), מלא (1:22, 28 [FLOOD] 9:1).

179. כבש (1:28) and רדה (1:28) are not reissued after the flood, while שרץ (8:17) and רבה (9:7) only occur after the flood. This unique distribution against an otherwise cohesive backdrop has brought proposals for emendation that we will consider in chapter four.

4

Exegetical Analysis of the Mandate in Genesis 1–11

INTRODUCTION

THE GOAL OF THIS chapter is two-fold: an exegetical analysis of the individual "text plots" on the one hand, and an identification of their thematic reverberations running through Genesis 1–11, on the other. These themes will be examined for their theological contribution to the Creation Mandate. Eventually we will explore how these texts intersect with the "image of God" and "male and female" language. We believe this will enable us to better understand the *significance* of the Mandate, where it rises in intensity (i.e., 1:28; 9:1) and how these junctures develop the author's message (chapter five).

In chapter three we isolated three clusters of terms that "define" the Creation Mandate, collecting and assessing their semantic uses in Gen 1:22, 28; 8:17; 9:1 and 9:7. We concluded by noting several emphases: (1) abundance, (2) governance, and (3) royal imagery in the manner of governance. Moreover, we observed a highly Theo-centric emphasis that saturates these terms in the Mandate texts.

Chapter four is a literary and theological analysis. Here, we will investigate the structure and contextual function of each Mandate text within the flow of Genesis 1–11. A conclusion will gather our research in these crucial texts.

Be Fruitful and Multiply

THE HEBREW TEXT PLOTS

Figure 1: Genesis 1:22		וַיְבָרֶךְ אֹתָם אֱלֹהִים לֵאמֹר
	פְּרוּ וּרְבוּ	
בַּיַּמִּים	וּמִלְאוּ אֶת־הַמַּיִם	
בָּאָרֶץ׃	וְהָעוֹף יִרֶב	

```
Then God blessed them <saying:>
              "Be fruitful and multiply,
                 and fill the waters           in the seas;
                 and let the birds multiply    on the earth."
```

Some scholars believe the text of Genesis 1 is the most "densely structured in the Hebrew Bible"[1] (see Appendix A). The text of Gen 1:22 is lodged within the 5th Day (1:20–23), the aquatic and aerial "filling" corresponding to Day 2, the separation and "forming" of sky and water (1:6–8).[2] As the literary backdrop, *horizontal symmetry* is wed with *vertical hierarchy*.[3] This symmetry connects the objects and life-forms to the created order while the hierarchy reveals the Creator's graded relationship with the three domains.[4]

Three days "populate" the "unpopulated" (1:14–31). Panel five (1:20–23) is the medial-day, stressing progression of autonomy with increasingly complex life. Of God's eight creative acts, Day 5 has one act with two aspects addressing fish and birds (cf. 1:6–8).[5] Two unique el-

---

1. W. P. Brown, *Structure*, 249 (see 59–112); idem, *The Ethos*, 35–58; S. E. Balentine, *The Torah's Vision*, 81–95; J. Blenkinsopp, *The Pentateuch*, 57–63; S. D. McBride, Jr., "Divine Protocol," 3–41; F. H. Polak, "Poetic Style and Parallelism in the Creation Account (Genesis 1:1—2:3)," in *Creation in Jewish and Christian Tradition*, ed. H. G. Reventlow and Y. Hoffman, JSOTSup 319 (Sheffield: Sheffield Academic Press, 2002), 2–31; B. W. Anderson, *From Creation to New Creation*, 42–55; M. Vervenne, "Genesis 1,1—2,4. The Compositional Texture of the Priestly Overture to the Pentateuch," in *Studies in the Book of Genesis: Literature, Redaction and History*, ed. A. Wénin (Paris: Peters, 2001), 35–79; Cassuto, *A Commentary*, 1:16–18; Waltke, *Genesis*, 55–78; M. Fishbane, *Text and Texture*, 10–11; Hamilton, *Genesis*, 103–50; Wenham, *Genesis 1–15*, 5–40; Walsh, *Style*, 38–38.

2. The creation account in the MT posits 7 panels: 1:1–5, 6–8, 9–13, 14–19, 20–23, 24–31, and 2:1–3. With seven panels corresponding to the seven days, English translations hardly represent this visual sculpture, often including further divisions between 1:25 and 26, for example (see NIV, NRSV, HCSB, etc.). See Appendix A.

3. Balentine, *The Torah's*, 85.

4. Ibid., 86.

5. The order of creation domains (heaven > water > earth) is implied in the poetic structure of Day 5: water/creatures (20a), birds/earth (20b); sea denizens/water (21a), birds (21b); "them" [= sea creatures] (22a), birds/earth (22b).

Exegetical Analysis of the Mandate in Genesis 1-11

ements highlight Day 5: the use of ברא ("create"; 1:21) and God's first blessing (ברך, 1:22). Strictly used with God as subject, ברא now highlights within the narrative the mythological connection to ancient creatures;[6] but in this case the narrator acknowledges pagan imagery devoid of pagan theology.[7] Secondly, ברך ("bless") occurs for the first time in the creation narrative (cf. 1:28; 2:3),[8] since a "utilizer" is postured to harness the "resources"[9] and rule the earthly domain.

God's creative agency is speech; his commands enact what he expresses.[10] Creation in Genesis 1 establishes the archetype of this "command—execution" pattern[11] (cf. Gen 6:13-22; Exod 39:32-43); the ordered cosmos has been worded—forth.[12] Without conflict or caprice, the reader observes a consistently obedient response to the Creator's *articulated* will.[13] Panel five surges through: creation (1:20), effect (1:21), and finally, blessing (1:22).

However, beginning with Gen 1:22 the reader is given more than a report of results from performative speech. Rhetorically, Gen 1:22 begins with God as the expressed subject in the *formal stem*: ויברך אתם אלהים

---

6. Cf. Job 3:8; Pss 74:13-17; 89:9-10; 104:26; Isa 27:1; 51:9-10; Jer 51:34; etc.

7. Waltke, *Genesis*, 63.

8. Days 1-3 find God consistently naming (cf. 1:5, 8, and 10), but letting Adam assume the naming of the blessed domains, Days 5 and 6 (cf. 2:19).

9. The terms of N. Sarna (*Genesis*, JPS Torah Commentary 1 [Philadelphia: JPS, 1989], 4).

10. E.g., Ps 148:5-6 reads, "Let them praise the name of the LORD, for He commanded, and they were created; He set them in position forever and ever; He gave an order that will never pass away" (HCSB), emphasis mine. Departing from Rahlfs' edition, A. Pietersma follows the *Göttingen Septuagint* by adding a parallel cola: "Let them praise the name of the Lord, for he spoke, and they came to be; he commanded, and they were created..." (*A New English Translation of the Septuagint: And other Greek Translations Traditionally Included Under That Title The Psalms* [Oxford: Oxford University Press, 2000], 146; expansion of 33:9).

11. Anderson, *From Creation*, 45-47.

12. Leading up to the performative blessing of 1:22, God has already "divided" (1:4; cf. 1:6, 7, 14, 18), "made" (1:7, 16), "fixed" (1:17), and "created" (1:21; cf. 1:1).

Not surprisingly, the OT can construe the "silence" of God as the judgment of God, leading to a punishment of spiritual "chaos" (cf. Amos 8:11-12). So Blenkinsopp, "The deluge is the time of the silence of God" (*Pentateuch*, 84). Similarly, silence can serve as a metaphor for famine, essentially "anti-blessing" (cf. Deut 8:3; 32:47; Job 33:31, 33; Pss 28:1; 35:22; 50:3; 83:1; 109:1; Isa 42:14; 62:1; 64:12; 65:6; Hab 1:13).

13. McBride, "Divine Protocol," 9. Emphasis original.

לֵאמֹר ("Then God blessed them saying"; see Figure 1).[14] The plural pronoun אֹתָם functions *resumptively*, referring to the sea creatures as the displaced object (cf. 1:21).

The blessing (ברך) of aerial and aquatic life is both *task* and *endowment*. A type of commission, since all other commands of God receive an immediate and positive response on the day they are issued.[15] This "blessing anticipates events beyond the 'creation week,'"[16] thus the text omits וַיְהִי־כֵן ("and it was so").[17] Endowment is also present since the blessing is God's *gesture* that enhances life. *Elohim* is the ultimate grantor of life officially enabled by the Creator's blessing.[18]

Closing the formal stem, לֵאמֹר ("saying") is the uninflected direct speech marker, framing the narrator's report.[19] The *ʾaṯnāḥ* divides the *declarative* comments of the narrator from God's *embedded quote* of blessing. While God has spoken throughout Genesis 1, לֵאמֹר occurs for the first time, signaling the *substance* of blessing.[20]

14. What might seem an axiomatic comment on a "genetic expression" (1:22) is given clarity next to 1:28: ויברך אתם אלהים ויאמר להם אלהים ("And God blessed them, and God said to them"). Amazingly, some scholars will still omit ויאמר להם אלהים in order to preserve the "genetic expression," when the author's rhetorical skill is arguably doing more. *BHK* finds the simplicity of the LXX attractive (λέγον), while *BHS* wisely forgoes any comment.

15. L. A. Turner, *Genesis*, 23. I take the *wāw consecutive* on ויברך as *resumptive* ("Then"; also אתם) as does NLT², while others take it as *logical/inferential* ("so"; HCSB).

16. Ibid.

17. See 1:7, 9, 11, 15, 24, 30. Reflecting a harmonizing plus, the LXX adds: καὶ ἐγένετο ουάτως," distorting the seven-fold use the phrase (cf. 1:6b [LXX]). In such cases, R. Hendel argues for a "proto-G" reading as indicative of scribal harmonization (*The Text*, 23; see 20–23). The LXX placement of the phrase (totaling 8x) seems schematized to trace God's creative commands.

18. Of this blessing, F. Delitzsch states: ". . . the wishing word is at the same time the imparting deed, the bestowal of generative power" (*A New Commentary on Genesis*, 96).

19. C. Miller breaks down ויאמר into several functions: (1) introducing information into the narrative without representing the entire exchange, (2) introducing speech acts of less than full characters, and (3) relating a series of embedded quotations from the perspective of the principal ("Discourse Functions of Quotative Frames in Biblical Hebrew Narrative," in *Discourse Analysis of Biblical Literature: What It Is and What It Offers*, ed. W. R. Bodine, SSS [Atlanta: Scholars, 1995], 155–82, 178).

Her desire to move beyond the "traditional" and "misleading" category of "direct speech marker" is noted. However, Gen 1:22 does not seem to fit within her categories (largely drawn from 2 Samuel), #2 coming closest (cf. *GKC*, §114o).

20. Similarly: ויברכם ביום ההוא לאמור בך יברך ישראל לאמר ("So he [Jacob] blessed them that day, saying, 'By you [sg.] Israel [col.] will pronounce a blessing, saying'"); Gen

Exegetical Analysis of the Mandate in Genesis 1–11

Unique to the fifth panel, 22b alludes to both aquatic and aerial creatures following the *ʾatnāḥ* (לֵאמֹר), the *proclamation* or focus of blessing. Two clauses comprise 1:22b, the initial in 1st person and the 2nd shifting to 3rd person. פרו ורבו forms the initial *charge elements*, the first two of three imperatives or *decretive* collocations.[21] פרו ורבו functions as a *hendiadys* meaning "be abundantly fruitful," and rhetorically represents the "core" charge. Here, the hendiadys connotes increase and abundance within the cosmic theatre, stipulating the *manner* of fecundity.

The *rebîaʿ* accent sets off the hendiadys from the third imperative that follows, ומלאו ("and fill"). Following the core charge (פרו ורבו), מלא denotes the spatial "domain" to be proliferated. The "sea" is not the *cause* of the creatures, merely their *element*.[22] Then the "secondary" charges are enumerated. Both Westermann's "explicative of conferral,"[23] and Wenham's notion of "divine promise"[24] help explain the use of the imperatives within the divine performative speech. Beginning with the domain of sea creatures, את־המים [בימים] ("the waters...") forms the direct object of ומלאו.[25] The *zāqēp̄* accent closes the first clause with the prepositional phrase, בימים ("in the seas"), stipulating the *sphere* or domain of vibrant animal life.[26]

48:20a). The *substance* of Jacob's blessing elevates Ephraim as the principle agent (בך), though ישמך that follows functions as a *distributive* singular (i.e., "the name of each of you"). The LXX changes the singular בך (MT) to the plural (ὑμῖν), referring to both sons. Wevers sees בך in reference to Joseph (*Notes*, 118). However, את־אפרים in 20b could be the author's note of prominence for "Ephraim" implied in 20a with בך ("by you [= Ephraim]"), the prominence already anticipated by Jacob when he summoned Ephraim *ahead* of Manasseh (cf. 48:5b).

21. We use "decretive collocations" because of the regularity of these three imperatives (1:28; 9:1; cf. 8:17; 9:7; Exod 1:7, etc.).

22. J. G. Murphy, *A Critical and Exegetical Commentary on The Book of Genesis with a New Translation* (Draper, 1868; reprint. Eugene, OR: Wipf and Stock, 1998), 64.

23. *Genesis 1–11*, 140.

24. *Genesis 1–15*, 33.

25. המים בימים ("the waters in the seas") also forms an attributive genitive of *specification* or *measure*, accentuated by cognate similarity.

26. Essentially a *locative* בְּ, "sphere" seems to capture the nuance better given the fluid substance coupled with divine performative speech. Within 1:20–22, birds always follow fish: beginning with the general terms נפש חיה ("living creatures," 20a) and עוף יעופף ("winged creatures of the wing," 20b). Then 1:21 gains specificity, shifting to the *inclusive* כל־נפש and כל־עוף (21b). Finally 1:22 uses more determined language: את־המים ("the waters") and the articular בארץ ("in the earth") and בימים ("in the water," 22b). Throughout panel five the usual words for "fish" and "bird" have been softened and outright avoided.

The second clause continues the discourse, but in a more opaque manner. Shifting to 3rd person, the force of direct address is blunted. To emphasize a new subject,[27] והעוף precedes the juss. (ירב). The singular juss. repeats רבה used earlier in the hendiadys (פרו ורבו), and continues the force of the three imperatives (רבה, פרה, מלא). Parallel expressions create intensity and aesthetic balance within the blessing. The 2nd clause ends as the 1st, with a prepositional phrase, בארץ ("in the earth").

In Gen 1:22 several "charge elements" or "directives" define the blessing.[28] The aquatic and aerial creatures are not only distinguished in blessing, but achieve fertility only through the performative word of God, not pagan ritual. Assonance[29] emphasizes the Creator's supremacy: ברא (*brʾ*), ברך (*brk*), פרה (*prh*), and רבה (*rbh*).

---

27. One translation renders והעוף *disjunctively*: "... but the fowl shall increase on the earth" (N. Scherman, *The Chumash*, 7; cf. SP, 4QGenᵍ: ירבה [imperf.], contra MT, 4QGenᵇ: ירב [juss.]. This is exegetically unnecessary, including the *descriptive* imperfect, since the author's emphasis is communicated through *domain*-distinctions.
   Similarly, Cassuto claims that רבה ("multiply") applied to the aerial creatures means they were not blessed with the "exceeding fertility as the fish" that received פרו ורבו. Again, this seems to be overloading one word within a larger performative speech (*A Commentary*, 1:52).

28. Hamilton's assessment is too simplistic, stating that: "God's blessing precedes his commands. He gives a blessing and then issues an order" (*Genesis*, 131). We're arguing that the blessing is the commands (better: *commission*); the order is inextricably part of the blessing (see chapter three). Kaminski agrees: "God did not bless the animals *and* give them commands. Rather, the imperatives are his blessing" (*From Noah*, 26; emphasis original); also D. Daube, *The Duty of Procreation* (Edinburgh: Edinburgh University Press, 1977), 3–4, 41–42.

29. L. S. Schökel defines assonance as: "Similarity of vowel sounds" (*A Manual of Hebrew Poetics*, Subsidia Biblica 11 [Rome: Pontifical Institute, 1988], 23). T. J. Murphy says, "Authors often use rhyme or similarity of sound in the accented vowels for the purpose of aesthetic appeal as well as unity, memorability and, occasionally, emphasis" (*Pocket Dictionary: For the Study of Biblical Hebrew* [Grand Rapids: InterVarsity, 2003], 32).

Exegetical Analysis of the Mandate in Genesis 1–11

```
Figure 2: Genesis 1:28                                    וַיְבָ֣רֶךְ אֹתָם֮ אֱלֹהִים֒
                                                          וַיֹּ֧אמֶר לָהֶ֣ם אֱלֹהִ֗ים
                                פְּר֥וּ וּרְב֛וּ
       וְכִבְשֻׁ֑הָ       וּמִלְא֥וּ אֶת־הָאָ֖רֶץ
                     בִּדְגַ֣ת הַיָּ֗ם        וּרְדוּ֩
                     וּבְע֣וֹף הַשָּׁמַ֔יִם    [ ]
עַל־הָאָֽרֶץ׃   וּבְכָל־חַיָּ֖ה הָֽרֹמֶ֥שֶׂת    [ ]

Then God blessed <them,>
And God <said to them:>
    "Be fruitful and multiply;
        and fill the EARTH     and subdue it,
        and rule over the fish of the SEA,
        and [ ] over  the birds of the SKY,
        and [ ] over  all animals that move   upon the ground."
```

Day Six (1:24–31; panel 6) is the most significant of the six. This day covers the creation of land animals and humans—the "filling" of what was formed on Day Three (1:9–13). The emphasis, however, is clearly placed on the creation of humankind (1:26–28) where 1:28 stands as the *vertical-zenith*. Humans are further dignified by the most "complex" blessing of the creation week (cf. 2:3).

The 6th panel begins with the creation of land animals (1:24–25), corresponding to the dry ground and vegetation of the 3rd day (1:9). Developing the earthly domain, the creation of animals and humans comprises the final two acts of creation in parallel to the two acts of Day Three (1:9–13). Similarly, the land now *produces* "living creatures" just as the end of the previous triad *produced* "vegetation;" both, however, occur strictly in response to the creative command of God, not by an independently fertile or deified ground.[30]

The author employs numerous "links," verbal and otherwise, to connect Days Five and Six: (1) נפש חיה ("living creatures," 1:20ff//24), (2) ברא ("create," 1:21//27ff), (3) ברך ("bless," 1:22//28), (4) מלא, רבה, פרה ("fruitful," "multiply," "fill," 1:22//28), (5) the sea and air are analogous to animal and human (1:20//24, 26), (6) the determinative construction ואת כל־/ובכל־ ("and [over] all"; 1:21//28),[31] (7) and the reproductive parameters

---

30. Several OT texts refer to people "slashing" themselves and draining their blood onto the ground in order to solicit action by their autochthonic fertility god (see Deut 14:1; 1 Kgs 18:28; Jer 16:6; 41:5; 47:5; Hos 7:14, etc.).

31. Whereas the *determinative* in 1:21[2x] summarizes the diversity within the domains on Day Five (1:20–23), the successive use in 1:28 occurs in God's blessing and the

for animals (1:20–22//24–25).³² To this fanfare of variety and multitude, God provides food (1:29–30) and exalts in His divine assessment with "very good!" (see Appendix 1).³³

Beyond the aquatic, aerial, and land animals, reflecting the three domains, the appearance of humankind is the trophy of God's creation (1:26–28). Human creation rises as the pinnacle of eight creative acts, though "rest" is the *goal* of the creative week (2:1–3).

To highlight this zenith of God's work, the author constructs a longer³⁴ and more intricate text.³⁵ These distinctives include: (1) God's

---

human *commission* when these same animals are now placed under human stewardship. The בכל of 1:28 signals the *actualization* of God's will expressed in 1:27 with startling lexical reiteration: (cf., ובכל־הארץ ["and over all the earth"], ובכל־הרמש הרמש ["and over every creeping animal"], and על־הארץ ["upon the earth"]).

32. In this inventory of animals three primary categories emerge: 1) domesticated, 2) reptiles, 3) and wild animals (1:24). See R. Whitekettle, "Where the Wild Things Are: Primary Level Taxa in Israelite Zoological Thought," *JSOT* 93 (2001): 17–37; idem, "Rats Are Like Snakes, and Hares Are Like Goats: A Study in Israelite Land Animal Taxonomy," *Bib* 82 (2001): 345–62; S. A. Reed, "Human Dominion Over Animals," in *Reading the Hebrew Bible for a New Millennium: Form Concept, and Theological Perspective*, vol. 1, THS, ed. W. Kim et al., (Harrisburg: Trinity Press, 2000), 328–48. This topic will be developed in later text plots (i.e., 8:17; 9:1ff).

33. In parallel with the closing of the first triad, the 6th panel has a *double announcement* (1:24, 26; cf. 1:9, 11) and a *double evaluation* (1:25, 31; cf. 1:10, 12).

34. Observe the mounting word count: Panel 1 (31), Panel 2 (38), Panel 3 (69)// Panel 4 (69), Panel 5 (57), and Panel 6 (149). While Panel 5 drops a little, both Panels 3 and 6 have *double* the text amount. The creation of humankind alone rivals Panel 5 with 52 words. The heavenly bodies of Panel 4 serves as a *Janis*, reflecting the inanimate creation of the first triad. Yet Panel 4 is placed within the human scope of the last triad and stands unique without blessing or name (see appendix 1).

35. Poetry dots the landscape with the narrator's reflective celebration of human creation (1:27) mimicked by the man's celebratory song of the woman's creation (2:23). Each poetic aside closes the thrust of the respective chapter. Whereas the narrator emphasizes their *uniqueness* with ברא ["create," 3x], the man emphasizes their *unity* with זאת ["this (one)," 3x] and מן [3x]. For information addressing this, see Alter's translation and discussion that highlights the poetics (*Genesis: Translation and Commentary*, [New York: W. W. Norton, 1996] 5, 9–10). Modern translations reflect this poetic scansion though its rhetorical significance is not appreciated. Regarding the 1:26–28 complex, Walsh agrees, noting that "the importance of the passage is emphasized by poetic language … an example of asymmetry of non-correspondence," referring to Day Six (*Style*, 105). However, Walsh breaks 1:28 apart to make a "chiasticaly organized quatrain that uses word order and wordplay to establish its pattern and express its theology" (ibid., 106; cf. 1:24, 26, 29):

A And God created (*wybrʾ*) humankind in his image.
   B In the image of God he created (*brʾ*) it.
   B' Male and female he created (*brʾ*) them.
A' And God blessed (*wybrk*) them.

Exegetical Analysis of the Mandate in Genesis 1-11

dialogue prior to human creation (1:26), (2) stylized performative speech with a *complex formal stem* (1:28a), (3) emphasis on male and female (1:27), (4) image of God (1:26-27), (5) additional *charge elements* added to proliferation (1:28), and (6) overt structural parallels between 1:22 and 1:28. Most of these elements we will address as we engage the text of 1:28. Some however, like image of God and gender, will be addressed in chapter five. Before analyzing the specifics of 1:28, it would be helpful to observe the shared textual structure between 1:22 and 1:28.

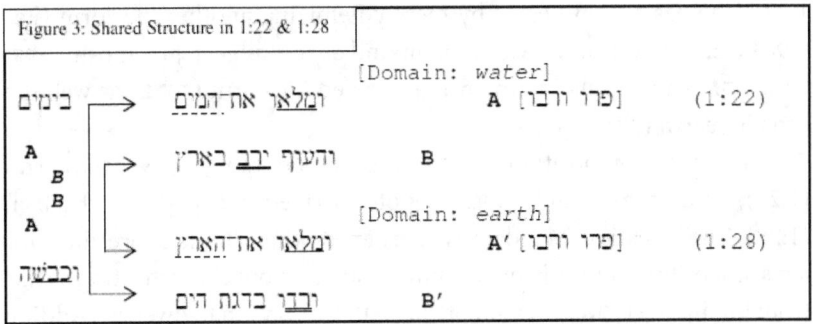

The initial lines excerpted from the preliminary text-plots (1:22, 28) reveal not only what is unique to each text, but also what spills over between them. These two portions contain the: *core charge* (פרו ורבו), *domain identification* ([הארץ/המים...]מלא), and *secondary charge elements* (ירב/כבש).

The four lines combine both *chiastic* (via nominal forms) and *paneled* elements (via verbal forms). The initial lines of each pair are verbal, forming a paneled structure (A, A'). In these clauses מלא initiates the "filling" of each respective domain, "the water," (המים, 1:22) followed by "the earth" (הארץ, 1:28). However, the interior lines of the four are chiastic, with articular references to "the earth" (B, B) framed by articular references to "water" on the outside (i.e., A, A: הים/המים). Taken together, fish fill the "sea" (A) and birds multiply on the "earth" (B); but humankind fills the "earth" (B) and rules the fish in the "sea" (A). This structure portrays order in proliferation; the sea is filled followed by multiplication over the earth. Humans, however, do not merely proliferate with the other crea-

---

By "splicing" part of the *formal complex stem* of 1:28a into 1:27 Walsh has construed *internal-synthetic parallelism*.

tures (i.e., enablement); humans also rule the creatures that multiply in their earthly domain.

A 3rd person juss. continues the *charge elements* in the 1st pair (1:22), whereas *two* unprecedented *charge elements* in the 2nd person define the 2nd pair (כבש, רדה, 1:28; A' and B'). While the 1st line terminates in a genitive of specification (מים), the 2nd מלא terminates in the potent verbal form, כבש (i.e., adverbial accusative of extent). Thus, the rise in intensity of 1:28 occurs with two additional verbs (כבש, רדה). Both lines in 1:28 pertain to "ruling," clearly an advance on the mere proliferation of 1:22. Whereas 1:22 B begins by merely itemizing another life-form (i.e., והעוף), 1:28 B' continues with humankind as the subject, juxtaposing רדה with כבש, and stipulating the fish as a ruled life-form (בדגת) as well the broader earth (הארץ, A').

The initial preposition (בארץ) denotes topography—"over the earth" (1:22), while the second (בדגת) denotes a ruled entity—"over the fish" (1:28). The Creation Mandate is sharpened when humans are the subjects, not only specifically mentioning "fish" now, but also reflecting a shift from inanimate (בארץ) to animate life (בדגת), domain to dwellers. Adding rulership to realm, humans are called to govern even as they grow (see Figure 3). Humans rule the earth, but celestial bodies rule the heavens (1:16–18).

The blessing of humans in 1:28 begins similar to that of the animals' blessing (1:22), but the outset reveals a fundamental difference (see Figure 2). The simple stem[36] is now a *formal complex stem*: ויברך ... אלהים, ויאמר ... אלהים ("Then God blessed ..., and God said ..").[37] While the repetition may prove suspect for some scholars,[38] this formal complex stem holds great significance. Unlike the blessing on animal life (1:22), this di-

---

36. That is: ויברך אתם אלהים לאמר ("Then God blessed them saying," Gen 1:22; see Figure 1).

37. Interestingly, the Syriac reflects the MT in this case, not the LXX. While ויאמר can function as לאמר (Joüon, §118j), in this case לאמר sets up an "object-less opening of a divine declaration" (Brown, *Structure*, 141, n.35). However, the reiterated אלהים strikes a greater note of intimacy in the *complex* stem, as we will argue.

38. When there is scope for simplification, linguists often speak of redundancy (S. C. Poole, *An Introduction to Linguistics* [New York: St. Martin's Press, 1999], 130). The presuppositions and adherence to a *Wortbericht* ("announcement") and a *Tatbericht* ("execution report") behind Genesis 1 and 2, does not reflect the internal structure or analysis of more recent synchronic studies. Hendel believes the difference between the MT and LXX is "slight," stating:

Exegetical Analysis of the Mandate in Genesis 1–11

vine injunction has "become a word of address, an act of communication."[39] Vanhoozer speaks of an "ethics of reading" in which the reader is responsible "to determine to what kind of act a text belongs, and to respond to this communicative act in an appropriate manner."[40] Here, God's word of blessing (ויברך)[41] has a unique goal tied to a specific situation of need that both distinguishes and prescribes the human role within the created order.

So from the outset the repetition in the *formal complex stem* sets a mood of authorization enacted through relational intimacy; the stewardship of human rule is initiated and defined within a dynamic relational framework. God's speech in their creation (1:26) culminates with the act of their commission. Humans called to a stewardship of governance find the very nature of their commission birthed in act and illustration—God has created His counterpart in dialogue, capable of dialogue.[42]

The *s^eḡôltā* accent concludes the first half of the *formal complex stem* with the *r^eḇîa͑* accent closing the second (see Figure 2). Both clauses

---

it is difficult to find a clear argument for the primary reading. The M reading is somewhat awkward in the repetition of אלהים twice in two short clauses; hence the shorter G reading may be preferred. (*The Text*, 30; so Westermann, calling it "stylistically improbable with P and syntactically harsh," *Genesis*, 79; also *BHK*; Skinner, *Genesis*, 33; Gunkel, *Genesis*, 114.)

However, we believe that the contributions of Speech-Act theory and rhetorical criticism offer not only exegetically viable but better explanations for the repetition of אלהים in 1:28. Wevers claims that the LXX's λέγων reflects 1:22, as the LXX "tends to repeat patterns even when the Hebrew changes" (*Notes*, 16). However, Hendel routinely disregards this kind of explanation, believing the reading existed in "proto-G" and was subsequently affected by "secondary harmonizations" (*The Text*, 30).

39. P. A. Bird, "Male and Female He Created Them," in *"I Studied Inscriptions from Before the Flood": Ancient Near Eastern, Literary, and Linguistic Approaches to Genesis 1–11*, SBTS, vol. 4 (Winona Lake: Eisenbrauns, 1994), 329–61, 353 n. 55.

40. *Is There Meaning in This Text? The Bible, the Reader, and the Morality of Literary Knowledge* (Grand Rapids: Zondervan, 1998), 395. Responding to Derrida and the attack on determinate meaning in a stable context, Vanhoozer responds, "I hope to show that what writing pulls asunder—author, context, text, reader—genre joins together" (ibid., 339).

41. Outside the text plots of Genesis 1–11, other examples of blessing initiated with the preterite form ויאמר ... ויברך include Gen 14:19; 24:60; 27:27; 35:9–10; etc.

42. Westermann, *Genesis*, 160. Defining the nature of personhood within community, the reader does not actually hear Adam speak until there is another with whom he can speak (cf. 2:23). Chapter 1 is reserved exclusively for God's performative speech, with his image bearer(s) speaking in chapter 2 (cf. 2:19). Adam does follow God's lead when he names the animals, arguably an expression of his "dominion" (1:26, 28).

stipulate a direct accusative (אתם, להם),⁴³ with אלהים occurring twice in a heightened use of performative speech.⁴⁴ The *core charge* in 1:28 (פרו ורבו) is more strongly tied to the *domain indicator* (ומלאו) with the *mêrᵉḵā* accents occurring with the initial three imperatives. This emphasis comes to rest on את־הארץ as the *domain-focus*, marked with the closing *ṭip̄ḥā* accent (cf. 1:22). At this point הארץ frames 1:28, broadly underscoring the domain of humankind (see Figure 2).⁴⁵ Prior to the *charge elements* or *decretive collocations* (1:28b), the *ʾatnāḥ* closes the first half of 1:28 with וְכִבְשֻׁהָ ("and subdue it"). The literary logic of this *ʾatnāḥ* separates the general *enablement* from the particular effects that follow. Unlike the animals blessed in 1:22, humankind has a concomitant responsibility to "subdue" while "filling,"⁴⁶ both imperatives coming before the *ʾatnāḥ*.

Within the charge elements, וְכִבְשֻׁהָ is crucial, requiring some nuance at several levels. The antecedent of the 3fs suffix (הָ) is הארץ ("the earth"), the object of the verb and the domain now in focus. As we have seen, כבש overwhelmingly pertains to subduing a people group,⁴⁷ and by extension their land, especially the Canaanites.⁴⁸ However, these semantic uses must be nuanced for the precise function of כבש within the Creation Mandate. Clearly, such meanings as "enslave" (2 Chr 28:10), "conquer" (Josh 18:1), and obviously "assault" (Esth 7:8) do not suit the Mandate context.⁴⁹ An adversarial relationship with the earth itself is unthinkable within the purview of the Creator's blessing. Instead, we propose that כבש in 1:28 pertains to harnessing and developing⁵⁰ the earth's resources, uti-

---

43. IBHS, §16.4f.

44. The *wāw* + prefixed conjugation can function *epexegetically* with the substance of the act of blessing coming in the 2nd clause (IBHS, §33.22a).

45. Whereas 1:22 seized upon את־המים as the domain-focus (see appendix 1), likewise the domain-focus of 1:28 is marked with את־הארץ. However, 1:28 does not proceed with a noun as 1:22 (cf. Figures 1, 2).

46. Almost every aspect of וְכִבְשֻׁהָ has generated passionate discussion. For example, is the ו functioning *epexegetically* (= "even subduing it"), *emphatically* (= "especially subdue it"), or *logically/inferentially* (= and so subdue it")? Though the functions may overlap, there is a reasoned connection in the human charge to "fill" and so "master," a development wholly absent in the blessing on the animals (1:22).

47. Cf. Jer 34:11, 16; 2 Chr 28:10; Neh 5:5, etc.

48. Num 32:22, 29; Josh 18:1; cf. 2 Sam 8:11; 1 Chr 22:18; Zech 9:13.

49. See the discussion of כבש in chapter three (see pp. 81–89).

50. T. E. Fretheim, "The Book of Genesis," in *The New Interpreter's Bible: A Commentary in Twelve Volumes*, vol. 1 (Nashville: Abingdon, 1994), 346.

Exegetical Analysis of the Mandate in Genesis 1–11

lizing them for one's benefit through cultivation, domestication, and even mining.⁵¹ Since the natural human need for food is addressed in 1:29, the force כבש is an authorization for accomplishment of God's design for *earthly* stewardship. The *commissional* aspect of the Mandate has the earth in view placed at the constructive disposal of humans.⁵²

However, to consider Genesis' time of writing is to acknowledge the historical "occasion" or "life-dynamic" in the interpretative process of כבש, a significant element we believe. This aims to wed the *historical* horizon that prompted the initial stages of writing with the final *literary* horizon in the shape that text assumed. Genesis adds "God-as-Creator" of the world to the nation's existential experience of "God-as-Deliverer" from Egypt (Gen 2:3; Exod 14:30). The creation of the world (1:1—2:25) anticipates the creation of the nation of Israel (Exodus 1–18).⁵³ Considering Exod 15:1–18, Dumbrell develops this theme of God as Creator-Redeemer:

> In Miriam's song, the redemption of the exodus is being advanced poetically as a new creative act, whereby Israel is brought into being as a political entity. Thus the developing theology of redemp-

---

51. R. Chisholm, *From Exegesis to Exposition: A Practical Guide to Using Biblical Hebrew* (Grand Rapids: Baker, 1998), 46; also H.-J. Zobel, "רָדָה," *TDOT*, 13:335.

While mining may seem strange, the idea is not new. Nahmanides writes: נתן להם כוח וממשלה בארץ לעשות כרצונם בבהמות ובשרצים וכל זוחלי עפר ולבנות ולעקור נטוע ומהררים לחצוב נחושת וכיוצא בזה וזה יכלול מה שאמר ובכל הארץ: (tran: "He gave them power and dominion over the earth to do according to their will with the cattle and with the swarmers and with all that crawl in the dust; and to build and to uproot what has been planted, and to hew out copper and such things from its mountains. All this is included in the words 'and over all the earth'") (*The Commentary of Nahmanides on Genesis Chapters 1—6:8*, Pretoria Oriental Series, trans. J. Newman, ed. A. Van Selms [Leiden: Brill, 1960], 57).

But J. Goldingay believes eatable produce rather than "mining for minerals" is the issue (*Old Testament Theology: Israel's Gospel*, vol. 1 [Downers Grove: Intervarsity, 2003], 113). However, food is clearly postponed until 1:29-30 that follows. Mining could fall within the purview of "earth" (1:28b).

52. Ibid. Holladay's "make subservient" in reference to the earth can include the consumption of the earth's resources (151). Exploitation will be addressed in upcoming chapters. Wagner states, "['To 'subdue'... [is] to make use of all the economic and cultural potential associated with the concept of 'land'" ("כָּבַשׁ," *TDOT*, 7:54).

53. Many of the stories in Genesis appear shaped with the national needs of Israel on the horizon. By showing the sovereignty of God in the events of universal history (Genesis 1–11), Moses can more effectively reveal a young nation that truly exists for a divine purpose, inaugurated in the earlier covenant with Abram (Chaps. 15, 17; cf. 12:1-3) and developed into Israel's national vocation as a "kingdom of priests" (Exod 19:3-6; cf. Isa 49:6; Luke 2:32).

tion is set positively within the more general purposes for humans and the world, as presented in Genesis 1–2.[54]

When Israel was born at Sinai (Exodus 19–24), Genesis answered for Israel the foundational geo-political and theological questions of a theocratic nation. For this reason, Genesis is laden with embryonic themes developed later in Scripture.[55] Thus, Genesis supports the Sinai Covenant by recounting specific events antecedent to but reflective of their national gathering at Mt. Horeb.[56] This in turn served to underscore Israel's identity and purpose (Exod 19:5–6; cf. 15:16–17). K. A. Kitchen defends the tie between the literary product and the Sinai occasion of writing, stating:

> [Genesis was] composed as we have it about the time of the Exodus ... Proclaimed to the tribes before the exodus or en route to Sinai ... The most fitting author would be the man mandated to lead them towards that Destiny, namely Moses.[57]

---

54. *Faith*, 37.

55. The garden narrative (chs. 2–3) and the lives of the patriarchs (chs. 12–50) cast long shadows toward the Sinai Covenant (Exodus 20). Key thematic elements anticipated include: divine blessings (1:28; cf. 27:27–29), apodictic law (2:16–17; 9:6; cf. 26:5), temple imagery 2:9–17; cf. 28:12, 22), curses (3:14–19; cf. 49:7), and religious codes (9:2–6; cf. 24:2–4). Hearing of Abraham's altars (12:7; 26:25), Isaac's burial (35:29), and Jacob's return to Canaan (31:3; 35:1), the nation is challenged to follow in the archetypical footsteps of their patriarchs with Joseph's bones leading the way (50:25; cf. Exod 13:19).

In his chapter entitled "Pre-Sinai Theophanies," J. J. Niehaus tries to develop this correspondence by comparing Gen 1:1—2:3 with the 2nd Millennium Hittite treaty format. Though ultimately unconvincing, Niehaus views Gen 1:28 as overlapping literarily and legally with the *Stipulations* and *Blessing/Curses* elements of the international treaty form (*God at Sinai: Covenant and Theophany in the Bible and Ancient Near East* [Grand Rapids: Zondervan, 1995], 143–47).

56. Regarding dating and the traditional connection of "document D" with the Josianic Reform (622 BC), Waltke builds on J. G. McConville and writes:

> historical and textual evidence supports an earlier date for the so-called Tetrateuch than the Exile. First, those books are written from the viewpoint of Israel's enslavement in Egypt, not from the viewpoint of its exile in Babylon. In Genesis the Lord predicts Israel's enslavement in a "country not their own" (15:12–16), and its author draws his history to conclusion with the entrance of the tribes into Egypt, where Moses single-handedly will forge them into a theocracy. In Genesis and Exodus the author faults the Egyptians for innocent Israel's troubles there, but the Deuteronomist finds Israel guilty of bringing the exile upon itself. (*Genesis*, 22–31; also Walton, *Genesis*, 41.)

57. "The Old Testament in Its Context 1," *TSFBul* 59 (1971): 9 [2–10]; also Mathews (*Genesis*, 80). Broyles addresses this hermeneutically ("Interpreting," 43). Most recently, Wenham contemplates three primary temporal "settings" for Genesis: (1) Mosaic era

Exegetical Analysis of the Mandate in Genesis 1-11

In our present argument, the issue is not when the text achieved its final stages, but the defining occasion of its initial stages and theological trajectories.[58] Written retrospectively, this anticipatory use of information achieved an integration of family history with international history (chap. 10); the writing reflects a powerful ante-Mosaic faith as the theological backdrop to Israel's covenant relationship with God.[59] The "seam" between Genesis and Exodus illustrates this retrospection rather well.

Historical and literary elements merge at this juncture. God declared to Moses: "I am the God of your ancestors—the God of Abraham ... Isaac ... Jacob" (Exod 3:6a).[60] Moses' very call was rooted in the dynamic tradition of Patriarchal History (Genesis 12-50). Significantly, this triad of patriarchal names is an expression of "territorial hope"[61] looking toward

---

(13th century BC), (2) united monarchy of David and Solomon (10th century BC), (3) and the post-exilic era (5th century BC). In the end, he is inclined to see the united monarchy, admitting, "This is not to say that it is not based on traditions of much older date" (*Story as Torah: Reading Old Testament Narrative Ethically* [Grand Rapids: Baker, 2004], 41, 43).

58. The well-known "scribal updatings," "a-Mosaica" (Waltke, *Genesis*, 207), or "ideological changes" (Emanuel Tov, *Textual Criticism of the Hebrew Bible* [Minneapolis: Fortress, 2001], 94) attest to the development and accretions the text took on, some of which may be indicative of the sources used in compilation, especially genealogies (see Gen 12:6; 14:14; 33:18-20; 36:31, etc.).

59. Hamilton, *Genesis*, 68; see also W. Eichrodt's description of Moses' role as a "founder" of the theocracy that brought in a new world order (*Theology*, 1:290-91).

60. See the instructive essay by R. A. Averbeck, addressing the historical, literary, and theological elements of the patriarchal narratives, particularly as genealogy is employed in the theological reflection of the biblical text ("Factors in Reading the Patriarchal Narratives: Literary, Historical, and Theological Dimensions," in *Giving the Sense: Understanding the Using the Old Testament Historical Texts*, ed. D. M. Howard, Jr. and M. A. Grisanti [Grand Rapids: Kregal, 2003], 126 [115–137]). Averbeck supports our argument, stating:

> The history of the patriarchs and the promises to them were too pivotal to the national existence, deliverance, and destiny of Israel as it was understood even in the wilderness period. (126 n.19)

61. Sarna, *Genesis*, 351. Cf. Exod 3:16; 6:3; 32:13; 33:1; Num 32:11; Deut 1:8; 6:10; 9:5, 27; 29:12; 30:20; 34:4. Citing the work of M. Köckert, P. Van Hecke notes several structural parallels operating at the nexus of Genesis and Exodus, one of which is the divine allowance given to Jacob to *enter* Egypt (Gen 46:2-4) which receives its counterpart in Moses' call to lead his people *out* (cf. Exod 3:4, 6, 12; "Shepherds and Linguists: A Cognitive-Linguistic Approach to the Metaphor 'God Is Shepherd' in Gen 48:15 and Context," in *Studies in the book of Genesis: Literature, Redaction and History*, ed. A. Wénin [Paris: Peters, 2001], 478-93, 488, emphasis original).

the land and is first used by Joseph only 54 verses earlier (Gen 50:24b).[62] Not surprisingly then, Moses' confirmation for the Israelites in Egypt is the same: "Tell them, 'The LORD, the God of your ancestors—the God of Abraham ... Isaac ... Jacob—has sent me to you'" (Exod 3:15a). It is from this organic "collection" of patriarchal stories that Genesis emerges.[63]

Viewed with this perspective, the broader militaristic denotation of כבש does have the nation of Israel in view, a nation en route to conquer a land promised by God and cherished by the patriarchs. Assessing the significance of the patriarch's sacred sites, G. Beale states:

> The patriarchs appear also to have built these worship areas as impermanent, miniature forms of sanctuaries that symbolically represented the notion that their progeny were to *spread out and subdue the earth* from a divine sanctuary in fulfillment of the commission in Genesis 1:26–28.[64]

We believe this is the existential reality at the time of the of text's inception, an interplay between the universal and national realities of

---

62. Joseph continues the pattern of the patriarchs by making his final concern the fulfillment of God's promise. "God will surely visit (פקד) you and bring you out of this land..." speaks of God's salvific intervention (cf. Exod 4:31). But Joseph continues: "to the land which he swore to Abraham, Isaac, and Jacob" (50:24-25). Wenham states: "Here the promises that constitute the theme of Genesis are linked to the exodus" (*Genesis 16–50*, WBC [Waco: Word Books, 1994], 491).

63. Cf. Gen 5:1; Num 21:14. Writing of Egypt at this time, J. K. Hoffmeier lays out several points of evidence that strengthen our argument: (1) the textual "seam" encompassing Gen 39—Exod 15 is compatible with Egyptian history, (2) Egypt contained people from western Asia at this time, (3) Israel's bondage is reflective of Egyptian practice with conquered people, (4) Semitic administrators like Joseph were known to take high offices, (5) foreign royalty were trained in the Egyptian court, (6) plagues 1-6 in particular fit Egypt's inundation setting, and (7) the geographical factors of that period are in keeping with a route for Israel from Egypt to Sinai. Thus, Hoffmeier argues that the historical viability of these narratives can be seen (*Israel in Egypt: The Evidence for the Authenticity of the Exodus Tradition* (New York: Oxford, 1996). For a more critical evaluation of Exodus 3 and 6, see T. L. Thompson, "How Yahweh Became God: Exodus 3 and 6 and the Heart of the Pentateuch" *JSOT* 68 (1995): 57-74.

64. G. K. Beale, *The Temple and the Church's Mission: A Biblical Theology of the Dwelling Place of God*. NSBT (Downers Grove: InterVarsity, 2004), 97. Emphasis added. Beale mounts the most vigorous attempt to date to extrapolate the cosmic significance of Gen 1:28 as initiated in the proto-typical garden-sanctuary with Adam's rule as priest-king and its growing eschatological manifestation in the temple theology of the NT. A *tour de force*, at times Beale's exegesis of the "local context" seems overrun by his "eschatological rubric," forcefully applied throughout his work. See especially, "The expanding purpose of Temples in the Old Testament," 81–97.

Exegetical Analysis of the Mandate in Genesis 1–11

the text that were more fluid. Linking God's grand purpose for the world with land served to prevent a preoccupation with land from supplanting Israel's national obligation to ethics and divine obedience.[65] By connecting creation and ethics with land Goldingay positions the Creation Mandate within a larger trajectory, and observes:

> The land (ʾereṣ) to which Yhwh directed Abram and which Israel comes to occupy is a particular segment of the land (ʾereṣ) God created . . . The completion of the occupation of the land is the completion of the *creation project of subjugating the land*. It is described in terms that recall God's own completion of the work of creation. (Josh 18:1; 19:51; cf. Gen 1:28, 2:2)[66]

Cognizant of this existential backdrop, the reader is equipped to understand a fuller significance of כבש since every occasion of military force exercised by כבש is ultimately commissioned or permitted by God.[67] This is also why כבש typically assumes that the group "subdued" is a hostile force to the one subduing, thereby requiring a degree of force.[68]

Following the ʾatnāḥ, the verb רדה ("rule") continues the *charge elements* (cf. 1:26). Within the performative speech of divine blessing, it is the verbs כבש and רדה that constitute the sharpest departure from the blessing on the animals (cf. 1:22). Moreover, maintaining the shift from 3rd (1:22) to 2nd person, 1:28 communicates an imperatival, and contextually moral "oughtness" for humankind that is wholly lacking in the animals' blessing. The "subduing" (כבש) is the *task* for utilization of the earth, whereas the "ruling" (רדה) grants humankind the necessary *posi-*

---

65. Goldingay, *Theology*, 512. The argument of the Decalogue (Exod 20:1–17) powerfully combines themes of land (20:2, 12), creation (20:4, 11), and progeny (20:5, 6). A similar argument is well stated by J. Oswalt:

> The land without the presence of God would be worthless . . . The people's primary need was not for deliverance from bondage or for possession of a land; it was for a face-to-face relationship with the personal, fatherly God. ("Theology of the Pentateuch," *DOTP*, 854.)

66. Ibid., 512–13. Emphasis added.

67. M. Wagner, "כָּבַשׁ," *TDOT*, 7:56. The LXX renders כבש with κατακυριεύσατε [αὐτς"], a more positive word than the MT (Wevers, *Notes*, 16), however the *GELS* gives the definition: "to gain dominion over" with "the earth" (τῆς" γῆς") in the genitive (299). *LEH* defines the word as, "to be master over, to rule" (317). "The Three" employ the more literal: ὑποτάξατε, the form translating Ps 8:7 (= שָׁתָּה תַחַת).

68. J. Oswalt, "כָּבַשׁ," *TWOT*, 1:430.

tion[69] to achieve the harnessing of earthly life, with emphasis on the animals. Fulfilling this divine commission "requires the energy of strength and the art of wisdom."[70]

To the *endowment* for reproduction (1:22; 28a) is distinctly added the *commission* of ruling (1:28b). In this way, divine blessing follows specific acts of creation, and is intended to extend that creation-work in the human realm (cf. 5:3). Thus the endowment of fertility works alongside the commission to rulership (רדה).[71] The goal of the Creation Mandate lies closest to the commission that organizes the life-forces of fertility; here animate and inanimate creation merge.

The goal of human fertility lies not in the fact of multiplication, but multiplication within an ordered world.[72] God's will has presented man's goal to him.[73] Humankind experiences death when order gives way to

---

69. The terms of Bird ("Male and Female," 352).

70. F. Delitzsch, *Genesis*, 101.

71. Regarding MT וּרְדוּ ("and rule"), Wevers states:

The Revisers all render רדו differently. Aq has the literal ἐπικρατεῖτε "rule over," (cf. also v.26). Sym uses χειρόω in the middle voice "conquer, subdue," while Theod renders by παιδεύετε "correct, discipline, train." Aq and Theod continue with ἐν constructions to modify their verbs; thus "(in) the fish (plural in Theod) of the sea and (in) the birds (singular in Aq) of the sky and (in) every ζῴῳ," which Aq then modifies by τῷ κινουμένῳ, but Theod, by ἕρποντι. (*Notes*, 16)

72. There is poignant irony in the wordplay surrounding רבה ("multiply") in 1:28 and 3:16. What is initially expression of endowment for fertility within God's blessing (1:28a) becomes shockingly convoluted as God's *futility curse* uttered in the 1st person, הַרְבָּה אַרְבֶּה ("I will surely *multiply* [your pain . . .]"; LXX: πληθύνων πληθυνῶ [see *BDF*, §198.6]). While one might expect הַרְבֵּה, it does not communicate the intensity of the judgment oracle, with the Hiphil infinitive absolute, as "God actively intervenes to sentence the woman" (S. Kempf, "Genesis 3:14–19: Climax of the Discourse?" *JOTT* 6 [1995]: 362; see H. C. White, *Narration*, 142).

Within the same *tôlᵉdôt* (2:4—4:26), life has gone from blessing to diminishment (= curse), a departure noted by the Masoretes, framing 3:16 with the *sᵉtumah* (ס). This is interesting for at least two reasons: (1) the oracle to the woman is *asyndetic* [*IBHS*, §689, 635], functioning appositionally, (2) and the independent *wāw*—consecutive of 3:14 (cf. 3:9, 13) initiates one literary unit uniting the entire discourse of 3:14–19. See A. Niccacci, "Analysis of Biblical Narrative," 175–97.

For helpful discussions on the genre and literary significance of the discourse in 3:14–19, see: C. J. Collins, "What Happened to Adam and Eve? A Literary-Theological Approach to Genesis 3," *Presby* 27 (2001): 12–44; A. Bartor, "The 'Jurdical Dialogue': A Literary-Judicial Pattern," *VT* 53 (2002): 445–64; N. Levine, "The Curse and the Blessing," 189–99.

73. W. Eichrodt, *Man in the Old Testament*, SBT 4 (Chicago: Henry Regnery Co., 1951), 33.

disorder,[74] when dominion degenerates into mutual diminishment of all life within its domains.[75]

In 1:28b, רדה has in mind a rule of human agency,[76] without the oppressive notions visible in other texts.[77] Within the purview of the Mandate, רדה stipulates the human responsibility of the commission toward the created order. The commission in 1:28b is the enactment of the "rule" (רדה) envisaged in anticipation of human creation (1:26b).

רדה ("rule") is not only the last *charge element* of 1:28, but the construction of רדה ב defines three final object clauses: "rule over [בְּ] the fish ... [בְּ] the birds ... [בְּ] the animals" (see Figure 2). The Hebrew structure *gaps*[78] the verb רדה for the final two objects—"birds" and "animals," but repeats the order of animals in the initial blessing (1:22).[79] This triad and clausal structure serves to extend the application and significance of רדה ("rule"), connecting each clause with the conjunction: "and over ... and over" (see Figure 2).

Following the *core charge* ("be fruitful and multiply"), the *charge elements* begin with reference to הארץ ("the earth"). The following two clauses

74. B. Lemmelijn argues that the "Plague Narrative" of Exodus 7-11 can be viewed as "anti-creation," such that the LORD of creation is exalted precisely thorough his ability to reverse order into chaos ("Genesis' Creation Narrative: The Literary Model for the So-Called Plague Tradition?" in *Studies in the Book of Genesis: Literature, Redaction and History*, ed. A. Wénin [Paris: Peters, 2001], 407-19, 408-11).

75. Rev 22:1-3 portrays the New Jerusalem from the perspective of a restored Eden (cf. Ezek 47:1-12). Eden's river is recast with its original intention as a fructifying force for a "New Eden." With the curse removed, the cosmic scope (i.e., for nations) is restored after the pattern of Genesis 1 and 2. This supports the "heart" of theology as being *creation*. The cross does not conclude history, but enables its completion with humankind's return to another garden-paradise (Rev 22:1-3; see W. J. Dumbrell, *The Search for Order: Biblical Eschatology in Focus* [Grand Rapids: Baker, 1994], 345. For the universal effect on humanity at large, see R. Bauckham, *The Climax of Prophecy: Studies in the Book of Revelation* [Edinburgh: T. & T. Clark, 1993], 34, 37, 135, 139, 168, 241, 312, 316-18).

76. H.-J. Zobel, "רָדָה," *TDOT*, 13:331.

77. *HALOT*, 3:1190; cf. *BDB*, "dominate," 921; P. J. Nel, "רָדָה," *NIDOTTE*, 3:1055. The Israelites are warned against "dominating" (רדה) their own countrymen (cf. Lev 25:43, 46, 53; Ezek 34:4; ibid.).

78. Scanning this Hebrew phrase, Polak employs similar terminology: "semant-synt-gapping" ("Poetic Style," 25).

79. Investigation of Psalm 8 proves very fruitful as it is a theological reflection on Genesis 1-2 broadly, and 1:16, 28-30 in particular. For now, it should be noted that the animals are listed in *reverse* order to that of Gen 1:28 (cf. Ps 8:6-8). This reversal not only emphasizes human solidarity with the animals (cf. Gen 9:1-7), but moves from the most to the least visible creatures symbolic of all creation "placed under his feet" (8:6b).

develop the final charge element of רדה.⁸⁰ Thus the structure of the Creation Mandate to humans envelops all three domains of Genesis 1:

Domain 3: הארץ (= "the earth")   with humans,
Domain 2: הים   (= "the sea")   with fish, and
Domain 1: השמים (= "the sky")   with birds.

However, the order of the domains in 1:28 is reversed, vis-à-vis the days of creation (cf. Appendix A). This thematic order underscores human solidarity with the animals that share the 6th day of creation with humankind, beginning with the earthly domain (1:24–31). Beyond this, the inclusion of all three creation-domains points to the scope of the supervisory role of humankind for creation *in toto*, "making them to rule (משׁל) over what your hands have made; having set all things under his feet" (Ps 8:6).

Additionally, the "earth" (הארץ) and "sky" (השמים) represented the domains from which God brought animals for Adam to name (2:19–20), an extension of the dominion God designed for humankind⁸¹ that required the powers of discernment.⁸² Before considering the royal notions of רדה and their significance for the Mandate, we must observe the final clause of Gen 1:28.

---

80. Additionally, the two clauses following the *core charge* stipulate new information moving from the 5th (1:22) to the 6th panel (1:28). Whereas aquatic life (אתם) is only implied and aerial life is identified "on the earth" (בארץ; 1:22), 1:28 specifies "fish" (דג) for the domain of water and "the sky" (השמים) as the more particular domain name of birds.

81. Fulfilling his role, Adam follows God's lead and assesses the nature/character of the animals to give an appropriate name—God had named created elements in the initial triad of days (1:5, 8, 10), which evidenced his sovereign role. Though naming is embroiled in some scholarly debate, naming *can* indicate exercise of dominion (cf. Num 32:38; 2 Kgs 23:34; 24:17, etc.).

J. D. Currid states: "Man now demonstrates his lordship over the animal through the medium of the word" (*Genesis 1:1—25:18* [New York: Evangelical Press, 2003], 110). Hamilton adds: "For to confer a name (*qārāʾ lᵉ*) is to speak from a position of authority and sovereignty . . . In acting as name-giver, the man exhibits a quality of discernment" (*Genesis*, 176, 177). For a discussion of creation and the significance of naming, see Reichenbach, "Genesis 1," 62–63; Cassuto, *A Commentary*, 1:170; Gerhard von Rad, *Genesis*, OTL, rev. ed. (Philadelphia: Westminster Press, 1972), 49–51, 80–83.

82. G. Ramsey, "Is Name-Giving an Act of Domination in Genesis 2:23 and Elsewhere?" *CBQ* 50 (1988): 24–35.

Exegetical Analysis of the Mandate in Genesis 1–11

The final clause, "and over all the animals which move upon the ground,"[83] follows the disjunctive *zāqēp̄*, and functions as a *summary*. The *expansive* construction בְּכָל ("over all") concludes with the "roving animals." This final clause may constitute an indirect blessing on the animals curiously absent in the prior blessing (cf. 1:22), possibly included now for their association with humankind.

כל lends a determinative notion to the clause with the substantive (הָרֹמֶשֶׂת) acknowledged through כל,[84] making the anarthrous חַיָּה (MT) preferable to הַחַיָּה (SP).[85] The closing reference to הָאָרֶץ ("the earth") reiterates the domain-focus of הָאָרֶץ as the object of מלא (see Figure 2). הָאָרֶץ within the summary clause forms an inclusio around the charge elements, further highlighting the principle domain of humankind.[86] Within

---

83. ובכל־חיה הרמשת על־הארץ along with the prior phrase: ובעוף השמים ("and over the birds of the sky") raises some unexpected difficulty among the versions. To ובעוף השמים the LXX adds: καὶ πάντων τῶν κτηνῶν, καὶ πάσης τῆς γῆς ("and all cattle and all the earth"). The Syriac also has the harmonistic plus, "and all cattle."

Reconstructing proto-G, Hendel compares three texts:

v. 26	M = G	ובבהמה ובכל הארץ ובכל הרמש על הארץ
v. 28	M	ובכל חיה הרמשת על הארץ
v. 28	G	ובכל הבהמה ובכל הארץ ובכל הרמש על הארץ

According to Hendel, while M varies in the specification of land animals, proto-G is essentially identical otherwise. He concludes, "The harmonizing scribe in the proto-G tradition further expanded -וב to -ובכל ה in v. 28 to make the mention of בהמה consistent with the other species in this sequence, all of which are modified by -ובכל ה" (*The Text*, 31). As our analysis has shown, however, such reconstruction obscures subtle points of inner-textual development. Brown argues that this is a case of *homoioarchton*, with the phrase representing the LXX's *Vorlage*, "since the first two letters *waw* and *bet* at the beginning of the omitted material are identical to the following word in the MT" (*Structure*, 141 n.36).

Additionally, the MT חיה is made articular in the SP, but the MT כל already contains the determinative sense (*GKC*, §117).

84. *GKC*, §126x; cf. Joüon, §138d; Gib, 135; also 1:21; 9:10.

85. The article on הָרֹמֶשֶׂת has the force of a relative (= "animals that..."). The substantival participle, being definite itself, stands in apposition (see S. R. Driver, *A Treatise on the Use of the Tenses in Hebrew and Some Other Syntactical Questions*, 3rd ed. [Oxford: Clarendon Press, 1892], §209.2; A. B. Davidson, *Introductory Hebrew Grammar: Hebrew Syntax* [Edinburgh: T&T Clark, 1912], §99 and R. 1; *GKC*, §138).

86. Thematic emphasis can be traced through form and structure. Gen 1:28 is the most domain-inclusive and elaborate blessing of the creative week. The Hebrew word count totals 22, the letters of the alphabet. Similarly, the Psalm of creation and "universal praise" (148) delineates 22 items to typify the "earth" (148:7–12), and distinguishes the "heavens" by 7 items (Schökel, *Poetics*, 185–86). Within Ps 148, "heavens/earth" functions as a compositional device in order that "praise *in* the world is united with praise *above*

the larger discourse, space itself has been arranged into vertical layers, chronologically delineated through a pattern of symmetrical triplets that climax on the 6th Day.[87] After the grand blessing of creation's stewards (1:28), divine speech falls silent.

The care-giving aspect of רדה in the commission carries with it the significant notion of *royal status*;[88] this too is woven into the fabric of the Creation Mandate. The theme and imagery of royalty is evident not only in the semantics surrounding רדה, but also through inter-textual and *ANE* parallels. We will consider these briefly.

---

the world so that the name of the LORD is declared as the truth about all reality" (J. L. Mays, "'Maker of Heaven and Earth': Creation in the Psalms," in *God who Creates*, 86. Emphasis original).

87. McBride, Jr., "Divine Protocol," 12.

88. This argument is convincing and more soberly supported in recent scholarly literature. See, Goldingay, *Theology*, 99–100; Reichenbach, "Genesis 1," 47–69; K. W. Whitelam, "King and Kingship," *ABD*, 4:40–48; Beale, *The Temple*, 29–121; G. H. Wilson, *Psalms*, vol. 1, NIVAC (Grand Rapids: Zondervan, 2002), 198–220, esp. 213–14; Waltke, *Genesis*, 79–96; Walton, *Genesis*, 130–31, 147–53, 181–83; McBride, Jr., "Divine Protocol," 3–41; Callender Jr., *Adam*, 25–38, 50–65; Brown, *Ethos*, 35–132; R. Matthews, "Kings and Kingship," in *Dictionary of the Ancient Near East* ed. P. Bienkowski and A. Millard (Philadelphia: University of Pennsylvania Press, 2000), 170–71; Mathews, *Genesis*, 168–76; O. Keel, "The Temple: Place of Yahweh's Presence and Sphere of Life" (111–76), "The King" (243–306) in *The Symbolism of the Biblical World: Ancient Near Eastern Iconography and the Book of Psalms*, trans. T. J. Hallett (Winona Lake: Eisenbrauns, 1997); J. Van Seters, "The Creation of Man and the Creation of the King," *ZAW* 101 (1989): 333–42; J. D. Levenson, *Creation and the Persistence of Evil: The Jewish Drama of Divine Omnipotence* (San Francisco: Harper & Row, 1988), 111–17; W. W. Hallo, "Texts, Statues and the Cult of the Divine King," in *Congress Volume: Jerusalem 1986*, ed. J. A. Emerton, VTSup 40 (Leiden: Brill, 1988), 55–66; O. Keel and C. Uehlinger, *God, Goddesses, and Images of God in Ancient Israel*, trans. T. S. Trapp (Minneapolis: Fortress, 1998), 88, 266–67; P. Machinist, "Literature as Politics: The Tukulti-Ninurta Epic and the Bible," *CBQ* 38 (1976): 455–82; Westermann, *Genesis*, 158; G. Wenham, "Sanctuary Symbolism in the Garden of Eden Story" *PWCJS* 9 (1986): 19–25; idem, *Genesis 1–15*, 44–86; S. Mowinckel, *The Psalms in Israel's Worship* (Oxford: Basil Blackwell, 1962; reprint, Grand Rapids: Eerdmans, 2004), 50–61.

Exegetical Analysis of the Mandate in Genesis 1–11

Within רדה is semantic evidence of royal imagery[89] that does not make רדה simply synonymous with כבש.[90] Within the Mandate itself, רדה pertains to the quality of *position* and *agency* as a means of enacting the commission to rule, not merely for the "earth" as a domain (i.e., כבש), but for all life that defines that domain (i.e., רדה).

Additionally, it is not surprising to find rich terminology and metaphor for royal ideology in the OT, such as "crown" (2 Sam 1:10; Ps 89:39), "throne" (2 Sam 14:9; 1 Kgs 2:12) and "scepter" (Gen 49:10; Ps 45:6). Through the Creation Mandate God's persona as cosmic King[91] is democratized[92] to the ranks of humankind, enacted through their stewardship of dominion. In this way, human rule and dominion was a reflection of the

---

89. Cf. 1 Kgs 4:24 [5:4]; Pss 8:5–6; 72:8; 110:2; Isa 14:2. Of Ps 72:8, Wilson writes:

[Psalm 72] is essentially a series of entreaties that God will establish and extend the righteous rule of the monarch so that all nations will submit to his reign and experience the blessings of God's kingdom through him ... Using the creation image, the Psalmist describes the monarch as fulfilling the intended role of humanity: "he will rule" (72:8a). The verb for "rule" (*rdh*) is the same as used in Genesis 1:26 to describe the intended role of all humanity in creation ... The monarch is here envisioned as establishing the intended creation order—God's kingdom—throughout the whole earth: "from sea to sea and from the River to the end of the earth." (*Psalms*, vol. 1, 985, 987, 988)

90. Contra Westermann, *Genesis*, 161. Bird concurs with this distinction ("Male and Female," 353). See chapter three's discussion of רדה.

91. Exod 15:18; Num 23:21; Judg 8:23; 1 Sam 8:7; 10:19; 12:12.

92. A term B. W. Anderson has popularized alongside royal ideology ("Human Dominion Over Nature," in *Biblical Studies in Contemporary Thought* [Burlington: Trinity College Biblical Institute, 1975], 27–45, 43).

Be Fruitful and Multiply

rule and conquest[93] of the heavenly king[94] since subduing opposition and securing order[95] is fundamental to royal ideology in kingship.[96]

As cosmic king, God was able to sustain world-order[97] through his royal delegates, a celebration of themes combining creation and histo-

---

93. The LORD's *basis* of kingship emerged from his conquering of the "chaos waters" (cf. Exodus 15) and their rebellious denizens (cf. Pss 74:12–14; 89:10–11, etc.).

94. At times the relationship between the human throne and its divine counterpart were construed as equivalent, and the LXX (B, *Codex Vaticanus*) shows overt reaction to the imagery in the MT of 1 Chronicles 29: "Then David said to the whole assembly, 'Praise the LORD your God.' So they all praised the LORD, the God of their fathers; they bowed low and fell prostrate *before the LORD and before the king*" (לַיהוָה וְלַמֶּלֶךְ׃, 29:20). In this ceremonial and royal context, the dual use of the ל functions beyond direct object to *specification*. This is a bold statement, putting prostration to the earthly king and to God on the same level, implying concord between the two. In LXX B, the article τ῀ (= "*the* king") is deleted, rendering an appositional relationship: "before the LORD and K/king [= וְלַמֶּלֶךְ]"; cf. *Ec* 12, 1–4 Leningrad Firk II 1547. Fragment ex 1 Chr 29:9–2 Chr 6:25. As a form, וְלַמֶּלֶךְ only occurs again in Esth 3:8 (cf. *BHQ masorah parva*).

Similarly one reads: "So Solomon sat *on the throne of the LORD as king* [עַל־כִּסֵּא יְהוָה לְמֶלֶךְ | ǀ] in place of his father David. He prospered and all Israel obeyed him" (29:23). Again, the LXX recognized and rejected this concord, deleting "of the LORD as king" (LXX = "So Solomon sat on the throne of his father David and prospered, and all Israel obeyed him"; cf. 29:1). The *Paseq* [ǀ] ("divider") may serve to safeguard the LORD (cf. M. Fishbane, *Biblical Interpretation in Ancient Israel* [Oxford: Clarendon, 1985], 40 no.64). Theologically, the earthly temple was an extension of the heavenly cosmic one—the enthroned human king representing God in Heaven (cf. "Shulgi's Coronation" [21–27], *COS*: I, 553). Inter-textually, this reenacts the exodus occasion (cf. Exod 25–31; 35:4–29) with David's assembly mirroring the preparation, gathering, and construction under Moses (cf. 1 Chr 3:2–8).

95. Order and security were procured through the king's interrelated functions of *warrior* (1 Sam 8:20), *judge* (2 Sam 12:1–15; 1 Kgs 21:1–20; 2 Chr 19:4–11) and *priest* (2 Sam 6:13, 17; 24:24; 1 Kgs 3:4, 15; 8:62; 9:25; 12:32; 31:1).

96. Whitelam, "King," *ABD*, 4:43. This relationship might best be illustrated through the "Eternal Kingship of YHWH" Psalms (see H. Bullock, *Exploring the Book of Psalms: A Literary and Theological Introduction* [Grand Rapids: Baker, 2001], 187–97), cf. Pss 47:6–8; 93:1; 96:10; 97:1; 98:6; 99:1. Also classified among the Psalms of "Eternal Kingship," 95 illustrates how the Cosmic Creator (vv. 3–5) is also National Creator/Redeemer (vv. 6–7), combining themes of Royal Kingship (v. 3) with Royal Shepherd (v. 7); cf. *COS*: I, 397 ("Epic of Creation").

97. Pss 24:1; 74:15–17; 89:11–12; 68:9, etc.

ry.⁹⁸ Human justice, order, fertility, and even truth were viewed in cosmic terms that penetrated the whole of society.⁹⁹

A vertical relationship measured the earthly counterpart or microcosm by the standards of God's universal kingship. The key element here is *relationship*. Established through God's initiation¹⁰⁰ the delegator constrained the delegated. What God "chose" in sovereignty, the king sustained through *humility*, possibly the *sin qua non* of kingly rule.¹⁰¹ The earthly ruler is accountable to God for the character of that rule.¹⁰² The justice and order provided by the earthy ruler are all contingent upon a righteous rule.¹⁰³

Any rulership (רדה) entrusted to humans then, had as its backdrop the LORD who *is already* king (cf. Exod 15:18; Num 23:21; Deut 33:5),¹⁰⁴ since any loss of cosmic authority would necessarily impugn notions of

---

98. Dumbrell, *Faith*, 213. J. Muilenburg states:

The way of Israel is historical. It is historical to a maximum degree because its history belongs to God. History is God's gift to Israel and to the world. (*The Way of Israel: Biblical Faith and Ethics*, vol. 5, ed. R. N. Anshen [New York: Harper & Brothers, 1961], 44.)

99. Whitelam, "King," *ABD*, 4:44.

100. Cf. Deut 17:15a; 2 Sam 7:18–29; 1 Chr 28:4, 5; 29:1, etc. Following Mettinger, Dumbrell states:

the anointing constructs a relationship between the king and Yahweh, not between the king and people, whereby the Israelite king is then called Yahweh's messiah. (*Faith*, rev. ed., 84)

101. Muilenburg, *The Way*, 124. Such royal humility is anticipated in Gen 44:14–34 where a new Judah exemplifies kingly qualities. Of this, Waltke states:

Jacob will crown Judah with kingship because he demonstrates that he has become fit to rule according to God's ideal of kingship that the king serves the people, not vice versa. Judah is transformed from one who sells his brother as a slave to one who is willing to be the slave for his brother. With that offer he exemplifies Israel's ideal kingship. (*Genesis*, 567)

Deut 17:20a establishes this. National tenure and dynastic succession are rewards for covenant fidelity (cf. Deut 5:32—6:2; 2 Sam 7:10–16; 1 Kgs 2:4; Ps 132:11–18, etc.). For a dissenting view, see J. P. Dickson and B. S. Rosner, "Humility as a Social Virtue in the Hebrew Bible?" *VT* 54 (2004): 459–79.

102. Muilenburg, *The Way*, 122.

103. Ibid., 123.

104. Celebrated in Pss 47, 93, 96–97, and 99, יהוה מלך is *durative* rather than *inceptive*. For some of these Psalms Pietersma prefers the translation: "The Lord became king!" (e.g., Ps 97:1; *Septuagint*, 96). Other English translations vary between "The LORD reigns!" (ESV, HCSB), and "The LORD is king!" (NAB, NLT²).

his eternal kingship and his reputation as historical deliverer.[105] Such a rupture would undercut foundational OT postulates and nullify the heart of OT worship, profoundly expressed in the royal theology of the Psalms:[106]

> [Ps 47:8–10] portrays God seated on his throne, ruling over the nations who have now become one with the people of the God of Abraham. The Lord of history has become Lord of all the earth. The promise to Abraham, the father, has been fulfilled (Gen 12:1-3), a glorious finale![107]

---

105. Cf. Ps 10:16; Hab 1:12; 3:11–15, 19.

106. Dumbrell, *Faith*, 213; cf. G. H. Wilson, "Psalms and Psalter: Paradigm for Biblical Theology," in *Biblical Theology: Retrospect and Prospect*, ed. S. Hafemann (Downers Grove: InterVarsity, 2002), 100–10. As the most common type of Psalm, the very structure and language of the lament mirrors the lodging of a complaint before royal K/kingship. This is all the more pointed when the earthly king himself pleads the One "enthroned between the cherubim" [יֹשֵׁב הַכְּרֻבִים] on behalf his nation (Isa 37:16–20) or what E. Gerstenberger wishes to call, "Royal Lament" ("Psalms," in *Old Testament Form Criticism* [San Antonio: Trinity University Press, 1977], 198–207; see also R. W. L. Moberly, "Lament," in *NIDOTTE*, 4:866–84). As lament of the king, the significance of Isa 37:16–20 would be heightened if it were construed as such in the translations. Muilenburg states:

> The responsibilities of power weigh so heavily upon the king that he must hasten to the sanctuary for help in his weakness . . . For to whom could the afflicted go when there was no helper in the land but to the place where his glory dwelleth? In the Presence of the Invisible One Enthroned, he could hear the holy name spoken, and to him he could address his miseries and fears. (*The Way*, 124)

G. T. Sheppard argues that laments reveal a "seeking of refuge" in God ("Theology and the Book of Psalms," *Interp* 46 [1992]: 143–55, esp. 149–54).

107. Muilenburg, *The Way*, 121. Written on a "heavenly stage," the Psalms allow eschatology and doxology to merge in a manner foreign to historical narrative. With Muilenburg, I maintain many "messianic" texts should be initially read within their historical "context of ancient anticipation and hope" (ibid., 140). Emerging from *progressive revelation* is the flowering messianic significance of such texts "*vaticinia post eventum*, prophecies after the event" (ibid.). W. H. Rose quotes S. Greidnaus who helpfully distinguishes seven ways the OT can point to Christ. Appropriately, this acknowledges the complexity of many of these texts ("Messiah," *DOTP*, 565–68).

Articulating his own "canonical" approach, Waltke isolates four successive stages that culminate in the overtly Christological fourth stage ("A Canonical Approach to the Psalms," in *Tradition and Testament: Essays in Honor of Charles Lee Feinberg*, ed. J. S. Feinberg and P. D. Feinberg [Chicago: Moody, 1981], 9). Given that the Psalter reflects this very process of growth as evidenced through a *colophon* (cf. Ps 72:20), Broyles comment is apropos:

> The principle of "progressive revelation" means not only that God gradually unfolds his self-manifestation, but also that the *process itself* is revelatory, including

Exegetical Analysis of the Mandate in Genesis 1–11

As a crucial inter-textual parallel, Psalm 8 (esp. vv. 5–6) presents some of the richest theological reflection on Genesis 1 and 2, celebrating "the centrality of human agents in creation."[108] Broadly, the writer's awe-inspired praise moves in two directions: (1) the stupendous quality of God's creative work, (2) and the great honor given to humble humankind, to *rule* over God's creation.[109]

Psalm 8 is framed[110] by the exclamation: "O LORD, our Lord, how magnificent is your name in all the earth!"[111] (8:1a, 9). A *paratactic* style covers such elements as LORD, heavens, and infants (vv. 2–3) with humankind, earth, and animals (vv. 4–8). The distribution of the *inclusive* or *absolute* כל ("all")[112] knits the beginning, middle, and end together.[113]

However, more significant cohesion comes through the repeated *anaphora-like*[114] expressions: מָה ("who, what," vv. 1, 4, 9).[115] Whereas the

---

each stage and its progression from previous stages. ("Interpreting," 40. Emphasis added.)

108. Brueggemann, *Reverberations*, 41. Elsewhere in the Psalter, humankind is essentially *recipient*, not agent.

109. Contextually, Psalm 8 portrays a vibrant celebration immediately following the laments of Psalms 3–7 that plead for deliverance, arguably using the same speaker. The nature of this Cosmic King is then extolled with royal language in Psalms 9–10 that immediately follow. For its part, Psalm 8 is the only Psalm composed in hymnic form of direct address to God (M. E. Tate, "An Exposition of Psalm 8," *PRSt* 28 [2001]: 343–59, 344).

110. For a discussion of inclusion, see V. M. Wilson, *Divine Symmetries: The Art of Biblical Rhetoric* (New York: University Press of America, 1997), 38–39; A. Schökel, *A Manual*, 78, 83, 191–92. J. P. Fokkelman's discussion is creative and engaging (*Reading Biblical Poetry: An Introductory Guide*, trans. I. Smit (Louisville: Westminster John Knox, 2001), 142–44.

111. These are examples of one-line strophes, only occurring 41x in the Psalter (Fokkelman, *Reading*, 38).

112. *BDB*, 482.2.

113. Moving from "earth" (v. 1), to "all things" (v. 6), "all [domesticated] animals" (vv. 7–8), and closing with the repeated refrain (v. 9). See the discussion of R. Alter, *The Art of Biblical Poetry* (New York: Basic Books, 1985), 119.

114. Schökel, *Poetics*, 198. While generally "pointing back," *anaphora* (also *anadiplosis*) used in poetry refers "to the linking of verses into bicola, tricola, and so forth by employing the same word or phrase at the beginning of each line" (Murphy, *Dictionary*, 25).

115. The following triad of exclamations emerge:

"How (מָה) magnificent is your name!" (v. 1)
"What (מָה) importance is mankind that you are mindful of him?" (v. 4)
"How (מָה) magnificent is your name!" (v. 9)

first and last envelope the Psalm with admiration for the regal Creator;[116] the medial interrogative ("what") poses the essential question addressing the scope of the Psalm.[117] It is this medial "question" (v. 4) that has behind it the force of the Creator's work (vv. 1–3) that is then immediately followed by the "answer" (vv. 5–8). Observe the following rhetorical structure:

    A Refrain: "O LORD, our Lord, <u>how</u> magnificent . . ." (8:1a)
        B Question: <u>what</u> is humankind in light of your <u>glory</u> (הוֹד), <u>works of your fingers</u> (מַעֲשֵׂה אֶצְבְּעֹתֶיךָ?; 8:1b–4)
        B' Answer: humankind is God's designated regent, sharing the LORD's <u>glory and honor</u> (כָבוֹד וְהָדָר), made steward of the <u>works of your hands</u> (מַעֲשֵׂי יָדֶיךָ; 8:5–8)
    A' Refrain: "O LORD, our Lord, <u>how</u> magnificent . . ." (8:9)[118]

Several points should be noted. At the core of the question—"What is humankind" (v. 4)—is a wisdom motif that elsewhere grapples with the quest for justice amid the reality of human mortality.[119] That God has shared such heavenly glory with earthly beings is baffling and verges on paradoxical for the Psalmist. Secondly is the theme of God as craftsman, with related imagery in the Creation Hymns that reference God's skill.[120] The יצר ("to form"; cf. Gen 2:7)[121] language places God atop a cosmic guild of "crafts and skills."[122] Thirdly, and most significantly, the royal imagery contained in the commission of Gen 1:28 becomes an assumed reality in Psalm 8.[123] Within this structure, Schökel observes several ingredients of royal imagery:

---

116. W. Brueggemann, *The Message of the Psalms: A Theological Commentary* (Minneapolis: Augsburg, 1984), 36.

117. Schökel, *Poetics*, 198.

118. Adapted from Dorsey, *Literary Structure*, 177.

119. Gerstenberger, *Psalms*, Part 1, 69, 71; cf. Job 7:17; 15:19; Ps 144:3–4.

120. Cf. Pss 33, 104, 144; cf. Job 38; *llQPs*; COS: I, 46 ("The Great Hymn to the Aten").

121. Cf. Gen 2:21–22; 6:5; 2 Sam 17:28; Job 10:8–9; Isa 29:16; Jer 18:2–4, etc.

122. Schökel, *Poetics*, 137.

123. According to Tate, "Psalm 8 affirms the powerful and majestic Creator and King of the heavens and the earth . . . Intertextually, it is proper to read Psalm 8 with Genesis 1–2 ("Exposition," 344, 356); J. H. Tigay believes there is an echo of Gen 1:16, 18 ("What Is Man That You Have Been Mindful of Him" [On Psalm 8:4–5]," in *Love and Death in the Ancient Near East: Essays in Honor of Marvin H. Pope*, ed. J. H. Marks and R. M. Good [Guilford: Four Quarters, 1987], 170–71); Wilson asserts, "The creation account is clearly

> The central part of the Psalm is a kind of rite of enthronement of man: his rank is: "little less than God," he is crowned "with glory and majesty," he has power "over the works of your hands," he places his feet over "animals, birds and fish."[124]

B. W. Anderson agrees, noting that 8:5 is the coronation of humans.[125]

In sum, Psalm 8 both illustrates and advances the royal imagery surrounding Gen 1:28 through *allusions*. Discussing the biblical use of citations, allusions, and reminiscences Schökel writes:

> The *allusion* points from a distance to a known fact, a shared tradition, a well-known text; the allusion makes these things present in a discrete kind of way. More so than with citation, the allusion needs the intelligent collaboration of the reader; sometimes it can be a showing off of culture, on other occasions a challenge to the sharpness of the reader.[126]

Constituting royal language, several "allusions" to Gen 1:26–30 emerge in Ps 8:5–6. First is the allusion to 1:26–27 in the phrase: "You made him a little lower than the heavenly beings" (8:5a).[127] This reflects the Creator's resolve: "let us make humankind in our image" (1:26).[128]

Secondly is the language of humankind's royal status reflected in the phrase "and crowned him with glory and honor" (8:5b). These allude to the royal standing of humankind as the vice-regent of God (Gen 1:26–30).[129]

---

the text our Psalmist has in mind here ... It is certain in my mind that the Psalmist has the account of creation in Genesis in 1:28 clearly in mind here" (*Psalms,* vol. 1, NIVAC, 206, 208); P. C. Craigie, *Psalms 1–50.* vol. 19, Word (Nashville: Thomas Nelson, 1983), 106, 108; H-J. Kraus, *Psalms 1–59,* trans. H. C. Oswald, vol. 1 (Minneapolis: Fortress, 1993), 179, 180.

124. Ibid., quoting *Treinta Salmos,* 111–18.

125. "Human," 121.

126. Schökel, *Poetics,* 143. Emphasis original. Acknowledging the "escalating" nature of the biblical text, Schökel comments, "Reminiscences and allusions are more probable at the end of a period of development, when a tradition has been built up" (ibid.).

127. An analysis of אלהים ("God," "heavenly beings," "angels" [LXX]) lies beyond our discussion though the fact of allusion can still be argued (cf. Gen 3:5; 22; with Ps 82:1, 6; see Tate, "Exposition," 354–55; Wilson, *Psalms,* vol. 1, 206–7; Craigie, *Psalms 1–50,* 104–14).

128. The parallel to Gen 1:26 is clearer if one construes Ps 8:5a as an *independent* clause (cf. *GKC,* §111.*m*).

129. The imperfect forms in 5b–6a are difficult to classify, most translations rendering "you made ... crowned," etc. [descriptive, unique?]; some, however, prefer "will crown" (Craigie, *Psalms 1–50,* 105). I prefer to construe the *imperfect + perfect* sequence with a

"Glory and honor" (כבוד והדר) are terms tied to the LORD's kingship (Ps 145:12), yet qualities extended to human royalty (Ps 21:5).[130] Concerning כבוד, von Rad states, "This gives us a mysterious point of identity between God and man, for on the OT view כָּבוֹד belongs supremely to Yahweh."[131] Of these terms, Tate concludes, "Thus it is clear that in Psalm 8 humanity is empowered with divine royal qualities."[132]

A third allusion is found in the phrase, "You made him ruler over" (תמשילהו ב; 8:6a), which is an allusion to the commission of "rulership" and "dominion" (רדה) in Gen 1:28b.[133] While משל ב and רדה ב are semantically synonymous in this context (= "rule over"),[134] the verbal form of משל is causative (i.e., "make one exercise dominion over), meaning humans implement a *derived* rather than *autocratic* authority, limited and accountable to the Creator from whom their authority and status is derived.[135] In keeping with the ruled domain of 1:28 is the "all things under his feet" (8:6b). A symbolic act in the *ANE* was the king's foot placed on an enemy's neck, comparable to imagery found elsewhere (cf. Ps 99:5).

Important implications arise from this. Clearly, humanity is God's viceroy with one foot planted in the creaturely world and the other uniquely in the divine realm.[136] Far from a despotic rule, human dominion "should imitate God's own dominion over creation and should have as its goal the fulfillment of God's good purpose for creation."[137]

---

past nuance that acknowledges the allusion to the human creation and blessing of Gen 1:26–28 (so Wilson, *Psalms*, vol. 1, 208).

130. Cf. Pss 45:2–3; 96:2; Isa 2:10, 19, 21. The "crown" (cf. עטר, Ps 8:5b) served as a metonymy for the bestowal of "glory" on the royal figure: "He has stripped me of my glory [כְּבוֹדִי] and removed the crown [עֲטֶרֶת] from my head" (Job 19:9).

131. "εἰκών," *TDNT*, 2:391.

132. "Exposition," 355.

133. Ps 8:6 lays out a sequence of imperfect (תַּמְשִׁילֵהוּ, "caused to rule") + perfect (שַׁתָּה, "placed). The perfect communicates on-going effects of the original Creation Mandate (1:28).

134. משל was used of the heavenly bodies in Gen 1:16. Elsewhere רדה describes the king's dominion (Ps 72:8), which also mentions the submission of his enemies (v. 9), cf. *COS*: II, 156 ("The Hadad Inscription").

135. Wilson, *Psalms*, vol. 1, 208.

136. Ibid, 206.

137. M. M. Wilfong, "Human Creation in Canonical Context: Genesis 1:26–31 and Beyond," in *God Who Creates*, 45–46.

Exegetical Analysis of the Mandate in Genesis 1-11

Commission and royal honor have combined giving humankind both gift and responsibility.[138] Significantly, this gift and responsibility establishes a divine-human relationship, one just below the heavenly beings. Moreover, Ps 8:7-8 mirrors Gen 1:28 by defining human dominion most immediately in terms of the animals.[139] Wilson believes that the placement of the 1:28 blessing following the creation of humans links them with the preceding land animals.[140] This exercise of royal authority is limited, derived from God, and ultimately accountable to the Creator who commissioned it.[141] It is precisely this royal language of Psalm 8 that allows its application to Christ.[142] As Childs explains:

> Psalm 8 when read in the LXX (Heb.2.5ff), allows him the possibility of seeing in the description of man's being made slightly lower than the angels, a temporal description of Christ's incarnation, humiliation, and ultimate fulfillment of the promise to put everything in subjection to him.[143]

---

138. Wilson, *Psalms*, vol. 1, 206.

139. As part of Habakkuk's 2nd prophetic lament (1:12-17) he writes in v. 14: "You have made men like the fish of the sea, like sea creatures that have no ruler over them [col.]" (:וַתַּעֲשֶׂה אָדָם כִּדְגֵי הַיָּם כְּרֶמֶשׂ לֹא־מֹשֵׁל בּוֹ); cf. 1QpHab: למשל, "[for him] to rule over"). Numerous lexemes are shared between Gen 1:28; Ps 8:7-9; and Hab 1:14. While unique, this רמש refers to sea creatures (cf. Ps 104:25). With irony verging on sarcasm, Habakkuk uses the "lowest" and most remote creature ruled by man to upend the creation ideal (Gen 1:28). Habakkuk vividly illustrates the defenseless destruction of Jerusalem by the Babylonians through a reversal of the theology of Psalm 8 (cf. vv. 6-8)—creation's ruling order overwhelmed by another chaos.

Jesus' temptation in the wilderness has cosmic proportion, also a harbinger of creation/cosmic reordering, typified by his presence with "wild animals" (Mark 1:13b; cf. Isa 11:6-8; 65:25; see Dumbrell, *The Search*, 183).

140. *Psalms*, 206, n.9. However, this is not to minimize the distinctions the narrator draws between humankind and animals. These are distinct identities within multi-tiered relationships, all of which are marred in the human rebellion (Gen 3:1-13; cf. vv. 14-19).

141. Wilson, *Psalms*, vol. 1, 209. God reserves the right to remove and replace royal figures, foreign or Israelite (cf. Lev 26:17; Neh 9:28; Isa 14:6; Ezek 29:15).

142. Anderson, "Human," 123-35. J. J. Roberts states:

> [The] claim that God had chosen David and his dynasty as God's permanent agent for the exercise of the divine rule on earth was the fundamental starting point for the later development of the messianic hope." ("In Defense of the Monarchy: The Contribution of Israelite Kingship to Biblical Theology," in *Ancient Israelite Religion: Essays in Honor of Frank M. Cross*, ed. P. D. Miller, [Philadelphia: Fortress, 1987], 377-96, 378.)

143. *Biblical Theology*, 311.

However, the *ANE* parallels are just as illuminating since they exhibit overt similarity through a shared "cultural environment." Throughout the *ANE* it was believed that kings were the patron deities of their countries. Even though the Pharaoh was held up as Re's offspring,[144] the Pharaoh was still divine, identified with Horus in life and Osiris in death.[145] Official documents employ the language of "sonship"[146] and "image," as found in Amon Re's charge to Amenophis II:

> Thou art my beloved son, come forth from my limbs, my very own image, which I have put upon the earth. I have permitted thee to rule over the earth in peace.[147]

Among the Canaanites, deities "adopted" royal personages as their official "sons." In turn, these "sons" functioned as intermediaries or vice-regents, performing the interests of their gods. This royal "persona" also extends to cultic and official functions of the king.

One cannot underestimate the significance in the Temple-Palace complex,[148] the building of which was the responsibility of the king, "the symbolic expression of the god as the guarantor of the state and the dynasty (2 Sam 5:12)."[149] Whitelam explains:

> The temple above all else defined the political, economic, and religious center. It was, thereby, a symbolic statement of the king's relationship with the god and his divine right to rule. The temple, among other things represented heaven upon earth (Ps 1:4). As the dwelling place of the deity upon earth, situated next to the king's palace and part of the same complex, it symbolized the king's

---

144. Whitelam, "King," *ABD*, 4:45.
145. Mathews, *Genesis*, 169.
146. Cf. Exod 4:22–23; 2 Sam 7:14; Pss 2:6–7; 89:26–27, etc.
147. Westermann (*Genesis*, 153), citing W. H. Schmidt.
148. Beyond the mere Temple, הבירה in 1 Chr 29:1, 19 arguably has a larger "temple-complex" in mind. Used 10x in Esther (1:2—9:12; cf. Dan 8:2; Neh 1:1; 7:2), *HALOT* defines the word as "citadel, acropolis, and temple" (1:123–24). Following J. Schwartz, G. N. Knoppers assesses its use in 1 Chr 29:1 and concludes:

> there is reason to believe that *bîrâ* refers here to a complex of buildings, including the temple, rather than to a single structure. (*1 Chronicles 10–29: A New Translation with Introduction and Commentary*, AB [New York: Doubleday, 2004], 944; see Bush, *Ruth/Esther*, 343–44; BHQ, 137.)

149. Whitelam, "King," *ABD*, 4:45.

Exegetical Analysis of the Mandate in Genesis 1-11

special relationship with the divine world and the political and religious center of the state.[150]

Comparing the Gudea Cylinders with the biblical text, Averbeck lists fifteen parallels that highlight the relationship of the king with temple building.[151] Here we can observe four key elements that illustrate this relationship:[152]

> 1) The close association between temple building and fertility, abundance, and prosperity in the ancient Near East and the Bible,[153] 2) Royal wisdom in association with temple building,[154] 3) Social justice, equity, and purity in association with temple building and dedication,[155] 4) and the close association of temple building with the blessings and responsibilities of kingship.[156]

Not surprisingly, the temple also became the locus of God's military protection within the cult,[157] "the matrix for the divine warrior's victory in battle."[158] This imagery is clearly seen in the Gudea Cylinder when it describes Gudea's god, Ningirsu, officially taking up residence in the new temple built for him:

> The *warrior*, Ningirsu, was entering into the *temple*; the *king* of the house came. Being (like) an eagle gazing at a wild bull; the *warrior*,

---

150. Ibid., 47.

151. The pertinent biblical texts are: Exod 25-40; 1 Kgs 5-9; 2 Chr 2-7 and Ezek 40-48.

152. "Sumer," 119-20. Averbeck's discussion is directly tied to his analysis of Gudea Cylinders A and B (see "The Cylinders of Gudea," *COS*: II, 417-33).

153. The parallels are: Cyl. A I 5-9, xi 5-11; *COS*: II, 419 n.4, 2.423 n.26; 2 Sam 7:1-2 (= 1 Chr 17:1); 1 Kgs 5:1-8[4:20-28], 18[4] (= 2 Chr 1:14—2:10); Ezek 47:1-12; Hag 1:2-11; 2:15-19; Zech 9:9-13 (ibid., 119).

154. Cyl. A I 12-14; *COS*: II, 419 n.6 1 Kgs 3:3-15; 5:9-14[4:29-34] (= 2 Chr 1:7-13); 1 Chr 28:6-10 (ibid., 119).

155. Cyl. B xviii 6-11; *COS*: II, 432 n.75; Ezek 42:13-14, 20; 43:6-12 (ibid., 120).

156. Cyl. B xxiii 18—xxiv 8; *COS*: II, 433 n.79; 2 Sam 7:4-17 (= 1 Chr 17:3-15); 1 Kgs 8:14-21; 9:1-9 (= 2 Chr 7:11-22); Ps 78:68-70 (ibid., 120).

157. When the "horns of the altar" are "cut off" God has removed his protection and Israel's asylum at the very site that symbolically celebrates it (Amos 3:14; cf. Exod 21:14; 1 Kgs 1:50-51; Ps 118:27).

158. G. N. Knoppers, "Jerusalem at War in Chronicles," in *Zion: City of Our God*, ed. R. S. Hess and G. J. Wenham (Grand Rapids: Eerdmans, 1999), 76.

his entering into *his temple* being (like) a storm roaring into *battle*, Ningirsu was coming into *his temple*.[159]

This excerpt from Cyl. B demonstrates the fluidity of military and royal ideology that defined both deity and earthly vice-regent. Furthermore, *ANE* royalty ideology also characterized their reigns in terms of wisdom[160] and shaking-of-mountains descriptions,[161] royal themes well known in the OT.[162]

In sum, the semantic, inter-textual, and *ANE* evidence not only constructs a clear portrait of royal imagery, but serves to underscore kingship and ruling notions that find their inception in the OT with רדה and the Creation Mandate (Gen 1:[26], 28). It is this exegetical weight that רדה contributes to the Mandate that justifies a more trenchant analysis. Aside from its first use in 1:26, which we will consider in our discussion of "image," the following four occurrences of רדה are all negative and relationally oppressive,[163] making a marked departure from its royal and more programmatic role in 1:28.[164]

It is precisely this tension surrounding the function of רדה with כבש in 1:28 that has led to some seminal, albeit disputed, proposals for their significance in the Mandate.[165] The analysis of N. Lohfink,[166] in particular, intersects with our study and so we will briefly consider his arguments.

159. Cyl. B v. 1–6; *COS*: II, 431. Emphasis added.

160. Cf. *COS*: III, 45d, 46c ("The King to Kaššū in Tapikka 2, 3").

161. Cf. *COS*: II, 427a ("The Cylinders of Gudea" [A]).

162. Cf. Gen 41:39; 1 Kgs 4:29[9:9]; 4:34[5:14]; 5:7[21]; Isa 11:2, etc. (= wise/wisdom); Pss 68:16; 87:1; 95:4; Isa 40:4; Ezek 17:22–23; Mic 7:12; Zech 14:4; Heb 8:5, etc. (= mountain(s)).

163. Cf. "do not rule [רדה] over them ruthlessly, but fear your God" (Lev 25:43); "but you should not rule [רדה] over your fellow Israelites ruthlessly" (Lev 25:46); "you must see to it that his owner does not rule over [רדה] him" (Lev 25:53); "those who hate you will rule over [רדה] you, and you will flee" (Lev 26:17).

164. The proposed emendation of וּרְבוּ (9:7b) for וּרְדוּ (cf. 1:28b) is acknowledged and will be discussed in our analysis of 9:7 (cf. *HALOT*, 3:1190.2; *BHK*, *BHS*, and the commentaries).

165. P. Bird sees in רדה the notion of "subordination," unnecessarily giving the term a negative connotation since a given context determines the type of rule ("Male," 356). B. Vawter, on the other hand, takes כבש and רדה as "absolute subjugation" (*On Genesis: A New Reading* [Garden City: Doubleday, 1977], 60).

166. "Macht euch die Erde untertan?" *Orientierung* 38 (1974): 137–42; reprint, "'Subdue the Earth?' (Genesis 1:28)," in *Theology of the Pentateuch: Themes of the Priestly Narrative and Deuteronomy* (Minneapolis: Fortress, 1994), 1–17; idem, *Great Themes from the Old Testament* (Chicago: Franciscan Herald, 1982), 176–79.

Exegetical Analysis of the Mandate in Genesis 1–11

Lohfink concentrates on the Priestly source, what he specifies as P⁰.¹⁶⁷ For Lohfink, this historical narrative was written at the end of the exile,¹⁶⁸ and views Israel as a sacral rather than military community. Far from notions of force and occupation, Israel's move into Canaan was analogous to establishing God's sanctuary.¹⁶⁹ However, it is the presence of P⁰ within Universal History (Genesis 1–11) that raises key implications for the Mandate.

According to Lohfink, Gen 1:26–30 expresses the ideal—one that knows no human force over the animals. In fact, it is because such brute force was exercised in the P⁰ material that God was impelled to bring the flood at all. Thus, the post-flood allowances for meat consumption amounts to a divine compromise for human rejection of God's ideal.¹⁷⁰ It is the necessity of sacrifices to preserve a sacral and oppression-free community that actually lay behind the permission to eat meat (cf. Gen 9:1–7).¹⁷¹

Lohfink's interpretation of the Mandate stems from a different definition of key terms, including רדה, namely, "to wander around" with semantic notions that include: "pasture" and "guide" along with "rule" and "command." Thus, for Lohfink, רדה does not mean "to have dominion over," but "to shepherd" and "domesticate" the animals.¹⁷² Moreover, כבש does not mean "conquer" or "subjugate," that is, "subdue"; rather כבש in Gen 1:28 pertains to people groups "taking possession" of their own regions.¹⁷³

Assessing Lohfink, it is important to realize that his argument turns on pitting P⁰ against J and D within Israelite history. P⁰ is anti-war, essentially contrary to the mode of the exodus and method of possessing Canaan. This in turn surfaces the contemporary social issues Lohfink is

---

167. P⁰ (Priestly historical narrative, with "g" = *Geschichtserzählung*).

168. P⁰ runs counter to J and D with respect to history and the sanction of war ("Die Schichten des Pentateuch und der Krieg," in *Gewalt und Gewaltlosigkeit im Alten Testament*, ed. N. Lohfink, Quaestiones Disputatae 96 [Freiburg im Breisgau: Herder, 1983]; reprint, "The Strata of the Pentateuch and the Question of War," in *Theology*, 173–226).

169. Ibid., 199–201.

170. "Subdue," 13.

171. "The Priestly Narrative and History," in *Theology*, 168.

172. "Subdue," 12.

173. Ibid., 8, 9, 10, 11.

responding to, issues strongly felt at the close of the twentieth century such as human oppression, international movement of nations, land division, and the general use of resources surrounding post-war Europe.

For Lohfink, the Mandate text of Gen 1:28 is firmly fixed in the milieu of post-exilic Israel. This life of Israel was characterized by a "peace-loving" and temple-based remnant whose "updated" sacrificial cult militated against human oppression. It is within this framework that כבש and רדה represent aspiring[174] if not prophetic words that depict:

> an ideal that no longer exists: an ideal of human society in which there is no war, and no exploitation of the created order, and in which human responsibility is to act as a shepherd to the created order.[175]

What Lohfink has contributed is a reminder of the place of shepherding imagery[176] in the OT theology of leadership, imagery that begins in Genesis.[177] However, this is more accurately tied to the royal ideology mediated through God's image that defines the *representative rule*[178] of humankind.

In the end, Lohfink is at pains to articulate a "pacifist theology" (= P^g) that shifts the emphasis of the Mandate's ruling language (1:26–30) from "dominion" to "nurture."[179] But to carve out a "Priestly strata" focused on

---

174. We agree with Goldingay that Lohfink's attempt to rehabilitate כבש and רדה is unconvincing (*Israel's Gospel* [Downers Grove: InterVarsity, 2003], 113 n.124).

175. J. Rogerson, *Genesis 1–11*, 19.

176. Tate agrees with this theme raised by Lohfink and states: "The model of the Shepherd-King seems to be appropriate for the dominion-having role of humanity" ("An Exposition," 358).

177. The OT never glorifies hunting, and the author of Genesis draws out this significance by aligning the non-chosen individuals with hunting and weaponry (i.e., Ishmael, 21:20; Esau 25:27; 27:2). Even within Genesis, the "hunter" (= Esau) finds the "archer" (= Ishmael) and marries into the clan (28:6–9). The patriarchs themselves are consistently depicted as shepherds with prosperous flocks (26:12–14; 30:25—31:42). Cast in the role of "ideal king," Joseph not only saves the land of Egypt, but their flocks and cattle as well (47:15–18). Not surprisingly, Jacob describes God in similar terms (49:24b-25a). The might of Israelite leadership came as "shepherd-kings" (cf. Gen 46:32–34; 1 Sam 16:11; Isa 40:11; Heb 13:20), who were not distinguished as hunters but routinely drew on pastoral imagery in the darkest of times (cf. 2 Sam 24:17; Psalm 23). By contrast, the Assyrian kings are often depicted as hunter-conquers in self-exaltation.

178. The term preferred by A. J. Köstenberger, *God, Marriage and Family: Rebuilding the Biblical Foundation* (Wheaton: Crossway, 2004), 33.

179. This is pervasive in Lohfink's biblical theology where both *family* (father and mother) and *institution* (king, priest, prophet, judge) are defined as sharing power equally

the land and committed to pacifist notions smacks of anachronism. In Brown's words:

> The Priestly tridents do not envision a situation of peaceful coexistence with the inhabitants of the land; the latter must be evicted from the land by Yahweh as landlord. (cf. Exod 14:26–28; Lev 18:24–25; 20:25)[180]

As discussed earlier, we do not believe is it necessary to place the Creation Mandate text of Gen 1:28 within a post-exilic context of Judah's social recovery. Rather than weighting the Mandate with political might, we believe 1:28 has in view a nation about to conquer the land of Canaan promised earlier to their ancestors. B. R. Reichenbach explains this significance:

> In short, whether P's treatment in Gen 1 is based on much older material or is of postexilic theological construction, it is quite appropriate to interpret the Genesis narrative from the perspective of a writer justifying possession of a land that was allotted to Israel by a powerful monarch who established his kingdom by creation and thereby justifies his claim to whatever exists in it ... Conquest is the means of Israel's occupation, not its ultimate justification. Israel's continued residence depends on continued allegiance and obedience to the King whose land it is.[181]

(cf. "Distribution of the Functions of Power," in *Great Themes*, 55–75). However, this is overplayed in Lohfink's theology, since leadership also brings equilibrium to the cult, not just land.

180. *Ethos*, 101 n.179.
181. "Genesis 1," 68, 69.

> **Figure 4: Genesis 8:17**
>
> כָּל־הַחַיָּה אֲשֶׁר־אִתְּךָ   מִכָּל־בָּשָׂר
> בָּעוֹף
> וּבַבְּהֵמָה
> וּבְכָל־הָרֶמֶשׂ   הָרֹמֵשׂ עַל־הָאָרֶץ הוֹצֵא אִתָּךְ
> וְשָׁרְצוּ בָאָרֶץ
> וּפָרוּ וְרָבוּ עַל־הָאָרֶץ:
>
> ```
> Every living thing that is with you—from all flesh:
>     <namely> birds
>     and <  > animals
>     and <  > every creeper   that creeps on the earth
>                                 shall come out with you;
>                              that they may swarm on the EARTH
>                              and be fruitful and multiply
>                                 upon the ground.
> ```

The *ideal function* of creaturely relationships within orderly domains (Gen 1:28) has given way to the more practical function of Gen 8:17. Between these points (1:28; 8:17) lie cycles of "chaos" that have left the original "edenic state" far behind, yet what remains is a theological pattern and moral ethic that will be reestablished.

Blatant "murder" (הרג; Gen 4:8, 23, 25) is followed thematically by "increase" via genealogy (Genesis 5). This genealogy reveals God's commitment to creation by legitimizing specific descendants, focusing divine blessing, and holding the narrative of Genesis together by preserving a family's continuity through redemptive history. Westermann explains how genealogy sustains divine blessing:

> Genealogies ... occur in the Bible only after creation of humankind; primeval events have been shifted from divine to human history ... The genealogies in Genesis depict all of humanity as the effect of the creator's blessing.[182]

Thus, the genealogy reveals God's on-going commitment to His creation.

However, not all "increase" in 1–11 is a result of divine blessing. Gen 6:1 functions as a *postscript*, with the temporal phrase ויהי כי ("when") referencing the initial blessing given to humankind to "be fruitful and

---

182. "Genealogies," in *The Oxford Companion to the Bible*, ed. B. M. Metzger and M. D. Coogan (Oxford: Oxford, 1993), 243–45.

Exegetical Analysis of the Mandate in Genesis 1–11

multiply."[183] On the other hand, the "multiplying" (רב) of humankind in this context makes it clear, with great irony, that "sin" is also multiplying.[184]

After the intervening genealogy (Genesis 5), the blight of rebellion resumes, but this time it is sheer "violence" (חמס; 6:11, 13). Gen 6:11–12 forces the reader to view the earth from the Creator's perspective. Mentioned 9x (cf. 6:9–22), "earth" is a metonymy for people steeped in cruelty, oppression, and moral perversion.[185] Beyond general wickedness (6:5), "corruption" (שׁחת; 6:11a) and "violence" (חמס; 6:11b) cover a spectrum of crimes that have despoiled the earth.[186] P. J. Harland probes the significance of חמס for the flood account and beyond:

> this raises the interesting possibility as to whether in the flood God punishes humanity on the basis of life for life i.e., that the deluge is God's way of requiring a reckoning for the crimes of חמס committed by that generation. The wholescale corruption caused by the violence called for total destruction. God used the flood as a just punishment for the infringement of human life which had occurred earlier ... The placing of the solemn charge of Gen. 9:5 in the context of the deluge might suggest that the flood was the means whereby God sought the blood of the slain. The fact that חמס was the sin of the pre-diluvian world does suggest that the punishment of death did fit the crime. The people who sinned by killing, received their due punishment.[187]

This amounted to a "re-chaos" of the earth that encompassed the more vulnerable animal domain (cf. 6:17; 7:21; 8:17; 9:11). The fact that "all flesh" (כל־בשׂר) had "corrupted" its way is a bitter reversal of God's initial assessment that creation was "exceedingly good" (טוֹב מְאֹד; 1:31).

---

183. Wenham, *Genesis 1–15*, 139.

184. Mathews states:

> expanding procreation has been matched by an outbreak of worldwide immorality. Procreation is the realization of God's blessing (1:28) ... but human survival is not dependent on the mechanism of sexual procreation alone. There must be a concomitant obedience on the part of the human family to God's moral order (2:7 with 3:17; 2:24; *Genesis*, 323).

185. H. Haag, "חָמָס," *TDOT*, 4:478–87.

186. Cf. 16:5; Deut 19:6; Judg 9:24.

187. *The Value of Human Life: A Study of the Story of the Flood (Genesis 6–9)* (Leiden: E. J. Brill, 1996), 160.

Within 8:15–19, God again engages Noah who has consistently waited for God's commands before he acts.[188] Cast in the language of a second creation, God instructs Noah to disembark with the animals. Against this backdrop, the rhetorical function of Gen 8:17 is *renewal*. This time "God will release Noah, and Noah will release the family and the animals."[189] Like the previous Mandate texts (cf. 1:22, 28), 8:17 contains the *core charge* (ופרו ורבו), *domain identification* (הארץ), and, in this case, a new *secondary charge element* (שרץ; see Figure 4). However, unlike the previous text plots, 8:17 is not a blessing, nor is ברך used; instead, 8:17 represents God's *promise* of increase and repopulation. The verse renews the charge but not in the formal language of blessing.

Following the masoretic accents (i.e., *mêrᵉkā* and *ṭiphā*; see Figure 4), the initial clause reads: כָּל־הַחַיָּה אֲשֶׁר־אִתְּךָ, "every living thing that is with you." The original כל־חיה of 1:28b is now the more definite expression, כל־החיה of (8:17a).[190] The article is generic, referring to the surviving

---

188. Noah's complete silence throughout the flood account highlights his unswerving obedience to God's command (cf. 7:5, 9, 16), a stark contrast to Adam (cf. 2:16–17 with 3:11, 17). The repetition (cf. 8:18–19) serves to reinforce the obedience of Noah.

189. Hamilton, *Genesis*, 307. A *journey formula* is used to portray Noah's entry into the boat (cf. 13:1–3; 36:6; 3:11-13; see Y. Avishur, *Studies in Biblical Narrative: Style, Structure, and the Ancient Near Eastern Literary Background* [Tel Aviv: Archaeological Center Publication, 1999], 35, 99, 100; esp., "Literary Formulae in the Narration of a Journey in the Bible and in Ugaritic Literature," 235–38). The first two lists (6:18–21; 7:7-8) include seven items; the third has ten (7:13–15), with the ceremonial phrase, "that very day" that was used for memorable occasions (see 17:23; Exod 12:41; Deut 32:48). Of Noah's instructions in 6:18–21, Avishur explains:

> Here too the division into three and four items may be observed, a secondary clause separating them. First come four items, whose common feature is their being living things. The fourth and seventh item are described at greater length than those preceding them, this, as stated, for the purpose of the break and the division. Note, too, that in the last three items the word לְמִינֵהוּ "according to (its) kind" comes at the end of the sentence. This formula is repeated in the fulfillment of God's command by Noah. (*Studies*, 236)

The boarding and departure of the animals was written to reflect the creation account (cf. 1:24; 8:19).

190. *GKC*, §§127b,c. כל (MT) is rendered with the *wāw* (וכל) in the SP, LXX, and Syr. Not only does the conjunction create a smoother transition between humans (v. 16) and animals (v. 17), but it is also represented in v. 19 (וכל) among 2 medieval Hebrew MSS, SP, LXX, Syr, and V. However, the *wāw* is not only "unnecessary" (Wenham, *Genesis 1–15*, 154), but adding it obscures the asyndetic (cf. Joüon, §177) relationship of people and animals essentially in apposition to אֵצ (16a) as the *head verb* and framed by its repetition הַוְצֵא (17a).

Exegetical Analysis of the Mandate in Genesis 1–11

collection of animals with a *totalitive* nuance (= "all," "every"; cf. Gen 8:7; Ps 1:4).

As the relative clause, אשר־אתך ("that is with you") reveals the relational element of the ark-microcosm. The ark Noah built mirrored the structure of the cosmos itself with the boat's three tiers probably reflecting the earth, sky, and firmament (6:16; cf. 1:6–10).[191] In the flood, water is not viewed as a domain that nurtures life. Instead, the watery force is redeployed as the agent of the original "chaos," collapsing the upper and lower spheres of water back into its primordial state (1:2, 6–7, 9). Whether stemming from human violence or cosmic deluge, *chaos* dismantles boundaries and collapses domains designed to preserve and promote all forms of life.[192] "The very verb of proliferation [רבה] employed in the Creation story for living creatures is here attached to the instrument of their destruction" (cf. 7:17, 18).[193] אתך frames the first half of 8:17a with the objects of prepositions (i.e., "birds, animals, creepers") placed in the middle. This sharpens the obligation of Noah as the recipient of God's new directive while also delineating those recipients of care (see Figure 4).

The $r^eb\hat{\imath}^a{}^c$ accent sets off the following clause: מִכָּל־בָּשָׂר, "from all flesh," and modifies החיה as the antecedent (i.e., "living things"). The מן of מכל functions *explicatively* with בשר that follows, employing a *collective* notion for בשר after the initial *expansive*: כל־החיה. The role of the second expansive phrase (כל־בשר) is difficult. Alone, בשר can refer to animals or human life in general,[194] but its occurrence in 8:17 as כל־בשר requires further exploration. While the flood story does emphasize the sinfulness of "flesh,"[195] and כל־בשר is typically derogatory in reference to *mortal*

---

191. Brown, *Ethos*, 54–55. The 18 inches encircling the roof (6:16) seem to parallel the "lights" of creation (cf. 1:14f) given the structural portrayal of the ark.

192. Ibid., 60.

193. Alter, *Genesis*, 33. von Rad states, "The world judgment of the Flood hangs like an iron curtain between this world age and that of the first splendor of creation" (*Genesis*, 130).

194. N. P. Bratsiotis, "בָּשָׂר," *TDOT*, 2:318; B. Chisholm ("בָּשָׂר," *NIDOTTE*, 1:777–79) includes Gen 8:17 with other references that can refer generally to animals or humans (Gen 6:12–13, 17, 19; 7:16, 21; Lev 17:14; Num 16:22, etc.).

195. בשר is used 31x in Genesis, with 15 occurrences in and around the flood account (cf. 6:3, 12, 13, 17, 19; 7:15, 16, 21; 8:17; 9:4, 11, 15[2x], 16, 17). The difficult reference in 6:12–13 does appear to at least include humankind. Compared to "blameless" Noah, "the end of all flesh has come before me" (cf. 18:20–21; *GKC*, §127b,c.). Moreover, "wipe them all" (cf. 6:3) becomes an emphatic declaration to Noah—"Yes, I will wipe them all." Thus, God's statements construct a word play with his "destruction" (שחת; v. 13) responding to the moral "corruption" (שחת; v. 12) of an earth now "spoiled" (שחת; v. 11).

humans,[196] בשר in 8:17 arguably refers to animals.[197] Several elements verify this.

God's directives have already stipulated all surviving human lives (8:16) that are to disembark אִתָּךְ ("with you"; v. 16b). However, in 8:17 God now turns to the groups of animals, concluding this second list as the first, alluding to Noah's care and responsibility via אִתָּךְ ("with you"; v. 17a),[198] when the point of origin, מִן־הַתֵּבָה ("from the ark") could be expected.[199] Thus 8:17 is dedicated to the welfare of the animals to which this בשר refers.

Practically an idiom, the second *expansive* phrase, כל־בשר, takes in "the entire animal world"[200] as distinguished from humankind.[201] The effect of the preposition: מִן ("from [all]") stipulates "species of animals not mentioned are excluded."[202] The very portrayal of restoration assumes creation's structure and phyla, even among the animals.

When "chaos" reigns, sin pollutes nature, bringing judgment on the animals as part of the earthly domain of human care (cf. Lev 18:24–28). Both *substance* (= "ground," 2:7,19) and *stewardship* (= "dominion," 1:28–30) establish a moral tie between human and animal causing both to share in the consequences.[203] Not surprisingly, renewal must emphasize creation's order, again, for the flood was indicative of the complete rupture of created relationships on the part of the creature.[204]

---

196. N. P. Bratsiotis, "בָּשָׂר," *TDOT*, 2:326.

197. The death of this order is tied to dry land, the domain of humankind. The narrator startlingly portrays the flood's destructive power by reversing the order of creation for days 5 and 6 (1:20–31; cf. 7:21; Zeph 1:3).

198. If one reads 8:16 as having three groups ("you and your wife," "your sons," "your sons' wives"), then 8:17 rhetorically matches this triad with: "birds," "animals," "creepers."

199. מִן־הַתֵּבָה ("from the ark") is used by the author within our immediate context (cf. 8:10, 16, 19; *BDB*, 424–25.3), but אִתָּךְ ("with you") carries a note of oversight and intimacy becoming of the caretaker of a new creation (cf. 9:1–7). What begins as a promise of God's "covenant with you [אִתָּךְ]" (6:18) is extended to the helpless of creation (8:17[2x]) through Noah's stewardship of obedience. Only the animals saved during the flood are described as "those with him [אִתּוֹ]" (7:23; 8:1).

200. N. P. Bratsiotis, "בָּשָׂר," *TDOT*, 2:319; cf. 6:19; 7:15f; *GKC*, §127b,c.

201. Ibid., 327. While human and animal were destroyed together (6:7), appropriately the renewal of creation resumes the separate foci (cf. Gen 1:20–23; 24–31).

202. N. P. Bratsiotis, "בָּשָׂר," *TDOT*, 2:319.

203. Cf. Gen 8:1; Hos 4:3; Ps 36:7; Joel 1:21; Job 38:41.

204. W. J. Dumbrell, *Covenant and Creation: A Theology of Old Testament Covenants* (Nashville: Thomas Nelson, 1984), 14. According to G. Gerleman, "In a few passages

The *explicative* use of מן [מכל] isolates three nominal clauses that are set off by a ב preposition (see Figure 4).[205] The shift from מן to ב is one of *specification*, functionally itemizing the successive groups as a triad of animals: "namely birds, and [namely] animals, and [namely] every creeper."[206] Thus the "birds," "animals," and "creepers" detail the constituent parts in the collective expression: מכל־בשר, "—from all flesh."[207] "Birds," "[large] animals," and "creepers" reflect the basic structure of 1:28b, mimicking the reestablishment of the created order; however, the emphasis seems to be on the basic phyla of animals—wildlife, domesticated livestock, and reptiles.

הָרֹמֵשׂ עַל־הָאָרֶץ הַיְצֵא אִתָּךְ ends the first half of the verse (8:17a). הרמש employs the article as a relative with the active participle: "that creeps . . ." (cf. 1:28b).[208] הארץ functions as an *accusative* of *location*, emphasizing the theatre of animal life. הארץ is also the first of two occurrences in v. 17, each underscoring the domain-location for the halves of the verse (v. 17a, b).

With the change of usual V-S-O syntax, the only verb הוצא[209] in v. 17a is placed at the end of a nominal string creating an O-V-S marked

---

(mik)kol-bāśār can be translated "of all kinds, varieties (esp. in P: Gen 6:19; 7:15; 8:17; 9:16; Num 18:15)" ("בָּשָׂר," *TLOT*, 1:283–85).

205. Hebrew lists orient the shorter nominal forms at the head for the sake of euphony (e.g., "Shem, Ham, Japheth," see 5:32; 6:10; 7:13; 9:18), and this triad seems to reflect this linguistic tendency: בעוף, ובבהמה, ובכל־הרמש. Because Gen 6:19 contains the phrase: ומכל הבהמה ומכל הרמש, Hendel takes it as a "harmonizing plus" to: ובכל בבהמה הרמש in 8:17 (*The Text*, 89, 134), but his argument is ultimately unconvincing as "stock expressions" also explain such repetition (similarly: הרמש על הארץ [8:17] with 6:20; ibid., 90, 134).

206. The idea of "among" (i.e., "in the domain of") or "consisting of" also communicates the notion of *specification* (GKC, §119i). Hamilton captures this well in his translation: "—all flesh, be it bird, cattle, or any creeping thing" (*Genesis*, 306).

207. Cf. Gen 7:21; 9:10; Hos 4:3; Exod 12:19.

208. The verbal participle (הָרֹמֵשׂ) has a *present iterative/gnomic* nuance.

209. The MT הַיְצֵא is a Hiph impv., 2ms from יצא. The MT is "irregular" (= *hapax*) and the *qĕrê* reads: הַיְצֵא; *BHK* needlessly replicates *qĕrê* in the apparatus. *GKC* proposes הוֹצֵא as the expected imperative form with הוֹצֵא arising from הַיְצֵא on analogy with Gen 19:12, הוֹצֵא (cf. §§69v; 70b). The SP reads: הוציה, a linguistic modernization according to Hendel (e.g., Juss. → Imperf.; *The Text*, 140). In light of other extant forms, it is not clear why the masoretic tradition should preserve the "irregular" הַיְצֵא. Hendel believes the *qĕrê* represents *graphic confusion* (י/ו; *The Text*, 140). However, the *qĕrê* seems to reflect the maintenance of a rare form alongside a more standard one (Hamilton, *Genesis*, 306–307, n.1, following J. Barr). It is possible that the *qĕrê* reads יצא as a I-י verb rather than I-ו, such

word order often termed *fronting* or *topicalization*.[210] Topicalization occurs when:

> a writer brings into prominence new information and places it into the given information slot or the topic position ... Topicalization takes what is normally nonsalient information, fronts that constituent, and places it in a position of informational prominence.[211]

The effect of this "object fronting" is to identify the particular phyla of animals (i.e., "birds," "[large] animals," "creepers") that are to disembark under the oversight of Noah. Our observations of this medial triad set off by the ב clauses, is developed further with the use of "object fronting" topicalization.

Whereas the three prepositional phrases modify בשר, the entirety of 17a modifies הוצא ("come out") as the imperative and *head verb*. This is the 2nd of four occurrences of יצא within the final "ark scene" (8:15–19).[212]

---

as יֹשֵׁר (so *GKC*, §§69v; 70b; Cassuto, *A Commentary*, 2:115). For Tov, the *qěrê* (הַיְצֵא) is simply "less plausible" than הוֹצֵא (*Textual*, 61). For related texts, see Lev. 24:14; Prov 5:25; Hos 7:17; 1 Chr 12:2; cf. Exod 2:9; Ps 5:9.

Within Rabbinic tradition, Rashi surmises:

> הַיְצֵא means "order them out," i.e., tell them to leave on their own, while הוֹצֵא carries with it the connotation that "if they refuse to leave, force them out." (*Bereishis/Genesis: A New Translation with a Commentary Anthologized from Talmudic, Midrashic and Rabbinic Sources*. vol. 1. N. Scherman and M. Zlotowitz ed. [New York: Mesorah Publishers, 2002], 276.)

With a different emphasis, Hirsch states:

> For the verb הוֹצֵא denotes passive acquiescence to the prodding of another while הַיְצֵא indicates the independent act of one who exits by choice: "merely give them permission and they will go" (ibid.); similarly Cassuto: "permit them to go forth." (*A Commentary*, 2:115)

210. Cf. *GKC*, §142f. This phenomenon is variously defined based on syntactical, discourse, or linguistic emphases. T. Murphy calls this "free inversion" (*Pocket*, 75); G. A. Long discusses "fronting" under "markedness" (*Grammatical Concepts 101 for Biblical Hebrew: Learning Biblical Hebrew Grammatical Concepts through English Grammar* [Peabody: Hendrickson, 2002], 157, 159, 160).

211. B. L. Bandstra, "Word Order and Emphasis in Biblical Hebrew Narrative," in *Linguistics and Biblical Hebrew*, ed. W. R. Bodine (Winona Lake: Eisenbrauns, 1992), 109–23, 120, 123. Bandstra lists twelve categories of "word-order topicalization" (120–21) of which our text (Gen 8:17a) most reflects his "object fronting" category (120, #2; cf. *GKC*, §142f.).

212. Used 2x by both God and narrator (8:16, 17, 18, 19), four forms of יצא can be observed, shifting from 2nd (= God's directives) to 3rd person (= narrator's report): 1) צֵא [Qal impv., 2ms], 2) הוֹצֵא [Hiph impv., 2ms], 3) וַיֵּצֵא [Qal pret, 3ms, with *wāw* cons], 4)

Exegetical Analysis of the Mandate in Genesis 1-11

In fact, God's two uses of יצא ("go/come," 8:16, 17) functions as a counterpoint to the twice-mentioned בוא ("bring/come," 6:19, 20), His initial instructions for the animals. Where בוא was used for embarking (7:1-5),[213] יצא now defines their departure (8:15-19).[214] Whereas בוא focuses on the *goal*, יצא typically focuses on the point of *departure*.[215] Repeating יצא in vv. 16, 17, 18, and 19, the author concludes the function of the ark by highlighting the animal's departure—"with" (אִתָּךְ) Noah. What follows

---

יָצְאוּ [Qal perf, 3cp] (cf. 9:10, 18). The narrator has reported what God commanded. While the two medial uses form truncated expressions ("bring out," "went out"), the extended expression is reserved for the final use, "they went out of the ark," revealing *stylistic symmetry* (Cassuto, *A Commentary*, 2:117). As elsewhere, the narrator "speaks" for Noah after God has issued His directives (cf. 6:13-22; 7:1-5). Gen 6:13 is the first time since God created humans that he has spoken to a person without judging them (cf. 3:14-19; 4:10-15). Ironically, Noah's 1st directive concerns the judgment of others, for Noah alone is "blameless" (6:9).

213. Cf. 6:18, 19; 7:1, 7, 13, 16.

214. Rather than lauding the "art of documentary analysis" (Skinner, *A Critical*, 147), the intricate textual variations of the flood narrative are better explained by Hebrew *epic* style that places possible sources under the control of the narrator (Waltke, *Genesis*, 125). While cordoning off "P" material, Speiser poetically describes "reshuffling the text" as that which "does violence" (*Genesis*, AB1 [Gordon City: Doubleday, 1980], 54). The literary structure of the flood account reveals an *extended palistrophe* (cf. 6:9—9:19; Wenham, *Genesis 1-15*, 156). Here, repetition serves a variety of effects such as God's "judicial sentence" to destroy human and animal (6:7) followed by the similar announcement in 7:4. However, 7:4 now reiterates the essential information *to Noah* giving him time to complete the instructions (cf. 7:10). Such repetition serves to advance the plot (Walsh, *Style*, 146-47). Similarly, the "I will wipe from" (6:7) that initiated God's speech graduates to "I will completely wipe out" (7:4; cf. כל), forming a "book-ending" effect. Moreover, the two numbering systems earmark the dates of Noah's age (i.e., day, month, year) on the one hand, and the span of days between flood stages, on the other (Hartley, *Genesis*, 100). The total days number between 365 and 370 days for each scheme. Therefore, it is not surprising that the "disembarkation" (8:15-19) can function as counterpoint to the "embarkation" (7:1-5). R. Chisholm refers to this practice in the flood narrative as "recapitulation" ("History or Story?," in *Giving the Sense: Understanding the Using the Old Testament Historical Texts*, ed. D. M. Howard, Jr. and M. A. Grisanti (Grand Rapids: Kregal, 2003), 54-73, 64-65. See esp., B. W. Anderson, "From Analysis"; Wenham, *Genesis 1-15*, 157-58; R. E. Longacre, "The Discourse Structure of the Flood Narrative," *JAARSup* 47 [1976]: 89-133; M. Kessler, "Rhetorical Criticism of Genesis 7," in *Rhetorical Criticism: Essays in Honor of James Muilenberg*, ed. J. J. Jackson and M. Kessler [Pittsburg: Pickwick, 1974], 1-17. Arguing for sources in the flood account based on the Gilgamesh account, see J. H. Tigay, "The Evolution of the Pentateuchal Narratives in the light of the Evolution of the *Gilgamesh Epic*," in *Empirical Models for Biblical Criticism* (Philadelphia: University of Pennsylvania Press, 1985), 21-52.

215. H. D. Preuss, "יָצָא," *TDOT*, 6:225-50; *IBHS*, 148, 616-17. C. H. Brichto describes יצא as "antipodal" to בוא (*Toward a Grammar of Biblical Poetics: Tales of the Prophets* [Oxford: Oxford University Press, 1992], 38).

the *'aṯnāḥ* is the designed proliferation of the animals (ופרו ורבו שרץ) and their domain identification (ארץ, 8:17b). Assessing the significance of Noah's accomplishment, Brown observes:

> Noah models primordial stewardship by sustaining all of life in its representative forms. His "subduing" of the earth entails bringing together the animals of the earth into his zoological reserve ... By fulfilling humankind's role as royal steward over creation (1:28), Noah is a beacon of righteousness in an ocean of anarchy. Noah exercises human dominion over creation by preserving the integrity and diversity of life.[216]

While Noah's relationship to the animals mimics Adam's (2:19–20), Noah's greatest achievement is the deliverance of an earth-bound "remnant" from the judgment of God.[217] Even in thanksgiving sacrifice, human and animal are inseparable as "the remnant" offers up their gratitude for passing through divine wrath (8:20–21).[218] Noah's cosmic deliverance has reestablished the global role of humankind in the preservation of the animal kingdom and its "kinds" (1:21; cf. 8:19).[219] Exactly what phyla or classes of animals are represented deserves brief mention.

---

216. *Ethos*, 60.

217. Brueggemann, *Reverberations*, 169. He states:

Perhaps the clearest case is that of Noah who, with his family, is a saved remnant from the flood (Gen 8:15–18; 9:8–17). In Isaiah 54:9, moreover, the poet likens exile in the sixth century to the flood, so that a remnant of displaced Jews will be protected from that disaster of exile as was Noah in the flood. (Ibid.)

In Isa 54:9, emending כִּי־מֵי [MT, LXX] ("like the waters of") to כִּימֵי [1QIsaᵃ, Cairo Geniza] ("like/indeed the days of") is attractive (so TNIV, NRSV, HCSB; contra JPS). The 2nd occurrence of כִּי־מֵי in v. 9 seems more straight forward though *BHS* suggests deleting it following the LXX. *BHK* emended the text outright (= כִּימֵי; *BHS* proposes כְּמֵי), justifying it largely through the Greek daughter versions, Syr, T, and V.

218. A. Ross, *Creation and Blessing: A Guide to the Study and Exposition of Genesis* (Grand Rapids: Baker, 1988), 197. Ross similarly speaks of "remnant" (196–97).

219. For both plants and animals God established boundaries separating the species (cf. Lev 19:19; Deut 22:9–11). In Gen 1:21–25, "kind" (לְמִינָהּ) is used 7x. The use of לְמִשְׁפְּחֹתֵיהֶם, "by their families/clans" (= "family by family," [8:19]) following their disembarkation reemphasizes the order and ideal of creation for a new era. For לְמִשְׁפְּחֹתֵיהֶם, the LXX has κατὰ γένος αὐτῶν ("after their kind"). Elsewhere, משפחה is used of "clans," "extended family," or "nations" (Deut 29:17; Josh 6:23) but never again of animals (so *HALOT*, 2:651.2.b). Wevers is convinced that the "MT has suffered in its transmission" (*Notes*, 109). Though משפחה modifies יצא, H. C. Leupold does not see actual species in departure, but a "great variety of species [that] all went forth intact" (*Exposition of Genesis*. vol. 1 [Grand Rapids: Baker, 1942], 320–21).

Exegetical Analysis of the Mandate in Genesis 1–11

Basic zoological classifications give conceptual order to a variety of animals.[220] Animals are a dominant presence in the Creation Mandate as it "matures" through Genesis 1–11. Their classifications or taxa are portrayed through a series of hierarchical schemes.

One of the most common is a *Threefold Primary Level Division*.[221] This inventory recognizes the triad of aquatic, aerial, and land animals, a schema we observed in the initial Mandate texts of 1:22, and 1:28 (see Figures 1, 3).[222] Whitekettle agrees with our observation of three domains, or what he calls "habitat descriptors" (i.e., השדה, הים, השמים):

> This threefold division of the animal kingdom is coordinated with the tripartite construction of the world (water, land, air) found in Israelite thought (e.g., Exod 20:4, 11).[223]

A second scheme is the *Fourfold Primary Level Division* that adds an additional tier of aerial animals.[224] These two tiers of animals are separated not only by two and four-legged species, but also by "שרץ movement."[225]

However, neither Wever's dogmatism or Leupold's figurative reading are convincing. While the sociological term does heighten Noah's relational-stewardship toward the animals, Skinner's observation that מין is typically not construed in the plural may also account for לְמִשְׁפְּחֹתֵיהֶם as a form (*Genesis*, 167).

Similarly, Gen 7:2 surprisingly uses איש ואשתו (lit. "a man and his wife" = "a male and his mate") in reference to animals rather then the more common זכר ונקבה ("male and female," cf. 1:27; 5:2; 6:19; 7:3, 9, 16). The reference to gender (rather than "kind") not only establishes seven "mated pairs" (after שבעה שבעה, 7:2a; so *distributive*), but also skillfully anticipates the renewal of the Mandate blessing (8:17; cf. 9:1f.) just as the stipulation of human gender (זכר ונקבה, 1:27b) directly precedes the blessing and endowment of v. 28 (so Mathews, *Genesis*, 371; Waltke, *Genesis*, 138).

220. Our discussion draws heavily from Whitekettle, "Where." For an illustrated refinement of his research see "Rats." For a broad but more "atomistic" treatment, see E. Firmage, "Zoology," *ABD*, 6:1109–51. For the symbolic significance of animals, see O. Keel, *The Symbolism of the Biblical World: Ancient Near Eastern Iconography and the Book of Psalms*, trans. T. J. Hallett (Winona Lake: Eisenbrauns, 1997), 85–95.

221. Whitekettle, "Where," 19.

222. "Aquatic" (= נפש חיה שרץ, 1:20–25; דגת הים, 1:28; cf. Zeph 1:3; Job 12:7–8); "Aerial" (= עוף השמים, 1:20–25; על-פני רקיע השמים/ עוף יעופף על-הארץ, 1:28; cf. Lev 7:26; Jer 12:4; Job 35:11; Ezek 31:6; Dan 2:38); "Land" (= נפש חיה, 1:20–25; כל-חיה הרמשת על-הארץ, 1:28; cf. Lev 20:25a; Ezek 31:13; Hos 4:3; Dan 4:11[14]).

223. Whitekettle, "Where," 20, following L. I. J. Stadelmann, *The Hebrew Conception of the World* (Rome: Pontifical Biblical Institute, 1970), 9–10.

224. Ibid., 23–24.

225. Ibid., 23. Whitekettle distinguishes between: שרץ movement (= Aerial II) and non-שרץ movement (= Aerial I), 24. Additional categories are needful since שרץ is used

שרץ is the final "secondary charge element" we encounter within our Mandate texts of 8:17 and 9:7.[226] As a subcategory, Whitekettle also identifies: *A Fourfold Division with Two Land Animal Classes*.[227]

While our Mandate texts can be situated within the "three" and "fourfold" schemes, Whitekettle has also found evidence for variations within "four" and "fivefold" schemes.[228] Every scheme contains a series of "truncations" or absent tier(s) inside the taxonomic schema. Whitekettle has found that aquatic animals are the tier most commonly truncated in listings,[229] with the absence of aquatic and aerial, less so. However "truncation never entails the absence of land animals."[230] Gen 8:17 then, can be situated within a truncated *Fourfold Division with Two Land Animal Classes*, consisting of "land animals I and II" with "aerial animals."[231] The two land classes of 8:17 are comprised taxonomically of: (1) רמש/שרץ, (2) and חיה/בהמה land animals.[232] Having short legs or no legs, the רמש/שרץ are "low carriage" animals while חיה/בהמה are "high carriage" animals, designations comprised of "habitat, anatomy and kinematics."[233]

Thus, the animals of 8:17 constitute Whitekettle's truncated "fourfold division" with the following breakdown: רמש represents "low carriage" land animals while בהמה represents "high carriage" land animals; with עוף representing aerial animals.[234] Significantly, the rhetorical function of 8:17 in the

---

of aquatic, aerial, and land animals (cf. Lev 11:9–12; 20–23; 41–45). While this line of argumentation concurs with M. Douglas' findings (*Purity*, 1966), Firmage disagrees ("Zoology," *ABD*, 6:1124).

226. Whitekettle's analysis does not address the significance of שרץ applied to *humans* in Gen 9:7 (cf. Exod 1:7).

227. Ibid., 24.

228. Gen 1:26 is an illustration of Whitekettle's "fivefold" scheme, as he emends the MT following the Syr. (29–31). Regardless, the MT (1:26) contains the following animal tiers: (1) בהמה (= high carriage land animals), (2) כל-הרמש הרמש על-הארץ (= low carriage land animals), (3) עוף השמים (= aerial animals), 4) דגת הים (= aquatic animals). In key respects, 1:26 seems to describe the animals in *ideal* and *inclusive* phyla, an ideal that will be modified (cf. 9:2–3).

229. According to Waltke, "there is no need for renewing fish" in such texts (*Genesis*, 129, n.25).

230. Whitekettle, "Where," 19, n.3.

231. Ibid., 24–25; cf. Gen 1:30; 6:7, 20; 7:8, 23; Lev 20:25b; Hos 2:20[18].

232. The addition of כל emphasizes *inclusion* within a given phyla of animals (cf. *GKC*, §127b,c).

233. Whitekettle, "Where," 27.

234. Whitekettle argues that animal taxon are found between שרץ and רמש on the one hand (= Land Animals I), and בהמה and חיה on the other (= Land Animals II); the

Exegetical Analysis of the Mandate in Genesis 1–11

post-flood scene is to anticipate the sacrifice of Gen 8:20 with עוֹף and בהמה referring to sacrificial animals (cf. Lev 1:4; 20:25a; Job 1:5). The language of whole burnt-offering is built on the phyla of animals that disembark in 8:17. A sacrificial ritual apparently anticipated by God himself.[235] Whitekettle argues a credible connection between 8:20 and Leviticus 20:

> Because Winged Insects, Bats and Wild Land Animals were not used in Israel's cult, עוֹף and בהמה must refer to Two-Legged Aerial Animals and Domesticated Land Animals in 8:20. Leviticus 20:25a refers to clean and unclean עוֹף and בהמה Animals. Because all animals were subject to the purity laws of Lev 11, עוֹף and בהמה must refer to all Aerial and Land Animals in Lev 20:25a.[236]

Following the *ʾaṯnāḥ*, וְשָׁרְצוּ בָאָרֶץ ("that they may swarm on the earth") begins the second half of 8:17b, and represents the next unit of thought.[237] The perfective form of וְשָׁרְצוּ, with *wāw* consecutive following the Hiphil imperative (הוצא, "come out") continues the force of that imperative.[238] Additionally, the nuance of the *wāw* is one of *purpose/result* determined by הוצא as the dominant verb,[239] "... that they may swarm."[240]

---

former are characterized by locomotory movement on the *horizontal* plane while the latter by locomotory movement in the *vertical* plane. That is, there was a perception of movement both *along* the ground and *over* the ground ("Rats," 361).

235. P. R. Williamson, "Covenant," 140.

236. Whitekettle, "Where," 21 n.7.

237. The viability of ושרצו בארץ at the outset of 8:17b is questioned among some text critics. To begin with, ושרצו בארץ is omitted in the LXX (contra, SP). Wevers devotes some attention to the LXX's "revised" translation of both 8:17a,b (*Notes*, 108–9). Of the omission Wevers explains: "In the tradition, the *n* text has added from 9:1 και πληρωσατε την γην as a third imperative. Hex has added under the asterisk και ερπετε επι της τας to make up for the ושרצו בארץ omitted by Gen" (*Notes*, 109). Following Skinner (*A Critical*, 167), Hendel sees MT as an example of a *harmonizing plus* "with the comparable blessing to humans in 9:7" (*The Text*, 41, 56). Since haplography can be excluded for the LXX, Hendel views the "archetype" of 8:17 to be: ופרו ורבו על הארץ (ibid., 56; similarly: אשר רמש על האדמה in 7:8 with 8:17, הרמש הרמש על הארץ, [ibid., 87; cf. 89, 90, 134])." While BHK issues two notes, BHS falls silent along with key modern commentators. Modern translations do not reflect the LXX omission.

238. Driver, *A Treatise*, §112; GKC, §112r; cf. Joüon, §119l.

239. Ibid. For Driver, such a *wāw* possesses a demonstrative element equivalent to "then" or "so" (cf. §108). Many contemporary scholars would question such genetic functions of the stems.

240. While some translations reflect a *descriptive* future-perfect aspect, "and they will spread over" (HCSB; so: NEB, JPS); it is better to stipulate *purpose*, "so that they may abound" (NKJV; so: NASB, NIV, NRSV, NLT, ESV, TNIV; *GBHS, A Guide*, 89 [3.5.2.c]).

שרץ represents the final "secondary charge element" we encounter in the Creation Mandate. Within our text plots it occurs once more in 9:7, however we will briefly consider its use in Exod 1:7. Ironically, שרץ in 8:17 refers to animals, whereas humans are the subjects in 9:7. Closing the phrase, וְשָׁרְצוּ בָאָרֶץ brings the formal "domain identification" set off by the *zāqēp* accent בָּאָרֶץ, "the earth" (see Figure 4). This is God's first such reiteration of the animals' domain following the flood (cf. 1:22b, 28b). The swarming of the animals will affirm the earth as their theatre of life. What seemed logical at first (1:22b) is now indispensable (8:17b).

The שרץ animals are those that "creep, teem," and "swarm,"[241] approximating innumerability.[242] What was initially used of aquatic life (cf. 1:20, 21) is now applied to land animals, the כל־בשר (8:17a, plus ב clauses). שרץ adds the notion of earthly profusion (i.e., quantity),[243] a crucial fact following the earthly desecration of life in the flood.

As the concluding phrase, וּפָרוּ וְרָבוּ עַל־הָאָרֶץ ("and be fruitful and multiply upon the ground") is familiar though not simple for 8:17b. Elsewhere, the "core charge" of וּפָרוּ וְרָבוּ has emphasized the *means* with מלא noting the intended *result* (cf. 1:22, 28). In fact, where ופרו ורבו and מלא occur together, מלא always connotes the intended result (1:22, 28; cf. 9:1).

ופרו ורבו continues the Qal perfect sequence that began with שרץ.[244] Whereas ופרו ורבו appears to fit the *core charge* function, it now becomes clearer why 8:17 is nonetheless, not the standard blessing we have come to know. Not only is ברך ("bless") absent for the first time,[245] the *core charge*

Syntactically, this Qal perf וְשָׁרְצוּ functions on *contingency* of a prior act, and does not represent a new isolated act (Driver, *A Treatise*, §112 no.2).

241. *HALOT*, 4:1655.

242. Hill, "שָׁרַץ," *NIDOTTE*, 4:251.

243. Ibid.

244. The LXX reads ופרו ורבו as imperatives (Αὐξάνεσθε καὶ πληθύνεσθε), and the V reads all three MT perfects as imperatives. The LXX reads the plural verb forms with Noah and the phylum of animals, but the MT pointed them as perfects with a different emphasis (see Figure 4). According to Westermann, "Such minor variants occur often in expressions that are frequently used" (*Genesis*, 451); Westermann incorrectly stipulates "imperf." rather than "impv." to describe the V (ibid., 392, n.17c).

Showing a deference for the LXX tradition, the JB interprets the three verbs as jussives (= "let them swarm ... be fruitful and multiply") with the NAB similarly translating, "and let them abound ... breeding and multiplying."

245. That is, 8:17 possesses neither the (1) *simple stem* (= לאמר ... ויברך, cf. 1:22a, Figure 1), nor the (2) *formal complex stem* (= אלהים ... ויברך, ויאמר ... אלהים, cf. 1:28a, Figure 2).

Exegetical Analysis of the Mandate in Genesis 1–11

is not cast in the imperatival mood, either (cf. 1:22, 28; 9:1, 7). Moreover the spatial element contributed by מלא is also lacking. Instead, the omission of these Mandate elements alongside the perfective aspect of שׁרץ, reveals God's *promise* for repopulation of the central phyla of animals.[246] Thus 8:17 renews the *commissional* aspect of the Creation Mandate whose goal and ideal still stand after the flood, the proliferation and diffusion of creation. This, however, does not constitute the original language of blessing. P. J. Harland concurs, stating:

> In 8:17, whilst God desires that animals multiply, he does not bless them as he does man in 9:1, 7. The blessing of 1:22 is not renewed.[247]

In 8:17 God promises the increase of the original creation to Noah, but the blessing of *endowment* for human proliferation and diffusion must await 9:1 and 7.[248] From a form critical perspective, G. Coats acknowledges these similarities and differences, and explains:

> speech is again a key structural element . . . In comparison with Genesis 1, only the last stage of re-creation involves a command-execution pattern. The detailed description of the execution in 8:18–19 is clearly part of the execution of the command.[249]

---

246. The land animals so prominent in 8:17 were precisely the phylum absent in God's initial blessing that focused on aquatic and aerial life (cf. 1:22). However, we suggested that the mutual domain of land animals and humankind (i.e., "earth") so central to Day Six (cf. 1:24–31), likely saw the animals' blessing postponed till the creation of humankind—scholars remain divided. Nonetheless, 8:17 now gives land animals a divine attention the reader has not yet seen. This not only anticipates their role in the sacrifice (8:20–21), it is crucial for God's pronouncement for moral equilibrium (9:2–6).

247. *The Value*, 151.

248. Not sensing these subtle changes, some commentators still describe 8:17 as a reiteration of 1:28 (Hartley, *Genesis*, 104), most others recognize that 8:17 is largely a repetition of 1:22, a focus on the animals (so Skinner, *Genesis*, 167; Leupold, *Genesis*, 1:319; Wenham, *Genesis 1–15*, 187; Sarna, *Genesis*, 59; Currid, *Genesis*, 1:209). However, Towner is correct to see God inaugurating a new world (*Genesis* [Louisville: Westminster John Knox, 2001], 86).

249. *Genesis: With an Introduction to Narrative Literature*, ed. Rolf Knierim and Gene M. Tucker, vol. 1, FOTL (Grand Rapids: Eerdmans, 1983), 78.

Be Fruitful and Multiply

> Figure 5: Genesis 9:1
>
> וַיְבָרֶךְ אֱלֹהִים   אֶת־נֹחַ וְאֶת־בָּנָיו
> וַיֹּאמֶר לָהֶם
>   פְּרוּ וּרְבוּ
> וּמִלְאוּ אֶת־הָאָרֶץ׃
>
> ```
> Then God blessed    <Noah and his sons,>
>     saying <to them:>
>         "Be fruitful and multiply,
>             and fill the EARTH."
> ```

Noah builds two structures: an ark to save life (6:14–16) and an altar to sanctify it (8:20–21). The common thread is the sovereign authority of God over life amid the human web of relationships.[250] The need to preserve life necessitated the ark, but the need to reestablish contact with God required a sacrifice of that life.[251] Noah's actions remain highly theocentric. Along with his characteristic obedience, Noah exhibits a God-like understanding, yet he has not spoken. God, however, makes blessing his inaugural words to humans, as with the first couple earlier (1:28).

To this sacrifice of Noah, God responds in two ways.[252] First, God issues an *oath of restoration* "in his heart [אֶל־לִבּוֹ]" (8:21) that echoes the earlier "grief to his heart [אֶל־לִבּוֹ]" (cf. 6:6).[253] The "heart" (לֵב) of human-

---

250. Between chapters 6–8, approximately 20 verses address the collection, preservation, and re-release of the animals.

251. The first mention of altar-building (מזבח) comes with Noah (8:20a), uniquely describes God's perspective (8:20-21), and lays out a generic pattern developed more fully in patriarchal history (cf. 12:7, 8; 13:18; 22:9; 26:25; 33:20; 35:1, 3, 7, etc.). Several thematic and form-critical elements connect the cultic scenes of Noah and Jacob, framing Genesis. Also facing a "new era" in his life (cf. 46:1-4), Jacob builds an altar (8:20a; 46:1) and seeks God's blessing (8:20b; 46:1b) through a sacrifice (זבח, cf. 31:54) that functions as preparation for divine revelation (8:21f; 46:2f; cf. Num 23:1; Ps 50:5). Just as this initiates God's final speech with Noah (9:1-17), so Jacob hears God's voice for the last time (46:2b-4). One could also argue that both Noah and Jacob assume prophetic roles (see Wenham, *Genesis 16–50*, 441). The next revelation from God will come to Moses (Exod 3:3—4:17).

252. Turner, *Genesis*, 50.

253. Similarly, human "thoughts and actions" echo "all their thoughts" (6:5). Yet commitment to a new order now replaces grief over the old. Additionally, God's *internal monologue* makes a personal pledge Noah never heard, corresponding to Noah's "silent sacrifice" (8:20). Patriarchal history "builds" on Genesis 1–11, it does not "out mode" Genesis 1–11.

Exegetical Analysis of the Mandate in Genesis 1–11

kind remains "bent toward evil," clearly Noah's righteousness is not hereditary (cf. 6:9; 7:1).[254] Secondly, God issues a blessing "to Noah and his sons" (9:1–7), which is our text of focus.

Moving chronologically, 9:1–7 is God's first post-Flood speech, and addresses human and animal relationships with numerous similarities to the Mandate context of 1:28.[255] Within the literary palistrophe that spans the entire flood account (6:9—9:19), 9:1–7 reflects God's positive resolve to bless a creation he once resolved to destroy—both times using an *interior monologue* (6:7; 8:21–22).[256] Following God's *oath of restoration* (8:21),[257] 9:1–7 is to be read within the broader context of divine grief (8:21–22), where the "one whose imagination is evil is also the one created in the image of God and now decreed to rule over the new creation."[258] Yet divine acceptance of sacrificial offerings will do nothing to mitigate humankind's treacherous impulses.[259] The new commands in 9:1–7 assume the old human disposition for violence (חמס; 6:11, 13). We agree with P.

For a discussion of the entire "palistrophe" (6:9—9:19) alongside Anderson's work (*From Creation*), see G. Wenham, "The Coherence of the Flood Narrative," *VT* 28 (1978): 336–48. Within this palistrophe, 9:1–7 is the fourth divine speech (cf. 6:13–21; 7:1–4; 8:15–17).

254. Ibid., 51.

255. God's words assume the ongoing intimacy of animal and human; pre-Flood designs remain operative in a post-Eden world (Fretheim, *The Book*, 398). The fact that both were "drawn" from the earth and created on the Sixth Day, share the same domain, and rely on similar food sources (1:24–31) is foundational to their relationship. Moreover, both share principle terminology (נפש חיה, 1:20, 24, 30; 2:19) and central characteristics that unite them: (1) mobility, (2) sexuality, (3) breath, and (4) blood (Anderson, *From Creation*, 107–8, 161).

Without the article, נפש חיה only appears in the creation and flood accounts and in Ezek 47:9. Such connections between Genesis 2 and Ezekiel 47 show "that the divine presence is the source of life for all the world" (S. Tuell, "The Rivers of Paradise: Ezekiel 47:1–12 and Genesis 2:10–14," in *God Who Creates*, 179).

256. Mulzac, "Genesis," 65–66.

257. From "negative resolution" (8:21) to "positive resolve" (8:22), a poetic flourish concludes God's oath (cf. 1:27). The seamless rhythm of seasons serves as a sign of God's personal promise. Four sets of terms (8:22) make up seasons, time, and temperature, signaling the return of a cosmic eco-system conducive to life. These terms mark the full agrarian year of essential phases that secure life, reaffirming the function of creation days (cf. Jer 33:20; Zech 14:7).

258. W. Brueggemann, *Genesis* (Atlanta: John Knox, 1982), 83.

259. Alter, *Genesis*, 36.

BE FRUITFUL AND MULTIPLY

Harland that: "the cause of the flood is met head-on in Gen. 9:1-7."[260] In other words, the flood was intended to "cleanse" the earth (אֶרֶץ) of violence (חמס) not reform the human heart (לֵב; cf. 8:21), for such violence cannot be extirpated, only controlled (9:5-6).[261] The Creation Mandate is reissued to Noah as a legal remedy to arrest the lethal nature of violence.[262] This time, the "chaos waters" were unleashed on a world in *moral disorder*, enabling the Creator to get "rid of a thoroughly polluted world and [start] again with a clean, well-washed one."[263] Simkins observes:

> This is the significance of the flood ending on New Year's day, for on this day God's creation of the world and victory over chaos is celebrated. The recreation of the world, necessitated by its pollution, entails first the destruction of the creation. Only through the catastrophic collapse of creation is a new creation possible.[264]

In 9:1-7 the arrangements of the first creation are modified and the sanctity of life is reasserted. While our focus lies specifically with 9:1 and 7, 9:2-6 presents a catalogue of declarations that governs the human-animal (9:2-5a) and human-human relationship (9:5b-6). By means of heightened accountability, this renewed Creation Mandate "establishes new limits for life in a disordered world."[265] Post-Eden, even blessing must contain new laws in order to safeguard relationships, animal and human.[266]

---

260. *The Value*, 145; see also R. W. E. Forrest, "Paradise Lost Again: Violence and Obedience in the Flood Narrative," *JSOT* 62 (1994): 3-18.

261. Blenkinsopp, *Pentateuch*, 85.

262. Brown, *Ethos*, 57.

263. T. Frymer-Kensky, "The Atrahasis Epic and Its Significance for Our Understanding of Gen. 1-9," *BA* 40 (1977): 147-55, 153.

264. R. A. Simkins, *Creator and Creation: Nature in the Worldview of Ancient Israel* (Peabody: Hendrickson, 1994), 204; following M. Eliade, *The Sacred and the Profane: The Nature of Religion*, trans. W. R. Trask (San Diego: Harcourt Brace Jovanovich), 77-80.

265. Dumbrell, *Faith*, 25. In a cursory manner, the catalogue stipulates that: (1) animals will fear humans (9:2), (2) animals will provide food for humans (9:3), (3) animal blood is banned from human consumption (9:4), and (4) animals and humans alike face capital punishment for taking a human life (9:5-6; Turner, *Genesis*, 51).

266. Harland, *The Value*, 145. Gen 2:16-17 amounts to the first prohibition, similar to Israel's later *apodictic* laws (i.e., "Ten Words," Exod 20:1-17). Prohibition tests human discernment and obedience through boundaries. The covenant-making LORD *God* built law and obedience into the very fabric of human relationship long before Sinai, as law enables relationship and defines the loyalty of the subject (Adam/Noah/Israel).

Exegetical Analysis of the Mandate in Genesis 1–11

Whereas the Mandate directed to the animals (1:22) is revisited in modified form in 8:17, likewise, the original blessing of humankind (1:28) is now reissued in tailored form to Noah, an Adam *redivivus* (9:1).[267] In Brueggemann's words:

> Noah is in any case the occasion for Yahweh's reversal of field, the reason whereby Yahweh may relove and reembrace the world as a system of blessing.[268]

Similarly, whereas God "saw" (ראה) that his creation was good (טוב, 1:25; 31) leading to the first blessing (ברך) of humankind (1:28), this time God "smelled" (ריח) a sacrifice and issues a renewed blessing (ברך)[269]—but God will never call creation "good" (טוב) again.[270] However, God will "see" (ראה) the rainbow, intended for *himself*, and reaffirm his commitment never to destroy the earth again (9:14–16).[271] God in his transcendence is omniscient, but in his immanence, casts himself with the affairs of fragile landlings, a common divine characterization of Genesis 1–11.[272]

In short, a reissuing to humankind of the original Mandate was necessary in light of the extreme degradation of the paradisiacal order through violence (חמס).[273] Therefore, the violence envisaged in 9:1–7

---

267. M. Fishbane, *Biblical*, 318. For Fishbane, 9:1–7 is a "typological repetition" of 1:26–30, a form of "aggadic exegesis" for legal texts (408, 424). The numerous thematic parallels between Adam and Noah will be considered later in this chapter.

268. Brueggemann, *Theology*, 545.

269. I cannot agree with Goldingay who reads 8:21 ("and the LORD smelled") as the climax rather than a *circumstantial* clause with "the LORD said" as an *independent* statement (*Theology*, 176, n.68). Rather, the masoretic accents propose the correct sequence, as we have argued above.

270. It is also significant that the divine *evaluation* of "very good" (טוֹב מְאֹד; 1:31) only comes after God has made humankind. Moreover, the key phrase occurs 2x on the day humankind is made (cf. 1:25, 31).

271. The rainbow is uniquely "God's"—he initiated it, he established it, and he perpetually gazes upon it as a reminder of his promise. Using the imagery of "storm," creation is reassured by a mnemonic "sign" of an "everlasting covenant" (9:9–11, 15). Pointing beyond itself, the bow is "hung" both meteorologically and transactionally "between God and every living creature of all flesh that is on the earth" (9:12–17), thus uniquely placed to comfort the earthbound (R. G. Branch, "Rainbow," *DOTP*, 667–686, 667; McBride, "Divine Protocol," 21; quoting M. J. Fox, "The Sign of the Covenant: Circumcision in the Light of Priestly *ʾôt* Etiologies," *RB* 81 [1974]: 568–73).

272. Waltke, *Genesis*, 146.

273. G. von Rad, *Genesis*, 131.

is no innovation,²⁷⁴ and the post-Flood world is no "Eden." Against the backdrop of cosmic disaster, the renewed Mandate provides a covenantal and *creational* framework for a post-Flood world.²⁷⁵

Three elements, among others, will create a notable profile in our analysis of 9:1–7: (1) the reinsertion of law into human life, (2) new terms for the role of human governance over animals (cf. 1:28), and (3) the anticipatory significance of legislation for the Sinai context, moving from *cosmic* needs in covenant (9:8ff) to *national* needs in covenant (Exod 20:1ff).²⁷⁶ Both the Abrahamic (Gen 17:7, 13, 19) and Mosaic covenants (Exod 19–24) "are set within the larger creational purposes of God announced in Genesis 9."²⁷⁷ "Israel's law becomes a more detailed form of the divine law for the whole world."²⁷⁸

Gen 9:1 is the verbal counterpart to the divine monologue (8:20–22). The earlier announcement of God's promise (8:20–22) is now amplified (9:1ff).²⁷⁹ Assessing Divine names, R. Longacre argues that יהוה operates in the strategic announcement of 8:20–22 while אלהים operates in the divine speeches themselves (9:1–17).²⁸⁰ Because deity is the "thematic participant" in 8:20–22, יהוה is used as the immanent, covenant-making appellation. However, 9:1–7 resumes the imperatival mood (contra, 8:17) amid 2nd person plural forms—the "thematic participant" has shifted and the transcendence of Creator-אלהים becomes secondary.²⁸¹ Yet in 9:8–11,

---

274. Turner, *Genesis*, 52.

275. Balentine, *The Torah's*, 100.

276. Harland states it well: "the history of Israel is bound up inseparably with that of the whole world" (*The Value*, 146; also, 147, 148, 149, 153, 154, 157). We find further evidence and advocate for reading the Creation Mandate texts as crafted against the historical horizon of Israel gathered as Sinai, the result of God's national creation, and existentially in need of law to establish equilibrium with God.

277. Balentine, *The Torah's*, 100.

278. Ibid., 147; similarly, Waltke, *Genesis*, 152; Mathews, *Genesis*, 399.

279. Hamilton, *Genesis*, 312.

280. See "The Discourse," 89–133, see also the chart highlighting repetitions within the discourse (95). Crucial to Longacre's argument is that אלהים is used when deity is not the "thematic participant" of the unit (cf. 128–29).

281. Within the "Noah account" (6:8—9:29) יהוה is used 8x (6:8; 7:1, 5, 16; 8:20, 21; 9:26), and אלהים 18x (cf. 9:1, 6). However, to the MT's 18x the LXX has 24. When the MT uses אלהים, the LXX employs κύριος ὁ θεός (cf. 6:8, 12, 22; 7:1, 5, 16; 8:15, 21[2x]; 9:12, 26), a collocation germane to the *immanence* of Genesis 2–3. Similar to the argument of Longacre (see above), one finds that where κύριος ὁ θεός occurs with Noah as the object, God is either commanding Noah or affirming his obedience. Yet where Noah is absent,

Exegetical Analysis of the Mandate in Genesis 1–11

both God and human are incidental to the thematic covenant. Finally, the sign of the covenant takes thematic prominence in 9:12–17. God's covenant will reestablish the integrity of creation, ensuring the efficacy of his blessing (9:1–7).[282]

Gen 9:1 begins with the stylized performative speech of God the reader has seen before (cf. 1:28a). It is not surprising then, to find the expression: וַיְבָרֶךְ אֱלֹהִים ("Then God blessed"), a modified form of the *formal complex stem* set off by the *zāqēp* accent (cf. 1:28a).[283] Again, ברך is laden with relational significance for the Creator now deputizing his new steward.[284] This preterite form with *wāw* consecutive (ויברך) denotes *result*: God responded by conferring a blessing (i.e., "Then God blessed")[285] because he was pleased with Noah's sacrifice (8:20).[286]

The phrase: אֶת־נֹחַ וְאֶת־בָּנָיו, "Noah and his sons," forms a double direct object that encompasses a new humanity while still maintaining emphasis on Noah as God's appointed agent.[287] The blessing for the animals has

---

κύριος ὁ θεός is posturing for judgment. In several ways, this literary design highlights the interaction of God and Noah on the pattern of God's interaction with Adam, earlier. God now works *through* Noah as his new steward of creation whereas his creative measures found God alone in Genesis 2. While יהוה אלהים once commanded Adam (2:16f) and resulted in disobedience, κύριος ο‚ θεός reissues commands to Noah that thrive in obedience. In the opinion of M. Kikawada and A. Quinn, this oscillation of divine names signifies a climax when they merge, for example, Noah's first speech of curse and blessing (i.e., יְהוָה אֱלֹהֵי שֵׁם, "Blessed be the LORD God of Shem," 9:25–26; *Before Abraham Was: The Unity of Genesis 1–11* [Nashville: Abingdon, 1985], 91–92). "God's words (9:1–17) pertain to human history in general; Noah's to redemptive history" (Waltke, *Genesis*, 149–50).

282. Brown, *Ethos*, 60.

283. ויאמר להם with ויברך . . . אלהים with ויברך . . . אלהים (1:28a), cf. אלהים . . . ויברך (9:1a, see Figures 2, 5). While sharing the preterite of the *simple stem* (ויברך, 1:22a), the *formal complex stem*, among other things, stipulates the object beyond the plural pronoun (אתם, 1:22a). Moreover, 9:1 uses the preterite ויאמר instead of the infinitival form, לאמר (1:22a).

284. As noted earlier (1:28a), the preterite (*wāw* + prefixed conjugation) can function *epexegetically*, denoting the *substance* of the act of blessing that follows (cf. *IBHS*, §33.22a).

285. Translations reflecting *result*: TNIV, NET, NLT, NIV, NKJV; contra: ESV, RSV, KJV, similarly: JPS, NEB, JB, HCSB.

286. Noah will close chapter 9 with his own blessing (ברך, v. 26). However, while Noah's role as blesser does mimic God's, Noah's blessing is a "doxological benediction" that stipulates Shem's line of governance in keeping with Gen 1:26–28 (Waltke, *Genesis*, 150–51).

287. Boarding the ark, we read: ויאמר יהוה לנח בא־אתה וכל־ביתך אל־התבה, "The LORD said to Noah, 'Go (2ms) into the ark, you (2ms) and your (2ms) whole family . . .'" (7:1a).

already been reiterated (cf. 8:17), so they are completely excluded in this Mandate blessing though they will be included in the upcoming covenant (9:10, 12, 15ff.).

The *ʾatnāḥ* sets off the addressees of God's blessing, with the *endowment* following (cf. 1:28a). As the endowment specifies "sons" (בני), a correspondence is established with the upcoming "seed" (זרע) of the covenant (9:9).[288] Shem's line in particular, transcends the Table of Nations (Chap 10), extending to Abram as Terah's son (11:10–26). With Noah's "sons" as progenitors, the nations of the world are ultimately in view—sons become nations (chap. 10).[289]

וַיֹּאמֶר לָהֶם, "saying to them," is unique because the masoretic tradition deliberately juxtaposes this phrase to God's speech rather than placing it before the *ʾatnāḥ* (cf. 1:28a) within the *formal complex stem* (cf. 1:28a,b). ויאמר supplies the *substance* of the blessing (the *endowment* following the *ʾatnāḥ* of בָּנָיו, "his sons"), and its semantic placement within the clause also brings a sharper note of intimacy to four men.

פְּרוּ וּרְבוּ is the *core charge*, arguably functioning as a hendiadys (i.e., "abundantly fruitful"). This is the second of three occurrences used expressly for people (cf. 1:28; 9:7), appropriately stipulating "sons" (בני) as future progenitors. It is intended that all descendant nations would be productive beneficiaries.[290] Cassuto observes:

> the first time *ûrᵉbû* (and multiply) forms part of the compound expression *pᵉrû ûrᵉbû* (be fruitful and multiply), it signifies the raising up of seed; the second time it is used by itself, and its primary use is to increase numerically.[291]

With the notion of "fertility on the increase," this collocation functions as the Creator's conferral on his creation of needed security for a continued existence,[292] extremely meaningful to the fledgling survivors of only four couples. The dynamic of the *core charge* (פרו ורבו) assumes

---

The closest repetition to 9:1a comes in 9:8a, with similar function, ויאמר אלהים אל־נח ואל־בניו אתו לאמר:, "Then God spoke to Noah and to his sons with him, saying."

288. Cf.: "you and your seed after you" (9:9 with 17:7–10, 19), "generations" (6:9; 9:12 with 17:7, 9, 12). Clearly, what begins in Universal History *matures* in Patriarchal History (cf.: 1:28a; 17:2b, 6a; 28:3a; 35:11a; 48:4a).

289. Brueggemann, *Theology*, 494.

290. Ibid.

291. *Commentary*, 1:129.

292. Eichrodt, *Theology*, 2:350, n.1.

survival is at risk.[293] God's commitment to creation is blessing and proliferation symbolizes that blessing.[294]

God has reissued his promise of divine *enablement*,[295] a guarantee of result; it is an enablement that is also his assurance. The *mêrᵉḵā* accent beneath וּמִלְא֥וּ ties this *secondary charge element* to אֶת־הָאָ֑רֶץ, the *domain identification*.[296] Here ארץ has in view universal rather than confined space.[297] Throughout our text plots, the *core charge* of פְּר֣וּ וּרְב֛וּ has emphasized the *means* with מלא noting the intended spatial *result* (cf. 1:22, 28).

It is clear that 9:1 repeats, in large measure 1:28, but it is also important to note how these two texts differ (see Figures 2, 5).[298] Where the MT of 9:1 ends with the *domain identification* (אֶת־הָאָ֑רֶץ:), the LXX adds a *secondary charge element*: καὶ κατακυριεύσατε αὐτῆς, "and subdue it" (= וְכִבְשֻׁ֑הָ). Not only is this a harmonization to the fuller thrust of God's initial blessing, but כבש in 1:28a is the sole occurrence among our five MT text plots (i.e., Genesis 1–11).[299] While the LXX plus may be logical, it is unnecessary in light of the "revised dominion" language in 9:2.

Because 9:1 practically mirrors the first blessing (cf. 1:28a), many have noted the absence of the *secondary charge elements* pertaining to land and the animals, i.e., "subdue" (כבש) and "rule" (רדה; see Figure 5). So

---

293. Harland, *The Value*, 148.

294. Simkins, *Creator*, 155.

295. Wenham, *Genesis 1–15*, 33; so Westermann, *Genesis*, 141.

296. Whether employing the *mêrᵉḵā* or *mahpāḵ* accent, מלא consistently reflects a *conjunctive* association with the *domain identifications* in our text plots (1:22, 28; 9:1). מלא is used once for the animals (1:22) and twice for the special expansion of humankind (1:28; 9:1; also Exod 1:7).

297. Hamilton, "אֶרֶץ," *TWOT*, 1:74–75.

298. For a discussion of semantic similarities and differences spanning 1:26–28 with 9:1–7, see Wenham, *Genesis 1–15*, 192; Mulzac, "Genesis 9:1–7," 68–69; Fishbane, *Biblical*, 318–21; Westermann, *Genesis*, 461–62; Skinner, *Genesis*, 169.

299. In C. L. Brenton's translation: "and have dominion over it" (*The Septuagint with Apocrypha: Greek and English* [Grand Rapids: Hendrickson, 2001], 10). According to Wevers, the LXX plus makes "the correspondence between the two creations complete" (*Notes*, 113). For Hendel, the LXX plus actually reflects the Hebrew phrase: ורדו בה, an *inclusio* with וּרְבוּ־בָהּ (9:7; cf. 1:28b [ב- ורדו]; *Text*, 92). While T. Muraoka indexes κατακυριεύειν under both כבש and רדה (*Hebrew/Aramaic Index to the Septuagint* [Grand Rapids: Baker, 1998] 67, 135), ורדו is already a serious text critical problem in 9:7 [MT] making Hendel's reconstruction more tenuous. The *GELS* surmises that the translator's Greek text probably had no Hebrew word corresponding to the Greek, and proposes deleting the Greek word for both 9:1 and 7 (299; cf. *LEH*, 317).

for most, this is indicative of the essential collapse of human governance due to the ravaging effects of sin, requiring a scaled-down blessing.[300] However, the ebb and flow of *creation-chaos-recreation* themes on the one hand, coupled with the structure of the 9:1-7 discourse on the other, reveals that "dominion" is *assumed* though its demonstration has changed.[301]

As 9:1 reiterated 1:28a (= enablement), so 9:2 picks up the "dominion" theme of 1:28b (= commission). However, the Edenic harmony (2:19-20; 3:1f.) and supervision is now replaced by "terror and dread" (9:2a; מוראכם וחתכם)[302] toward humankind, the negative side of the on-going dominion (1:26f.).[303]

"Yet [the] terror and dread" (ומוראכם וחתכם)[304] has replaced "rule" and "supervision" with a harsher idiom (see Figure 2) as ומוראכם וחתכם is unique military terminology.[305] Because Noah is granted permission to eat meat (9:2b-3a), the animals' fear not only checks their vicious behavior (6:12), but it also compensates for changed food laws among humans (9:3; cf. 1:29f.).[306]

300. So Leupold, *Exposition*, 1:328; Mathews, *Genesis*, 400-401; Hamilton, *Genesis*, 113-14; Hartley, *Genesis*, 109; contra: J. Calvin, *Commentaries on the Book of Genesis*, vol. 1, trans. J. King (Grand Rapids: Eerdmans, 1948), 290; Murphy, *A Critical*, 227; A. Dillmann, *Genesis: Critically and Exegetically Expounded*, trans. W. B. Stevenson (Edinburgh: T&T Clark, 1897), 291; Delitzsch, *Genesis*, 1:282-83; von Rad, *Genesis*, 131; Wenham, *Genesis 1-15*, 192; Sarna, *Genesis*, 60; Waltke, *Genesis*, 144; Skinner, *Genesis*, 117; Goldingay, *Theology*, 112-13; G. Goldsworthy, *According to Plan: The Unfolding Revelation of God in the Bible, An Introductory Biblical Theology* (Downers Grove: InterVarsity, 2002), 115; Kruger, "Subscripts," 436; Carr, *Reading*, 65.

301. Fretheim, *Genesis*, 398.

302. ומוראכם וחתכם (lit. "yet [the] terror and the dread") functions as a *disjunctive* clause (i.e., *wāw* + non finite form = *contrastive/antithetical*). However, I could find no English translation rendering 9:2a disjunctively, most treating the *wāw* as essentially *pleonastic*. מוראכם וחתכם could be translated as a *hendiadys* (so Speiser, *Genesis*, 58, n.2; Hamilton, *Genesis*, 311, n.1; NAB) though a *merism* seems better. Nonetheless, the phrase functions as a military collocation that is unnecessarily obscured in a hendiadys rendering, and one few English translations follow.

303. Westermann, *Genesis*, 462.

304. The 2mp suffixes [-כם -כם] function as objective genitives of *result/effect* (*GKC*, §135m), referring to the things feared (H.-P. Müller, "פַּחַד, *TDOT*, 11:518).

305. Harland, *The Value*, 149; so Westermann, *Genesis 1-11*, 462; Wenham, *Genesis 1-16*, 192; Waltke, *Genesis*, 144; Mulzac, "Genesis 9:1-7," 71; cf. Deut 1:21; 3:8; 11:25; 31:8, etc.).

306. As the 3rd Curse in the divine catalogue (Lev 26:14-39), Israel's discipline could also include attacks from wild animals (חית השדה), regarded as a divine punishment for sin (Lev 26:21-22; cf. Deut 32:24; 2 Kgs 2:24; 17:25; Isa 13:21, 22; Ezek 5:17; 14:15; contra:

Exegetical Analysis of the Mandate in Genesis 1–11

Instigated by God, the significance of the military collocation should not be missed. Both כבש ("subdue," 1:28a) and מוראכם וחתכם ("terror and dread," 9:2a) constitute *anticipatory* or *pre-Sinaitic* language that also operates at the level of Israel's national experience, including the exodus (cf. Exod 4:34; Deut 26:8; Jer 32:21). As J. P. Harland explains:

> Blessing is then put in an unusual light since it is set in the context of the permission to kill for food. מוראכם וחתכם is distinctive military terminology (Deut 1:21; 11:25; 31:8), which refers to the fear which falls on Israel's enemies so that she can take the land.[307]

Thus, just as כבש was also used of the Israelites conquering the nations in the Promised Land (Num 32:22, 29; Josh 18:1; 1 Chr 22:18), so "terror and fear" operates on dual horizons of Universal (Genesis 1–11) and National history. This language of "terror and dread" was also used to safeguard Jacob's journey to Bethel (35:5).[308] In the same way, God also incited the nations to "fear" the approaching Israelite company (Deut 2:25; 11:25). Significantly, the Israelites themselves are encouraged not to "dread" or "fear" their foes (cf. Deut 1:21). So the Mandate reissued to Noah not only renews a marred world, these stock terms also inform a broader message and inspire a weary people to "subjugate" their enemies

---

Isa 11:6–9; 35:9; Hos 2:20[18]). "I will release vicious animals against you" (Lev 26:22) shockingly reverses God prior statement: "I will remove vicious animals from the land" (26:6; see Milgrom, *Leviticus 23–27*, 2310; also R. Bauckham, "Jesus and the Wild Animals (Mark 1:13): A Christological Image for an Ecological Age," in *Jesus of Nazareth* [Grand Rapids: Eerdmans, 1994], 3–21).

307. *The Value*, 149. Similarly, Harland writes:

> there are two concentric circles which are operating; the outer in Gen. 9 includes the whole world and is the blessing which is given to Noah. The smaller of the two circles is the specific blessing and promise to Israel through Abraham, and Israel's existence is dependent on that of the whole world. (Ibid, 148)

308. The warring context of Genesis 34, with the rape of Dinah (34:2) and the slaughter of the Shechemites (34:25), highlights this language of "holy war" (cf. Exod 23:27; Josh 2:9). For their part, peaceful shepherds (34:21) have become rapacious warriors (Waltke, *Genesis*, 473), and the narrator describes the city inhabitants as: כל־יצאי שער עירו, "all those going out of the gate of his city" (34:24), also a military collocation for battle-ready warriors (*DCH*, 4:260; *HALOT*, 2:425.4.c; Preuss, "יָצָא," *TDOT*, 6:227–28; so Speiser, *Genesis*, 265; Alter, *Genesis*, 193; see also 2 Sam 18:4; Jer 17:9; C 3 Cairo Geniza, ed. Kline, Schocken Bible, NAB with text note).

and create a nation defined in Edenic terms (cf. Ps 8:2; Isa 51:3; Ezek 36:35).[309]

Alongside "terror and dread," (9:2a, מוראכם וחתכם), humans' modified relationship to the animal world is further explained by: "into your hand they are given," (9:2b, בידכם נתנו).[310] This too, is the language of holy war,[311] signifying the power of life and death and, again, the language of Israel's national conquest is on the horizon (cf. Deut 9:12).[312] The listing of animals that "creep" is merismatic, pivoting on the "ground" [ארץ/אדמה] as the human theatre of action for both: (1) upper [= "sky"] and (2) lower [= "sea"] phyla of animals.[313]

---

309. Dumbrell writes:

Canaan is, in its totality, presented as divine space (cf. Exod. 15:17; Ps. 78:54) . . . Eden is thus presented in the narrative as the earthly center where God was to be found. Such presentation is clear from Isaiah 51:3, where Eden/garden of God are paralleled (cf. also Gen. 13:10). The garden is thus sacred space, as the world is to become—that much becomes clear as divine revelation develops (cf. Rev. 21–22). We are thus, in terms of biblical eschatology, moving from a localized Eden in Genesis 2 to the new creation as a universal Eden in Revelation 22:1–5. (*Faith*, 2nd ed., 20)

310. Gen 9:2 is a compound sentence using *apposition* for the purpose of *explanation* (Gen 1:27; 6:9; 9:5; 16:12; 27:36; 41:13; Gib, 178).

311. Westermann, *Genesis*, 462; cf. Deut 19:12; 20:13; Lev 26:25, etc; cf. *HALOT*, 2:735.

312. The MT plural passive emphasizes that "they are given" (נתנו), but the LXX puts the discourse in the 1st person: "I have given" (δέδωκα; so SP: נתתי). The LXX form is an intensive perfect with *present* aspectual emphasis, with ὑπό denoting the agency of the action expressed by the verb. For Wevers, the emphatic δέδωκα is preferable to the MT: נתן (*Notes*, 114). Regardless, נתן means "bestow, appoint, assign" with God as the subject. Likewise, when God is the subject of "give," it pertains to the "bestowal of blessing" (Westermann, *Genesis*, 463, following J. Milgrom).

313. Thus: *ground* ↑ "sky" [upward]; *ground* ↓ "sea" [downward]. The MT of 9:2 exhibits a chiasm: (A) "terror and dread" of you, (B) "all animals" ∥ (B') "all animals," (A') "into your hand." The first half of the verse uses על clauses modifying יהיה; while the two ב clauses establish dominion in 2b, employing כל that functions as the *hanging nominative* with the grammatical subject in the pronominal suffix of נתנו (cf. *GKC*, §27. Rem.2.a). The ב of *accompaniment* or *concomitance* may not be strong enough. In this context כל carries a *qualitative* nuance (= "all sorts"; so LXX: παντοῖος) rather than *distributive* (= "each"; cf. SP: ובכל, "and on all" for בכל, "on all").

Exegetical Analysis of the Mandate in Genesis 1–11

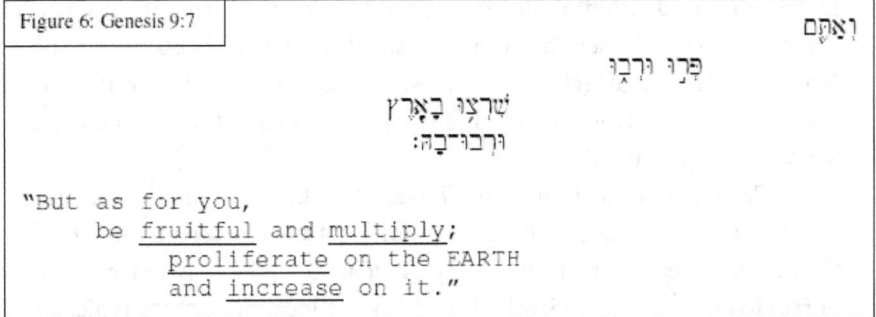

Figure 6: Genesis 9:7

"But as for you,
 be fruitful and multiply;
  proliferate on the EARTH
  and increase on it."

Gen 9:7 signals a "break" from the "poetic formulation of the principle of talion"[314] (9:6) resuming a more personal direct address (cf. 9:1f.). What the poetic genre of 9:6 implies,[315] the syntax of וְאַתֶּם (9:7a) establishes, namely, a sharpened focus on the subject: "But as for *you*" with the personal pronoun (אַתֶּם).[316] With the *waw* and the pronoun, וְאַתֶּם creates an *adversative* force,[317] contrasting with 9:5b–6. For Fishbane, this shifting of grammatical person in vv. 5, 6, 7 (1st, 3rd, 2nd) is indicative of the narrator and *his* aggadic *tradito*, drawing from Gen 1:26–28.[318]

With 9:7, the divine rhetoric of blessing officially resumes for humankind, in keeping with the precedent of 1:28. The plural pronoun

---

314. Wenham, *Genesis 1–15*, 193. The "accountability" for life established in 9:5 is explained in 9:6 as an obligatory system of retributive justice that bridles violence and preserves the moral order (i.e., capital punishment, cf. Exod 21:12–14; Num 35:16–32; Deut 17:6–7; 19:15). While revenge is condemned (Rom 12:17), state retribution is prescribed (Rom 13:17). The Hebrew chiastic order: A "shed," B "blood," C "humankind" ‖ C' "humankind," B' "blood," A' "shed" mirrors the concept of reprisal with the punishment matching the crime (Walsh, *Style*, 27–28; Fokkelman, *Narrative*, 34–35; so NIV, ESV, TNIV).

315. While some translations mark the genre "break" between 9:6 and 7 (NEB, NAB, NRSV, NIV, JPS, NET, ESV, HCSB, TNIV), others confusingly construe 9:7 as also poetic (NASB, NKJV, Hamilton, *Genesis*, 311; Alter, *Genesis*, 38–39). Still others regard no poetic form even for 9:6 (KJV, RSV, Berkeley, CEV, NLT).

316. *GKC*, §135a.

317. I.e., *waw* conjunction + pronominal subject + verb (so LXX: ὑμεῖς δε, "But as for you").

318. *Biblical*, 321; emphasis original. Sensing this tension, the LXX uses the 1st person for greater continuity in the pericope (i.e., ἐποίησα, "I have made [humankind]"). Dillmann may be correct when he states:

the use of the third pers. is for the same reason that in ch. i. 26 נַעֲשֶׂה is put for אֶעֱשֶׂה, because the narrator does not wish to make God say בְּצַלְמִי. (*Genesis*, 1:296)

(אֹתָם) resumes the Mandate to Noah and his sons (לָכֶם). God's design is the *positive* production of life (9:7) to be distinguished from its *negative* defacing (9:5b-6). Absent from this blessing is the Creator's assessment of "good" and "excellent" (cf. 1:25, 31), reserved for a world where no blood is shed (cf. 1:29f). However, the life Noah has preserved now has a legal basis for being fostered.

9:7a concludes with the *core charge*, פְּרוּ וּרְבוּ, as the *ʾaṯnāḥ* indicates (see Figure 6). As a hendiadys collocation, פרו ורבו consistently portrays the notion of "enablement" for every Mandate text, the only reoccurring phrase to do so (cf. 1:22, 28; 8:17; 9:1, 7). As a collocation, פרו ורבו typically initiates God's directive for proliferation (1:22, 28; 9:1, 7), often employing מלא as the *secondary charge element* to explicate spatial coverage. In fact, מלא never precedes פרו ורבו in the Mandate texts.[319]

What follows the *ʾaṯnāḥ* in 9:7 is the *result* of divine "enablement," namely, the *profusion* of life. This time, however, שרץ is used for the expected מלא (cf. 1:22, 28; 9:1).[320] Whereas שרץ denoted the *abundance* of animal life in 8:17b, here it anticipates human abundance. Like מלא, however, שרץ prefaces the *domain identification* of the "earth" (ארץ; so 1:28; 9:1, 7) as the *mêreḵā* and *ṭip̄ḥā* accents show (see Figure 6).

An obvious *inclusion* is struck between 9:1 and 9:7 (see Figures 5 and 6), employing: (1) the imperatival mood (9:1a, 7a,b), (2) stipulation of subject (להם, אתם), (3) followed by *core charge* (פרו ורבו), (4) use of *secondary charge elements* (מלא, שרץ), and (5) closing with *domain identification* (ארץ). Ultimately, 9:1 must be read with 9:7 as part of the same discourse.[321] 9:7 serves to underscore the continuity of life against the threat of death. Patterned after 1:28, the Mandate texts of 9:1 and 7 portray God blessing

---

319. As the essential counterpart of שרץ מלא does precede פרו ורבו once in 8:17b: וישצו בארץ ופרו ורבו, "that they may <u>swarm</u> the earth and be fruitful and multiply." However, this is neither the standard blessing formula nor is it directed to humans. By contrast, 9:1 and 7 resume with imperatival verbs, not only for the *core charge* (contra, 8:17b: Qal perf), but the *secondary charge elements* as well (מלא, 9:1; שרץ, רבה, 9:7), unlike 8:17.

320. Among the Mandate texts, only 9:7 closes the 1st half with the פרו ורבו collocation. For Hendel, the whole clause (שרצו בארץ) represents a "harmonization" to 1:28 (*Text*, 140). Regardless, 9:7 is also unique in its *asyndetic* clause that immediately follows the *core charge*, שִׁרְצוּ, "proliferate." Some Hebrew MSS and the SP insert the *wāw*: וּשׁרצו (= και πληροσατε [LXX, so V]). While this is logical (cf. 8:17b), it is not necessary and obscures imperatival nuances highlighted by two pairs of hendiadys: ורבו ... || פרו ורבו שרצו (Anderson, *Sentence*, 99).

321. Observe the delimitation of the discourse by the *sᵉtumah* (ס) (i.e., "closed paragraph") following 9:7 (MT) reflecting an ancient interpretive tradition.

Exegetical Analysis of the Mandate in Genesis 1-11

a new community in restatement more than re-instatement.[322] "There is no other life but that which continues generation after generation and expands over the earth."[323]

As the final phrase of 9:7b, וּרְבוּ־בָהּ ("and increase on it") is steeped in critical discussion because of the verb רבה (MT). Since שרץ ("proliferate") and רבה ("multiply") have already been employed as terms for "abundance" (i.e., פרו ורבו) it is argued that רבה is redundant and would make better sense if emended to רדה ("rule"), thus more accurately reflecting the stock lexemes and structure of 1:28b.[324]

B. Porten and U. Rappaport mount a forceful defense of the MT over against the וּרְדוּ emendation.[325] While some evidence exists for וּרְדוּ in a few Greek manuscripts, Porten and Rappaport show the combined weight of the LXX manuscripts and other versions favor the MT reading.[326] Internally, Porten and Rappaport observe a verbal sequence of four verbs in 9:7 (פרה ← רבה ← שרץ ← רבה) that they believe makes 1:22 the structural parallel to 9:7 rather than 1:28.[327] This shared verbal pattern (a → b → c → b) ostensibly removes the grounds for emending רבה ("multiply") to רדה ("rule") in 9:7b.[328]

---

322. G. W. Coats, *Genesis with an Introduction to Narrative Literature.* FOTL 1, ed. Knierim, R. and G. M. Tucker (Grand Rapids: Eerdmans, 1983), 78.

323. Westermann, *Genesis*, 462.

324. *BHK* and *BHS* suggest the emendation וּרְ[דּ]וּ (Qal imper, mpl), "and rule" on analogy with 1:28 (some OG MSS: καὶ κατακυριεύσατε [so Brenton], "and rule/gain dominion"). Yet the better critical editions of the LXX reflect the MT (so Rahlfs, *Larger Cambridge Edition*, *Göttingen Edition*). But Hendel believes "a reconstructed archetype can be ascertained with some confidence" with ורבו "explicable as an assimilation by reminiscence" (*The Text*, 9), however, the S, SP, Tg. Onq., Tg. Ps.-J, C 3 (Cairo Geniza), and 911 (*Berlin Fragment*) reflect the MT with the LXX similarly reading: καὶ πληθύνεσθε ἐπ' αὐτῆς [= τὴν γῆν, so A] (= ומלאו את הארץ, so V), a harmonization to the MT of 1:28 (ibid, 140). Those supporting the emendation include: Gunkel, *Genesis*, 150; Skinner, *Genesis*, 171; Speiser, *Genesis*, 57; Vawter, *On Genesis*, 133; Westermann, *Genesis 1-11*, 460; Alter, *Genesis*, 39. Against the emendation includes: Cassuto, *A Commentary*, 1:128; Wenham, *Genesis 1-15*, 155; Hamilton, *Genesis*, 311 n.4; Mathews, *Genesis*, 406; Harland, *The Value*, 147; Currid, *Genesis*, 1:217; Goldingay, *Israel's*, 290 n.15.

325. "Poetic Structure in Genesis IX," *VT* 21 (1971): 363-69.

326. Ibid., 364-65.

327. Other examples Porten and Rappaport use include: Isa 28:23; 30:10; Jer 22:20; 34:4 (see chapter three and the discussion of פרו ורבו).

328. Not many translations adopted the emendation. The first was the JB (1966, "and be lord of it") followed by the NEB (1970, "and rule over it") and the NAB (1970, "and subdue it"). Yet three decades since has not seen other translations embrace this emendation.

In light of our analysis of these Mandate texts, several observations favor retaining the MT. Firstly, רדה is not necessary for 9:7b since our analysis of the broader discourse has shown that "governance/rule" is contextually addressed in the technical phrases of 9:2a,b (i.e., "into your hand they are given," 2b). G. Coats agrees, stating:

> The reference to subduing the earth and having dominion over the subhuman creatures is not paralleled here in the same words, *but 9:2 must represent an extension of that clause.*[329]

Secondly, the connections to 1:28 are both lexical and thematic, requiring precise definition and function of these words. רדה in 1:28b applied to the governance of the animals via three object clauses (רדה ב), not the earth (see Figure 2).[330] This is at cross-purposes with the emendation and the MT of 9:7b that has ארץ ("earth") as the antecedent of the 3fs suffix (בה).

The third observation is tied to the Porten and Rappaport method. Generally, their argument is too linguistically genetic, ignoring the contextual function of these terms in differing contexts. רבה is part of a hendiadys (פרו ורבו) that they consistently ignore. This leads them to wrongly uphold 1:22 as the template for 9:7. However, we have already observed that the counterpart of 1:22 is more arguably 8:17, with the 9:1 and 7 texts forming the counterpart to 1:28. There are substantial implications in the Mandate directed to humankind (1:28; 9:1, 7) compared to Mandate texts with animals in view (1:22; 8:17). Linguistic connections must also be defined by genre and discourse pragmatics (e.g., ויאמר להם אלהים [1:28a]; ויאמר להם [9:1b]; see above).[331]

CONCLUSION

Our analysis of the five text plots moved in semantic, thematic, and theological directions (cf. 1:22, 28; 8:17; 9:1, 7). Within these trajectories the texts both overlap and distinguish themselves. We can highlight several significant points that have defined the Creation Mandate in our analysis.

---

329. *Genesis*, 78, also H.-J. Zobel, "רָדָה," *TDOT*, 13:336. Emphasis added.
330. E. Blum, "רַב," *TDOT*, 13:282.
331. This in turn has rich implications for the language and theology of Exod 1:7.

Exegetical Analysis of the Mandate in Genesis 1–11

We isolated repeated elements that reveal the literary logic and semantic character of these five texts, functioning as highly "stylized components" (see Figures 1–6). As direct discourse they generate narrative movement rather than reflect it. From these texts, the following units were assembled: (1) *Formal Stem* (= "Then God blessed them saying"), (2) *Core Charge* (= "Be fruitful and multiply"), (3) *Secondary Charge Elements* (= "fill," "subdue," "rule," "swarm"), (4) and *Domain Identification* (= "earth," "sea," "sky").

Throughout these Mandate texts, God's blessing is "worded forth" in performative utterances or speech acts; initiated by the *Formal Stem* (. . . ויברך; 1:22a, 28a; 9:1a).[332] What follows is the substance or declaration of that blessing (. . . לאמר, 1:22a; 9:1b). The *Core Charge* specifies abundance as the manner of productiveness (פרו ורבו; 1:22b, 28a; 8:17b; 9:1b, 7a). The *Secondary Charge Elements* explicate the result of increase relative to the sphere (מלא, 1:22b, 28a; 9:1b), manner (כבש, רדה, 1:28a,b), and extent (רבה, שרץ, 1:22b; 8:17b; 9:7b) of that fertility. Finally, the *Domain Identification* stipulates the spatial theatre of proliferation, whether "sea," "land," or "sky" (cf. 1:22, 28, etc.).[333]

The Creation Mandate given to humankind in 1:28 brings subtlety and detail not seen in the other text plots. Here the power of blessing is heard in God's first words to humankind, here is felt the obligation of task, the privilege of royal assignment in the sanctity of work; all this is a gift reflective of the Giver. For humankind, the realm of God's Mandate remains distinctly earth-bound. To produce and care is to mimic the Creator.

We argued that the *Formal Complex Stem* of 1:28a is a potent upgrade, signifying an act of communication to humankind with a unique relational dynamism.[334] Additionally, we observed the presence of all three domains in 1:28 ("earth," "sea," "sky"), reversing the order of Genesis 1 to emphasize the solidarity of humankind with the earthly domain and

---

332. See chapter three for the discussion of ברך as illocutionary speech rather than mere command.

333. For a recent argument for the OT conception of the world as *bipartite* or dualistic, see J. T. Pennington, "Dualism in Old Testament Cosmology," *SJOT* 18 (2004): 260–77. Regardless, we have referred to "earth, sea, sky" under the rubric of *functional* cosmology in creational narrative rather than *ontological* cosmology, a notion resumed in the very structure and purpose of Noah's ark.

334. Refer to the discussion in this chapter of ויברך אתם אלהים ויאמר להם אלהים (1:28a) that we termed the "formal complex stem."

its creatures (cf. Psalm 148).³³⁵ We argued that God's blessing to humankind (1:28) is a composite or "theological hendiadys"³³⁶ of *endowment* and *commission*, the former for reproduction and the latter for ruling. By genre and substance, the Mandate reaches beyond mere "command" to "produce children," it adds the influential stewardship of governance.³³⁷ Through *task* ("subdue") and *royal installation* ("rule"), humankind is called to imitate their Creator through production and care.

We also argued that כבש ("subdue") functions on dual horizons. On the one hand is God's authorization for accomplishing earthly stewardship through a harnessing of its resources. On the other is the anticipation of Israel's "subduing" of the nations in the Conquest. The design of historical creation is completed in the national occupation of the land, a removal of chaos and extension of creation. The task of "subduing" (כבש) works in tandem with the position of "ruling" (רדה) in order to utilize earthly life.

While some would hold that governance is omitted in the Mandate re-issued to Noah, we argued that 9:1 reiterates 1:28a (i.e., *enablement*) with 9:2 resuming the language of dominion in 1:28b (i.e., *commission*). In 9:2a, we argued that "terror and dread" (מוראכם וחתכם) is the language of legal dominion for a new era, joining "subdue" (כבש, 1:28a) as pre-Sinaitic terminology, written retrospectively, for Israel's national experience. Couched in different form and language the original "commission" is cast as *assurance*, a promise³³⁸ needed for a new world. This merging of universal and national horizons is further emphasized with the language of 9:2b, "into your hand they are given" (בידכם נתנו), militaristic language for holy war (cf. Deut 19:12).³³⁹

---

335. This solidarity between human and animal reappears in the *futility curses* through the shared language of "dust" (עפר), "ground," (האדמה), "eating" (אכל), "curse" (ארר), and temporality ("all the days of your life"; כל ימי חייך) that punctuate the oracles to the serpent (Gen 3:14) and man (3:17, 19). The death of the man eventuates in the food of the serpent. No longer providing security and identity, the domain of their origin (האדמה) is now both ominous and ironic.

336. R. F. Capon, *Genesis: The Movie* (Grand Rapids: Eerdmans, 2003), 140.

337. Unfortunately the genre of blessing within the performative speech of God is commonly reduced to a mere "command to procreate" even in contemporary scholarship (see A. J. Köstenberger, *God*, 133, 174, 203; cf. 142 regarding infertility). However, we agree with J. Sailhamer who does not view this as command due to ויברך (*Genesis*, 38).

338. The language of Goldingay, but with differing argumentation (*Theology*, 180).

339. According to D. W. Baker, 9:2 makes "more explicit a connotation of military

Exegetical Analysis of the Mandate in Genesis 1–11

On the national horizon, we believe 1:28 has in view a nation called to conquer the land of Canaan. Rather than its ultimate justification, conquest is the means of Israel's occupation. Such conquest was fundamentally a religious notion tied to their covenant in which God as Sovereign provided defense and protection (cf. Ps 8:2b).[340] "The land is, on the one hand, God's bounty to Israel, hers by right. On the other hand, she must take it by conquest."[341]

Thus, earthly stewardship not only anticipates Israel's "subduing" of nations in conquest (Josh 18:1), but "terror and dread" reiterates the initial "ruling" (רדה, 1:28b) via legal terminology. This, we argued, is pre-Sinaitic language written *retrospectively* with Israel's national conquest in view.

We also argued that the Mandate blessing of 1:22 is reenacted in 8:17, with 1:28 reoccurring in 9:1–7, the very order reminiscent of creation itself. While the former maintains its focus on animals, the latter addresses human life. Though the terminology becomes more expressive in 9:1–7, governance is passed on to Noah as an Adam *redivivus* (9:1). In this way the dominion of Adam is preserved, for the Creator's design is needed for life itself, even if its expression must be modified.

Defining the commission, we also observed the thematic and theological significance of royal imagery surrounding רדה ("rule"). רדה stipulates the quality of *agency* and *position* as a means of enacting the

---

conquest [cf. Deut 11:25]" ("God, Names of," *DOTP*, 364). This is a concept inadequately considered for this text in scholarly literature, see G. von Rad, *Holy War in Ancient Israel*, trans. M. J. Dawn (Vandenhoek, 1991; reprint, Eugene: Wipf and Stock, 2000); J. J. Niehaus, *God* ("Theology and Theophany," "Pre-Sinai Theophanies," 17–42; 142–80); T. Hiebert, "Warrior, Divine," *ABD*, 6:876–80; T. Longman III, "Divine Warrior," *NIDOTTE*, 4:545–49; A. C. Emery, "Warfare," *DOTP*, 877–81; see above for discussion.

According to M. Weinfeld, a *Kulturkampf* lies behind Israelite ḥērem (esp. Deut 20:18). For Weinfeld, such a policy of obligatory extermination (i.e., automatic decree) is utopian, not defined by vow, akin more to theory, and unheard of in Israel's historical accounts ("Deuteronomy, Book of," *ABD*, 2:179).

Weinfeld's stance might be stronger if there were not the clear example of Achan stealing from the ḥērem (Josh 7:1–26; cf. "There is a devoted thing (חרם) in your [pl, contra MT] midst" (7:13); 4QJosh^a), on the one hand, and Rabshakeh's bluster that" "the kings of Assyria have annihilated (חרם) all the lands" (Isa 37:11a; cf. *HALOT*, 1:354). But in such uses, according to C. Brekelmans, ḥērem (Hiph) "had become a profane expression for 'to annihilate (totally),' and only then are gentiles or YHWH subjects of the verb" ("חָרַם," *TLOT*, 2:474–77; BDB, 355.b,c; see further Fishbane, *Biblical*, 199–208).

340. W. S. LaSor, "War," in *The Oxford Companion to the Bible*, ed. B. M. Metzger and M. D. Coogan (Oxford: Oxford, 1993), 791.

341. Dumbrell, *Faith*, 64, following P. D. Miller.

commission to rule. Both verbs כבש and רדה ("subdue," "rule") "indicate that humanity is seen as the ruler, one might say as king, over creation."[342] In fact, כבש and רדה include notions of force, but never of a king against his own people.[343] Divine kingship animated its earthly counterpart borne out through both royal dominion and royal notions of conquest, suppression of opposition, and securing of the created order.[344]

This dominion reflects a relationship established through divine initiation—a realty assumed elsewhere in Scripture (cf. Psalms 8, 72). This "human coronation," however, is not an autocratic but a *conferred authority* stemming from the Creator. Royal honor and commission have combined producing responsibility and gift. The *ANE*, semantic, and inter-textual evidence not only highlights a royal portrait, it also constructs a programmatic role for 1:28 built on that portrait.

---

342. H. Wildberger, "צֶלֶם," *TLOT*, 3:1082.

343. F. Crüsemann, *The Torah: Theology and History of Old Testament Law*, trans. A. W. Mahnke (Minneapolis: Fortress, 1996), 291 n.75.

344. Israelite reference to war had God's agency in mind and appropriated a well-defined "shepherd-king" imagery for her rulers (see, O. Keel, *Symbolism*, esp. "Defense Against Enemies," 291–306; K. W. Whitelam, "King and Kingship," *ABD*, 4:40–48).

5

Themes, Image of God, and Gender in Genesis 1–11

INTRODUCTION

CHAPTER FOUR HELPED DEFINE the Mandate by isolating an aggregate of terms within Genesis 1–11. Investigation of five different texts surfaced highly stylized units (see Figures 1–6). Endowment and commission (1:28a, b) comprise a "theological hendiadys" encompassing both reproduction and ruling. Now, chapter five will build on this, bringing into relief those themes that reverberate between Genesis 1 and 9.

Significantly, royal imagery rooted in the terms of the Mandate is extended in the image of God language. Here we will seek to understand how the "image of God" and gender-language contributes to the theological *gravitas* of the Creation Mandate. We will summarize our findings and look back in our conclusion.

Thematic Relationships Surrounding Genesis 1 and 9

Lying within broader literary criticism is the significant interpretative tool of Rhetorical Criticism.[1] Its classical focus on the "aesthetic of the final

---

1. J. Muilenburg had proposed two fundamental canons for Rhetorical Criticism: (1) delineating, and describing the *structure* and boundaries of a literary unit, and (2) articulating the poetics that define the *texture* of that text ("Form Criticism and Beyond," *JBL* 88 [1969]: 1–10). T. B. Dozeman explains this shift away from Form Criticism:

> An overemphasis on similarity in the study of the *Gattungen* created an abstraction for the reader so that the uniqueness of the individual text was not sufficiently included in interpretation. The result of such abstraction was that the integral relation between form and content was severed, which not only obscured the thought and intention of the writer or speaker, but even more seriously, produced a skepticism of all attempts to read a pericope in its historical context. ("Rhetoric and Rhetorical Criticism," *ABD*, 5:713)

product" intersects well with exegetical interests in "original meaning." Where Form Criticism looks for the typical and preliterary,[2] Rhetorical Criticism seeks out the unique and extant to discern the literary logic and flow of thought.[3] According to Wenham, "Rhetorical criticism links the concerns of literary and historical criticism."[4] An understanding of the historical culture and setting must be analyzed alongside textual expression, as rhetorical sensitivity illuminates both the author's literary skill and force of argument,[5] one capable of mastering the reader's mind.[6]

For our purposes, Rhetorical Criticism helps elucidate the text's argument by means of persuasion without overturning the historical context.[7] Our application of Rhetorical Criticism to Genesis 1 and 9 will not only highlight elements in repetition, but in so doing will ascertain the author's ethical stance vis-à-vis those recurring elements. By means of such replication the author defines new levels of significance for the reader through emotional involvement, intellectual reaction, and dramatized events.

See also D. Greenwood, "Rhetorical Criticism and Formgeschichte: Some Methodological Considerations," *JBL* 89 (1970): 418-26; M. Kessler, "A Methodological Setting for Rhetorical Criticism," *SemeiaSt* 4 (1974): 22-36; I. M. Kikawada, "Some Proposals for the Definition of Rhetorical Criticism," *Semitics* 5 (1977): 69-91; W. Wuellner, "Where Is Rhetorical Criticism Taking Us?" *CBQ* 49 (1987): 448-63; J. J. Jackson and M. Kessler, *Rhetorical Criticism: Essays in Honor of James Muilenburg*, PTMS 1 (Pittsburgh: Pickwick, 1974).

2. R. A. Taylor, "Form Criticism," *DOTP*, 336.

3. R. N. Soulen, "Rhetorical Criticism," *Handbook of Biblical Criticism*, 2nd ed. (Atlanta: John Knox, 1981), 169.

4. *Story*, 3. Wenham has recently harnessed the approach of rhetorical criticism to articulate the ethical stance of the writer that is in turn built on the theological message (see "The Rhetorical Function of Genesis," 17-43; "Ethical Ideals and Legal Requirements," 73-107 in *Story*; similarly "Theme of the Pentateuch," 145-58; "Composition of the Pentateuch," in *Exploring the Old Testament: A Guide to the Pentateuch*, vol. 1 [Downers Grove: InterVarsity, 2003], 159-85).

5. *Story*, 18.

6. Y. Gitay, "Rhetorical Criticism" in *To Each Its Own Meaning: An Introduction to Biblical Criticisms and Their Application*, ed. S. L. McKenzie and S. R. Haynes (Louisville: Westminster, 1993), 136. M. Weinfeld also speaks of the rhetorical technique used "to capture and maintain the interest of his listeners" (*Deuteronomy and the Deuteronomic School* [Winona Lake: Eisenbrauns, 1992], 172).

7. Here, *structure* and *texture* merge in contribution (i.e., *structure* [= acts, scenes, episodes, strophes, dialogue, discourse, pericope indicators, inclusio, chiasm, extended palestrophe, symmetry and order variation, motif repetition, quotation, subordinate and parenthetical description, etc.]; *texture* [= paronomasia and phonetic wordplay, syllables, words, phrases, allusion and foreshadowing sentences, groups of sentences, etc.]).

Themes, Image of God, and Gender in Genesis 1–11

In varying measures, Genesis 1 and 9 contain three types of repetition, what we can call: figural representation, concept/event reversal, and concept/event renewal.[8] Sternberg notes:

> What kind of text is the Bible, and what role does it perform in context? ... the question of the narrative as a functional structure, a means to a communicative end, a transaction between the narrator and the audience on whom he wishes to produce a certain effect by way of certain strategies.[9]

In figural representation, an author uses real historical events known to the readers to represent past, present or future realities.[10] Figural representation is not dreary reiteration of events but insightful reflection on them, employed as a literary strategy for thematic purpose, and one often eschatologically oriented.[11] In the end, figural representation is not what the reader does, but detecting what the author has already done; it is compositional in nature rather than interpretative.[12]

A second type of repetition is concept/event reversal. This form overturns a precedent in some way, either by gaining literary momentum or losing it. Thus concept/event reversal represents an inversion of an earlier event/concept.[13] In this way, "an event may be given a more dynamic meaning in subsequent references, or a less forceful meaning."[14]

The third type of repetition is concept/event renewal. Here a theme or motif finds some form of development, an incremental or graded parallel to the initial concept/event. While these might appear as essentially reiteration, on closer analysis there is a kind of highlighting, a development that "intensifies" the concept/event.

---

8. Terms adapted from: M. J. Wells, "Figural Representation and Canonical Unity," in *Biblical Theology: Retrospect and Prospect*, ed. S. Hafemann (Downers Grove: InterVarsity, 2002), 111–25; H. G. Reventlow, "Creation as a Topic in Biblical Theology," in *Creation in Jewish and Christian Tradition*, ed. H. G. Reventlow and Y. Hoffman, JSOTSup 319 (Sheffield: Sheffield Academic Press, 2002), 153–71; H. A. G. Kruger, "Subscripts," 429–45.
Sailhamer identifies what he calls: recursion, contemporisation, and foreshadowing (*Introduction*, 290–97).

9. *Poetics*, 1.

10. Wells, "Figural," 113.

11. Ibid., 114.

12. Ibid., 115.

13. Kruger, "Subscripts," 431.

14. Ibid.

For concept/event reversal and renewal, some modification occurs to the initial occurrence. Alongside the author's literary convention, we are keenly interested in the ethical stance communicated by the author through these textual strategies. In this case "a theology derived from OT creation tradition depicts the human creature as the subject of moral responsibility"[15]—one that builds a moral relationship encompassing both environment and human community.[16]

The overarching repetition is between Adam (Gen 1) in the context of the first creation (Gen 2) and Noah (Gen 9) amid a world re-created (Gen 8).[17] While the fall and Noah's drunkenness share similarities of the event reversal type,[18] possibly more significant is the broader recurrence of a creation once given to Adam and subsequently "cleansed" for Noah. Genesis 1 and 9 lie lodged within a grand event-renewal repetition of pre and post-diluvian worlds. G. V. Smith demonstrates how meaning flows from structure, employing linguistic similarities.[19] His observations are compelling, noting that the author employs repeated phrases and concepts to form the structural cohesion between the narratives of Adam

---

15. G. W. Coats, "Theology of the Hebrew Bible," in *The Hebrew Bible and Its Modern Interpreters*, ed. D. A. Knight and G. M. Tucker (Minneapolis: Fortress, 1985), 255.

16. Ibid.

17. Pertinent literature addressing this repetition includes: Blenkinsopp, *Pentateuch*, 54–97; Brueggemann, *Genesis*, 89–91; Clines, *Theme*, 2nd ed., 66–84, 128; W. Gage, *The Gospel of Genesis: Studies in Protology and Eschatology* (Winona Lake: Carpenter, 1984), 9–15; Mathews, *Genesis*, 351; Sailhamer, *Introduction*, 290–97; Waltke, *Genesis*, 125–31; Wenham, *Genesis 1–15*, 157–58.

Similarly: B. W. Anderson, "From Analysis;" J. P. Fokkelman, *Reading Biblical Narrative: An Introductory Guide* (Louisville: Westminster/John Knox, 1999), 112–22; D. M. Gunn and D. N. Fewell, *Narrative in the Hebrew Bible* (Oxford: Oxford University Press, 1993), 148–58, 175–77; R. Longacre, "The Discourse Structure;" E. J. Revell, "The Repetition of Introductions to Speech as a Feature of Biblical Hebrew," *VT* 47 (1997): 91–110; J. T. Walsh, *Style*, 145–53; A. J. Tomasino, "History Repeats Itself: The 'Fall' and Noah's Drunkenness," *VT* 42 (1992): 128–30.

18. While one could argue for mere parallel events, such facts as one human cursing another (9:25), the first and only time Noah speaks, constitutes a negative shift. Following divine law (9:4–6//2:16–17), it now falls to God's agent in Noah to enact retribution following his own interrogation and curses, cf.: 3:8–13, 14–19//9:24, 25; 2:8//9:20; 3:6//9:21; 3:7//9:21; 3:7//9:23; 3:7//9:24; 3:14//9:25; 4:1–2, 5//9:25–27, so Sailhamer, (*Introduction*, 293), what he calls "the construction of 'reality'" (292).

19. "Structure and Purpose in Genesis 1–11," *JETS* 20 (1977): 307–19. On the relationship of meaning and structure, D. A. Dorsey is also persuasive (*Literary*, 15–20, 327–28).

Themes, Image of God, and Gender in Genesis 1–11

and Noah. Modifying Smith's list, even elements beyond Genesis 1 and 9 assume a richer significance:

- Both worlds emerge from primordial watery chaos through parallel stages (1:9//8:5).[20]
- Both are distinctly linked with the image of God (1:27//9:6).[21]
- Both uniquely "walk with God" (3:8; 6:9).
- Both relate to God through obedience to divine "commands" (2:16//6:22).[22]
- Both receive divine "law" or "legislation" intended to be fixed (2:16–17//9:4–6).
- Both "rule" the animals via naming and preservation (2:19//7:15).
- Both receive the *enablement* of the Mandate (1:28a//9:1).
- Both receive the *commission* of the Mandate (1:28b//9:2).[23]
- Both receive instructions regarding food (1:29//9:3)
- Both work the "ground" (2:4–7//9:20).[24]
- Both follow a similar sequence of transgression via consumption of a fruit (3:6//9:21).[25]

---

20. Cf. Precreation Status (1:2//8:1b–2); 2nd Day (1:6–8//8:2b); 3rd Day (1:9//8:3–5); 5th Day (1:20–23//8:6–12); 6th Day (1:24–25//8:17–19); Image of God & Gender (1:16–28//8:16, 18; 9:6); Royal Blessing (1:28//9:1, 7).

21. Cf. 5:1–3; ביום ברא אלהים אדם, "when God created humankind" (5:1b) employs the past aspect of ברא along with the same telic verb employed in God's creation of humankind (cf. 1:27; also עשה, אדם). Moreover, "image" (בדמות) continues as Adam replicates God's man-making in his son, Seth, the only son explicitly connected with "image."

22. Cf. 3:11, 17//7:5, 9.

23. "Rule over the fish of the sea" (1:28b) is reiterated as "all the fish of the sea, they are given into your hands" (9:2; see discussion above).

24. Cf. 2:7; אִישׁ הָאֲדָמָה ("man of the ground") is a *hapax* used to recall Adam's work (cf. 2:15; 3:23). Death is a return to the ground, the point of origin and thus definitive reference point which is probably why the man rather than the woman receives the "death oracle" (3:19, cf. 4:11; Job 4:19). Animals are also made from the "ground" (2:19), establishing a link to humankind. Noah's "ground-working" is probably appositional to the proper name (contra, *GKC*, §120b).

25. The wine of the Noah story (9:21) is fundamentally viewed as God's gift and in the story's context the wine implies a new era, not ground free from its curse (so Mathews, *Genesis*, 416; Waltke, *Genesis*, 148; contra, Fretheim, *The Book of*, 393; cf. Gen 27:28; Deut 7:13; 11:14; Ps 4:7; Joel 2:19, 24; Hos 2:8, 21–22; John 2:1–11; Luke 22:14–20, etc.).

- Both experience a "knowing" and shameful "nakedness" (3:5, 7//9:21, 24).[26]
- Both are "clothed" by another in their helpless state (3:21//9:23).[27]
- Both have three named sons (4:1–2, 25//9:18).[28]
- Both instigate consequences of "cursing" from a transgression (3:17//9:25).[29]
- Both speak in oracular form of future destiny within a close relationship (3:20//9:26).
- Both perform "priestly" roles as oracle-givers, neutralizing some encroaching force of chaos.[30]

This example of event-renewal repetition demonstrates that retelling may be the most powerful form of theological discourse in the OT.[31] Similar to figural representation, the thematic repetition involving Adam and Noah employs narrative typology wherein the earlier character (= Adam) provides the pattern for the later character (= Noah) in the

---

26. Ham's role is analogous to the serpent; both tempt others with forbidden knowledge and end up cursed (אָרוּר) in subjugation to the offspring (cf. 3:14–15; 9:25; Tomasino, "History," 129, 130). In both cases, eyes are opened and nakedness is seen (3:7; 9:22; Carr, *Reading*, 236).

27. The inadequate state including nakedness, is ameliorated by "skins" and a "garment" (3:21//9:23). The article on אֶת־הַשִּׂמְלָה ("the garment," 9:23) either functions *anaphorically* (Cassuto, *A Commentary*, 2:162) or as *definite in the mind* of the characters/narrator (so *GKC*, §126r; cf. Exod 22:26; Deut 24:13).

28. Elements of hope and judgment are distributed among Adam and Noah's three sons. As Adam's three sons are divided around Seth, so are Noah's around Shem. Moreover, "as the Cainites from Adam sought their security in cities, the Canaanites from Ham son of Noah will seek theirs in a tower" (Waltke, *Genesis*, 128 n.20).

29. In each case, the offended party seeks to rectify the situation (3:14–19//9:25–27). Moreover, these are the only oracular curses within Genesis 1–11.

30. Callender, *Adam in Myth*, 207. For Adam, it was the chaos of his "death oracle" from God (3:19) that prompts his immediate naming of Eve as "life giver" (3:20). Similarly, Noah views Ham's actions as a representative of moral chaos, prompting an oracle of moral segregation (9:25; cf. vv. 26–27). For both, some form of "chaos" is ameliorated in the only recorded occasions of their speech.

31. Reventlow, "Creation," 158. Employing "ark," and "flood" imagery, the infancy narrative of Moses (cf. Exodus 1–2) illustrates how Noah's life can be rehearsed in figural representation with eschatological force (see I. M. Kikawada, "Noah and the Ark," *ABD*, 4:126–27).

narrative.³² This forms a dynamic correlation the author exploits for ethical emphasis—literary structure corresponding to theological meaning.³³ E. E. Ellis explains this typology, stating:

> The OT displays a hermeneutical progression in which ... sacred accounts of God's acts in the past provided models for later accounts of his present and future activity ... It represented a typological correspondence that is not a mere cyclical repetition but rather a progression in which the new surpasses the old.³⁴

Among other observations, the author underscores that God's good creation is increasingly languishing under sin whose impact is no longer "local," nor will exile prove the antidote for post-diluvians it was for Adam (Gen 3:23–24). With Ham (9:24), Noah experiences what God's internal monologue already revealed—the sinful disposition of humankind also survived the flood (8:21). Yet something of that creation ideal is salvaged through the very convention of repetition.

The defining acts of creation, though diminished, continue to resonate between Genesis 1 and 9, the highpoints of movement in Genesis 1–11. Such strategic repetition tethers key characters and concepts to God's intended design. The dry earth (8:6–14) along with human and animal relationships (8:15—9:7) represents a renewal of Days 3 and 6, the domain pertaining to land and creature interaction. It is the presence of human wickedness that displaces the original "goodness," taking the narrative to a more desperate level—it is, in the end, an imperfect renewal.³⁵ Here God blesses and the reader is left wondering how the future will improve; can re-creating and pro-creating adequately renew?³⁶ However fragile, the episode of 9:1–7 stands as the first glimpse of life under the re-

---

32. Chisholm, "History," 73.

33. Kruger, "Subscripts," 431.

34. "The Old Testament Canon in the Early Church," in *Mikra: Text, Translation, Reading and Interpretation of the Hebrew Bible in Ancient Judaism and Early Christianity*, ed. M. J. Mulder (Van Gorcum: Assen/Maastricht, 1990), 687.

35. T. L. Brodie, *Genesis as Dialogue: A Literary, Historical, and Theological Commentary* (Oxford: Oxford University, 2001), 180.

36. Following Fokkelman (*Narrative*, 11–45), the role of *leitwörter* plays a key role for repetition in co-textual plots (e.g.: ראה is pivotal, in many ways framing the Adam and Noah narratives: "discerning," 1:31//9:16; "appearance," 1:9//9:14; also ויטע, 2:8–9//9:20).

freshed blessing of the Creator.[37] Human frailty has aroused the Creator's fidelity.[38]

THEOLOGICAL CONTRIBUTION OF THE CREATION MANDATE TO GENESIS 1-11

The theological contribution of the Mandate will be considered under three heads: image of God, male and female, and the order of creation. Their combined voices have more to communicate together than individually vis-à-vis the Mandate. Here, co-textual data must be analyzed.

"Image of God" in Relation to the Mandate

An understanding of the image of God is confined to three texts: 1:26-27, 5:3, and 9:6. Significantly, 1:26-27 and 9:6 serve to frame the Mandate plots (i.e., 1:28; 8:17; 9:1, 7), adding contour to Genesis 1-11.[39] Within the rhetorical flow of Genesis 1-11, renewal must emerge from an epicenter of violence that both indicts and cleanses the earth (6:11, 13; 7:21-23).

---

37. Turner, *Genesis*, 54.

38. Brodie, *Genesis*, 180.

39. The focus of our analysis lies in the relationship of the image to the Mandate rather than the ontological nature of the image, per se, though they clearly overlap. For discussions on the nature of the image, see: D. J. A. Clines, "The Image of God in Man," *TynBul* 19 (1968): 53-103; J. R. Middleton, "The Liberating Image? Interpreting the Imago Dei in Context," *CSR* 24 (1994): 8-25; R. C. Van Leeuwen, "Form, Image," *NIDOTTE*, 4:643-48; F. J. Stendebach, "צֶלֶם," *TDOT*, 12:386-96; H. Wildberger, "צֶלֶם," *TLOT*, 3:1080-85; G. Wenham, *Genesis 1-15*, 26-33 (with bibliography); I. Hart, "Genesis 1:1—2:3 as a Prologue to the Books of Genesis," *TynBul* 46 (1995): 315-36; C. Westermann, *Genesis*, 142-60 (with bibliography); N. Jastram, "Man as Male and Female: Created in the Image of God," *CTQ* 68 (2004): 5-96; S. J. Grenz, "Jesus as the *Imago Dei*: Image-of-God Christology and the Non-Linear Linearity of Theology," *JETS* 47 (2004): 617-28; M. Miller, "In the 'Image' and 'Likeness' of God," *JBL* 91 (1972): 298-304; E. H. Merrill, "Image of God," *DOTP*, 441-45; A. A. Hoekema, *Created in God's Image* (Grand Rapids: Eerdmans, 1986); W. Loader, *The Septuagint, Sexuality, and the New Testament: Case Studies on the Impact of the LXX in Philo and the New Testament* (Grand Rapids: Eerdmans, 2004), 27-69; W. Bruegemann, *Theology*, 450-54; W. J. Dumbrell, *Faith*, 2nd ed. 15-18; Mathews, *Genesis*, 160-74; E. M. Curtis, "Image of God (OT)," *ABD*, 3:389-91; I. A. McFarland, *The Divine Image: Envisioning the Invisible God* (Minneapolis: Fortress, 2005); B. K. Waltke, "Relating Human Personhood to the Health Sciences: An Old Testament Perspective," *Crux* 25 (1989): 2-10; P. Bird, "Male and Female He Created Them: Genesis 1:27 on the Context of the Priestly Account of Creation," *HTR* 74 (1981): 129-59; K. E. Borresen, *The Image of God* (Minneapolis: Fortress, 1995); J. F. A. Sawyer, "The Meaning of בְּצֶלֶם אֱלֹהִים ('In the Image of God') in Genesis I-XI," *JTS* 25 (1974): 418-26.

Violence and creation form a staple in *ANE* cosmogonies and mythology, with "echoes" of this emerging in God's re-creation (i.e., Gen 9:1–7).[40] With 9:1–7 comes a blessing that strains to recapture Eden's ideal (cf. 1:26–28). Yet, regardless of one's view of "image," some interpretative harmony must be struck between all three texts.[41] To the royal imagery already discovered in 1:28 further evidence is added through key terms (i.e., רדה, 1:26b)[42] and metaphor.[43] "ANE modes of representation are highly metaphoric and symbolic."[44]

Against the backdrop of God as "cosmic king" in Genesis 1 comes the potent imagery of the *imago Dei*. Here, צֶלֶם (1:26a) supports the relational analogy between God as cosmic king on the one hand, and his regal vice-regent, on the other. While this relationship is constrained by two different domains,[45] Creator and creature are, nevertheless intimately linked by a vibrant communion and communication.[46] "The creature who will bear a divine resemblance cannot be conceived apart from divine

---

40. T. L. Thompson, "Kingship and the Wrath of God: Or Teaching Humility," *RB* 109 (2002): 163. While trenchant, Thompson's discussion is too Epigenetic-Historical, minimizing conscious authorship and the independent identity of the Genesis text itself within its *ANE* milieu.

41. The appropriate reminder of F. J. Stendelbach ("צֶלֶם," *TDOT*, 12:394). Interpretive extremes of "image" are due, in part, to reading one text in isolation from the others.

42. Language and structure so foundational to the Mandate of 1:28 actually finds its inception in 1:26 (i.e., בדגת, ובעוף, ובבהמה, הרמש, על־הארץ, etc.). For an analysis of royal ideology in human creation against the backdrop of ANE culture, see D. E. Callender, Jr., *Adam in Myth and History: Ancient Israelite Perspectives on the Primal Human* (Winona Lake: Eisenbrauns, 2000), esp. 21–39.

43. See C. G. Bartholomew and M. W. Goheen, *The Drama of Scripture: Finding Our Place in the Biblical Story* (Grand Rapids: Baker, 2004), 36. For helpful discussions on language and metaphor, see: G. B. Caird, *The Language and Imagery of the Bible* (Grand Rapids: Eerdmans, 1997), 17–18, 44–59, 66, 90–91, 131–33; J. C. L. Gibson, *Language and Imagery in the Old Testament* (Peabody: Hendrickson, 1998).

44. Van Leeuwen, "Form, Image," *NIDOTTE*, 4:643–44. For discussion of "image" in Egyptian and Mesopotamian environs, see H. Wildberger, "צֶלֶם," *TLOT*, 3:1083; Van Leeuwen, "Form, Image;" F. J. Stendelbach, "צֶלֶם;" E. M. Curtis, "Image;" A. Schüle, "Made in the 'Image of God': The Concepts of Divine Images in Gen 1–3." *ZAW* 117 (2005): 1–20.

45. In the rhetorical logic of Genesis 1, the heavens, or cosmological "firmament," represent the domain already awarded to the celestial bodies (1:16–18).

46. D. J. A. Clines, "Genesis 6.1–4," in *The Theme*, 2nd ed., 81.

self-involvement."[47] The creation of humankind ultimately results from a dialogical act.[48]

The boundary between the human and divine is not absolute, somehow humankind represents God.[49] This dynamic relationship is effectively communicated through metaphor in "image"-language. Through image humankind is "explained,"[50] though there is little agreement as to what constitutes the "content" of this image, a situation, according to Childs, that "remains unclear and contested."[51] Whether "image" refers to a speech-creature, rational being, relational counterpart, or upright posture; all such, we maintain, are complementary *aspects* of "image" rather than mutually exclusive or alternative definitions.[52] What defines image is a more rich and multivalent concept; ironically, one that plays no role in the OT view of humanity, nor does it "constitute a major theological datum for Israel's reflection on the topic."[53]

---

47. Bird, "Theological Anthropology in the Hebrew Bible," in *The Blackwell Companion to the Hebrew Bible*, ed. L. Perdue (Malden: Blackwell, 2005), 258–75, 263. For Bird, the structure of vv. 26-28, with "the divine plurals of v. 26 [reveals] a rhetorical device of the author to emphasize the solemnity and deliberative nature of this final act of creation" (ibid.).

48. T. E. Fretheim, *The Pentateuch*, IBT (Nashville: Abingdon, 1996), 74.

49. Clines, *The Theme*, 81. Clines discusses the intriguing view that Gen 6:1-4 is a distortion of royal representation:

> In 6.1-4, on the contrary, we find a satanic parody of the idea of the image of God in humankind. Far from God being present on earth in the person of humankind as his *kingly representative exercising benign dominion* ... we now have the presence of the divine on earth in a form that utterly misrepresents God through its exercise of *royal violence* and *despotic authority* over other humans (ibid; emphasis added).

50. C. G. Bartholomew, "A Time for War, and a Time for Peace: Old Testament Wisdom, Creation and O'Donovan's Theological Ethics" in *A Royal Priesthood? The Use of the Bible Ethically and Politically: A Dialogue with Oliver O'Donovan*, vol. 3, ed. C. Bartholomew et al. (Grand Rapids: Zondervan, 2002), 106-7.

51. *Biblical Theology of the Old*, 112.

52. Ibid., 107. See Brueggemann's helpful discussion of personhood, *Theology*, 452–54. See also the recent discussion of D. Sheriffs ("'Personhood' in the Old Testament? Who's Asking?" *EvQ* 77 [2005]: 13–34), looking for insight into personhood in light of conceptual tools available in (post)modern culture.

53. Brueggemann, *Theology*, 452. Investigation in the physiology of "image" is rewarding since the "earthling" indeed emerges from the "earth" (cf. Gen 2:7; Pss 103:14; 104:29-30, etc.).

From the throng of heavenly beings comprising the "heavenly court,"[54] YHWH reigns supreme; kingship is his central image in the Old Testament.[55] "It is the sovereignty of God in all the affairs of heaven and earth that makes his court the universal court of appeal."[56] From this vantage, "Let us make humankind in our image" (1:26a) portrays God's intention amid the vibrant relatedness of the Creator.[57] Here, "the voices of the heavenly court join that of the Deity without revealing their identity or compromising the authority of the sole God (cf. Isa 6:8)."[58] Though "image" via צֶלֶם does not occur in Hebrew, the related derivations of "chop off, hew, cut, carve" can be validated through several cognate languages.[59]

---

54. The "angelic view" best addresses the issues of the pronoun, which always functions as a *countable plural*. This is why, grammatically, the pronoun (= "us") cannot be a plural of intensification, majesty or polytheistic hold-over (so Joüon, §113e, §136d; Gib., §120c; Stendebach, "צֶלֶם;" cf. Gen 3:22; 11:7; 1 Kgs 22:19–23; Job 1:6; 2:1; 38:7; Pss 29:1–3; 89:5–6; 103:20–21; Isa 6:8; 40:1–6 Jer 23:15–22; Amos 3:7; Dan 10:12–13; Luke 2:8–14; also B. W. Anderson, *Contours of Old Testament Theology* [Minneapolis: Fortress, 1999], 67–68).

55. Gibson, *Language*, 121; J. G. McConville calls kingship "the root metaphor" ("The Judgment of God in the Old Testament" *ExAud* [2004], 25). It is the *universal* kingship of God that animates his national influence, e.g.,

> "The Lord has established <u>his throne in heaven</u>,
>   and his kingdom <u>rules over all</u>.
> Bless the Lord, you <u>his angels</u> . . .
> Bless the Lord, all his heavenly hosts,
>   his servants that <u>do his will</u>!
> Bless the Lord, all his works,
>   in all places of <u>his dominion</u>"

(Ps 103:19–22a; emphasis added; cf. Judg 8:23; Pss 5:2,4; 29:3,10; 74:12,14,17; 95:3–5; 96:10; Isa 6:5; Zech 14:6–9, etc.). W. P. Brown contends that God's kingship "is undeniably central in the Psalter" (*Seeing the Psalms: A Theology of Metaphor* [Louisville: Westminster/John Knox, 2002], 29).

56. McConville, "Judgment," 25.

57. Brueggemann, *Reverberations*, 56; also, P. D. Miller, "Cosmology and World Order in the Old Testament: The Divine Council as Cosmic-Political Symbol," *HBT* (1987): 53–78; E. T. Mullen, *The Assembly of the Gods: The Divine Council in Canaanite and Early Hebrew Literature* (Cambridge: Harvard University Press, 1980).

58. Bird, "Theological Anthropology," 263. The *authorizing formula*, "thus says the LORD" reflects both decision and dispatch "to announce the verdict of heaven upon the affairs of earth" (Brueggemann, *Reverberations*, 56).

59. Of its 17 occurrences in the OT, 11 refer to physical images (e.g., statues) and 5 relate to humankind in God's image. In Daniel 2–3, one also finds the Aramaic term 17x. For etymological discussions, see: *HALOT*, 3:1028a; F. J. Stendebach, "צֶלֶם," *TDOT*, 12:387–88.

These derivations are revealing, and, coupled with ṣalmu (Akk.), ṣᵉlēm (Aram.), and ṣalama (Arab.) express the idea of "statue."[60] In Egypt the articular form of the word "image" is often written with a hieroglyphic statue.[61] In the context of Genesis 1–11, image has a sense of adequate representation where "that which is depicted is itself present."[62] As a holistic term, Bird claims that "image of God" reflects a Mesopotamian royal epithet, and has a specific "notion of physical resemblance" when applied to humans.[63] This is appropriately nuanced by observing key points of structure and syntax in the biblical text of 1:26–28.[64]

Verse 27 is typically scanned as three clauses:

> So God <u>created</u> (A) humankind in his <u>image</u> (B; צלם), in the <u>image</u> (B'; צלם) of God he <u>created</u> (A') him: male and female he <u>created</u> (A") them.

60. See, H. Wildberger, "צֶלֶם," *TLOT*, 3:1080–81; Van Leeuwen, "Form, Image," *NIDOTTE*, 4:646; F. J. Stendebach, "צֶלֶם," *TDOT*, 12:387, 389; P. Bird, "Male and Female He Created Them: Genesis 1:27 on the Context of the Priestly Account of Creation," *HTR* 74 (1981): 129–59.

61. J. K. Hoffmeier, "Some Thoughts on Genesis 1 and 2 and Egyptian Cosmology," *JANES* 15 (1983), 47.

62. H. Wildberger, "צֶלֶם," *TLOT*, 3:1081. D. J. A. Clines discusses several distinguishing characteristics of humans made in God's image: (1) "image" refers to a statue in the round, (2) "image" expresses more than depicts, thus is not a facsimile, (3) "image" possesses the life of the one being represented, (4) "image" represents the presence of the one represented, (5) "image" functions as ruler in the deity's stead, (6) "image," within Genesis, encompasses the plurality of male and female within a unity of humanity ("The Image," 53–103; similarly, Wenham, *Genesis 1–15*, 29–32).

63. "Theological Anthropology," 261; cf. Num 33:52; 1 Sam 6:5, 11; 2 Kgs 11:18; 2 Chr 23:17; Ezek 7:20, 16:17; Amos 5:26, etc.

64. Thematic emphasis reveals the following profile (adapted from Wenham, *Genesis 1–15*, 27):

26a:	*Announcement*: (1p) of intention	[direct]
26b:	*Purpose*: of humankind's creation	[direct]
27a:	*Report¹*: (3p) fact of human creation	[indirect]
27b:	*Report²*: unity of humankind	[indirect]
28a:	*Blessing¹*: (2p) endowment =reproduction	[direct]
28b:	*Blessing²*: commission =ruling	[direct]
29:	*Assignment*: (1p) food for humankind	[direct]
30:	food for animals	
31a:	*Evaluation*: (3p) excellence & pinnacle	[indirect]
31b:	*Conclusion*: temporal frame	[indirect]

Significantly, God does not speak to the animals, and even their sustenance is part of the direct discourse given to humankind, their caretaker.

Themes, Image of God, and Gender in Genesis 1–11

Without key elements present in the other creation days, emphasis emerges through *asymmetry* and poetic language.[65] Of the key terms employed in God's earlier goal (v. 26: דמות,[66] צלם), only צלם (v. 27) is reiterated (2x), with *anaphoric* force.[67] These three clauses function in apposition, highlighting the significance of human life.[68] The two initial clauses form a chiasm with ברא and צלם (see above), the third clause emphasizes the unity of the genders in that image.[69]

There is, however, another semantic connection that exposes broader associations, one extending beyond the immediate structure v. 27 and connecting with v. 28. In this case a *chiastic quatrain* emerges, employing both word order and wordplay to communicate theological weight:[70]

A   So created (ויברא) God (אלהים) humankind in his <u>image</u>,
 B   <in the <u>image</u> of God> he created (ברא) him:
 B' <male and female> he created (ברא) <u>them</u>.
A' Then blessed (ויברך) God (אלהים) <u>them</u>,

Subunits "A" begin with the inflected verb (ברא, ברך) followed by the reiterated subject (אלהים), "normal" Hebrew word order.[71] Together, ויברא and ויברך not only reflect paronomasia (*wybrʾ, wybrk*) but they under-

---

65. I.e., fulfillment statement, cohortative replacing the command ("Let us make" rather than "Let there be"), etc. (Walsh, *Style*, 74,105; Coats, *Genesis*, 44).

66. דמות, from the verb (I) דמה ("resemble"), is used of a "model" (2 Kgs 16:10), "likeness" (Ezek 23:15), and "shape" (Gen 1:26; Ezek 1:22; *HALOT*, 1:225–26). דמות occurs 25x, and according to E. Jenni has in mind "equivalence" or "total comparability" (cf. Isa 40:18) rather than "diminished similarity" ("דָּמָה," *TLOT*, 1:340).

67. We can loosely scan 1:26 as follows:

ויאמר אלהים
נעשה אדם בצלמנו   כדמותנו
וירדו   בדגת הים
ובעוף השמים
ובבהמה   ובכל־הארץ
ובכל־הרמש הרמש   על־הארץ:

68. Significantly, ברא occurs 1x in each poetic line, emphasizing the *uniqueness* of the human creation.

69. See F. I. Anderson's discussion (*Sentence*, 55).

70. Adapted from Walsh (*Style*, 106).

71. The LXX places greater emphasis on the creation of humankind (τὸν ἄνθρωπον) in 27a by omitting κατ' εἰκόν (= בְּצַלְמוֹ), using εἰκόν only in 27b (W. Loader, *The Septuagint, Sexuality, and the New Testament: Case Studies on the Impact of the LXX in Philo and the New Testament* [Grand Rapids: Eerdmans, 2004], 28–29).

score the fact that human creation is beyond a simple, neutral cosmogonic event, it is salvific and doxological.[72] With increasing intimacy,[73] the 3rd person report of the narrator (v. 27) sets up the 2nd person blessing of God (v. 28a), connecting the exercise of dominion with the function of image.[74] Conversely, *topicalization* is stressed in the order of subunits "B," namely, "in the image of God" and "male and female." This chiastic structure coordinates these phrases with an atypical word order. By structure, subunits "B" are explicative,[75] yet in function they are transitional, moving from the descriptive "him" (v. 27) to the dialogical "them" (v. 28).

This structural profile of 1:26–28 provides a rich theological setting for the "image (צלם) of God," elucidating significant "textual ligaments." First, as terms, בצלמנו כדמותנו ("in our image, according to our likeness," v. 26a) are adverbial constructions and essentially "interchangeable,"[76] including their prepositions (cf. בדמותו כצלמו, 5:3).[77] Appositionally placed,

---

72. Ibid. Similarly, Gen 1:21–23. Brueggemann asserts that creation is:

a majestic liturgical poem, a vigorous doxology as an act of worship at the beginning of Israel's canonical text. Its cadences of grandeur enunciate the main claims of Israel's creation faith ... Israel's doxology asserts that every aspect of the cosmos is derivative from, dependent upon, and obligated to the rule of the creator God. (*Reverberations*, 40–41)

73. As a juxtaposition, את־האדם | אלהים formed a relational dynamic too blatant for the masoretes, who insert the *paseq* accent (|) to assure appropriate separation between the Creator and his creation.

74. Unlike the creation of the animals using the 3rd person (cf. 1:20f), 1st person dialogue is the hallmark of human creation (1:26), employing 1st person pronouns *three* times ("let us make," "in our image," "after our likeness").

75. Westermann agrees, "The twice repeated resumption of the imperf. consec. with the inverted perf. ברא is to be understood in an explicating sense" (*Genesis*, 79, n.27a).

76. Jenni, "דָּמָה," *TLOT*, 1:341; Stendebach, "צֶלֶם," *TDOT*, 12:394; Curtis, "Image of God (OT)," *ABD*, 3:389; E. W. Bullinger's hendiadys rendering ("in the likeness of our image") is too brash, even for modern translations (*Figures of Speech Used in the Bible: Explained and Illustrated* [Grand Rapids: Baker, 1991], 659).

For the Hebrew בְּצַלְמֵנוּ כִּדְמוּתֵנוּ ("in our image, according to our likeness"), the LXX employs coordinating prepositional phrases: κατ' εἰκόνα ἡμετέραν καὶ καθ' ὁμοίωσιν ("according to our image and according to [our] likeness"). To the double κατά ("according to") is also added the conjunction, καί ("and," so SP, V). The former removes the MT possessive to avoid redundancy and reflects precedent in Gen 1:11 [κατὰ γένος καὶ καθ' ὁμοιότητα, "according to their kind and according to their likeness"], while the latter removes the MT appositional construction. However, the dual κατά phrases may achieve the sense of the Hebrew synonyms since both εἰκών and ὁμοίωσις mean "likeness, resemblance" (Wevers, *Notes*, 14). However, καί could also be *explicative*.

77. Anderson, *From Creation*, 121 n.21. In fact, the nouns and prepositions of 1:26 (בְּצַלְמֵנוּ כִּדְמוּתֵנוּ, "in our image, according to our likeness") are reemployed *precisely* in

the abstract noun + כְּ (כְּ-דְמוּת) serves to explicate בְּ-צֶלֶם,[78] yet the lexemes express core similarity.[79] The collocation,[80] "to make 'A' in conformity to 'B'" is employed elsewhere (cf. Exod 25:40), precluding an appeal to "בְּ-*essentiae*" for Gen 1:26.[81] The collocation highlights the Creator's activity over the creature's nature.[82] Significantly, the pronouns signal a change as "our image" (צַלְמֵנוּ) and "our likeness" (דְּמוּתֵנוּ) fix their point of reference in God, not in "him" or "herself" (cf. מִין).[83]

---

opposite placement in 5:3 (cf. בִּדְמוּתוֹ כְּצַלְמוֹ, "in his likeness, according to his image"). This analogy of "Adam" reflected in his "son" views Adam as the "prototype" for following generations and is probably the force represented in the LXX choice of ἰδέαν (cf. 1:26 [LXX]; so Gunkel, *Genesis*, 112–13).

78. As evidenced in the bilingual statue from Tell Fekheriye (northern Syria, late ninth century BC), the Akkadian term (ṣalmu, "image, statue") is rendered in the Aramaic cognate as ṣalmu [lines 12, 16] and also as dĕmûta [lines 1, 15] in reference to the statue of the king:

(1.1f.) This is the image [דמותא] of Hadduyiṯi which he has erected in front of Hadad-Sikannu, the lord of heaven and earth.

(1.12–15) [This is] the image/statue [צלם] of Hadduyiṯi, king of Guzana, Sikannu, and Arzan. For the glory and the consolation of this dynasty and for the continuance of his life and for his words to be agreeable to the gods and to the humans he has made this image/statue [דמותא]. (Quoted in Schüle, "Made," 10.)

(Van Leeuwen, "Form, Image," *NIDOTTE*, 4:644; Curtis, "Image of God (OT)," *ABD*, 3:137–38, following Millard and Bordreuil 1982, 137–38. Similarly, בְּצֶלֶם אֱלֹהִים ("in the image of God," v. 27) develops the earlier בְּצַלְמֵנוּ ("in our image," v. 26), and is likewise employed as בִּדְמוּת אֱלֹהִים ("in the likeness of God") in 5:1 (cf. Ps 8:6). In the LXX, εἰκών consistently translates צלם, however, דמות takes a number of Greek forms.

Aquila and Theodotion partially mimic the MT with ἐν εἰκόνι ἡμῶν ("in our image" [= בְּצַלְמֵנוּ]), though Aquila retains the καί (Wevers, *Notes*, 15, n.48).

79. Gib., §118 Rem.2. In both 1:26a and 5:3a the Masoretic accents imply the presence of syntactical apposition between the words with the major disjunction (ʾatnāḥ) following. We also agree with Wildberger that the terms are not "essentially distinct statements ... such that they should be distinguished" ("צֶלֶם," *TLOT*, 3:1082).

80. That is, עשׂא [+ dir. obj.] + preposition בְּ.

81. For discussion of the בְּ-*essentiae*, see: Joüon, §133c; *GKC*, §119h. While Arnold and Choi appeal to the בְּ-*essentiae* to explain the usage in Gen 1:26 (*GBHS*, 106; so Merrill, "Image of God," *DOTP*, 443), Westermann is less convinced, preferring to translate "after, according to" (*Genesis*, 145); *DCH*, 2:84–85; similarly: *IBHS*, §11.2.9.b; Fishbane, *Biblical*, 352–53.

82. Bird, "Theological Anthropology," 261.

83. E. J. van Wolde, "Rhetorical, Linguistic and Literary Features in Genesis 1" in *Literary Structure and Rhetorical Strategies in the Hebrew Bible*. ed. L. J. de Regt, J. de Waard, and J. P. Fokkelman (Winona Lake: Eisenbrauns, 1996), 149.

Secondly, וירדו ("[so] that they may rule," v. 26b) following the cohortative (נעשה, "let us make," v. 26a) expresses clear *purpose*.[84] Divine intention for rule (רדה בְ ... וַיֹּאמֶר, v. 26b) resounds in audible blessing to rule (רדה בְ ... וַיְבָרֶךְ, v. 28b) on the earthly stage once humankind appears. God's unique image is a precondition for humankind's unique rule.[85] Verse 26b in both the MT and LXX are alike, suggesting to W. Loader "that the God-like aspect consists in ruling the world of creation."[86] This purpose is distilled in the representative agency of humankind who personifies "God's lordship over the lower orders of creation"[87] (vv. 21–25) and are also obligated to preserve the sanctity of their own lives (9:6). Rulership, then, emerges as the consequence of image rather than its definition, underscoring the responsibility of representation bound up in the Mandate.[88] The ethics of the Mandate are reciprocal and reflexive, administrative and personal. Yet Genesis stresses an "image-functional" over "image-ontological," though the pattern is analogous it is also qualitatively inferior.[89] The one who is modeled on the divine is, in turn, to model the divine to the

---

84. The prefixed verbal form with *wāw* conjunctive denotes *purpose/result* (*GKC*, §109f; Van Leeuwen, "Form, Image," *NIDOTTE*, 4:645; Stendebach, "צֶלֶם," *TDOT*, 12:394; Wildberger, "צֶלֶם," *TLOT*, 3:1083; T. O. Lambdin, *Introduction to Biblical* Hebrew [New York: Charles Scribner's Sons, 1971], 119; Dumbrell, *The Search*, 19; T. J. Meek, "Result and Purpose Clauses in Hebrew," *JQR* 46 (1956): 40–43; so Gen 34:23; 2 Sam 3:21). Regarding נַעֲשֶׂה, it is helpful to recall that 3rd-*hê* verbs do not distinguish between the cohortative and imperfective form, God's dialogue with the "heavenly court" informs our interpretation. Thus, the syntax portrays the phenomenological function of humankind more than the ontological constituents of image reserved for later inter-textual development (see Reichenbach, "Genesis 1," 61–64).

85. P. Bird, "Theological Anthropology," 260.

86. *The Septuagint*, 28.

87. Clines, "The Image," 101. K. Barth is right to highlight the relational element in image. However, the *Zeitgeist* of his time takes Barth too far when he claims that relationship constitutes the definition itself (= "thou"), whether between male and female or within community. As Childs assesses Barth, he emphasizes that "there is virtually no explanation of the term within the Old Testament," with Barth's notion surfacing after the OT period (*Old Testament Theology*, 97). Additionally, this not only exchanges an entailment (= relationship) for the broader constitution of the human person, it also ignores the function of image in Gen 9:6 where retributive justice is meted out for the destruction of "אדם-generic," not "אדם-gender" (*Church Dogmatics: The Work of Creation*, vol. 3.1, trans. and ed. G. W. Bromiley and T. F. Torrance [Edinburgh: T&T Clark, 1960], 182–206).

88. S. J. Grenz, "Jesus," 621.

89. Merrill, "Image of God," 443.

world.⁹⁰ Their divine origin makes their rule of the earth "God-like," yet localized as "landlings."

Additionally, the OT knows no hypostasis of the human person, but views personhood primarily through a demonstrable service that is relationally accountable.⁹¹ That is, the human being "is *a person in relation to Yahweh.*"⁹² Thus, like God, humankind rules through speech, identification in personal (pronoun) reference, exercise of authority, analogous creation (5:1–3), and capacity for choice (2:17).⁹³ In the words of McBride:

> This unifying image in humankind has a sacramental as well as an essential corporeal function: Adamic beings are animate icons; they are empowered by the "image" and its correlative blessing to be a terrestrial counterpart to God's heavenly entourage.⁹⁴

Thirdly, humankind is ennobled in this mission through a kingly pattern, imaged after God with a "mandate" to accomplish the rule of a domain. Dumbrell asserts:

> The description of humankind in Genesis 1 is in royal terms. The species is God's vice-regent, placed over all creation to have dominion over it and rule it. Under God humankind is king over all creation.⁹⁵

Theirs is not a dominion of power, but power for dominion, the commission is dignifying, but for divine reflection rather than human exaltation. According to Van Leeuwen:

> The vocabulary, the ANE parallels, and the royal language of Ps 8 (which does not use the term "image of God" but clearly presupposes it) all confirm that this dominion is to be understood in terms of kingship, which has been "democratized" to refer to all humans. The meaning of image, thus, does not lie in the mere

---

90. Bird, "Theological Anthropology," 261.

91. "Man is a compound that cannot exist without a body; therefore, one tries to preserve the body by embalming" (F. Maass, "אָדָם," *TDOT*, 1:78; cf. Gen 50:2–3, 26). Even the idiom for death, "gathered to his people," retains community orientation (Gen 49:33b).

92. Brueggemann, *Theology*, 453. Emphasis original.

93. Merrill, "Image of God," *DOTP*, 443.

94. "Divine Protocol," 16.

95. *The Search*, 19; idem, "Creation," 156. "The verbs indicate that humanity is seen as the ruler, one might say as king, over creation" (Wildberger, "צֶלֶם," *TLOT*, 3:1083; Bird, "Theological Anthropology, 262, 266; McBride, "Divine Protocol," 16; Mathews, *Genesis*, 169; Brown, *Ethos*, 44).

terms used, but in Israel's, or more precisely, the priestly tradition's, understanding of representative kingship.[96]

Within the context of the Creation Mandate, the commission amounts to royal investiture of humankind, divine image animates human mission.[97] Gen 1:26–28 contributes the notion of royal agency to a profile of humankind that includes priestly (Ezek 28:11–19) and prophetic imagery (Job 15:7–8). Common to all three roles is the function of an intermediary.[98]

Fourthly, image also pointed to the *place* of God's presence, for Adam, the garden-sanctuary of Eden. Specifically placed in Eden (Gen 2:8), it was the locus of divine presence from which one could only be "exiled" (3:23–24; cf. 4:14,16). Developing *ANE* notions of sacred space and portrayal of deity, Curtis states:

> The significance of the image did not lie in the way it described or depicted the god (though that was not totally unimportant); rather, it lay in the fact that the statue was in a place where the deity was present and manifested himself. Thus, the presence of the god and the blessing that accompanied that presence were affected through the image. It was the function of the image rather than its form that constituted its significance.[99]

McBride's explanation is also helpful:

> The peculiar purpose for their creation is "theophanic": to present or mediate the sovereign presence of deity within the central nave

---

96. Van Leeuwen, "Form, Image," *NIDOTTE*, 4:645.

97. Cf. Ps 2:7. Reflective of the Mandate terms in Genesis 1, royal imagery recurs in the narratives of Abraham and Joseph, defining *national promise* and *inception* of an earlier blessing. Abraham's "walk throughout Canaan" (Gen 13:14–18 [כָּל־הָאָרֶץ, 14; הִתְהַלֵּךְ בָּאָרֶץ with אֶתְּנֶנָּה, 17]) and Joseph's ceremonial "ride throughout Egypt" (Gen 43:41–46 . . . וַיֵּצֵא [מִצְרָיִם], 41]) נָתַתִּי ; also 46, וַיַּעֲבֹר בְּכָל־אֶרֶץ מִצְרַיִם ;45 ,עַל־אֶרֶץ מִצְרָיִם) is illustrative of such legal and royal investiture texts with clear description of "expansive," albeit international, domain.

Both the Mesopotamian and Egyptian texts viewed the king, more so pharaoh, as the "image" of deity (see discussions of Curtis, Van Leeuwen, Wildberger, Westermann, and Stendebach in the above literature).

98. Callender, *Adam in Myth*, 206.

99. Curtis, "Image of God (OT)," *ABD*, 3:390; Anderson, *From Creation*, 120–21; Schüle, "Made," 5–6; R. S. Hess, "Adam," *DOTP*, 18.

or the cosmic temple, just as cult-images were supposed to do in conventional sanctuaries.[100]

Thus, the image did not constitute God's real appearance, but His presence and primary activity vis-à-vis human function.[101]

For Gen 5:3, image-as-dominion is not the point; instead, 5:3 recapitulates "likeness" and "image" as Seth is in the image of Adam since "he functions both like his father and on behalf of his father"[102]—reversing the terms of 1:26.[103] Here, Adam is the point of reference, not God (cf. 1:26).[104] Within the theology of Genesis, sin has not defaced the image (5:3) or derailed the commission (9:6); image is passed on through filial relationship (i.e., father to son). Image retains its potent worth (9:6), since harming an image-bearer "injures the majesty of God"[105] as its Creator, denigrating his counterpart, the only creature capable of response.[106] Whether through divine creation (1:26, 27), human procreation (5:1–3), or community preservation (9:5–6), image reflects a relational dynamic

---

100. "Divine Protocol," 16. Similarly, it is worth noting von Rad's classic expression:

Just as powerful earthly kings, to indicate their claim to dominion, erect an image of themselves in provinces of their empire where they do not personally appear, so man is placed upon earth in God's image as God's sovereign emblem. He is really only God's representative, summoned to maintain and enforce God's claim to dominion over the earth. The decisive thing about man's similarity to God, therefore, is his function in the nonhuman world. (*Genesis*, 58)

101. Reichenbach, "Genesis 1," 61. The emphasis on "function" reflecting ANE concepts is common in recent literature, see: Walton, *Genesis*, 131; Sheriffs, "'Personhood,'" 17, for example.

102. Curtis, "Image of God (OT)," *ABD*, 3:390.

103. The following genealogy of Adam through Seth (5:3–32) signifies the initial installment of multiplication envisioned in the Mandate to Adam (1:28). Bird comments:

What this notice asserts is that the divine image identified with humankind at creation also characterizes successive generations. This distinguishing feature of the species is not lost or diminished, nor can it be won; it is a birthright. That it is immutable is brought out in Gen 9:1–7. ("Theological Anthropology," 264)

104. As Callender observes:

From the standpoint of the genealogical structure, to place God at the beginning of the genealogy, as the text has done, is to place him in the position of 'father' to Adam." (*Adam in Myth*, 33)

105. Ibid; cf. Prov 14:31; Jas 2:9. In the NT, Christ is identified with the image and he reigns preeminently (see Rom 8:29; 1 Cor 11:7; 15:49; 2 Cor 3:18; 4:4; Col 1:15; 3:10; Heb 1:3).

106. Stendebach, "צֶלֶם," *TDOT*, 12:395.

that transcends its earthly stage, yet is demonstrated through social ethics. On the one hand image is vertically defined by the Creator, but on the other, it is to be horizontally guarded for God by a human community that stands accountable to the "owner" and guarantor of sanctity.[107]

In sum, several observations on image can be made in light of the Mandate context. The "image of God" pertains more to authority and prerogative than physical resemblance per se, though a psychosomatic whole ultimately defines the human person, not one particular aspect.[108] Brueggemann claims:

> I shall insist that this physiology, which largely participates in the standard articulation of its ancient social environment, is to be understood as a way of speaking about the human person in order to say *theologically* what was important for Israel to say.[109]

The image (1:26, 27) serves as the judicial and royal authorization for humankind to perform the requirements of the Creation Mandate (1:28) on behalf of God as the Cosmic King.[110] "This means that the analogy between Yahweh's reign and human activity relates to the whole gamut of human 'being.'"[111] For humans, "imaged-life" is necessarily temporal, defined by a responsibility of stewardship that began as a breath-gift (2:7). Yet "image" also defines a contingent relationship, a physical and functional dependence of humankind upon God who gives life and delegates its jurisdiction.[112]

Through divine image, humankind possesses the moral vision and functional capacity to effect order on earth that is worthy of its Creator. In the image, both representation for dominion, and counterpart for

---

107. When Jesus asked whose "image" (εἰκών) was stamped on the coin, he established an *a fortiori* principle, namely, God owns that which bears His image; they were to give themselves to God (Mark 12:13–17; M. J. Erickson, *Christian Theology* [Grand Rapids: Baker, 1990], 515).

108. Van Leeuwen, "Form, Image," *NIDOTTE*, 4:644; Stendebach, "צֶלֶם," *TDOT*, 12:392; Curtis, "Image of God (OT)," *ABD*, 3:390; Schüle, "Made," 7. Goldingay states, "Human beings are souls animating dispensable bodies. It is not surprising that what they do to the body affects the whole person (e.g., overeating, overworking, sex)" (*Old Testament*, 99).

109. *Theology*, 453. Emphasis original.

110. Bartholomew states, "in the context of Genesis 1:26-28, 'image' clearly refers to the human reign over the creation that images Elohim's reign" ("A Time," 107).

111. Ibid.

112. McBride, "Divine Protocol," 16–17.

dialogical relation, merge. According to Clines, image is the only representative that is actually in spiritual union with the one it represents.[113] Representation and counterpart comprise a function initiated in 1:26 where image and dominion are joined. Through the Creation Mandate, this dominion is to be viewed as a blessing.[114]

The combination of 1:26, 5:3, and 9:6 creates a portrait in which "the image of God is a representative function transmitted through procreation."[115] Adam's creative work (5:3) mimics God's (1:26) in fulfilling the initial intent of the Mandate (1:28). This is an expression of personhood requiring guardianship and retribution (9:6); both the horizontal (5:3) and vertical (9:6) aspects are required for "image-life." All are "imposed" with life lest one should die. God has endowed humankind with a representative vocation to enforce order and claim dominion;[116] they preside as His "under-kings,"[117] his "sovereign emblem."[118] These three texts serve as prologue for the following biblical narrative.

Male and Female, Image, and Mandate

The controversy over "gender" vis-à-vis the image essentially emerges from Gen 1:26–28. Again, 1:27–28a proves to be crucial, both lexically and rhetorically:

---

113. "The Image," 93.

114. Zobel, "רָדָה," *TDOT*, 13:335.

115. Dumbrell, *The Search*, 18. Though Adam is exiled from God's garden-sanctuary, qualifying their relationship, the function of the image remains—to extend God's kingdom, even as Eden's rivers marched to the "four corners" of the world (2:10–14).

116. Grenz, "Jesus," 622.

117. C. G. Bartholomew and M. W. Goheen, *The Drama of Scripture: Finding Our Place in the Biblical Story* (Grand Rapids: Baker, 2004), 37.

118. Brueggemann, *Genesis*, 32.

Figure 7: 1:26–28

[DIRECT DISCOURSE—1st per]

Announcement: "Let us make humankind (אדם) in our <image"> (26a)
Purpose: "So that they (ו–) may rule . . ." (b)

[NARRATED DISCOURSE—3rd per]

A So created God humankind (האדם) in his <image> (27a)
Report: B in the <image> of God he created him (אתו, b)
B' male (זכר) and female (נקבה) he created them (אתם, c)
A' Then God blessed them (אתם, 28a*a*)

Blessing[1] **(formal complex stem)**: And God said to them (להם, 28a*b*)

[DIRECT DISCOURSE—2nd per]

Blessing[2] **(endowment)**: "Be fruitful and multiply . . ."

God's direct discourse within the heavenly court (1:26) proves a harbinger of theological intent and terms that are immediately developed in 1:27–28. Significantly, "the creation of humankind results from a dialogical act,"[119] language that fosters theological richness and complexity. Indeed, the trajectory of the ensuing narrative takes its cue from this vital portion.

Oscillating between direct and indirect discourse (see diagram), the narrator reports the *fact* of human creation (27a,b), but culminates with the *depiction* of genders in unity (27c). This distribution of lexical terms supports unified genders in אדם ("humankind").

As the structure reveals tight juxtaposition (1:26–27, see Figure 7), it is clear that: (1) the human being is made in God's "image" (1:26a, צלם), (2) this image is directly tied to ruling, (1:26b, רדה), (3) and image inculcates a plurality of genders, both "male" and "female" (1:27c, זכר, נקבה). God's following blessing to "them" (1:28a, אתם) recapitulates His earlier intention that "they" rule (1:26b, וירדו).[120]

119. B. C. Birch, et al., *Theological Introduction to the Old Testament* (Nashville: Abingdon, 1999), 49.

120. It is intriguing that all speech in this context is strictly God's; to hear either the heavenly court (cf. 1 Kgs 22:20–22) or the humans talk (cf. Gen 2:23; 3:10–13) would diminish the theocentric focus of Divine will in 1:26–31. Supporting this, God remains the subject in all three movements (1:26–30), and humankind the object; so too, in the dismantling of primary relationships (3:14–19).

Themes, Image of God, and Gender in Genesis 1-11

The ruling community anticipated at the outset (1:26b ["they"] וְיִרְדּוּ) is officially confirmed through an elaborate and corporate blessing at the end (1:28a ["them"; cf. וּרְדוּ, 28b]). Use of the plural pronouns ("us," "our," 1:26a) is matched by the pronouns at the close ("them," "them," 1:28a), resuming divine speech (see diagram). "Divine plurals" from the heavenly stage (= "our" [נוּ-]) initiate a *cause* that the "human plurals" *validate* on the earthly stage (= "to them," [לָהֶם]), bracketing the entire unit (1:26-28). Both the narrator's report (3rd person, 1:27) and the divine blessing (2nd person, 1:28a) confirm the accomplishment of the Creator's goals (1st person, 1:26b). The narrator's detail not only celebrates the Creator's success, it also informs the issue of "gender" (see Figure 7).

From this, several key points should be noted. Rooted in God's dialogue (1:26a), אדם initiates "stages" in the textual movement of 1:26-28.[121] This אדם refers to the category of "human being," "humanity," or "humankind" to which the individual belongs.[122] אדם carries the notion of humanity's position as a dependent creature on God.[123] The OT does not use אדם to distinguish one individual or group from another,[124] but for אדם in a particular aspect of its creatureliness; אדם is simply human, outside

---

121. אדם occurs 554x in the OT (such texts as Deut 32:8; Job 31:33; Hos 6:7; 11:4, and 13:2 make precise cognate determinations difficult). It is only used in the masc., sg., and abs.; never with suffixes. Next to Ezek (132x) the highest concentrations occur in Eccl (49x) and Genesis 1-11 (46x). Apart from Gen 16:12, it does not occur in Genesis 12-50. The majority (30x) of the Genesis 1-11 uses occur in chaps. 2 and 3 (where אִישׁ is used 2x; 2:23-24). The articular form (הָאָדָם) occurs 24x in Genesis 2 (all the occurrences in this chapter except 2:5). R. Rendtorff claims that the articular form has in view the first created man ("Creation and Redemption in the Torah," in *The Blackwell Companion to the Hebrew Bible*, ed. L. G. Perdue [Oxford: Blackwell, 2005], 314). It is used 14x in Genesis of relationship between human and animal.

Exactly where the proper name "Adam" (אדם) is first used finds no agreement in the translations: 2:19 (KJV, NKJV); 2:20 (NASB, JPS, NIV, NET, ESV, TNIV); 3:17 (RSV, HCSB); 3:21 (NEB), and 4:25 (JB, REB, NRSV, etc.). Aside from God's declaration (1:26a), the first anarthrous occurrence of אדם is in Gen 2:20.

122. Maass, "אָדָם," *TDOT*, 1:75; C. Westermann, "אָדָם," *TLOT*, 1:33; R. Rendtorff, "Creation and Redemption," 314. Unfortunately, the etymology of אָדָם remains contested (see Hess, "Adam," *DOTP*, 18; Maass, "אָדָם," *TDOT*, 1:78; Westermann, "אָדָם," *TLOT*, 1:31-33; H. N. Wallace, "Adam," *ABD*, 1:62, 63; V. P. Hamilton, "אָדָם," *NIDOTTE*, 1:262-64.

123. M. J. Paul, "Adam and Eve," *NIDOTTE*, 4:360.

124. Hess, "Adam," *DOTP*, 19.

all relationships.¹²⁵ The overwhelming emphasis in Genesis 1 is on the uniqueness of אדם as the appointed *agent* of the Creation Mandate.¹²⁶

The shift to the articular האדם ("humankind") in 1:27a in parallel to אתו ("him," 1:27b) suggests that זכר ("male") and נקבה ("female") in 1:27 are two types of the same generic human being (cf. אתם ["them"], 1:27c). Without reference to "male" and "female" the reader would intuit the gender of human beings.¹²⁷ However, with gender stipulation the narrator not only gives sexuality special weight but also anticipates their ensuing roles in the blessing (1:28).¹²⁸

This inclusiveness is confirmed by the narrator's subsequent report that "male" (זכר) and "female" (נקבה) were created (1:27c); rhetorically, an amplified expression corresponding to the preceding צלם ("image," 1:27b; see Figure 7). Thus, the closing reference in 1:27c to "male" and "female" functions to prefigure the events that follow.¹²⁹

Secondly, it is significant that אדם ("humankind") is explicated by זכר ("male") and נקבה ("female"), not איש ("man") and אשה ("woman").¹³⁰

---

125. Westermann, "אָדָם," *TLOT*, 1:34. "God's History with His People Does Not Concern the ʾādam" (ibid.).

126. Hamilton, "אָדָם," *NIDOTTE*, 1:265.

127. Loader, *Septuagint*, 29-30.

128. The LXX follows this shift with τὸν ἄνθρωπον, "humankind." This makes better sense than presuming a bisexual, androgynous, or even two persons for האדם. Rabbinic midrashim view the first human as a "golem" (= גלם), an unanimated lump of matter (Ps 139:16; cf. Job 10:10; E. L. Greenstein, "God's Golem: The Creation of the Human in Genesis 2," in *Creation in Jewish and Christian Tradition*, ed. H. G. Reventlow and Y. Hoffman, JSOTSup 319 [Sheffield: Sheffield Academic Press, 2002], 230]). That some would argue for man and woman being created from an original bisexual, or asexual being (around 2:23) is unfounded and historically naïve (so P. Trible, *God and the Rhetoric of Sexuality* [Philadelphia: Fortress, 1978, 17-23; M. Bal, *Lethal Love: Feminist Literary Readings of Biblical Love Stories* [Bloomington: Indiana University Press, 1987], 113-16; J. C. de Moor, "The duality in God and Man: Gen 1:26-27," in *Intertextuality in Ugarit and Israel: Papers Read at the Tenth Joint Meeting of the Society for Old Testament Study and Het Oudtestamentisch Werkgezelschap in Nederland en Belgie, Held at Oxford, 1977*, OTS 40 [Leiden: Brill, 1998], 124). Against such a reading, see E. Noort, "The Creation of Man and Woman in Biblical and ancient Near Eastern Traditions" in *The Creation of Man and Woman: Interpretations of the Biblical Narratives in Jewish and Christian Traditions*, ed. G. P. Luttikhuizen, Themes in Biblical Narrative: Jewish and Christian Traditions 1 (Leiden: Brill, 2000), 6-10.

That said, Trible wishes to avoid sexist assumptions and her use of rhetorical criticism brilliantly plumbs the "density" of the text to expose its complexity.

129. Loader, *Septuagint*, 30.

130. With איש decidedly used of particular individuals (427x), "Adam's" elation in 2:23 over the woman appropriately employs איש and אשה. He celebrates their unity of

Themes, Image of God, and Gender in Genesis 1–11

This differentiation of sex rather than individual (= איש/אשה) is important for at least two reasons: (1) its direct connection to the preceding image (צלם, 27a,b; cf. 1:26a), (2) and the generative blessing that follows (1:28a).

The former means that human sexuality, in its generative capacity, is fundamentally linked to the *imago Dei*,[131] key elements unspecified for the animals.[132] While "procreation is shared by humankind with the animal world (1:22, 28); sexuality is not."[133] As incest collapses family structures, bestiality collapses the created organization of creatures, blurring the uniqueness of an image-bearer. As such, biblical prohibitions intend to keep the categories of "male" and "female" distinct.[134] Among living creatures, humankind is the "great exception."[135] Animals may multiply "according to their kind" (למינה; 1:25), but humans, "according to our likeness" (כדמותו; cf. 5:3). In the latter case, this sexual distinction of אדם ("humankind"; cf. 5:1) establishes the crucial thematic bridge to the Mandate blessing. The narrator's specification of אדם (1:26a) as "male" and "female" (1:27c) supplies the necessary prerequisite for the Mandate

---

"shared flesh" (מבשר). While the narrator has defined the אדם ("human") relative to the אדמה ("humus"; 2:7; cf. 3:19; 4:11–12; 5:29), the man uses a similar paronomasia to define the אשה ("woman") relative to איש ("man"; cf. Sym ἀνδρός / ἀνδρίς; V *virago/viro*). Moreover, identifying the woman as a feminine "אדם" (= אדמה) would create a redundancy with the man's point of origin. For איש and אשה, the LXX employs τοῦ ἀνδρός αὐτῆς and γυνή, respectively. Unfortunately, this not only dismantles the MT wordplay, it alters the meaning with the genitive pronoun, "she is called *woman* because she was taken *from her husband*," anticipating the point of marriage in 2:24.

131. Childs, *Old Testament Theology*, 97.

132. I am not arguing here for the "gendered" nature of God as possessing "male" and "female" aspects, nor is this intended to address the ethical equality of men and women per se, ostensibly within a patriarchal society of the biblical world. Such issues must draw on more than Gen 1:26–28 (see Trible, *God and the Rhetoric*, 1–30).

133. Trible, *God*, 15.

134. T. Frymer-Kensky, "Sex and Sexuality," *ABD*, 5:1145]. Both sex with a daughter-in-law and an animal is called תֶּבֶל "(improper) mixing," "perversion" (Deut 17:21; cf. Exod 22:28; Lev 18:23; 20:15–16). Homosexuality (between men) is not labeled תֶּבֶל, but given the extreme prohibition of death (Lev 19:13; cf. 18:22).

135. F. Maass, "אָדָם," *TDOT*, 1:85.

blessing (1:28a).¹³⁶ The male-female model for sexual union is fixed in creation itself.¹³⁷

Thirdly, the Mandate blessing specifically states that: "they rule" (1:28b), but the route to this climactic sanction should not be overlooked. While the ruling (רדה ב) image-bearer is God's intention from the outset (1:26a,b), it is human sexuality (1:27c) that is medially juxtaposed to the image (1:27a,b). This sexuality (1:27c; זכר/נקבה) directly leads to the expression of fertility (1:28a; i.e., *endowment*), and closes with their "ruling over" (1:28b; רדה ב) the animals, a reiteration of the Divine goal (1:26b; i.e., *commission*).¹³⁸

In sum, אדם in 1:26–28 refers to collective humankind as "male" and "female." "God chose to create two different forms of humanity for different functions within his creation."¹³⁹ As such, the Mandate is given to both *man* and *woman*. The poetic repetition of 1:27b,c juxtaposes אדם (27b) with "male" and "female" (27c) for emphasis. It is their gendered identity that "embodies the potency of divine blessing."¹⁴⁰ Fertility through sexuality (= *endowment*) is crucial for dominion but does not itself define dominion (= *commission*).¹⁴¹ More broadly, אדם in Genesis 1–11 is plainly generic "humanity," with the individual "Adam" (5:3–5) viewed as an ar-

---

136. Bird, "Theological Anthropology," 263; idem, "Male," 349, 356. For similar reproductive emphasis vis-à-vis זכר ("male") and נקבה ("female"), see 6:19 and 7:9 where reproduction is at issue.

137. D. Wold, *Out of Order* (Grand Rapids: Baker, 1998), 8.

138. To be sure, it is their capacity for fertility that to some degree enables accomplishment of the Mandate. That said, a "ruling by mating" is reductionistic and hardly explains: the relationship to "image" (1:27a,b), the significance of 1:28 with its terms of governance, canonical context, royal ideology, and the theology of representation (see prior discussion of the 1:28 text plot).

139. Childs, *Old Testament Theology*, 192. Childs is attempting to realign distortions that either accentuate "*mores* of a fallen society into the kingdom of God" or "a modern egalitarian ideology which would simply identify the sexes in every respect with the same roles, goals, and capacities" (ibid. Emphasis original).

140. Brown, *Ethos*, 48.

141. The esteem attributed to generative fertility can be appreciated in Deut 25:11–12 where a woman injures an offender's genitals in a brawl between her husband and another man (cf. Exod 21:22–25; Deut 7:14). These injuries are associated with reproductive physiology, either impeding his ability to sire children or amounting to a breech of dignity. Such cases bring the penalty of *lex talionis*, having her hand severed from her body (cf. Lev 24:19–20).

chetype.¹⁴² In Genesis 2, "ʾādām who is representative man is instantiated in Adam."¹⁴³

As אדם ("human being") is tied to צלם ("image"), the emphasis in 1:26–27 is on male and female as a *composite*, not the "first couple" per se.¹⁴⁴ At two levels, it is clear that human gender does not define image. Firstly, its use in 9:6 as the basis of retributive justice is tied to a vertical assault on God's image and humanity in relationship with God¹⁴⁵ not a horizontal defacing of abstract gender.¹⁴⁶ Secondly,

> The sexual differentiation in 1:27 shows that being made in the divine image is not meant in the sense of a physical replica, for Israel's God transcends the sexual polarity characterizing the creaturely world.¹⁴⁷

God himself is not gendered and is never construed with a consort,¹⁴⁸ making the connection to image essentially a functional element in the Mandate and not one of ontology.¹⁴⁹ As divine intent (1:26, נעשה) culmi-

---

142. Paul, "Adam and Eve," *NIDOTTE*, 4:360. Gen 8:21 is driven by this representative sense of אדם, recalling the curse 3:17–19.

143. Childs, *Old Testament Theology*, 191.

144. Wallace, "Adam," *ABD*, 1:62,63. Such insistence is at pains to explain the "apparent discrepancy" to the creation of man and woman in Genesis 2.

145. The *ground of reason* follows the disjunctive ʾatnāḥ and the following כי clause: כִּי בְּצֶלֶם אֱלֹהִים עָשָׂה אֶת־הָאָדָם ("for in the image of God he made 'humankind,'" 9:6b); וַיִּקְרָא אֶת־שְׁמָם אָדָם ("and He called their name 'humankind'" ["Adam," HCSB; "man," NIV; "mankind," NET]).

146. The collective notion of "humankind" is emphasized by the use of אדם/ה 3x in 9:6 (5x in 9:1–7).

147. Stendebach, "צֶלֶם," *TDOT*, 12:394.

148. Sexuality is absent from the divine realm. God does not represent "male virility," nor is He imaged "below the waist." His relationship with "wife-Israel" is impassioned though not erotic. While priests were always married, strict separation of sexuality from sacred space was maintained (cf. Lev 15:16–18; 1 Sam 21:4–5; [Frymer-Kensky, "Sex and Sexuality," *ABD*, 5:1146]).

149. In the portions of Genesis classified as "P," the narrator uses "male" terminology for God, harnessing a use of metaphor that deserves further exploration in light of "female" terms occasionally used for God elsewhere (cf. Deut 32:18; Isa 42:14; 66:13). J. Oswalt makes a good case for the use of male terminology for God since both *transcendence* and *personhood* would be compromised with the standard association of fertility/sexuality of female deities who were "at one" with their creation ("Theology of the Pentateuch," *DOTP*, 849).

That said, the *Zeitgeist* of our time is reflected in the *SBL Handbook* articulating their concern for a standard of "bias-free language," meaning "gender-free":

nates in human Mandate (1:28; וַיְבָרֶךְ), "the blessing establishes the right of its subject to fertility."[150] אדם is the human being engendered, yet God's blessing to "them" dignifies and activates human sexuality, moving reproduction toward its goal.[151]

The combination of both צלם ("image") and רדה ("rule") means "this genus is assigned a special role within the creation ... but above all is given a special relation to God."[152] According to Callender, "it is most natural to accept the idea of ruling as an important aspect of image and likeness, and not as incidental."[153] "Man in marriage" is not taken up until Genesis 2 where אדם is used as an individual and proper name, Adam (2:20), the "male" partner (2:18).[154]

The Mandate in the Order of Creation

It is in the consideration of the Mandate in the order of creation, its inception and development within Genesis 1–11, that OT ethics forcefully partners with biblical theology. Whether confessional or not, how one views the Mandate constitutes a foundational decision within "essentialism," that is, the transfer of terms and concepts from one culture to another without distortion.[155] In this section we will consider several implications

---

The generic use of the masculine nouns and pronouns is increasingly unacceptable in current English usage. *The assignment of gender to God is likewise best avoided.* (*The SBL Handbook of Style for Ancient Near Eastern, Biblical, and Early Christian Studies*, ed. P. H. Alexander et al. [Peabody: Hendrickson, 1999], 17. Emphasis added.)

150. Coats, *Genesis*, 47.

151. Bird, "Male," 359. See Bird's helpful conclusion (356–61). She is at pains to separate the social from the biological aspects of reproduction in the account (1:26-28), a sentiment echoed by several other feminist writers (for example, J. C. Exum, "Feminist Study of the Old Testament," in *Text in Context: Essays by Members of the Society for Old Testament Study*, ed. A. D. H. Mayes [Oxford: Oxford University Press, 2000], 88–115). See Child's assessment of Trible's arguments pertaining to ʾādām and an original androgynous "earth creature" (*Old Testament Theology*, 189–91); S. Scholz's assessment of evangelical's analysis of gender: "The Christian Right's Discourse on Gender and the Bible," *JFSR* 21 (2005): 81–100.

152. Childs, *Old Testament Theology*, 189.

153. *Adam in Myth*, 29.

154. Both the LXX and V begin to render MT הָאָדָם as "Adam" in 2:19. Hess maintains that: "ʾādām is a title that reflects a middle point in the continuum from the general usage of ʾādām in Genesis 1 to the personal name Adam at the end of Genesis 4" ("Adam," 19).

155. J. W. Rogerson, "Old Testament Ethics," in *Text in Context: Essays by Members of*

under two heads: the literary logic of the Mandate within Genesis 1-11 and its theological significance. What emerges is the Mandate as a "moral vision."

The context of the Mandate is a Cosmic Creator in deep-seated relationship with humankind (1:26-27). Within 1:1—3:31, humankind is the apex of several divine "separations" (1:27; 2:21-22). In the words of C. Plantiga Jr., "God orders things into place by sorting and separating them."[156] The garden-sanctuary in turn defines essential bonds between human and ground, human and animal, man and woman, and the human pair with God (2:4-24).

A key aspect of the created order is the enlivening tension of this separation and binding.[157] With the creation of humans there is a fundamental binding to earth as its stewards (2:5b, 15), a binding to God through His image (1:26-27), and a binding of man and woman as perfect complements (2:24).[158] What follows this is a sketch of the "undoing" of creation's principal relationships (4:1—7:24) and the reissuing of the Mandate (9:1-7).

Through both terms and topic, Genesis 1-11 serves as a prologue to the ensuing Patriarchal History (Genesis 12-50).[159] This Universal History (Genesis 1-11) focusing on אדם (46x) covers thousands of years through twenty generations in a world overwhelmed by sin. Deadly responses to a Mandate of life begin to unravel the created order (cf. 4:8, 23; 7:22). Five

---

the Society for Old Testament Study, ed. A. D. H. Mayes (Oxford: Oxford University Press, 2000), 132.

156. *Not the Way It's Supposed to Be: A Breviary of Sin* (Grand Rapids: Eerdmans, 1995), 29.

157. J. Holloway, "'From the Beginning,' The Moral Vision of Genesis 1-11," *SJT* 44 (2001), 87.

158. Plantiga, *Not the Way*, 29.

159. Helpful in Genesis 1-11 are both T. Hiebert's discussion of "The Primeval Age" (*The Yahwist's Landscape*, 30-82), and S. Niditch's *Chaos to Cosmos: Studies in Biblical Patterns of Creation* (Atlanta: Scholars Press, 1985), esp. "Initial Creation and Ordering," 13-24. Both employ a rather epigenetic-historical approach, especially Hiebert, whose discussion is rather positivistic at times, focusing more on textual strata (e.g., P, J) than literary strategy. Discovering cultural parallels in the literature still does not elucidate the strategy of the biblical Hebrew author. For this reason, Niditch admits in her introduction that: "Genesis 1-11 is to be respected as literature, treated as a composition made of many narrative themes each of which has a definable structure of content and various levels of meaning" (3).

Be Fruitful and Multiply

genealogies serve as visual representations of restoration,[160] and move history toward a divine goal.[161] This is accomplished in a basic pattern of *sin-exile-restoration* in Genesis 1–11, written retrospectively as *theological etiology* for a nation "born" at Sinai (Exod 19–24). This pattern (*sin-exile-restoration*) will be played out in Israel's own history (cf. Mic 4:8).

If Genesis 1–2 establishes the model of human Mandate and divine presence (1:26, 28), this relationship is increasingly ruptured in Genesis 3–11 requiring the Mandate's eventual reassertion (9:1–7). The contribution of Genesis 1 is to equip humankind with a Charter intended to further the development and ordering God began in his garden-sanctuary.[162] This blessing is animated through unparalleled inter-relationship in creation: God's blessing with humankind (1:28) and humankind reproducing their own (5:2–3). Consequently, cursing functions as counterpoint to blessing (3:14–19), as is exile to installment (3:23–24; cf. 2:15). God's futility curses in 3:14–19 serve to personalize the downturn of the Mandate, both in fertility and dominion.[163] "The two who once reigned as one attempt to rule each other."[164]

Continuing God's creation through proliferation (4:1; 5:3; 6:1)[165] may reflect an aspect of design, but experiences of death (7:21–22) and barrenness (11:30) only highlight the Creator's power and the creature's dependence. Any advancement in fertility (15:4) or dominion (22:17b; 35:5) requires another act of God's blessing and creation. With such divine interventions a young Israelite nation could identify (Exod 1:9, 19). Among other things, the stories of Universal History (Genesis 1–11) were written to anticipate national appropriation of this Charter (Genesis 12—Deuteronomy 33). The moral choices of Cain, however, exasperate rebellion (4:8), turning "dominion" and "mastery" over to sin (4:7b;

---

160. C. M. Pate et al., *The Story of Israel: A Biblical Theology* (Downers Grove: InterVarsity, 2005), 31.

161. Cf. 2:4—4:26; 5:1—6:8; 6:9—9:29; 10:1—11:9; 11:10–26.

162. A point forcefully made by W. J. Dumbrell (*The Search*, 23–26) and most recently developed by G. K. Beale ("Eden, the Temple, and the Church's Mission in the New Creation," *JETS* 48 [2005]: 7–15).

163. Hamilton states, "Far from being a reign of co-equals over the remainder of God's creation, the relationship now becomes a fierce dispute, with each party trying to rule the other" (*Genesis*, 202).

164. Ibid.

165. The language of Gen 6:2 recalls Eden's transgression of God's vice-regents (cf. ראה, טוב, לקח; 3:6) as the subjects abuse royal power in some form.

Themes, Image of God, and Gender in Genesis 1–11

cf. 3:16b). Breaking even brotherhood (4:8), the farmer of the "ground" (אדמה)[166] kills the keeper of sheep, contaminating all spheres of God's original blessing (4:11). Not surprisingly, Lamech marks hope by relief from the "ground" (אדמה) God cursed earlier (3:17).[167] In the end, the reissued Mandate (9:1, 7) represents God's perspective of an earth cleansed through re-ordering more than Lamech's hope of toil removed. God's re-creating inaugurates a history conducive for life. According to Reventlow:

> God's guarantee for the cosmic order (Gen 9:1–7, including the protection of human life) is the presupposition for human history ... Israel's history, seen under the aspect of Yahweh's salvific actions, can be regarded, first, as the realization of מנוחה, the rest in the land in the form of an agrarian existence, embedded in the cyclic order of creation ... 'Israel perceived the structure of the world as the ultimate theodicy of Yahweh. If this structure fails, Yahweh fails, and nothing matters any more.'[168]

By the time Noah presides over a microcosm in the ark (6:14ff.), the various relational "bindings" between "all flesh" (6:13) have been dismantled in "violence" (6:11; חמס). Sin may have expelled (3:23; 4:16) and death destroyed (4:25), but the "seed" for a new world survives adrift in another watery chaos (7:18), one chaos (מבול) revokes another (חמס).[169] Noah is a *moral exemplar* for a refreshed world, a transitional name and role that casts him in priestly light.[170] The original relationship now survives in preservation (8:1), but gone are divine place, presence, and benediction of "good" (טוב). Silent during the cleansing flood, God never abandoned his relationship of blessing and invigorates life by renewing the Mandate (9:1, 7) in a post-sin, pre-Abrahamic world. Like Adam earlier, Noah's life is defined by the ground, a curse he can relieve but not remove (cf. 5:29).[171]

---

166. For a helpful discussion of "Adam" (אדם) related to the "ground" (אדמה) alongside *ANE* parallels, see Hiebert, *The Yahwist's Landscape*, esp. 32–41.

167. Among the key terms Lamech reiterates from the initial futility curses are עצבון ("pain," "toil"; cf. 3:16,17), arguably a hendiadys here וּמֵעִצְּבוֹן מִמַּעֲשֵׂנוּ (= "toilsome work," so NLT², HCSB). Lamech's speech (Gen 5:29) reveals his pathos, not a programmatic change.

168. "Creation," 164; also following Knierim, *The Task*.

169. For Niditch, "A cosmos floats on chaos" (*Chaos to Cosmos*, 23).

170. Mathews even calls Noah a "mediating priest" (*Genesis*, 394).

171. Though it is common to view the Noahic Covenant (9:1–18) as a "reverse of the curse," or a suspension, the flood actually went beyond the judgment of 3:17. Of 8:21,

Be Fruitful and Multiply

The covenant with Noah (9:8–17) is a precursor to later covenants in Israel's national history, covenants built on a Creator's promissory relationship with the world and the original "binding" of its life forms.[172] Thus, cosmic blessing antedates national blessing, setting the parameters for the universal influence of a nation called to "serve the world by her separateness" (Exod 19:3b-6).[173] More particularly, it is the Creation Mandate itself (9:1, 7) that in turn lays the foundation for the Cosmic Covenant through Noah (9:8–17). The biblical theology of God's blessing reissued to Noah (9:1, 7) portrays the Creator in some degree of accommodation, *recalibrating* the original Mandate for a new era (cf. 1:26–30).[174] McBride explains this covenantal development:

> Each such accommodation is sealed by a covenant. The primordial commission, which is at once solemn command and blessing, has precedence in this broad scheme of divine providence ... The five covenants ... are subordinate measures ... They are formal instruments by which supplementary decisions are integrated into the cosmic design of God who creates. These supplements are introduced to facilitate and sustain the efficacy of the protocol's benedictory commission, on behalf of all created life and in spite of demonstrated weakness in the human agents whose formation in the divine image is endangered but never abrogated.[175]

Wenham astutely points out:

> It is important to note the position of עוד in this sentence, coming after לקלל to "curse," not after אסף "do again" [= "I shall not curse the soil any further"] ... God is not lifting the curse on the ground pronounced in 3:17 for man's disobedience, but promising not to add to it." (*Genesis 1–15*, 190)

Mathews agrees, but his argumentation is connected to 6:5b rather than 3:17 (*Genesis*, 394).

172. T. E. Fretheim, "Which Blessing Does Isaac Give Jacob?" in *Jews, Christian, and the Theology of the Hebrew Scriptures*, ed. A. O. Bellis and J. S. Kaminsky, SOBLSS 8 (Atlanta: SBL, 2000), 283.

173. Dumbrell, *The Search*, 45. Against the notion of Israel's international "priesthood," J. A. Davies argues that Exod 19:6 represents an unparalleled relationship with God, unlike standard suzerain treaties in that Israel is the main beneficiary of the agreement. As such Israel has no mission among the nations since her priesthood expresses her vertical tie to God (*A Royal Priesthood: Literary and Intertextual Perspectives on an Image of Israel in Exodus 19:6*, JSOTSup 395 [London: T&T Clark, 2004]).

174. McBride, "Divine Protocol," 18. Emphasis added.

175. Ibid., 18–19.

Themes, Image of God, and Gender in Genesis 1–11

It is because of God's renewed blessing to Noah that Eden's original "binding" of human, animal, and divine relationships is dignified afresh—"all flesh" is once again secured within the created order (9:12).

This recalibrated Mandate to Noah must not only develop a reordered world, it must *sustain* it. To accomplish this, law is heightened (9:3–5; cf. 2:16–17).[176] God's discussion of animals in immediate proximity to new legislation for life (9:4–5) advances an earlier "ruling" (1:28b) by means of a "guarding" that treasures animal life along side the sanctity of human life.[177] This extension of human authority (9:6) refurbishes an old "binding" (2:19–20). Renewal is necessary to maintain Mandate stewardship, enabling image-bearers themselves to criminalize "violence" (6:13; חמס) that had earlier polluted God's cosmic temple.[178] Not surprisingly, the one found "blameless" (6:9; תמים), "righteous" (7:1; צדיק), and obedient to God's "command" (7:5; צוה) soon implements moral justice himself by cursing "Canaan" (9:25), the only time Noah speaks in the narrative.

The significance of a *recalibrated* Mandate is illustrated by brief reflection on the themes of *work* and *fulfillment* as they relate to the Mandate. These themes are played out in the wider trajectories of Genesis, with "work" located at the outset of the Mandate (Genesis 1–2) and "fulfillment" straddling Genesis 49—Exodus 1. Consideration of these not only fills out humankind's representative aspect in the Mandate, it also shapes the moral task bound up in the Mandate.

The Mandate is cosmic mission, and mission is responsibility. The theological thrust of the Mandate weds divine *instruction* with human *responsibility*.[179] God's instructions (2:15–17; cf. 9:3–4) establish boundaries that define Mandate stewardship (1:28; cf. 9:1, 7); law identifies relationship "as a tangible symbol of their moral nature."[180] Moreover, law shapes this moral order to reflect the created order, preserving God's own cre-

---

176. The statement of divine retribution for murder in 9:5: מִיַּד אִישׁ אָחִיו ("at the hand of every man's brother") is a direct connection to the death of Abel, Cain's "brother" (4:2a). Not only is "brother" used 7x in 4:1–11, but the narrator, Cain, and God all speak of אח ("brother"), and it is always "his brother [Abel]," highlighting Cain's responsibility.

177. A. Philips, "Animals and Torah," in *Essays on Biblical Law*, ed. D. J. A. Clines and P. R. Davies (Sheffield: Sheffield Academic Press, 2002), 135.

178. Ibid., 21.

179. Hess, "Adam," *DOTP*, 19.

180. Hartley, *Genesis*, 61.

ative work.[181] Thus localized obedience in the garden-sanctuary takes on both ecological and eschatological proportion through its cosmic effect. Here canonical trajectories come into view.

Mandate stewardship (1:28) intended localized work in Eden: לְעָבְדָהּ וּלְשָׁמְרָהּ[182] ("to work and guard it," 2:15).[183] The Mandate in Genesis 1 prescribed both כבשׁ ("subdue," 1:28a) and רדה ("rule," 1:28b) as obligations of humankind relative to the ארץ ("earth," 1:28a,b; see discussion). Gen 2:5 points to a core human function as cultivation ("there was not yet any human to work the ground").[184] The narrative scene of Geneses 2 confirms this connection in which *sacred space* is combined with *sacred*

---

181. T. E. Fretheim, *The Pentateuch*, 49. God not only remains the "Cosmic Artisan" in Israel's theology (cf. Psalms 8; 33; 104; 145), but Mark intentionally reflects this "good creation" (Gen 1:31) when he writes that "He has done all things well" (7:37, LXX).

182. The ָהּ suffixes on these forms are best taken as feminine with גַּן ("garden") as the *feminine* antecedent (so Dillmann, *Genesis*, 136; Delitzsch, *A New Commentary*, 137; GKC, §122l). For further support: (1) Song 4:16 contains the only unambiguous masc. use of גַּן, (2) gender is fluid in place names, and (3) the Hebrew phenomenon of *constructio ad sensum* (= according to sense; *IBHS*, §6.6.b). In this case עֵדֶן is an *explicative genitive*, specifying the proper noun (i.e., specific member of a class), appropriately translated: "the garden, Eden" (GBHS, 12; Gib. argues for עֵדֶן functioning adjectivally (§35a).

The proposal for הָאֲדָמָה ("the ground," 2:9) as the antecedent, is a less viable option since it is displaced from the immediate discourse (contra Hamilton [*Genesis*, 171]). גַּן־עֵדֶן ("garden of Eden," 2:15), is also a possible referent, but appeals to exception. In this possibility, the gender of the bound form is derived from עֵדֶן ("Eden" [f.]), not the head noun (גַּן [m.]); (Gib., §17a; *IBHS*, §6.4.1d, citing 2 Kgs 2:16; Isa 27:2; Ezek 21:21; Hos 10:1 as egs.; so Westermann, *Genesis*, 184, n.15a; Mathews, *Genesis*, 209, n.96).

183. The literature overwhelmingly identifies work with Gen 2:15 and 2:5, but inadequately explores its connection to the Mandate of 1:28. See Wilfong, "Human Creation," 46; Bartholomew and Goheen, *The Drama*, 38–39; Brown, *Ethos*, 138, 217; Birch, et al., *Theological Introduction*, 42, 50; Anderson, *From Creation*, 12, 131; Goldingay, *Israel's*, 118, 127, 220; Hess, "Adam," *DOTP*, 19; Beale, *Temple*, 66–70, 83–84; Hartley, *Genesis*, 60–61; Blenkinsopp, *The Pentateuch*, 64; S. R. Driver, *The Book of Genesis: With Introduction and Notes*, ed. W. Lock (London: Methuen & CO, 1904), 40–41; Mathews, *Genesis 1—11:26*, 209–210; Fretheim, *The Pentateuch*, 75; Dumbrell, "Creation, Covenant and Work," 160–67; idem, *Faith*, 2nd ed., 21–22; Turner, *Genesis*, 28; Gunkel, *Genesis*, 5–7; Greenstein, "God's Golem," 232; Balentine, *The Torah's*, 88, 236; J. A. Soggin, "The Equality of Humankind from the Perspective of the Creation Stories in Genesis 1:26–30 and 2:9, 15,18–24," *JNSL* 23 (1997), 24; R. B. Coot and D. R. Ord, *The Bible's First History: From Eden to the Court of David with the Yahwist* (Philadelphia: Fortress, 1989), 53; Gib., §107.

184. The verbs in 2:5 are preterites following the adverb טֶרֶם ("not yet," cf. GKC, §107c). This disjunction beginning with 2:5 is for backgrounding (cf. 1:2). Two causal clauses follow two negative (for explanation), concluding with a positive circumstantial clause addressing hydration (2:6; cf. 1:2).

Themes, Image of God, and Gender in Genesis 1–11

status (Genesis 1).[185] Royal language of the Mandate (1:28) now merges with priestly terms (2:15), but royal ideology runs through both chapters since Eden is God's, making Adam a divine servant.[186]

The literary logic of 2:5-17 shows that vv. 5-6 supply antecedent information for the narrative. Here, the אדמה requires the work of the אדם (2:5), lexemes specific to 2:4—3:24. אד (2:6),[187] a word for "ground flow," reveals the narrator's skill with similar terms, confronting the reader with another background issue of water (cf. 1:2).

The main narrative formally starts with 2:7 and ends with v. 9. It is in 2:7 that the lack of an אדם is formally resolved. Given the background of 2:5, God's next step is to create the garden designated for care by the אדם (v. 8), with a river supplying constant water.[188] In similar fashion, 2:10-14 supplies background information that sets up 2:15ff. While the setting in vv. 5-6 is necessary for the formation of the אדם, vv. 10-14 in turn capitalize on אדם (2:7) for the sake of distinct topography.[189]

The preterite of 2:15a (וַיַּנִּחֵהוּ, "place") functions *resumptively* (= "As stated . . ."). While הִנִּיחַ ("to place") is a semantic variant of the earlier שִׂים ("to put," 2:8b),[190] הִנִּיחַ contains some finer nuances in 2:15. As a form, הִנִּי(חַ) is the 2nd [B][191] of two Hiphil roots with the latter denoting "place (somewhere), set, lay."[192] Comparing this to 2 Sam 16:21, one reads: אֲשֶׁר הִנִּיחַ לִשְׁמוֹר הַבָּיִת "whom he has left *to keep* the house."[193] More than mere "putting," 2:15 views God *stationing* Adam *with a special task to*

---

185. Callender agrees, discussing the significance of this garden space (*Adam in Myth*, 65, 207).

186. Ibid., 59, 65.

187. Cf. *HALOT*, 1:11.

188. E. J. van Wolde, "Man and Woman in the Garden of Eden," in *Words Become Worlds: Semantic Studies of Genesis 1–11* (Leiden: Brill, 1994), 14.

189. A. Niccacci, "Analysis," 188. My structural argument has benefited from Niccacci's essay [175-98].

190. M. Vanoni notes that this term is used particularly with God's actions involving creation ("שִׂים," *TDOT*, 14:108). Its use in Gen 2:8 is a collocation with an adverb and prepositional object, a *causal-locative* connotation (240x, 59%; "שִׂים," *TDOT*, 14:100).

191. Cf. *HALOT*, 2:679.B; *BDB*, 628.B.

192. *HALOT*, 2:679.B, or "lay, set down, leave" according to H. D. Preuss ("נוּחַ," 9:277-86, 282; cf. Gen 19:16; Josh 4:3,8; 6:23; 1 Sam 6:18; 10:25; 1 Kgs 7:47; 8:9; 13:29, 31; 2 Kgs 23:18; 2 Chr 1:14; 9:25).

193. Cf.: "to take care of the palace" (HCSB); "to look after the palace" (NLT²).

carry out.[194] The instillation of Adam in the garden-sanctuary removes the second deficiency (cf. 2:5).

The cadence of 2:5–17 sees humankind created for the purpose of working God's garden-sanctuary in priestly fashion (cf. Ezk 28:13; Isa 51:3). The inference of Adam's *personal* deficiency, immediately observed by God (2:18), can be appreciated anew, in light of his appointed task; woman was also created to help in his stationed appointment (cf. "them," [2x] 1:28a). In this context, the fertility of the edenic land (2:10–14) assumes the fertility of the "edenic woman" made in its presincts.[195] This association is further illustrated when both (human and land) suffer the effects of rebellion to God's instruction.

The locution, לבדו ("by oneself") is clear enough in contexts of shared labor (cf. Num 11:14; Deut 1:9, 12; Qoh 4:9–12). But the addition of לֹא־טוֹב ("it is not good") heightens the gravity of the situation[196] and is only resolved after six verses (2:18–23). Again, emphasis comes in a wordplay: ʿ*bd* with *lbd* (vv. 15, 18). So Jethro counsels Moses: לֹא־טוֹב הַדָּבָר כִּי־כָבֵד מִמְּךָ הַדָּבָר לֹא־תוּכַל עֲשֹׂהוּ לְבַדֶּךָ... "this situation is not good ... for this matter is too burdensome for you; you are not able to undertake this by yourself" (Exod 18:17b, 18b).

In sum, a few points should noted. First, Adam's installation in Eden points to *positional* significance combining location with work. So pivotal is the garden-sanctuary that both the Adam's installation and banishment are recorded *twice* in their respective scenes (cf. 2:7, 15; 3:22–24).[197] The immediate context finds Adam "keeping and guarding" when he names the animals and shows voluntary obedience (2:15–19). Adam's place of service is the realm of the divine.

Just as Eden is God's garden-sanctuary, the prototypical temple, so the terms of "keeping and guarding" (לְעָבְדָהּ וּלְשָׁמְרָהּ) are used for priests who "serve" God in the temple and "guard" it from all unclean things.[198]

---

194. Niccacci, "Analysis," 188; based on his illustration.

195. Hiebert, *The Yahwist's Landscape*, 71.

196. Greenstein, "God's Golem," 236–37 following Gunkel, *Genesis*, 8; similarly, Gelander, *The Good Creator*, 23.

197. J. T. Walsh, "Genesis 2:4b—3:24: A Synchronic Approach" in *I Studied*, 373.

198. G. K. Beale, "Eden," 7–8; cf. Num 3:7–8; 8:25–26; 18:5–6; 1 Chr 23:32; Ezek 44:14; or Dumbrell, *Faith*, 2nd ed., 19–21.

Beale's description of Eden as "the first sanctuary in sacred history" (*The Temple*, 10), also "Adam himself was cast out of the Garden and did not enjoy God's presence anymore and lost his function as God's priest in the temple" (11) suffers from an over realized

This was instructive narrative for a young nation about to "build" their own tabernacle.[199] Adam's work is construed around priestly description for a nation summoned to be "a kingdom of priests" (Exod 19:6a). Even Mesopotamian kings bore the epithet *nukaribbu* ("gardener"), and *ikkaru* ("farmer").[200] ANE myths address rituals of *investiture* and *expulsion*, both intriguing and supportive of our findings.[201]

Secondly, there is a universality and timeless nobility to the work inaugurated in Eden that begins to flesh-out core aspects of the Creation Mandate *prior* to rebellion. Human labor was to be an exercise of human dominion,[202] assumed in the context of creation's development and renewal (cf. 8:22).[203] As Stassen and Gushee explain:

> The dominion/stewardship mandate (Gen 1:28) requires human beings to exercise responsibility over the creation. This involves various forms of work, which, after the fall became arduous and difficult (3:19)—yet work itself remains rooted in God's design for human life. Work reflects and advances human dignity as our vocations become an outlet for creativity, self-development and even joy, an avenue to contribute to the common good and as a means of providing for ourselves, our families and those we can bless with our generosity.[204]

Analysis of 2:5, 15 with 1:28 reveals programmatic connections: the presence of royal ideology commingled with the purpose of "keeping and

---

emphasis on Temple constructs, minimizing *ANE* connections to the "sancta." One wonders if Eden is so easily reconstructed. Mythical nuance would not only help explain the biblical language in key places but provides a better transition "from Eden to (the new) Jerusalem." This language is prototypical and anticipatory, drawing more on theological distinctions than ontological realities of architecture.

199. See Fishbane's helpful analysis of God's "world-building" as the pattern for Moses' "shrine-building" in Exodus (*Text*, 11–12).

200. Callender, *Adam in Myth*, 65, 207. Callender states, "This is the most substantial link with kingship in the account of Genesis 2–3" (ibid.). It is significant to observe that both Saul (1 Sam 15:5) and Elisha (1 Kgs 19:19) are plowing when they are summoned, tying royalty and labor to the offices of king and prophet (cf. Acts 18:3; 2 Thess 3:10).

201. Callender (*Adam in Myth*, 213) and Greenstein ("God's Golem," 235 n.86) both refer to these myths as illustrative of Genesis 2–3.

202. M. G. Kline, *Kingdom Prologue* (Hamilton: Meridith Kline, 1993), 69.

203. Interestingly, Isa 66:22 alludes to Gen 8:22 in form and function as both are cultic. The pre-Sinaitic (8:22) issues forth in the eschatological (Isa 66:22) regarding true worship on an international scale.

204. G. H. Stassen and D. P. Gushee, *Kingdom Ethics: Following Jesus in Contemporary Context* (Downer Grove: InterVarsity, 2003), 420–41.

guarding" is not fundamentally abrogated in their expulsion.²⁰⁵ The reality of rebellion (3:14–19) does not occasion a withdrawal of the Mandate mission or the high status given to work. "Service" seen in this light is a better term. As Fretheim states, "Gen 3:22–24 exhibits no change in the divine commission of 2:15."²⁰⁶ W. Kaiser agrees, stating that in 2:15 "the mandate is intact."²⁰⁷ *Degree*, more than *kind*, is the issue, as "caring-work" (2:15) now becomes "painful toil" (3:17; 5:29), horticulture was diminished to exertion.²⁰⁸ God was the Master-Workman from the beginning (Exod 20:11; cf. Ps 8:4). Likewise, humans truly participate in God's rule over

---

205. Sailhamer's observation that עבד ("work") and שמר ("keep") are formally separated in 3:23–24, depriving humankind of "worship" (שמר) should not be pressed too hard (*Genesis*, 45). For one, cherubim already exist, the designated "keepers" (שמר) of God's presence (Exod 26:31). Secondly worship is evidence of life (Ps 30:9), and is the first mutual activity mentioned of Adam's sons, arguably at Eden's "cosmic mountain" (4:2b-5; cf. Ezek 47:1–12), requiring no description of cultic procedure (see Fishbane, *Text*, 111–20). Cain's disobedience merely brings further exile from sacred space (4:14, 16). That such access/worship is nonetheless diminished is also reflected in Cain's shirking of *moral* השמר ("keeping") for his brother—what Adam forfeited, Cain rejected (4:9b). Thirdly, while the priestly exercise of humans lost proximate access to God's "Edenic presence," nevertheless, divine representation continues through the elements of רדה ("rule," 1:28b) and צלם ("image," 5:1–3). Fourthly, mention of "cultivation" consistently has אדמה ("ground") in view, before (2:5), transitionally (3:17–19), and after garden residence (3:23). In our opinion, Sailhamer's strong bifurcation of the terms does not bear out.

206. "Which Blessing," 284.

207. W. C. Kaiser et al., *Hard Sayings of the Bible* (Downers Grove: InterVarsity, 1996), 90. Kaiser also supports my earlier claim that 1:28 has been divorced from 2:15 in his comment, "'What, then, happened to the cultural mandate . . .' it is found not here in Genesis 1:28 but rather in 2:15. There Adam is given the task to 'work' the Garden of Eden and to 'take care of it'" (ibid.).

208. Sailhamer's desire to translate וּלְשָׁמְרָהּ לְעָבְדָהּ as "to worship and serve" (*Genesis*, 45, 47–48) is not only a naïve adoption of Cassuto's earlier proposal (*A Commentary*, 1:122), it is rife with exegetical problems: (1) it requires dropping the *mappîq* (so Hendel, *The Text*, 44) which does not necessarily achieve his ends (cf. *GKC*, §91e). Additionally, the alternative infinitives construct Sailhamer would have are essentially those of stative verbs, not active such as we have (*GKC*, §45d; cf. Joüon, §45d); (2) Sailhamer (and others) wishes to read a different Hiph root (נוח A, "cause to rest"; *HALOT*, 1:11), which is not the MT form with a doubled 1st radical, insisting this represents the original purpose for humankind (cf. *Tg. Onq.*); (3) moreover, this interpretation constitutes an aversion to "work" existing pre-fall, an ideology unsupported in the literature and an avoidance of the holistic concerns of the 1:28 Mandate. Behind the notion of worship is a desire to connect Eden with Israel and articulate a purpose for which the Garden no longer exists. Significantly, not one English translation has adopted the Sailhamer/Cassuto rendering nor do they even entertain an alternative translation as a text note.

creation in their creative-workmanship (cf. Exod 31:1–11).[209] Dumbrell captures this element of the Mandate, stating: work is not an end in itself but the means to an end which is our wider participation in the activities of the Kingdom of God.[210]

In duty, the Mandate requires the family unit, externally, and assumes the family unit, internally. "Through marriage and family God enables human beings to participate in his creative activity and redemptive purposes."[211]

The question also arises as to when or in what fashion the Creation Mandate is fulfilled within the OT.[212] While the question is appropriate, the answer takes us beyond our purview of Genesis 1–11 to its initial realization in the national context of Exod 1:7.

Our prior analysis of five text-plots (1:22, 28; 8:17; 9:1, 7) surfaced semantic patterns or "stylized components" (see Figures and discussion). This reaps benefits that validate fulfillment occurring in Exod 1:7. However, the Mandate "matures" in its transition through successive patriarchs. The Mandate's shift from Adam to Noah (9:1, 7) enabled its national focus to emerge from the cosmic with the characterization of elect individuals over mythic archetypes. The patriarchs illustrate a more personal and less cosmic stewardship, though worldwide reform is initiated on a different plane with Abraham. Moreover, the emphasis falls more on God's elective promises with the patriarchs, rather than the formative blessing structure in the early Mandate texts. God's presence is more opaque as Mandate stewardship (Genesis 1–11) "advances" to a stewardship of promises (Genesis 12–50). In the latter, for example, the global life of creation is more *beneficiary* than partner, a barometer of moral stewardship[213] rather than its primary arena.

---

209. A. Richardson, "Work," in *A Theological Word Book of the Bible*, ed. A. Richardson (New York: Macmillan Publishing, 1962), 287.

210. "Creation," 167.

211. Stassen and Gushee, *Kingdom Ethics*, 275, following V. Guroian.

212. See, for example, Kaminski, *From Noah*, esp. 124–38; Beale, *The Temple*, 95, 106, 265–66. This question also seems driven by a truncated reading of "command" for some imperatives in Gen 1:28 (= enablement), while minimizing imperatives of the commission, rather than understanding elements of blessing, relationship, and speech act (see earlier discussion).

213. Gen 18:17–19 is a powerful illustration of moral responsibility on the human plane working in tandem with divine promise. While Abraham bears obligation, the wickedness of Sodom must also be purged from the land if the impact of blessing is to be effective.

Be Fruitful and Multiply

The Creation Mandate gifted to Adam and Noah becomes a mandate of national creation for the patriarchs; obedience is not merely reported (6:22), instead, vast narrative units "flesh out" their moral ethos making the characters anything but "flat" (e.g., Jacob). Gen 1:28 is the theological impetus and pedigree for the commission reiterated to Abraham (12:2–3; 17:2, 6, 8, 16; 22:18), Isaac (26:3–4, 24), and Jacob (28:3–4, 14; 35:11–12; 48:3, 15–16), and ultimately to the Israelite nation itself (Gen 47:27; Exod 1:7; Deut 7:13; Ps 107:38; and Isa 51:2).

Exod 1:7 is strategic among four other texts (Deut 7:13; Ps 107:38; and Isa 51:2) that clearly define the fulfillment of the patriarchal promises in national Israel.[214] Yet it is also evident that this fulfillment never breaks loose from its creational moorings that serve as the local and eschatological foundation.

Significant elements emerge from the language of Exod 1:7.[215] Firstly, five lexemes directly tie Exod 1:7 to the theological stream of the Mandate text-plots (cf.: מלא, רבה, שרץ, פרה, and ארץ). Exod 1:7 "contains a very strong climax"[216] to this stream of terms.

Secondly, these shared lexemes all reflect the *endowment* within the Mandate, as commissional rule has already been granted through divine land promises to the patriarchs, and recognized early by them (cf. Gen 49:29–32 [Jacob]; 50:24–25 [Joseph]).

Thirdly, five verbs are employed to communicate a veritable population explosion (פרה, שרץ, רבה, עצם, מלא). Nowhere else do these five verbs occur together, a powerful expression only heightened by במאד מאד ("exceedingly"). "Density in population is a sign of YHWH's blessing."[217]

Fourthly, the use of שרץ ("swarm") is rather startling as it is only used of humans here and in the Mandate text of 9:7 ("teeming multi-

---

214. Beale, "Eden," 13, following N. T. Wright (*The Climax of the Covenant: Christ and the Law in Pauline Theology* [Minneapolis: Fortress, 1992]).

215. Note the layout:

ובני ישראל   פרו וישרצו
וירבו ויעצמו במאד מאד
ותמלא הארץ אתם:

"But the people of Israel were fruitful and swarmed/ and they multiplied and they grew exceedingly numerous/ so that the land was filled with them" (Exod 1:7).

216. C. Houtman, *Exodus*, HCOT, vol. 1 (Kampen: Kok Publishing House, 1993), 231.

217. Houtman, *Exodus*, 233 who lists: Gen 16:10; 17:20; Lev 26:9; Deut 1:10f.; 6:3; Jer 3:16; 23:3; Ezek 36:11, 37f.; Mic 2:12; Zech 8:10; Ps 72:16.

tude"), but elsewhere of animals (cf. 8:17b).[218] This usage sharply fits the contest where the Egyptians had a vermin-like fear of the Israelites (cf. Exod 1:12; 5:5).[219]

Fifthly, the tenor of Exod 1:7 most clearly echoes the initial Mandate to humankind in Gen 1:28. This combination of blessing theology and divinely-aided "swarming" "hints that the events of the Exodus represent a new beginning for Yahweh and humanity."[220] Exod 1:7 not only fulfills Gen 1:28, but is built on the promises made to the patriarchs.[221]

Sixthly, one should observe that Exod 1:7 is a "report" and therefore the *Formal Stem* of divine discourse is not needed, the other three elements are directly or indirectly present. The *endowment* has been successful and the narrative discourse celebrates it.

Propp list several reasons for this bald description of fertility:[222] (1) [practical]: only 70 had arrived; (2) [theological]: God is pictured as redeeming promises made to the patriarchs; (3) [ecological]: Egypt was renown for its agricultural fertility and Egypt is the place where the nation finally overcomes the sterility of her Matriarchs and Patriarchs who guarded the promises; (4) [political]: prodigious fertility worked as a threat to host Egypt, manifesting "the fear and dread" (9:2) intended to operate on the international horizon (see previous discussion); (5) [type-scene]: stories of barren women producing gives way to the temporary danger to the offspring (so Isaac, Jacob, Joseph). Israel belongs to this corporate "person,"[223] as her time of incubation in Egypt has come full term.

In sum, Exod 1:7 represents fulfillment of patriarchal promises because the language harkens to creation, God's initial venture on behalf of a dependant world. The Creator originally created swarming groups (Gen

---

218. For וישרצו, the *wāw* is *sequential*, emphasizing the result of a "teeming hoard."

219. W. H. C. Propp, *Exodus 1-18*, AB (New York: Doubleday, 1998), 129-30, following Knight.

220. Ibid., 134.

221. Contra W. Brueggemann who wants to view Gen 1:28 against the backdrop of the returning exiles soon to populate the promised land ("The Kerugma of the Priestly Writers," *ZAW* 84 [1972]: 397-414). Hautman also disagrees with Brueggemann, connecting Exod 1:7, instead, to the patriarchs (*Exodus*, 232-33).

222. Five distinct statements underscore this "fertility explosion:" (1) "fruitful," (2) "swarmed," (3) "multiplied," (4) "exceedingly numerous," (5) "simply filled" (J. I. Durham, *Exodus*, WBC [Waco: Word Books, 1987], 4).

223. Propp, *Exodus*, 134-35.

1:21; cf. 8:17).²²⁴ The theological trajectories of Genesis and Exodus cannot be untied—creation was redemption and redemption will be a new creation. In the main, the thrust of Exod 1:7 passes over Abraham to align with Adam in the Creation Mandate. It is the relationship begun with Adam (אדם) that Abraham reenacts in his faithful "walk with God" (Gen 17:1; cf. 24:40). Amid the Mandate mission, Abraham emerges through elective relationship for the sake of all אדם (Gen 12:3b).

Secondly, fertility highlights the Mandate's *endowment* (1:28a) since the national horizon is about to dawn when "subduing" will fulfill the *commission* (1:28b; 9:2). As such, fulfillment is at least inaugurated in Exod 1:7, to be completed with Israel's "subduing" entrance into the Promised land (Josh 18:1). When the "land of Eden" is redeemed in national conquest (cf. Isa 51:3; Zech 14:8), divine law will once again become operative:

> Israel at Sinai is in effect addressed as humans were on the sixth day of creation. In the law, Israel is given a task in the tradition of Genesis 1:26–28: have dominion over the earth. Mosaic law is a fuller specification of the law for a newly redeemed people, a law implicitly or explicitly commanded in creation. (Gen 1:28; 2:16–17; 9:1–7)²²⁵

Thirdly, the patriarchal stewards were bearers of a creation theme ultimately deposited in Egypt.²²⁶ With the stewards, there was no quick "fulfillment," only stages of a maturing promise. One such stage is Gen 47:27, where the Israelites "were fruitful and multiplied exceedingly." This text pointed to signaled fulfillment.²²⁷ But 47:24 uses modest terms and has only Goshen in view. Exod 1:7, on the other hand, applies Goshen's localized fertility to the entire country of Egypt.²²⁸ The Egyptians will experience the "anti-creation" that will effect Israel's grand redemption. Exod 1:7 signals that, once again, God is near.

If Gen 12:1–3 is transitional, closing Universal History and inaugurating Patriarchal History, Exod 1:7 is a receptacle of those themes of blessing and promise—they now "swarm" (cf. Gen 1:21). Yet Exod 1:7 is also transitional, pointing back to patriarchal fulfillment, on the one

---

224. P. Enns, *Exodus,* NIVAC (Grand Rapids: Zondervan, 2000), 41.
225. Birch, *Theological Introduction,* 158.
226. Kaminski, *From Noah,* 142.
227. Ibid., 143.
228. Hautman, *Exodus,* 231.

hand, and ahead in international scope on the other.[229] Moreover, if the climactic promise was to bless "all nations of the earth" (12:3b); one isolated group is now a "microcosm" reminiscent of Noah's endeavor, and poised to mediate blessing on the world scene.

God created a world dynamic in its order. His representative image-bearers act as agents for the betterment of creation entrusted them. To these moral agents, defined by royal status, the Creation Mandate is their map. These royal image-bearers are: (1) themselves embodied in creation—they are dependent, they are sexual, and bear creaturely responsibility.[230] Law's role was both preventative and preservative, enabling the Mandate's responsibility of representation. Royal image-bearers are also (2) embedded in history. Humans receive from the past and plan for their future necessitating moral responsibility. Neither passivity nor selfish-ambition qualifies as Mandate stewardship. Finally, (3) royal image-bearers are engendered in sexuality. By design and blessing, there is no neutral role; commission creates community and collective function—sameness with difference. These constitute the "moral task" within the Mandate, namely, representing the sovereign Creator on behalf of His "good creation" armed with His Mandate.

CONCLUSION

Our analysis of Mandate repetition isolated pivotal interplay between Genesis 1 and 9. Here we observed *event-renewal* at work, re-telling creational themes through and for theological discourse. Amid this substantive re-enactment surrounding these chapters, the author has successfully excluded all other material except that which echoes between them. In this way, Adam, through narrative typology, provides a "pattern" for Noah. This movement within Genesis 1–11 showed that sin was no longer localized as entire political groups are blighted under the shadow of a renewed Mandate. In spite of God's reissued blessing, human wickedness, yet again, assures the original "goodness" remains a memory.

Our investigation of image, focusing on 1:26 while considering 5:3 and 9:6, found its significance was broadly functional, yet to some degree multivalent. For the Mandate, image further supports the unique rela-

---

229. B. S. Childs, *The Book of Exodus: A Critical, Theological Commentary*, OTL (Louisville: Westminster, 1974).

230. The categories of J. Holloway, "From the Beginning," 84–87.

tionship between God and humankind; it is intermediacy through divine investiture. The relational orientation of "image" is reciprocal, fixing the human reference point in God rather than the earthly stewards themselves (i.e., reflexive and terminal).

Significantly, for the Mandate, image, as God expresses it in Gen 1:26, denotes *purpose*—the function of ruling as God's vice-regent. Image makes representative rule possible. It is a consequence more than a definition. Image serves as the judicial and royal authorization for humankind to perform their obligations set out in the Mandate—a power for dominion, not mere dominion of power. Furthermore, "image" points to the garden-sanctuary of Eden as the *locus* of divine presence; uniting divine will (1:26) with topography (2:8) and service (2:15).

Throughout Genesis 1–11, image not only retains its potent dignity (9:6), but it is passed on, in some sense, through procreation (5:3). It is image as "under-kings" that gives humankind both moral vision and functional capacity to achieve an order worthy of its Creator. While 1:26 carries notions of representation and counterpart, it is in these that function is animated in royal dominion. 1:26, 5:3, and 9:6 share various elements, the portrait of which defines image in Genesis 1–11.

We found that there is a tight interface between image and "male and female."[231] Key lexica and syntax of Gen 1:26–27 argues that אדם (contra אשה/איש) is composite "human being," dependant creature outside relationship yet the appointed *agent* of the Creation Mandate (1:26). "Male" (זכר) and "female" (נקבה) are two types of the same generic human being.

It is precisely in this gender stipulation that the narrator (1:27) points to sexuality as it prefigures their ensuing roles in the divine blessing (1:28). In 1:27, "male" and "female" (1:27c) amplify the preceding "image" (צלם, 1:27b). The semantic emphasis on sexuality (= זכר) over the individual (= איש) highlights the generative capacity linked to the image.

The male-female model for sexual union is rooted in creation itself—collective אדם is "male and female." Because אדם is the human being *engendered*, it is the divine blessing that in turn, establishes the right to

---

231. An important implication for men and women ethically has to do with the exercise of authority. There is great freedom alongside ethical obligation, but all actions are "in service" *for* and oriented *to* "mandating-purpose." Mutual servanthood defines freedom and unleashes gifting that brings, among other things, moral order to human community (G. H. Stassen and D. P. Gushee, *Kingdom Ethics*, 324).

Themes, Image of God, and Gender in Genesis 1–11

fertility. Divine intention for human "rule" (רדה) is enabled through the engendered image-bearers (1:26a,b).

The sexuality of "male" (זכר) and "female" (נקבה, 1:27c) is medially juxtaposed to the "image" (צלם, 1:27a,b), not only setting up fertility in the *endowment* (1:28a) but also the "ruling over" (רדה ב) in the *commission* (1:28b), a reiteration of the Divine goal (1:26b).[232] The engendered identity of men and women ensures the "potency" required for the Creation Mandate. While sexuality is crucial for dominion, Mandate-dominion is not itself a sexual enterprise. Sexuality has an accountable-function. Biblically speaking, there is no autonomous "sex life." For the Mandate, gender is functional and does not define "image" for life (1:28a) or in death (9:6).

Within the order of creation, the Mandate constructs a moral vision. The "goodness" of God's creational separations collapses under waves of human rebellion. The Mandate carries forward the Creator's design, but sin stymies the Mandate-mission by severing programmatic relationships: human to God, human to animal, human to human, and human to ground.

The renewed Mandate blessing to Noah (9:1–7) is God's gracious *recalibration* of lost equilibrium, evident in all strata of relationships. The Noahic Covenant has a foundational and sustaining aim, stabilizing human stewardship around the original "bindings" of cosmic life with a view toward God's redemptive program.

The Mandate is *cosmic mission* that requires royal responsibility. Here, divine law (i.e., instruction) sets boundaries for community under obligation (cf. 2:15–17; 9:3–4). Renewed law assures moral order reflects created order thereby sustaining God's creative work.

For Adam, Mandate stewardship was temporally oriented through localized obedience in God's garden-sanctuary, an obedience that included physical service within a priestly context. Mandate stewardship included work described in Gen 2:15 relative to Eden. "To work and guard it" (לעבדה ולשמרה, 2:15) captures the harnessing of resources encountered fifteen verses earlier in כבש ("subdue") and רדה ("rule"), royal and priestly language (cf. Num 3:7–8). These were obligations with the

---

232. The occurrence of אדם is uniquely clustered in Genesis 1–11 (see previous discussion) with 1:26; 5:2; 6:1; and 9:5–6 being crucial uses (cf. איש/אשה with sg./pl. interplay used in the "dissolve" of their relationship in Genesis 3).

earth (ארץ) in view. With *inanimate* objects such as "ground" (אדמה), עבד ("work") means to work on, develop, and cultivate.²³³

Thus, Adam's instillation (2:15) combined location with work in God's garden-sanctuary, significant narrative for the Israelite nation needing to "build" their tabernacle and "subdue" their enemies. The Creation Mandate required the inauguration of work in Eden itself (2:5, 15). Human labor was a core performance of dominion. However, banished from God's presence, Adam's caring-work of horticulture was reduced to the painful-toil of exertion. The context of Adam's service (עבד, 2:15; 3:17) must now run its course in the ground worked *outside* Eden (עבד, 3:23; cf. 4:2).

Our analysis also revealed that Exod 1:7 represents the ostensible "fulfillment" of the Mandate through the patriarchal promises, employing the language of creation (1:21; 8:17).²³⁴ As such, a fulfillment matures in Egypt (Exod 1:7) and will be fully realized with Israel's "subduing" entrance into the land. The patriarchs, themselves covenant stewards, sustained the Mandate mission through successive stages. Exod 1:7 is a receptacle of Mandate blessing, fulfilling its inter-textual trajectory.

---

233. H. Ringgren, "עָבַד," *TDOT*, 10:382.

234. Just what numerical count one can justifiably attach to the Israelites in Egypt at this time is beyond our discussion (J. J. Davis claims around two million, in *Moses and The God's of Egypt: Studies in Exodus*, 2nd ed. [Grand Rapids: Baker, 1986], 52). Our point is taking notice of theological themes borne out through lexical repetition.

6

Key Currents in the History of Interpretation

INTRODUCTION

THE EXEGETICAL ANALYSIS SURROUNDING the Creation Mandate is aided by investigation into the history of interpretation. Against the backdrop of exegetical theology that focused on five text-plots in the MT (chaps. four, five), we now turn our attention to the contribution of key "historical currents" essentially revolving around Judaism and rooted in the OT Scriptures.

The combination of culture and *Zeitgeist* reveal unique hermeneutical interests that have interacted with the Creation Mandate (Gen 1:28). Chapter six will summarize key strands, from *ANE* literature to Rabbinics, all of which relate with the Creation Mandate in some form.

CONTRIBUTION OF ANE LITERATURE

In Mesopotamia alone, the passage of over two millennia meant that "Mesopotamian cities developed substantial literary traditions,"[1] much of which was stored in state archives. Whether trade letters or cultic documents, the value and popularity of this literature largely survived into the Hellenistic period.[2]

Looking at Gen 1:28, *ANE* literature, including mythological elements,[3] are prevalent enough to study alongside the biblical creation text. The organizational focus between *ANE* and the biblical text is some-

---

1. N. P. Lemche, *Prelude to Israel's Past: Background and Beginnings of Israelite History and Identity*, trans. E. F. Maniscalco (Peabody: Hendrickson, 1998), 154.

2. Ibid.

3. See Batto, *Slaying the Dragon*, esp. "The Yahwist's Primeval Myth," 41–71; Mullen, *Ethnic Myths*, 87–122.

what generic. It is, for example, in the non-combative nature of God's creation, the *reason* for humankind's creation, the existence of the image of God, etc., where the biblical text stands out. Israel's connection to her *ANE* environment was cosmological; her departure was *theological*.

Myth was integral to *ANE* literature and essentially functioned to *explain*,[4] affording a ritualized accessibility to the transcendent; as such, it was also performative. G. B. Caird states:

> [myth committed] its adherents to a pattern of life ... a fund of powerfully emotive language on which creative thinkers could draw "along morally persuasive lines," to lead their people into ever deepening appreciation of the significance of their national history.[5]

What the biblical text shares with its *ANE* counterparts is, in large measure, the dynamism of myth.

Concerning "time" and history, myth is tied to Israel's own history and reaches even farther back into the cosmic framework of Divine acts, all of which remain firmly *historical*. The creation account enveloping the Mandate, views time as necessarily preceding both space and status, rooting Israel's national experience *in* history.

Regarding origins, comparison to *ANE* texts confirms that the future never actually "breaks free" of the past, but is defined by it, giving vital perspective and identity to life in the present. There is a continuity of meaning between primordial acts and future fulfillment, "between the *Urzeit* of origins and the *Endzeit* of hope."[6] Myth served to guard the aspirations and expectations of that people group.

It is with creation and origins that the greatest affinity to *ANE* literature is seen. Whether one considers the Babylonian myth of *Enuma Elish*[7] with Marduk, the god of cosmic order, doing battle with Tiamat, the ocean monster, or *Ras Shamra*[8] where Leviathan is the ocean monster in Canaanite mythology, or the Babylonian cosmological epic of Atrahasis[9]

---

4. J. Ellull, *The New Demons*, trans. C. E. Hopkins (New York: Seabury, 1975), 93–94.

5. *The Language*, 224, 232.

6. Fishbane, *Biblical*, 356.

7. 12th century BC (B. R. Foster, "Epic of Creation," *COS*, 1:390–402).

8. In this, twelve kings of Ugarit have been identified by name, covering the 18th to 13th centuries BC (M. Yon, "Ugarit," trans. S. Rosoff, D. Pardee, and P. Bordreuil, *ABD*, 4:695–721).

9. Seventeenth century BC (B. R. Foster, "ATRA-HASIS," *COS*, 1:450–53).

and its depiction of creation in early human history; common to all such *ANE* creation stories is a coherent articulation of forces acting upon the visible world.[10] Several documents give some illustration.

An excerpt from the Memphite Theology reads:

> So were the *male life-principles* made and the *female life-principles* set in place—they who make all food and every *offering* through ...[11]

This document not only stipulates the male and female, it alludes to their worship obligations. From the Instruction of Merikare, one also reads:

> Well tended is mankind—god's cattle,
> He made *sky and earth for their sake*,
> He subdued the *water monster*,
> He *made breath* for their noses to live.
> They are *his images*, who came from his body,
> He shines in the sky for their sake;
> *He made for them plants and cattle*,
> *Fowl and fish to feed them* ...
> He has *built his shrine around them* ...
> He made for them *rulers in the egg*,
> Leaders to raise the back of the weak ...
> *Do not neglect my speech*,
> Which lays down all *the laws of kingship*,
> Which instructs you, *that you may rule the land* ...[12]

This text not only includes a reference to the primordial monster defeated in creation, but mentions many other recognizable elements: "sky and earth," "breath," "his images," "plants, cattle, fowl, fish," "shrines," "speech," and "kingship" alongside "law." Similarly, the document of Enki and Ninmah reads:

---

10. Regarding creation and the flood, see also: "Eridu Genesis," "Enki and the Ordering of the World," "Enki," "Ninmakh," and the "Creation of Humankind," "Baal Cycle," "Heliopolis Pyramid Text," "Memphis Creation Story," and "Song of Ullikummi" (B. T. Arnold and B. E. Beyer, *Readings from the Ancient Near East*, EBS [Grand Rapids, Baker, 2002], 13–70; also, J. H. Walton, *Ancient Israelite Literature in its Cultural Context: A Survey of Parallels Between Biblical and Ancient Near Eastern Texts*, LBI [Grand Rapids: Zondervan, 1990], 19–44).

11. J. P. Allen, COS, 1:21–23, esp. 22, Col 56–58. Emphasis added.

12. M. Lichtheim, COS, 1:61–66, esp. 65–66, Col 130–35. Emphasis added.

> [Thus(?)] *she created mankind*
> *ma[le and female(?)* ...].
> By the male inseminating [the female(?)]
> mankind [will beget(?)] an *offspring*,[13]

Another document with intriguing parallels is the Mesopotamian *mīs pī* ritual or incantation text, known as the "washing" or "opening of the mouth."[14] This ritual describes stages of making a divine image (i.e., *alādu*, "being born"), beginning with a material object, then a statue, with its culmination in the image of a living deity.[15] Schüle outlines the steps as: (1) "in the workshop," (2) "to the river," (3) "in the garden," and (4) "to the Temple."[16] With core similarities, the biblical account differs in that the creation of woman is also included; moreover, the couple eats from the tree in the garden.[17] The "instillation for service" (Gen 2:15) may reflect this same notion.

These texts are not only reminiscent of God making male and female (Gen 1:26–27), but also of His food provision (Gen 1:29–30) and the formation of man (Gen 2:7; cf. 2:5). That said, the *ANE* texts see a slave in humankind and therefore lack the royal dignity attributed to the humankind in Genesis vis-à-vis God's "image" (Gen 1:26–27).

Additionally, both Canaanite and Mesopotamian cosmologies portray creation through violence and destruction,[18] a significant departure from the stayed momentum and order of the Genesis creation account. Even the Mesopotamian hero, Utnapishtim receives immortality rather than regency. Compared to the biblical account of Noah (Gen 9:1–7), Utnapishtim is removed from meaningful agency in human society. Noah, on the other hand is to be intentionally resourceful and fertile.[19]

---

13. J. Klein, *COS*, 1:516–18, esp. 517, Col 38–39. Emphasis added.

14. Schüle, "Made," 11–14; also Greenstein, "God's Golem," 225–26; T. Jacobsen, "The Graven Image" in *Ancient Israelite Religion: Essays in Honor of F. M. Cross*, ed. P. D. Miller, Jr., P. D. Hanson, and S. D. McBride (Philadelphia: Fortress, 1987), 15–32.

15. Ibid., 11.

16. Ibid., 13.

17. Ibid., 14. Schüle minimizes the comparative role of the biblical tree. Like the Most Holy Place, the tree is not only in the middle of the garden, and thus controlling it, but is directly associated with the tabernacle implements (Wenham, *Genesis 1–15*, 62–64).

18. See the discussion of Thompson, particularly regarding the *Akitu*-festival in the Babylonian epic ("Kingship," 168–77).

19. Sarna, *Genesis*, 60.

Key Currents in the History of Interpretation

SEPTUAGINT WITNESSES

M. Hengel calls the Septuagint "the first complete and pre-Christian 'commentary' to the Old Testament,"[20] utterly formative for the early church. But Hengel nevertheless laments:

> Due to the overwhelming orientation toward the original Hebrew text of the Old Testament and the Greek text of the New Testament, larger related passages in the Septuagint, let alone one or more books, are seldom read with the aim of ascertaining their style, translation technique and historical locus.[21]

The challenges the Septuagint poses for the exegete are daunting and no uniform approach to the *LXX* has emerged, to say nothing of understanding its translation technique and exegesis.[22] Jobes and Silva recommend ascertaining the "interpretative bias" of the translators under three heads: (1) the theological influence of translators' time, (2) the translators' respect for the oral tradition that had developed in tandem with Scripture, and (3) the social and political pressures of the translators' era that motivated an actualization of Scripture.[23] Similarly, Tov lists: (1) theological exegesis, (2) midrash-type exegesis, and (3) actualizations.[24] According to N. F. Marcos, "we find reflected in the *LXX* a whole gamut of translation techniques which run from literal translation (including transliteration) to paraphrase."[25]

Against this backdrop, Tov believes that the significance of the *LXX* for biblical studies lies in "the fact that it reflects a greater variety of important variants than all the other translations put together."[26] He states:

---

20. *The Septuagint as Christian Scripture: Its Prehistory and the Problem of Its Canon*, trans. M. E. Biddle (Grand Rapids: Baker, 2002), xi.

21. Ibid.

22. A theoretical linguist, J. M. Hoffman observes three areas where "the *LXX* completely fails to confirm" key aspects of the Masoretic system: (1) in the Masoretic stop/fricative, (2) Masoretic vowels, and (3) the Masoretic distinction between consonantal and vocalic *wāw* (*In the Beginning: A Short History of the Hebrew Language* [New York: New York University Press, 2004], 90–102).

23. *Invitation to the Septuagint* (Grand Rapids: Baker, 2000), 93–101.

24. "The Septuagint" in *Mikra*, 176–78.

25. *The Septuagint in Context: Introduction to the Greek Versions of the Bible*, trans. W. G. E. Watson (Leiden: Brill, 2000), 22–26.

26. *Textual Criticism*, 142; cf. 14, 15.

The *LXX* also reflects much important information about the exegesis of its translators. Some books are of particular importance in this regard since their exegetical traditions reveal much about the cultural and intellectual background of their translators.[27]

In sum, Tov sees the translators' exegesis comprised of both *linguistic* and *exegetical* components.[28] In Wevers opinion, the *LXX* of Genesis should be viewed "as an exegetical document."[29] Just what "exegetical" means would require extended explanation as the translators' work involved complex issues through an extended period of text production, all of which moves beyond mere "divergence." While some scholars see platonic influence[30] and others targumic paraphrase,[31] most acknowledge that where the *LXX* differs from the MT, the text of the DSS can often be validated.[32]

Our analysis of the Mandate texts and the image of God interacted substantially with *LXX* variants, but largely for text-critical purposes (see chapter four). Here we will distill some of the translation techniques observable in the *LXX* text of Genesis,[33] noting a key illustration.

According to J. Cook's analysis of *LXX* Genesis 1–11, the translator was relatively literal, though neither slavish nor free in his work.[34] While

---

27. "Some Thoughts on a Lexicon of the Septuagint" in *The Greek and Hebrew Bible: Collected Essays on the Septuagint* (Leiden: Brill, 1999), 95–108, esp. 95.

28. "The Septuagint," *Mikra*, 173.

29. *Notes*, xx, cf. xxi.

30. Loader, *The Septuagint*, esp. 5–25.

31. Marcos, citing a Leipzig lecture of R. Kittel who stated that the *LXX* amounted to theological commentary (*Septuagint*, 23, n.18).

32. C. A. Evans, *Noncanonical Writings and New Testament Interpretation* (Grand Rapids: Hendrickson, 1992), 73. Evans also notes many *LXX* readings are reflected in the NT, which follows the *LXX* over the MT in over half of occurrences (ibid., 73–74).

33. See, S. P. Brock, C. T. Fritsch and S. Jellicoe, *A Classified Bibliography of the Septuagint* (Leiden: Brill, 1973), esp. 98–100; E. Tov, *The Greek*, esp. "The Rabbinic Tradition Concerning the 'Alterations' Inserted into the Greek Translation of the Torah and their Relation to the Original Text of the Septuagint" (1–20), "Greek Words and Hebrew Meanings" (109–28), "The Impact of the Septuagint Translation of the Torah on the Translation of the Other Books" (183–94), and "The Nature and Study of the Translation Technique of the Septuagint" (239–46); T. V. Evans, *Verbal Syntax in the Greek Pentateuch* (Oxford: Oxford University Press, 2001).

34. "The Exegesis of the Greek Genesis," in *VI Congress of the International Organization for Septuagint and Cognate Studies*, ed. C. E. Cox (Atlanta: Scholars Press, 1986), 97. According to Cook, Genesis has one of the fewest quantities of "minuses," only 48

Key Currents in the History of Interpretation

examples could be given for *transpositions/inversions, additions/omissions, explicative/harmonizing* or *theological exegesis*,[35] we find an apt illustration of *harmonizing* or *leveling* of distinct elements in the *LXX* of Gen 2:18-24. As such we approach the *LXX* as a translation vis-à-vis the MT rather than a base source.[36]

In the formation of the woman (Gen 2:18-23), the *LXX* echoes Gen 1:26-27 in a startling way. The MT עֵזֶר כְּנֶגְדּוֹ ("a helper corresponding to him," 2:18, 20) is rendered in the *LXX* as βονθὸς κατ' αὐτόν ("a helper like him," 2:18). But the same MT phrase in 2:20 finds the *LXX* rendering βονθὸς ὅμοιος αὐτ ͡ ("a helper similar to him"), a stronger phrase. Both "like him" (= κατ' αὐτόν) and the more emphatic "similar to him" (= ὅμοιος αὐτῷ) are cast as a fulfillment of 1:26-27 where a dual κατὰ phrase is employed (see chapter 4).

This connection of *LXX* 2:18-23 with 1:26-27 is confirmed in the *LXX*'s "leveling" of אֶעֱשֶׂה ("I will make," 2:18) for ποιήσωμεν ("Let us make"), thereby mirroring 1:26.[37] Moreover, the *LXX*'s use of ποιέω ("do, make") over πλάσσω ("form, mold") only underscores the connection to Gen 1:26. Thus, not only is there a shift from the singular (MT, 2:18) to the plural (*LXX*, 1:26), but the generic ἄνθρωπος ("human being," 2:24) was chosen instead of ἀνήρ (= אִישׁ, 2:24), likewise in keeping with 1:26, 27 (ἄνθρωπον).

These lexical choices of the *LXX* translators are used retrospectively to Genesis 1, but not to avoid any misunderstanding,[38] but as part of the "leveling" or attuning of Genesis 2 with Genesis 1 in the *LXX*.[39] Both Loader and Tov help explain the exegetical and methodological significance:

> The result is that the forming of the woman is being set more closely in parallel to the creation of ἄνθρωπος in 1:26. That, in turn, creates an analogy. As ἄνθρωπος, understood as the male, is in the likeness of God (but subordinate), so the woman is in the

---

in Genesis 1-11 (345 for the book), but substantially more "pluses" with 193 in Genesis 1-11 (800 for the book; ibid., 98-99).

35. See ibid., 100-109; Tov, *The Greek*, 257-69.
36. Tov, *The Greek*, 260.
37. Cook, "Exegesis," 105.
38. Contra, Cook, 113.
39. Loader, "Septuagint," 35. Marcos notes that Symmachus' translation of Gen 1:27 plays down anthropomorphism related to deity and avoids comparisons between God and man (*Septuagint*, 131; cf. n.34).

likeness of the male (and, by implication and analogy, subordinate in the chain of being) . . . because the need is seen as relating to this particular male, *LXX* uses the name, "Adam," in 2:20, whereas in 2:18 it had used ἄνθρωπος. Adam is the ἄνθρωπος of 1:26 who now has someone in his likeness beside him . . . By implication as man seeks oneness with God, so woman seeks oneness with man.[40]

Tov helpfully notes:

In a way, all forms of exegesis might be called "contextual exegesis," because the translators' concept of "context" was wider than ours. They referred to the relationship between not only in their immediate, but also in remote contexts. Furthermore, the translation might contain any idea the source text called to mind . . . Most exegetical elements, however, are reflected in the lexical choices themselves, which were influenced by the immediate context and the conceptual world of the translators.[41]

ARAMAIC WITNESSES

In biblical studies, the Targumim[42] constitute early Jewish interpretative translations[43] of the Bible into Aramaic.[44] According to Tov, Aramaic *trgm*, means "explanation, commentary, and even translation."[45] Alexander states, "The root *trgm*, then like Gk *hermēneuō*, Lat *interpretor*, and English

---

40. Ibid., 35–36, 120. Loader concludes:

All of this lent itself to being interpreted according to Platonic models of thought so that Genesis 1 depicts either the creation of ideas or the creation of each genus, after which the second account describes the concretization. (Ibid., 120)

41. "The Septuagint," 173, 174.

42. To the Pentateuch, include: Onqelos [*Tg. Onq.*], Pseudo-Jonathan [*Tg. Ps.-J.*; Jerusalem Targum I/Targum Yerushalmi], Fragment Targum [*Frg. Tg.*; Jerusalem Targum II,III], Vatican Neofiti I [*Tg. Neof.*], Cairo Genizah Fragments [C], 4QtgLev, and Samaritan Targum [*Sam. Tg.*]. See Evans, *Noncanonical*, 97–113; P. S. Alexander, "Jewish Aramaic Translations of Hebrew Scriptures," in *Mikra: Text, Translation, Reading and Interpretation of the Hebrew Bible in Ancient Judaism and Early Christianity*, ed. M. J. Mulder (Van Gorcum: Assen/Maastricht, 1990), 217–54; idem, "Targum, Targumim," *ABD*, 6:320–31; Tov, *Textual*, 148–51.

43. Evans, *Noncanonical*, 97.

44. Alexander, "Targum," 320.

45. *Textual*, 149.

Key Currents in the History of Interpretation

"interpret," covered both "translation" and "explanation."[46] Because Targum fragments were found at Qumran, interest in them for biblical studies is on the rise.[47]

According to Alexander, the translation techniques include: (1) treatment of anthropomorphism, (2) actualization, (3) doublets, (4) associative translation, (5) complementary translation, and (6) converse translation.[48]

The more literal *Tg. Onq.* shows the following readings:

Tg. Onq. Gen 1:22: פושו ("be many," so 1:28; 8:17; 9:1, 7) translates a more concrete idea of *numerical* increase rather than the metaphorical expression of the MT פרו ("be fruitful").[49]

Tg. Onq. Gen 8:17: ויתילדון ("they shall be reproduced") normally employs רחש (= שרץ, MT), but here avoids the MT וישרצו ("and they shall swarm") for dignity, since humans rather than animals are being addressed.[50] Similarly *Tg. Onq.* translates Exod 1:7: ובני ישראל נפישו ואתילדו ("Now the sons of Israel became numerous and prospered").[51]

Tg. Neof. shows the following readings:

Tg. Neof. 1:22 reads: "Be strong" (תקף, so 1:28; cf. Exod 1:7 תקפו, "grew strong")[52] for MT פרה ("be fruitful").

Tg. Neof. 1:28 reads: "And *the Glory of the Lord* blessed them, and *the Memra of the Lord* said to them: ["Be strong ..."]."[53] Contra *Frg. Tg.*,[54] *Tg. Neof.* divides the *Formal Complex Stem* into two expressions with "the Glory" functioning as a superlative for the usual targumic designation for

---

46. Alexander, "Targum," 321.

47. Tov, *Textual*, 149; Evans, *Noncanonical*, 98.

48. "Jewish Aramaic," 226–29.

49. M. Aberbach and B. Grossfeld, *Targum Onkelos to Genesis: A Critical Analysis Together with an English Translation of the Text* (Denver: Ktav, 1982), 25, n.16.

50. Ibid., 62–63.

51. An aversion also followed by *Tg. Ps.-J.*, *Tg. Neof.*, *Sam. Tg.*, and S.

52. תקף ("be strong") is rather consistent in TN for MT פרה ("be fruitful," so 1:28; 2:8; 8:17; 9:1, 7; 26:22; 35:11; 47:27; 49:22; Exod 1:7, etc.).

53. *Targum Neofiti 1: Genesis: Translated, with Apparatus and Notes*, vol. 1A (Collegeville: Liturgical, 1992), 54.

54. *Frg. Tg.* 1:28: וברין מימריה דיי יתהון ואמר להון מימרא דיי ("And the *memra* of the Lord blessed them, and the *memra* of the Lord said to them ..."; cf. 1:22). M. L. Klein, *The Fragment-Targums of the Pentateuch According to their Extant Sources*, vols. 1, 2 (Rome: Biblical Institute Press, 1980), 5.

deity ("the Memra," 1:22).⁵⁵ According to *Tg. Onq.*, Noah was protected by the "Memra" of the LORD when he entered the ark (Gen 7:16).⁵⁶ It is the periphrastic use of "Memra" for God himself that warrants it's essential use in other texts such as John 1 (i.e., Logos). The utility of "Memra" allows the divine-human relationship to be preserved.⁵⁷ He is the "speaking God."

Tg. Neof. 8:17 reads: "Let them *reproduce* on the earth and *grow strong* and multiply . . ." With animals in reference, "reproduce" matches MT "swarm" (שרץ), with "grow strong," a consistent rendering in *Tg. Neof.*, more demonstrative then MT פרה.

Tg. Ps.-J. shows the following readings:

Tg. Ps.-J. 1:28 reads: ". . . fill the earth *with sons and daughters*, and become powerful *in possessions* . . ."⁵⁸ The element of fertility is clearly concretized in *Tg. Ps.-J.*, extending even to material advance.

Tg. Ps.-J. 8:17 reads: "Let them reproduce" (ויתילדון) reiterating the targumic expression (cf. *Tg. Onq.*, *Tg. Neof.*).⁵⁹

In sum, the major Targumim, concretize propagation through quantitative terms. The esteem of "family" and "progeny" was so high that employing שרץ of animals (MT 8:17) in close proximity to Noah's own family (8:16) was still viewed as debasing the role of fertility by associating it with the non-human. The context of 8:16–17 is completely "humanized" around ילד (= "childbearing") in esteem of fertility. Not surprisingly, the Targumim also depart from the MT's use of שרץ in association with national Israel in Egypt (Exod 1:7). What the MT held in tension, namely the blessing of animal and human fertility, was in the Targumim, "leveled" to correspond solely to human fertility.

---

55. According to M. McNamara, "the Memra of the Lord" is a "buffer word," used for theological purposes such as avoiding anthropomorphisms or avoiding making God the formal subject of acts associated with creation. It is found 314 times in *Tg. Neof.*, 178 in *Tg. Onq.*, and 322 *Tg. Ps.-J.* (*Targum Neofiti 1*, 37–38).

56. Elsewhere "God made a covenant between Abraham and His Memra" (Gen 17:2); and Moses "brought forth the people to meet the 'Memra' of God" (Exod 19:17; cf. Deut 3:2; 4:24).

57. B. F. Wescott, *The Gospel According to St. John: The Authorized Version with Introduction and Notes* (Grand Rapids: Eerdmans, 1971), xvi.

58. M. Maher, *Targum Pseudo-Jonathan: Genesis. Translated, with Introduction and Notes*, vol. 1B (Collegeville: Liturgical, 1992), 20.

59. Ibid., 43.

Key Currents in the History of Interpretation

RABBINICS

"Rabbinics" is an amalgam of religion and literature, the religion codified in the literature as a sacred worldview preserved in distinct and complex literary forms.[60] Within "rabbinics," two essential hermeneutical outlooks operate: (1) the biblical text is a "code" which appropriate hermeneutic rules could crack,[61] and (2) the biblical text contains potentially unlimited meanings.[62]

A dialectic emerged between a "maximalist" interpretation (= דרש, *dāraš*) and a "minimalist" form (= פשט, *pĕšat*). The former interpreted even the "crowns" on Hebrew letters, while the latter believed God had accommodated to human language, requiring a logical exegesis.[63] Furthering this dialectical tension was the rabbinic conviction that Moses simultaneously received a written *and* oral Torah at Sinai, the oral being an exhaustive revelation of all possible interpretation of the written record.[64] God's Sinai revelation was transformed from a singular moment

---

60. Helpful literature for our discussion of "Rabbinics" includes M. A. Singer, "How the Bible Has Been Interpreted in Jewish Tradition," in *The New Interpreter's Bible*, vol. 1 (Nashville: Abingdon, 1994), 65-82; Evans, *Noncanonical*, 114-48; R. Kasher, "The Interpretation of Scripture in Rabbinic Literature" in *Mikra: Text, Translation, Reading and Interpretation of the Hebrew Bible in Ancient Judaism and Early Christianity*, ed. M. J. Mulder (Van Gorcum: Assen/Maastricht, 1990), 547-94; P. Stern, "Torah" in *The Oxford Companion to the Bible*, ed. B. M. Metzger and M. D. Coogan (Oxford: Oxford, 1993), 747-48; A. J. Avery-Peck, "Jews, Judaism" in *Eerdmans Dictionary of the Bible*, ed. D. N. Freedman (Grand Rapids: Eerdmans, 2000), 711-13; B. L. Visotzky, "Hermeneutics, Early Rabbinic," *ABD*, 3:154-55; L. R. Helyer, *Exploring Jewish Literature of the Second Temple Period: A Guide for New Testament Students* (Downers Grove: InterVarsity, 2002), esp. 27-41; 449-84.

61. Visotzky, "Hermeneutics," 155; *b. Sanhedrin* 34a; *m. Aboth* 5.22. Hillel's basic seven rules were later expanded to 32+ (*t. Sanhedrin* 7.11): (1) *Qal wa-homer* (lit. "light and heavy"; cf. 2 Sam 4:9-11; Jn 10:31-38); (2) *Gezera shawa* (lit. "an equivalent regulation"; cf. 1 Sam 21:6; Mk 2:23-28); (3) *Binyan 'ab mikkatub 'ehad* (lit. "constructing a father [principle] from one [passage]"; cf. Exod 3:14-15; Mk 12:26); (4) *Binyan 'ab mishshene ketubim* (lit. "constructing a father [principle] from two writings [passages]"; cf. Deut 18:1-8; Mat 10:10); (5) *Kelal uperat uperat ukelal* (lit. "General and particular, and particular and general"; cf. Deut 6:4-5; Rom 13:9-10); (6) *Kayotze bo mi-maqom 'aher* (lit. "To which something [is] similar in another place [passage]"; cf. Dan 7:13-14; Gal 3:8-16); (7) *Dabar halamed me'inyano* (lit. "word of instruction from the context"; cf. Gen 1:27; Rom 10-11) (see Helyer, *Exploring*, 456; Evans, *Noncanonical*, 117-18).

62. Evans, *Noncanonical*, 116.

63. Singer, "How the Bible," 66; *Sipre* 112.

64. God said to Moses:

into Israel's universal revelation,[65] for it even preceded creation itself.[66] In this way, "Torah study became the process for resolving the contradictions between the contemporary world of the interpreters and the written and oral Law."[67]

Rabbinic literature is vast, but our primary concern here is the Talmud and Midrash. The Talmud consists of the: Mishnah, Tosepta, Jerusalem Talmud, and the Babylonian Talmud.[68] The time period is divided into Tannaitic (50 BC to 200 AD) and Amoraic (220 AD to 500 AD). While the contribution of the Tannaitic (= *tenāʾ*, "teachers") period was the production of the Mishnah;[69] the Amoraic (= *ʾamar*, "expounders") contribution was the writing of two Talmuds and various Midrashim.[70] While the "Mishnah indicates the centrality of Scripture in religious practice,"[71] it is rabbinic exegesis itself that is called "midrash" (= *dāraš*, "allegorization").[72] Because of this on-going dialectic, there was a hermeneutical drift from the original context of the text and some rabbis were startled to realize that Scripture does not lose its "plain sense" (= *pěšat*).[73]

"Write these things, for it is by means of these things that I have made a covenant with Israel" (Exod 34:7). When God was about to give the Torah, He recited it to Moses in proper order: Scriptures, Mishnah, Aggadah, and Talmud, for God spoke all these words (Exod 20:1), even the answers to questions which distinguished scholars in the future are destined to ask their teachers did God reveal to Moses! (*Ki Tissa* 58b; quoted in Signer, "Jewish Interpretation," 66.)

65. Singer, "How the Bible," 69.

66. Stern, "Torah," *Oxford Companion*, 748; cf. *m. Aboth* 3.14; *Sifrie Deut* 37; *Sir* 24:1–23.

67. Signer, "How the Bible," 66.

68. Evans, *Noncanonical*, 115.

69. In rabbinic tradition, the Mishnah was compiled by Rabbi Judah the "prince/patriarch" (135–217 AD), based in the oral tradition of his predecessors, the Tanniam. Approximately in this time the early academies emerge: *Bet Shammai* ("House of Shammai") and *Bet Hillel* ("House of Hillel"). It is midway through this period that official sages were given the title "Rabbi" ("my master"; Signer, "Jewish Interpretation," 67; Evans, *Noncanonical*, 115).

70. Ibid., *Noncanonical*, 115.

71. Singer, "How the Bible," 67.

72. Similarly, Greek: *ereunan* ("to search"), employed in the 1st Cen (cf. 1QS 8:15, "This is the study [*midraš*] of the Law"; Evans, *Noncanonical*, 116). "Midrash" can be subdivided into *Halakic* and *Aggadic* midrash.

73. Visotzky, "Hermeneutics," *ABD*, 3:155; *m. Sabbat* 63a.

Key Currents in the History of Interpretation

According to Fishbane, however, midrash drew on operative techniques used by the biblical text itself.[74]

In practice, rabbinic interpretation is a religion of dual-canon that moved through three formative stages of interpretative concentration: (1) lexical/philological, concerned with translation for the benefit of the community, (2) sequence/coherence, enlivened by advances in grammar and syntax, and (3) harmonization.[75] The first stage brought together community and vernacular; the second, contemporary concerns with classical explanation, and the third harmonized traditional concern with contemporary culture. According to Signer:

> Midrash as a literature encouraged the continuing dialogue between the Jewish people and their past as embedded in the biblical texts. *It permitted the past to be eternally present.*[76]

It is to these two principle genres of creative rabbinic interpretation, the Talmud and Midrash, that we turn our attention. The diverse views and cultural implications that emerge from a reading of Gen 1:28 is enlightening. They contain both *Halakic* (= legal, behavioral) and *Aggadic* (= literary, nonbehavioral) exegesis, addressing didactic, ethical, and moral concerns.[77]

This "classical period" of rabbinic literature distinguishes itself through two characteristics: (1) documents as compilations of multiple traditions rather than singly produced and focused, and (2) the *utopian* and *atemporal* nature of the literature. This transcendence reinforced the written and oral Torah as twin repositories of divine wisdom.[78]

The loss of cult, temple, and land was a dramatic turning point in Judaism.[79] Through an adaptive hermeneutic, however, every generation could still hear the authoritative instruction applied to their community and time. As Avery-Peck explains:

---

74. "Inner Biblical Exegesis: Types and Strategies of Interpretation in Ancient Israel," in *Midrash and Literature*, ed. G. H. Hartman and S. Budick (New Haven: Yale University Press, 1986), 19–37.

75. Singer, "How the Bible," 66.

76. Ibid., 69. Emphasis added.

77. Visotzky, "Hermeneutics," 155.

78. Singer, "How the Bible," 70.

79. See Helyer, *Exploring*, 17–41.

In this way, rabbinic Judaism put each individual at the center of creation—where the temple and Jerusalem has always been conceived to stand—and ascribed to him or her the power to impart to the world order and meaning.[80]

According to the Mishnah,[81] "no man may abstain from keeping the law [to] be fruitful and multiply," except if he already has children.[82] According to Rambam, "We are thus commanded to be fruitful and multiply for the perpetuation of the species. This is the law of propagation."[83] According to Shammai, it should be two sons,[84] but Hillel stipulates a son and daughter, for he reasons: "it was written, 'male and female created he them.'"[85] With Noah, God remained committed to blessing His people as He had begun with Adam (1:28), however, according to *Midrash Tanhuma*, it was said to Noah (Gen 9:1), "From now on you are responsible for the blessing" (cf. Gen 12:2).[86]

In Rabbinic literature, the responsibility of propagation essentially resides with the man.[87] The reasoning is circuitous. Rashi sees Gen 1:18 as a blessing, but his view is an exception.[88] While others recognize that "be fruitful and multiply" is not counted among the "ten sayings" which created the world, it nonetheless stands as a command for men, which contains a blessing for women.[89] One compilation states, "The verse is

---

80. "Jews, Judaism," 713.

81. H. Danby, *The Mishnah: Translated from the Hebrew with Introduction and Brief Explanatory Notes* (Oxford: Oxford University Press, 1983).

82. *m. Yebamoth* 6.6; See J. T. Townsend, *Midrash Tanhuma*, vol. 1 (Hoboken: Ktav, 1989), 1.38.

83. *Ishus* 15.1; *m. Mo'ed Katan* 18b, 23a; *m. Bezah* 36b; *m. Pesahim* 72b; cf. *Sefer Hamitzvoth*, positive commandment 212, cited in Sherman, *The Chumash: Bereishis*, 73, n.1; *m. Shabbath* 111a.

84. On analogy of Moses with "Gershom and Eliezer" (1 Chr 23:15; *Yerushalmi Yebamoth* 6.6.1.A in *The Talmud of the Land of Israel: A Preliminary Translation and Explanation*, vol. 21, trans. by N. Neusner (Chicago: University of Chicago Press, 1987), 219.

85. *m. Yebamoth* 6.6. Only after a man has been married ten years without children is he free from the command (*m. Yebamoth* 6.6).

86. *Midrash Tanhuma Genesis*, 3.5.

87. In terms of obligation, both the study of the Torah and procreation exempt women (*m. Kiddushin* 34b).

88. Scherman, *The Chumash: Bereishis*, 73 citing *Kesuboth* 5a; cf. *m. Sanhedrin* 59b; *m. Yebamoth* 65.b.

89. Ibid., noting the views of Vilna Gaon and Harav Gifter (73). Ibn Ezra and Radak recognize the essential blessing but also attach a symbolic command (ibid., 74).

Key Currents in the History of Interpretation

a blessing, but also a command that is to be implemented by conscious propagation."[90] Most others believe Gen 1:28 constitutes the foundational commandment:

> This is a great Mitzvah upon which all the *mitzvos* of the world exist, because it was given to man not angels ... One who neglects this has neglected a Positive Commandment, incurring great punishment, because he thereby demonstrates that he does not wish to comply with the divine will to populate the earth.[91]

On the whole, however, the rabbis teach that the duty to "be fruitful and multiply" falls to the man rather than the woman.[92] But R. Johanan b. Baroka, for example disagrees, reciting that, "God blessed *them* and said to *them*,"[93] thus the woman is co-recipient with the man. Some, however, recognized that there are two parts to the "blessing," proliferation and governance.[94] However, even the notion of governance (כבש) is, in the literature, viewed in light of the dominant role of the male.[95]

The rape of Dinah (Genesis 34), for example, serves as foil for the rabbinic teaching that the woman is not to walk about with her jewelry lest her jeweled appearance prove an occasion for transgression.[96] The *Midrash Tanhuma Genesis* justifies this in a surprising turn:

> There is already an allusion in the Torah about this thing, that a woman should not go about a lot in a marketplace. Where? Where it is so written (in Gen. 1:28): "Then God blessed them, and God said to them: 'Be fruitful and multiply, fill the earth, *and subdue her.*' [*and subdue her* is written here]. The man subdues the woman, and the woman does not subdue the man. But, if she walks about a lot and goes out into the marketplace, she finally comes to a state

---

90. Ibid., 74.

91. Ibid., 73, n.1.

92. Ibid., 2.18; cf. 5.1; *m. Yebamoth* 61b, 65b.

93. *m. Yebamoth* 5; *m. Gittin* 43b. While the *Levirate* function (Deut 25:5–6) is discussed in detail (cf. *m. Yebamoth* 5), the modern practice of "insemination" is now more accepted than the male performing חלצה (*halîtā*).
Moreover, R. Johanan says the command is fulfilled if children were born while the man was a heathen and later became a proselyte, but R. Simeon b. Lakish disagrees (*b. Bekoroth* 47a). Emphasis added.

94. Scherman, *The Chumash: Bereishis*, citing the view of Avrohom ben HaRambam (74).

95. *Midrash Tanhuma-Yelammedenu Genesis* (Hoboken: KTAV, 1998), 12.

96. *Midrash Tanhuma Genesis*, 8.12 (cf. 8.5; Job 31:1).

of corruption, to a state of harlotry. And so you find in the case of Jacob's daughter Dinah.⁹⁷

The interpretation of "subduing the woman" is based on a revocalization of MT: וְכִבְשֻׁהָ ("and subdue it"), referring to אֶת־הָאָרֶץ, "the earth" that immediately precedes וְכִבְשֻׁהָ. Without the *wāw* (וְ, cf. כִבְשׁוּהָ), however, the form could be read as 1st-person imperative singular masculine (= וְכִבְשָׁהּ) with pronominal suffix, "and subdue *her/it*,"⁹⁸ especially in light of Gen 3:16 (וְהוּא יִמְשָׁל־בָּךְ), "and he shall rule over you."⁹⁹ It is reasoned that because warfare is also bound up in "subduing," this would necessarily exclude women who do not share the man's nature for battle.¹⁰⁰ Therefore, fertility vis-à-vis 1:28 is a directive for the man rather than the woman. Consequently, since the last part of the clause is directed to the man (i.e., "subdue"), so must the first part (i.e., "be fruitful").¹⁰¹ The Gemara thus concludes:

> It is therefore necessary to teach specifically that a woman is obligated to propagate, even though she does not wage war, and that she must fear her parents, even though her husband has a superior claim to her attention.¹⁰²

---

97. Ibid. Emphasis added. The discussion continues, noting that "like mother, like daughter," Dinah merely followed the practice of Leah who "went out to meet him" (Gen 30:16), ibid, 8.14, referencing *y. Sanhedrin* 29d; *'Arakh* 17a.

98. *Midrash Tanhuma-Yelammedenu*, 12; *m. Rabbah* 12; *m. Yebamoth* 65b; J. Neusner, *Genesis Rabbah: The Judaic Commentary to the Book of Genesis. A New American Translation*, vol. 1 (Atlanta: Scholars Press, 1985), 85 (8.3.A); 1cf. GKC §110c.

99. Sherman, *The Chumash: Bereishis*, 75; *m. Yebamoth* 65b.

100. *m. Kiddushin* 35a; *m. Yebamoth* 65b. Adam's original "dominion" over the earth creatures was a dominion that made the animals work for him (*m. Sanhedrin* 59b). Moreover, it is argued that the restoration of the blessing to Noah (Gen 9:1–2) excludes the original "dominion" given to Adam and was regained only in the politically ideal reign of Solomon: "When did it return? In the days of Solomon, as it is written, *For he had dominion over all the region*" (1 Kgs 5:4; *m. Rabbah* 12. Document emphasis).

101. *Midrash Tanhuma-Yelammedenu*, 12; *Genesis Rabbah*, 1:86 (8.4.A); *m. Rabbah* 12. The ideology of sexual design within created boundaries is emphasized precisely via its perversion in the Flood when the animals copulated outside their own species (e.g., serpent with the bird). This, it is explained, is why the text says "all flesh" (כל־בשׂר) rather than "all men" were in "corruption" and, apparently, an argument for Noah only taking pure animals "after their families" into the ark (ibid.).

102. *b. Bavli* 35a; cf. 43b.

Key Currents in the History of Interpretation

In spite of this tradition of the man "subduing" the woman, R. Johannan b. Berokah is cited as a corrective authority in *Midrash Rabbah* stipulating *both* man and woman under God's blessing and command.[103]

The rabbinic tradition also teaches that every precept given to Noah and repeated at Sinai was intended for both groups, both circumcision and propagation.[104] Their concern was to avoid the notion that the Sinai legislation canceled any antecedent code, so strong is their intention of preserving the earliest statements of propagation.[105] In fact, one question asks, "was not the world created only for propagation [since] 'He formed it to be inhabited.'"[106]

The counterpart of "be fruitful and multiply" given to Noah (Gen 9:7) is Moses' instructions that the Israelites should "return again to your tents" (Deut 5:27).[107] Even the sacred rite of circumcision was incumbent on Noah, before the Sinai legislation, for it is reasoned that Abraham and his descendants leading up to Sinai are all Noah's "sons."[108]

In sum, rabbinic literature addressing Gen 1:28 focuses on the wording and orthography of Gen 1:28 to support an all-encompassing ideology of procreation, an ideology that conditioned its own historiography. Rabbinic literature established that procreation is not only the man's role, according to Talmudic law, but its neglect is tantamount to a diminishment of the divine image in the world.[109] Within the literature this is ar-

---

103. *m. Rabbah* 12.

104. *m. Sanhedrin* 59a.

105. *m. Moe'd Katan* 8b. Not surprisingly, castration or other forms of sterilization are a sacrilege (*m. Shabbath* 111a). While the woman may use contraceptives, the man may not (*Genesis Rabbah*, 1:85 [8.3.B]).

106. *m. Hagigah* 2b.

107. *m. Sanhedrin* 59b. That is, resuming sexual relations suspended three days earlier prior to divine revelation (cf. Exod 19:15).

108. Ibid.

109. D. Sinclair, "Procreation" in *The Oxford Dictionary of the Jewish Religion*, ed. R. J. Z. Werblowsky and G. Wigoder (Oxford: Oxford University Press, 1997), 546, citing *m. Yebamoth* 63b.

J. Cohen explains the correlation with image:

If murder diminishes the image of God because it destroys one who embodies or represents that image, so too does the failure to procreate detract from the divine image because it prevents the representation of that image ... sexual reproduction transmits that image from one generation to the next." (*"Be Fertile and Increase, Fill the Earth and Master It": The Ancient and Medieval Career of a Biblical Text* [Ithica: Cornell University Press, 1989], 111.)

gued my means of elaborate syllogisms and constant appeal to proof-texts culled from the OT. Cohen elaborates:

> In the world view of classical rabbinic society, status and prestige were directly proportional to the degree of one's obligation to the laws of God; the more commandments bound an individual, the greater his or her claim to divined election. Talmudic master thus reformulated the primordial blessing as a precept of Mosaic law and then limited its application to free Jewish males, excluding slaves, women, and Gentiles.[110]

So all-encompassing is the "commandment" of Gen 1:28 that a staggering amount of life, indeed, a worldview was made to intersect with the formulaic significance of Gen 1:28 as the "first commandment." Bearing children is an act that produces merit, was a guarantee of divine providence and is, therefore, virtually divine—"whoever adds one soul to Israel is considered as if they had built a whole world."[111] That said, rabbinic Judaism couched Gen 1:28 as God's commitment to blessing and, one that properly belonged to the Jewish people.[112]

CONCLUSION

The *ANE* texts addressing creation, and humankind in particular, reveal numerous similarities to the Genesis text, albeit, generic. A strict emphasis on this "cultural connectedness," however, also runs the risk of minimizing the theological differences resident in those same texts. That polemic exists in the Genesis account is, then, not surprising.[113]

Additionally, the *role* played by the human being in the *ANE* texts (i.e., slave)[114] is in stark contrast to the divine "sharing," "representation,"

---

110. "Be Fertile," 310–11.

111. Sinclair, "Procreation," 546, citing Miamonides, *Hilkhot Ishut* 15.16. Cohen references the Zoharic Kabbalah that went a step further:

> Procreation exemplified not only human piety but also the mysterious and harmonious perfection of the deity; by complying with the divine mandate, a human couple replicated *and effected* the integration of the godhead, facilitating their own admission into the realm of the supernal as well. ("Be Fertile," 312–13; emphasis original.)

112. Cohen, "Be Fertile," 310. For a discussion of the "Noachihde Commandments" and their relationship to aliens, see Sarna, *Genesis*, 376–77.

113. E. C. Lucas, "Cosmology," *DOTP*, 136.

114. Ibid.

and, "provision" exemplified in the Genesis account, all on behalf of humankind. The *manner* of God's creative activity is also unique in the Genesis account, being devoid of consort, conflict, and residual antagonism from any competing pantheon.

The *LXX* employs routine harmonizing or "leveling" techniques in its translation as seen in its lexical choices. Among other things, the effect is to attune the more unique elements of Genesis 2 with that of Genesis 1, particularly as they relate to the creation of man and woman. This *retroversion* enables analogy: Adam made in the likeness of God receives his own subordinate counterpart with the creation of woman in his (i.e., Adam's) likeness. Adam's "oneness" toward the divine finds its correspondence in her "oneness" with man.

The Targumim portray a very *realist* epistemology toward Gen 1:28, which itself is woven into a far broader fabric that construes propagation in concrete and programmatic terms. שרץ ("swarm"), the unique term used for animals (Gen 1:22), is not translated in either Gen 8:17 or Exod 1:7 in reference to humans (so MT) in order to "humanize" notions of childbearing (i.e., ילד) and protect human dignity.

The notion of "fertility," emanating from Gen 1:28, forms a dominant profile in rabbinics. It is intriguing how sexual reproduction (Gen 1:28a) completely overwhelms the parallel injunction for "ruling" in the same verse (Gen 1:28b). Rabbinic literature surrounding Gen 1:28 clearly attempts to "sanctify" sexuality in an "evil" world by appealing to a *cosmic frontier* where human and divine actions intersect. It appears that because Judaism came to view "space" in terms of eschatological renewal and the cosmic, rather than through natural or existential rights, particularly after the exile, sexual reproduction itself became a quantifiable *means* of expressing "dominion;" progeny became the basis for land-claim.

SUGGESTIONS

Because our study focuses almost exclusively on five texts within Genesis 1–11, some elements were hardly addressed, or went unaddressed altogether, and these deserve mention as topics for further study. There is an eschatological element to the Creation Mandate that we could not delve into. Beale's analysis excels on this point.[115] Similarly, NT usage and theology, particularly Christology and image, build on the theology of image

---

115. See, *The Temple*.

broached in Genesis.[116] Nevertheless, we trust our analysis of image in light of the Creation Mandate has deepened the basis upon which NT theology builds its Christology.[117]

Later streams in the history of interpretation that bear on the Creation Mandate also deserve study, material including the Apocrypha, Pseudepigrapha,[118] Philo, DSS,[119] Josephus, and patristics.[120] Finally, contemporary discussion of "earth care" is much needed,[121] particularly as it intersects with Christian Tradition and the rise of natural law.[122] Medieval, Catholic, and Reformed traditions all uniquely enter this discussion, es-

---

116. See, for example, M. Endo, *Creation and Christology: A Study on the Johannine Prologue in the Light of Early Jewish Creation Accounts*, WUNT 149 (Tübingen: Mohr Siebeck, 2002); P. S. Minear, *Christian and the New Creation: Genesis Motifs in the New Testament* (Louisville: Westminster/John Knox, 2004).

117. See, for example N. T. Wright's insightful analysis of Jesus' interaction with the Sadducees regarding marriage and the resurrection (Matt 22:23-33; Mk 12:35-37; Luke 20:41-44). Noting how Jesus has bypassed the Deuteronomic command in favor of creation's ideal (cf. Mk 10:2-8) in previous discussions, Wright states:

> The Levirate law, quite explicitly, had to do with continuing the family line when faced with death; Jesus, in Luke's version, not only declares that this law will be redundant in a world without death, but that marriage itself, even with one husband and one wife, will likewise be irrelevant in such a world. A key point, often unnoticed, is that the Sadducees' question is not about the mutual affection and companionship of husband and wife, but about *how to fulfill the command to have a child*, that is, how in the future life the family line will be kept going. This is presumably based on the belief, going back to Genesis 1.28, that the main purpose of marriage was to be fruitful and multiply. (*The Resurrection of the Son of God*, vol. 3 [Minneapolis: Fortress, 2003], 423. Emphasis original.)

118. P. T. O'Brien, for example, writes:

> *Jub.* 22:14 and 32:19 deduce that the patriarchal blessings specifically apply to Israel the lordship of the world that was confirmed upon human beings (Adam) according to Genesis 1:26-28. ("Was Paul Converted?" in *Justification and Variegated Nomism: A Fresh Appraisal of Paul and Second Temple Judaism*, vol. 2, ed. D. A. Carson, P. T. O'Brien, and M. A. Seifrid [Grand Rapids: Baker, 2004], 384.)

119. See, for example, J. R. Davila, *Liturgical Works*, ECDSS (Grand Rapids: Eerdmans, 2000).

120. See, for example, *Epistle of Barnabas*, 6:18; *Clement of Rome (Letter to the Corinthians)*, 33:6; Justin Martyr (*Dialogue with Trypho*), 62:1; Philo of Alexandria (*Quaestiones in Genesim* [Aram.]), 2:56; Theophilus (*Ad Autolycus*), 2:11, etc.

121. See, for example, C. Park, *Caring for Creation*; R. J. Berry, *The Care of Creation: Focusing Concern and Action* (Leicester: InterVarsity, 2000).

122. See, for example, J. Schaefer, "Appreciating the Beauty of the Earth," *TS* 62 (2001): 23-52.

pecially with such dogma as celibacy and the esteem of virginity in early and modern Western church tradition. For each tradition, pre and postmodern,[123] the *raison d'être* shifts significantly.

---

123. See, for example, K. I. Parker, "Adam: The Postmodernist Bourgeois Liberal?" *JSOT* 29 (2005): 439–53.

7

Conclusion

SUMMARY

IN OUR STUDY, THE "Creation Mandate" was analyzed through five text plots within Genesis 1–11 (1:22, 28; 8:17; 9:1, 7). The result was an *exegetical theology* of the Mandate. In particular, we found Gen 1:28 to be a watershed for the investigation, wherein divine blessing of the Mandate established the right of the subjects to fertility within relationship (1:28; cf. 1:22).

The Creation Mandate (1:28) is God's functional blessing, a vitality of relationship, status, and capability for both propagation and governance. Within the blessing, "be fruitful and multiply" constituted human *enablement* (1:28a), the corollary of which is the *commission* to "rule" over creation (1:28b). The image of God (1:26) granted royal authorization for humankind to rule over creation as God's "under-kings." The context of the garden-sanctuary of Eden inaugurated the Mandate as mission, locally and practically (2:5, 15).

Key terms employed throughout the Mandate merged Israel's national horizon with creation's historical horizon in the broader textual trajectories. The language of "subduing" (1:28) along with holy war terminology used with Noah (9:2) ultimately move beyond the cosmic sphere of creation to the international theatre of Israel's conquest, with narratives employing the same terms (cf. Deut 19:12; Josh 18:1). Sinai was the existential occasion of a nation whose covenant and legislation were *retrospectively* grounded in the theological language of the Creation Mandate that called for fertility, dominion, and the imposition of a moral order. These are themes reiterated throughout the patriarchal narratives and ostensibly fulfilled with Israel's residence in Egypt (Exod 1:7).

Conclusion

A comparison with *ANE* literature, Septuagint, Targumim, and Rabbinics revealed a unique biblical text that exalts humankind with a dignified status and honorable stewardship to multiply and govern God's handiwork. The *LXX* revealed key harmonizations, essentially uncomfortable with lexical tensions and unique expressions in the MT. The Targumim elevate human propagation, on the one hand, but abandoned the MT's close juxtaposition of humankind with animals, on the other hand. Humankind is not allowed to "swarm" using terms for the animals (8:17; cf. Exod 1:7), contra MT. In rabbinics, fertility and propagation constitute their own end. Human dignity, identity, and purpose are defined by an all-inclusive fertility. Ruling is totally subordinated to propagation and seems to be the very means of expressing "national dominion."

IMPLICATIONS

Implications, exegetical and theological, emerge from our study. Regarding method and focus, it is acknowledged that in an era of increasing advocacy and ideological criticisms there is an equal need, if not more, for text-dominant studies, calling the imagination to begin with the biblical text. That is, exegetical commitment that respects the biblical text enough to listen to it with mind and heart willing to consider the text's emphases rather than dismiss it under the rubric of one ideology exerting its will over another.

Our analysis of the Creation Mandate is a plea to re-prioritize the biblical text as the "lead carriage" in the interpretative process. Brief analysis of Targumic and rabbinic literature alone reveals how wide the interpretative pendulum swings over time. Where is the analysis of the history of interpretation in an era of monolithic ideologies?[1] Is the biblical voice of the text less worth hearing? Are legitimate ethical pursuits biblically grounded or have they attached themselves to the moorings of presumed meanings? Cohen rightly states:

> In the case of Gen. 1:28, modern scholars have retrojected contemporary concern with domination over nature onto Scripture's call

---

1. See, for example, A. Linzey, *Animal Theology* (Chicago: University of Illinois Press, 1994); idem, *Animal Gospel* (Louisville: Westminster John Knox, 1998); S. McFague, *The Body of God* (Minneapolis: Fortress, 1993); idem, *Models of God*; H. Harrod, *The Animals Came Dancing* (Tuscon: University of Arizona Press, 2000).

to "fill the earth and master it," assuming that here lies the source of Western ecological attitudes that have flourished.²

The alternative is thoughtless participation, blinded by our *own Zeitgeist* that is overwhelmingly a political and "need-based" analysis of biblical texts, especially those addressing "earth" (= ecotheology), "male and female" (= gender studies), "ruling" (= social oppression), and "subduing the earth" (= ecological crisis). This has fostered a bias with scant interest in data. The question is not whether such ideologies deserve consideration, but the *grounds* for their address. Most advocacy approaches are fueled by a theology of "immanence" where the Creator is increasingly co-extensive with creation. In other words, minimizing the "thick work" of text-based exegesis has, we maintain, resulted in a parade of "thin ideologies" crying "foul."

From the outset, our analysis has been an exegetical theology of these biblical texts and, from there, interacting with some of the oldest versions and their interpretative traditions. Because Genesis 1–11, in particular, constitutes the "headstream" of biblical-theological tradition, we felt it necessary to concentrate on this biblical deposit, rooting the exegetical analysis of key portions, outside creed, concerned organization, and denomination.³

Appreciating the literary logic of our texts, borne along by the peculiarities of the text's rhetorical character, has returned a measure of respect for the narrator's strategy and a general awe for the text. Our commitment to the literary, historical, and theological investigation of the process made chapters four and five the most substantive and involved portions of our study. While text-dominant, our exegetical approach is hallmarked by several elements we only list in review:

- Semantic structure—this has elucidated the literary logic and contour of the texts, aiding appreciation for their "textuality."

- Lexical usage—analysis of the primary terms proved invaluable for each text plot, throwing into relief deviations and accentuations within larger portions.

---

2. "Be Fertile," 314.

3. Consider the *Journal of the Adventist Theological Society* (*JATS*), the latest edition of which devotes half of its entries (not entirely uncommon) to creation, but creation reflecting their ideological concerns and recurring names (see 15 [2004]). On "The President's Page" is listed "Creation—The Sine Qua Non of Adventism," 1–4.

Conclusion

- Masoretic accents—these proved enlightening, considered alongside our own syntactical analysis, and thrust us into an interpretative world largely abandoned today.
- Genre/Form Criticism—proved invaluable in light of terms such as ברך, dispelled certain interpretative views, and proved significant for discourse analysis.
- English translations—kept our exegetical analysis from becoming unduly abstract, interacting with existing readings, interpretations, and even translational trends.
- "Progressive hermeneutic"—that is, considering concentric circles of terms moving through Genesis and into the Pentateuch. This, we believe, helped surface additional layers of significance in light of the Sinai event.
- "Repeatable method"—the profile of these elements, whether one agrees or not, constitutes a repeatable method others can follow, learn from, and develop.

For theological implications several brief points may be noted. The phrase, "be fruitful and multiply" (פרו ורבו) not only functions as a hendiadys, but it runs through כבש ("subdue") as the thought unit, not merely מלא ("fill"). Too many studies merely consider the initial three verbs without the added nuances and contribution of "subdue" (כבש) and "rule" (רדה). Again, the masoretic accents deserve a hearing.

Additionally, it has proven significant to explore the domain of the earth, a domain shared between the animal (1:22) and human (1:28) realms. Additionally, one can appreciate the relational dynamism defined by God toward humankind. Reverberating between the earth and its Creator is an interplay rich in its similarities and distinctions. Mixing 1:22 with 1:28 collapses theological boundaries necessary for nurture and mission.

The lexical significance of כבש as a term of overt force, sanctioned by God for an assumed threat, represents a spate of nuances that interpreters continue to struggle with, especially in the creation context. It seems exegetically viable to read this as "harnessing" and "developing" relative its antecedent, "land" (ארץ), on the one hand, yet also view the "existential moment" in light of the Israelite nation at Sinai with a national "commission" of taking the Promised Land and thereby "extending" the work of creation. Similarly, comparing our lexical stock of Mandate terms with Exod 1:7 where the narrator uniquely describes the שרץ ("swarming") of an entire nation, a term used for animals, proved a rich comparison, and too much, ideologically, for the Targumim.

Breaking down the Creation Mandate into dual components of *endowment* and *commission* proved both necessary and helpful for several reasons: it dispelled the view that the Mandate is merely about "having children," and placed a cosmically oriented commission alongside propagation for the development of God's entire creation, animate and inanimate, human and animal. Missing the element of "commission" in "rule" (רדה) seems largely to stem from a lack of understanding as to the role of God's image in this context (1:26). Multiplication is a significant element that also requires the representative rule of the image. This is not to deny that image has an ontological basis, but our focus lay with its historical and biblical-theological function of image that operates in the crucial texts of 1:26, 5:3, and 9:6.

The role of the phrases in 9:2: "fear and terror" and "into your hand they are given" we believe has not been adequately explored. Not only is Adam's governance resumed in more technical language, but this language also anticipates, yet again, the conquest of the Israelite nation through holy war (Josh 18:1; Deut 19:12). This, along with the deeply royal notions surrounding the image were found to be crucial and need further exploration in the biblical theology of these texts within Genesis 1–11. Through analysis of these five texts with their vivid motifs, we hope our analysis has made a contribution to the on-going work in the literature of Genesis 1–11, bringing both credibility and contemplation.

Appendix A

The Rhetorical Structure of Gen 1:1—2:3

INCLUSIO (1:1-2):
- <u>Summary</u> (1:1): ("In the *beginning*") "created" → "God" → "heavens and <u>earth</u>"
- <u>Initial State of Cosmos</u> (1:2): "Now the <u>earth</u> was **formless** and **empty** ..."

Order by **FORMING** ...   Inhabitance by **FILLING** ...
(= unproductive becomes productive)   (= unpopulated becomes populated)

[Domain #3: *sky*]

<u>Day 1</u>: light & darkness   <u>Day 4</u>: sun, moon, stars
(1:3–5; *names*, 5)   (1:14–19)

[Domain #2: *water*]

<u>Day 2</u>: sky & waters   <u>Day 5</u>: birds & fish
(1:6–8; *names*, 8)   (1:20–23; *blesses*, 22)

[Domain #1: *earth*]

<u>Day 3</u>: a. land & seas   <u>Day 6</u>: a. beasts
        b. vegetation   b. humankind
      (1:9–13; *names*, 10)   (1:24–31; *blesses*, 28)

[2x *announcement*, 1:9, 11]   [2x *announcement*, 1:24, 26]
[2x *evaluation*, 1:10, 12]   [2x *evaluation*, 1:25, 31]

***Day 7*: REST**
(2:1–3)
└──→ [*sanctified* it as "holy time" 2:3]

INCLUSIO (2:1-3):
- <u>Summary</u> (2:1): ("Thus *finished*") "heavens and earth" → "God" (2:2) → "created" (2:3)
- <u>Final State of Cosmos</u> (2:2–3): "God finished ... rested ... blessed ... that *he had done*"

Bibliography

Aberbach, M. and B. Grossfeld. *Targum Onkelos to Genesis: A Critical Analysis Together with an English Translation of the Text.* Denver: Ktav, 1982.

Alexander, P. H. et al., eds. *The SBL Handbook of Style for Ancient Near Eastern, Biblical, and Early Christian Studies.* Peabody: Hendrickson, 1999.

Alexander, P. S. "Jewish Aramaic Translations of Hebrew Scriptures." Pages 217–54 in *Mikra: Text, Translation, Reading and Interpretation of the Hebrew Bible in Ancient Judaism and Early Christianity.* Edited by M. J. Mulder. Van Gorcum: Assen/Maastricht, 1990.

———. "Targum, Targumim." Pages 320–31 in vol. 6 of *The Anchor Bible Dictionary.* Edited by D. N. Freedman. 6 vols. New York: Doubleday, 1992.

Alexander, T. D. *From Paradise to the Promised Land: A Introduction to the Main Themes of the Pentateuch.* Grand Rapids: Baker, 1995.

———. *From Paradise to the Promised Land: An Introduction to the Pentateuch.* 2nd ed. Grand Rapids: Baker, 2002.

Alter, R. *The Art of Biblical Narrative.* New York: Basic Books, 1981.

———. *The Art of Biblical Poetry.* New York: Basic Books, 1985.

———. *Genesis: Translation and Commentary.* New York: W. W. Norton & Company, 1996.

Arnold, B. T., and B. E. Beyer. *Readings from the Ancient Near East.* Encountering Biblical Studies. Grand Rapids, Baker, 2002.

———, and J. H. Choi. *A Guide to Biblical Hebrew Syntax.* Cambridge: Cambridge University Press, 2003.

Anderson, B. W. "From Analysis to Synthesis: The Interpretation of Genesis 1–11." *Journal of Biblical Literature* 97 (1978): 23–39.

———. *From Creation to New Creation: Old Testament Perspectives.* Overtures to Biblical Theology. Minneapolis: Fortress, 1994.

———. "Human Dominion Over Nature." Pages 27–45 in *Biblical Studies in Contemporary Thought.* Burlington: Trinity College Biblical Institute, 1975.

Andersen, F. I. "Salience, Implicature, Ambiguity, and Redundancy in Clause-Clause Relationships in Biblical Hebrew." Pages 99–116 in *Biblical Hebrew and Discourse Linguistics.* Edited by R. D. Bergan, Summer Institute of Linguistics. Winona Lake: Eisenbrauns, 1994.

———. *The Sentence in Biblical Hebrew.* New York: Mouton, 1974.

Assmann, J. *The Mind of Egypt: History and Meaning in the Time of the Pharaohs.* Translated by A. Jenkins. New York: Metropolitan Books, 1996.

Averbeck, R. E. "Clean and Unclean." Pages 477–86 in vol. 4 of *New International Dictionary of Old Testament Theology and Exegesis.* Edited by W. A. VanGemeren. 5 vols. Grand Rapids: Zondervan, 1997.

Bibliography

———. "Factors in Reading the Patriarchal Narratives: Literary, Historical, and Theological Dimensions." Pages 115–37 in *Giving the Sense: Understanding the Using the Old Testament Historical Texts*. Edited by D. M. Howard, Jr. and M. A. Grisanti. Grand Rapids: Kregal, 2003.

———. "Sumer, The Bible, and Comparative Method." Pages 88–125 in *Mesopotamia and the Bible: Comparative Explorations*. Edited by M. W. Chavalas and K. L. Younger, Jr. Grand Rapids: Baker, 2002.

———. "The Sumerian Historiographic Tradition and Its Implications for Genesis 1–11." Pages 79–102 in *Faith, Tradition, and History: Old Testament Historiography in Its Near Eastern Context*. Edited by A. R. Millard, J. K. Hoffmeier, and D. W. Baker. Winona Lake: Eisenbrauns, 1994.

Avery-Peck, A. J. "Jews, Judaism." Pages 711–13 in *Eerdmans Dictionary of the Bible*. Edited by D. N. Freedman. Grand Rapids: Eerdmans, 2000.

Avishur, Y. *Studies in Biblical Narrative: Style, Structure, and the Ancient Near Eastern Literary Background*. Tel Aviv: Archaeological Center Publication, 1999.

Baker, D. W. "God, Names of." Pages 359–68 in *Dictionary of the Old Testament: Pentateuch*. Edited by T. D. Alexander and D. W. Baker. Downers Grove: InterVarsity, 2003.

———, V. P. Long, and G. J. Wenham, eds. *Windows into Old Testament History: Evidence, Argument, and the Crisis of "Biblical Israel."* Grand Rapids: Eerdmans, 2002.

Balentine, S. E. *The Torah's Vision of Worship*. Overtures to Biblical Theology. Minneapolis: Fortress, 1999.

Bandstra, B. L. "Word Order and Emphasis in Biblical Hebrew Narrative." Pages 109–123 in *Linguistics and Biblical Hebrew*. Edited by W. R. Bodine. Winona Lake: Eisenbrauns, 1992.

Barr, James. "Remembrances of 'Historical Criticism': Speiser's Genesis Commentary and Its History of Reception." Pages 59–72 in *God Who Creates: Essays in Honor of W. Sibley Towner*. Edited by W. P. Brown and S. D. McBride, Jr. Grand Rapids: Eerdmans, 2000.

———. *The Semantics of Biblical Language*. Oxford: Oxford University Press, 1961.

Bartholomew, C. G. "A Time for War, and a Time for Peace: Old Testament Wisdom, Creation and O'Donovan's Theological Ethics." Pages 91–112 in *A Royal Priesthood? The Use of the Bible Ethically and Politically: A Dialogue with Oliver O'Donovan*. Vol. 3. Edited by C. Bartholomew et al. Grand Rapids: Zondervan, 2002.

———, and M. W. Goheen. *The Drama of Scripture: Finding Our Place in the Biblical Story*. Grand Rapids: Baker, 2004.

Barton, J. "Form Criticism (OT)." Pages 838–41 in vol. 2 of *The Anchor Bible Dictionary*. Edited by D. N. Freedman. 6 vols. New York: Doubleday, 1992.

———. *Holy Writings, Sacred Text: The Canon in Early Christianity*. Louisville: Westminster/John Knox, 1998.

———. *Reading the Old Testament: Method in Biblical Study*. London: Darton, Longman, and Todd, 1984.

Bartor, A. "The 'Jurdical Dialogue': A Literary-Judicial Pattern" *Vetus Testamentum* 53 (2002): 445–64.

Batto, F. F. *Slaying the Dragon: Mythmaking in the Biblical Tradition*. Louisville: Westminster/John Knox, 1992.

———. "Jesus and the Wild Animals (Mark 1:13): A Christological Image for an Ecological Age." Pages 3–21 in *Jesus of Nazareth*. Grand Rapids: Eerdmans, 1994.

Bibliography

Bauckham, R. *The Climax of Prophecy: Studies in the Book of Revelation*. Edinburgh, T&T Clark, 1993.

Beale, G. K. "Eden, the Temple, and the Church's Mission in the New Creation." *Journal of the Evangelical Theological Society* 48 (2005): 5–31.

———. *The Temple and the Church's Mission: A Biblical Theology of the Dwelling Place of God*. New Studies in Biblical Theology. Downers Grove: InterVarsity, 2004.

Bimson, J. "Old Testament History and Sociology." Pages 125–55 in *Interpreting the Old Testament: A Guide for Exegesis*. Edited by C. C. Broyles. Grand Rapids: Baker, 2001.

Birch, B. C., et al. *Theological Introduction to the Old Testament*. Nashville: Abingdon Press, 1999.

Bird, P. A. "Male and Female He Created Them." Pages 329–61 in *"I Studied Inscriptions from Before the Flood": Ancient Near Eastern, Literary, and Linguistic Approaches to Genesis 1–11*. Sources for Biblical and Theological Study. Vol. 4. Winona Lake: Eisenbrauns, 1994.

———. *Missing Persons and Mistaken Identities: Women and Gender in Ancient Israel*. Overtures to Biblical Theology. Minneapolis: Fortress, 1997.

———. "Theological Anthropology in the Hebrew Bible." Pages 258–75 in *The Blackwell Companion to the Hebrew Bible*. Edited by L. Perdue. Malden: Blackwell, 2005.

Blenkinsopp, J. "The Documentary Hypothesis in Trouble." *Biblical Research* (Winter 1985): 13.

———. *The Pentateuch: An Introduction to the First Five Books of the Pentateuch*. New York: Doubleday, 1992.

Block, D. I. "My Servant David: Ancient Israel's Vision of the Messiah." Pages 17–56 in *Israel's Messiah in the Bible and the Dead Sea Scrolls*. Edited by R. S. Hess and M. D. Carroll. Grand Rapids: Baker, 2003.

Blum, E. "רָבַב." Pages 272–93 in vol. 13 of *Theological Dictionary of the Old Testament*. Edited by G. J. Botterweck, et al. 14 vols. Grand Rapids: Eerdmans, 2004.

Bock, D. "Evangelicals and the Use of the Old Testament in the New." *Bibliotheca Sacra* 142 (1985): 209–23, 306–19.

Borgman, P. *Genesis: The Story We Haven't Heard*. Downers Grove: InterVarsity, 2001.

Branch, R. G. "Rainbow." Pages 667–68 in *Dictionary of the Old Testament: Pentateuch*. Edited by T. D. Alexander and D. W. Baker. Downers Grove: Intervarsity, 2003.

Bratcher, M. "The Pattern of Sin and Judgment in Genesis 1–11." PhD diss., The Southern Baptist Theological Seminary, 1984.

Bratsiotis, N. P. "בָּשָׂר." Pages 313–32 in vol. 2 of *Theological Dictionary of the Old Testament*. Edited by G. J. Botterweck, et al. 14 vols. Grand Rapid: Eerdmans, 1999.

Brekelmans, C. "חָרַם." Pages 474–77 in vol. 2 of *Theological Lexicon of the Old Testament*. Edited by E. Jenni and C. Westermann. 3 vols. Peabody: Hendrickson, 1997.

Brenton, C. L. *The Septuagint with Apocrypha: Greek and English*. Grand Rapids: Hendrickson, 2001.

Brichto, C. H. *Toward a Grammar of Biblical Poetics: Tales of the Prophets*. Oxford: Oxford University Press, 1992.

Brodie, T. L. *The Crucial Bridge: The Elijah-Elisha Narrative as an Interpretive Synthesis of Genesis-Kings and a Literary Model for the Gospels*. Collegeville: Michael Glazier, 1999.

———. *Genesis as Dialogue: A Literary, Historical, and Theological Commentary*. Oxford: Oxford University, 2001.

Bibliography

Brown, M. L. "בָּרָךְ." Pages 757–67 in vol. 1 of *New International Dictionary of Old Testament Theology and Exegesis*. Edited by W. A. VanGemeren. 5 vols. Grand Rapids: Zondervan, 1997.

Brown, W. P. *The Ethos of the Cosmos: The Genesis of Moral Imagination in the Bible*. Grand Rapids: Eerdmans, 1999.

———. *Seeing the Psalms: A Theology of Metaphor*. Louisville: Westminster/John Knox, 2002.

———. *Structure, Role, and Ideology in the Hebrew and Greek Texts of Genesis 1:1—2:3*. Society of Biblical Literature Dissertation Series 132. Atlanta: Scholars Press, 1993.

———. and S. D. McBride, Jr., eds. *God Who Creates: Essays in Honor of W. Sibley Towner*. Grand Rapids: Eerdmans, 2000.

Broyles, C. C. "Interpreting the Old Testament: Principles and Steps." Pages 13–62 in *Interpreting the Old Testament: A Guide for Exegesis*. Edited by C. C. Broyles. Grand Rapids: Baker, 2001.

———. "Traditions, Intertextuality, and Canon," Pages 157–75 in *Interpreting the Old Testament: A Guide for Exegesis*. Edited by C. C. Broyles. Grand Rapids: Baker, 2001.

Brueggemann, Walter. *Genesis*. Atlanta: John Knox Press, 1982.

———. *The Message of the Psalms: A Theological Commentary*. Minneapolis: Augsburg, 1984.

———. *Reverberations of Faith: A Theological Handbook of Old Testament Themes*. Louisville: Westminster/John Knox, 2002.

———. *Texts Under Negotiation: The Bible and Postmodern Imagination*. Minneapolis: Fortress, 1997.

———. *Theology of the Old Testament*. Minneapolis: Fortress, 1997.

Bullinger, E. W. *Figures of Speech Used in the Bible: Explained and Illustrated*. Grand Rapids: Baker, 1991.

Bullock, H. *Exploring the Book of Psalms: A Literary and Theological Introduction*. Grand Rapids: Baker, 2001.

Bush, F. W. *Ruth, Esther*. Word Biblical Commentary. Dallas: Word, 1996.

Callender, D. Jr. *Adam in Myth and History: Ancient Israelite Perspectives on the Primal Human*. Harvand Semitic Studies 49. Winona Lake: Eisenbrauns, 2000.

Caird, G. B. *The Language and Imagery of the Bible*. Grand Rapids: Eerdmans, 1997.

Calvin, J. *Commentaries on the Book of Genesis*. Vol. 1. Translated by J. King. Grand Rapids: Eerdmans, 1948.

Camp, C. V. "Metaphor in Feminist Biblical Interpretation: Theoretical Perspectives." Pages 3–36 in *Semeia* 61. Women, War, and Metaphor: Language and Society in the Study of the Hebrew Bible. Edited by C. V. Camp and C. R. Fontaine. Atlanta: Scholars Press, 1993.

Capon, R. F. *Genesis: The Movie*. Grand Rapids: Eerdmans, 2003.

Carr, David M. *Reading the Fractures of Genesis: Historical and Literary Approaches*. Louisville: Westminster/John Knox, 1996.

Carson, D. A. *Exegetical Fallacies*, 2nd ed. Grand Rapids: Baker/Paternoster, 1996.

Cassuto, U. *A Commentary on the Book of Genesis*. 2 vols. Translated by I. Abrahams. Jerusalem: Magnes, 1972.

Childs, B. S. *Biblical Theology in Crisis*. Philadelphia: Westminster, 1970.

———. *Biblical Theology of the Old and New Testaments: Theological Reflection on the Christian Bible*. Minneapolis: Fortress, 1992.

Bibliography

———. *The Book of Exodus: A Critical, Theological Commentary*. Old Testament Library. Louisville: Westminster/John Knox, 1974.

———. *Introduction to the Old Testament as Scripture*. Philadelphia: Westminster, 1979.

———. *Old Testament Theology in a Canonical Context*. Philadelphia: Fortress, 1985.

Chisholm, R. "בָּשָׂר." Pages 777–79 in vol. 1 of *New International Dictionary of Old Testament Theology and Exegesis*. Edited by W. A. VanGemeren. 5 vols. Grand Rapids: Zondervan, 1997.

———. *From Exegesis to Exposition: A Practical Guide to Using Biblical Hebrew*. Grand Rapids: Baker, 1998.

———. "History or Story?" Pages 54–73 in *Giving the Sense: Understanding the Using the Old Testament Historical Texts*. Edited by D. M. Howard, Jr. and M. A. Grisanti. Grand Rapids: Kregal, 2003.

Christensen, D. L. *Deuteronomy 21:10—34:12*. Word Biblical Commentary. Nashville: Thomas Nelson, 2002.

Church Dogmatics: The Work of Creation. vol. 3.1. Translated and Edited by G. W. Bromiley and T. F. Torrance. Edinburgh: T&T Clark, 1960.

Clines, D. J. A. *The Bible in the Modern World*, The Biblical Seminar 51. Sheffield: Sheffield Academic Press, 1997.

———. "The Image of God in Man." *Tyndale Bulletin* 19 (1968): 53–103.

———. *On the Way to the Postmodern: Old Testament Essays, 1967–1998*. Vol. 1. Journal for the Study of the Old Testament, Supplement 292. Sheffield: Sheffield Academic Press, 1998.

———. "The Significance of the 'Sons of God' Episode (Genesis 6.1–4) in the Context of the 'Primeval History' (Genesis 1–11)." Pages 75–88 in *The Pentateuch: A Sheffield Reader*. Edited by J. W. Rogerson. Sheffield: Sheffield Academic Press, 1996.

———. "Theme in Genesis 1–11." *Catholic Biblical Quarterly* 38 (1976): 499–502.

———. *The Theme of the Pentateuch*. Journal for the Study of the Old Testament, Supplement 10. Sheffield: Sheffield Academic Press, 1978.

———. *The Theme of the Pentateuch*. 2nd ed. Journal for the Study of the Old Testament, Supplement 10. Sheffield: Sheffield Academic Press, 1997.

———. *What Does Eve Do to Help? And Other Readerly Questions to the Old Testament*. Journal for the Study of the Old Testament, Supplement 94. Sheffield: JSOT, 1990.

———. "A World Established on Water (Psalm 24): Reader-Response, Deconstruction and Bespoke Interpretation." Pages 79–90 in *New Literary Criticism and the Hebrew Bible*. Sheffield: JSOT Press, 1993.

———. "אָדָם, The Hebrew for 'Human, Humanity': A Response to James Barr." *Vetus Testamentum* 53 (2003): 297–310.

Coats, G. W. *Genesis with an Introduction to Narrative Literature*. The Forms of the Old Testament Literature. Edited by Rolf Knierim and Gene M. Tucker. Vol. 1. Grand Rapids: Eerdmans Publishing, 1983.

———. "Theology of the Hebrew Bible." Pages 239–62 in *The Hebrew Bible and Its Modern Interpreters*. Edited by D. A. Knight and G. M. Tucker. Minneapolis: Fortress, 1985.

Cohen, J. *"Be Fertile and Increase, Fill the Earth and Master It": The Ancient and Medieval Career of a Biblical Text*. Ithica: Cornell University Press, 1989.

Collins, C. J. "What Happened to Adam and Eve? A Literary-Theological Approach to Genesis 3." *Presbyterion* 27 (2001): 12–44.

Bibliography

Cook, J. "The Exegesis of the Greek Genesis." Pages 91–125 in *VI Congress of the International Organization for Septuagint and Cognate Studies*. Edited by C. E. Cox. Atlanta: Scholars Press, 1986.

Craigie, P. C. *Psalms 1–50*. Vol. 19. Word Biblical Commentary. Nashville: Thomas Nelson, 1983.

Crüsemann, F. *The Torah: Theology and History of Old Testament Law*. Translated by A. W. Mahnke. Minneapolis: Fortress, 1996.

Currid, J. D. *Genesis 1:1—25:18*. New York: Evangelical Press, 2003.

Curtis, E. M. "Image of God (OT)." Pages 389–91 in vol. 3 of *The Anchor Bible Dictionary*. Edited by D. N. Freedman. 6 vols. New York: Doubleday, 1992.

Danby, H., tr. *The Mishnah: Translated from the Hebrew with Introduction and Brief Explanatory Notes*. Oxford: Oxford University Press, 1983.

Daube, D. *The Duty of Procreation*. Edinburgh: Edinburgh University Press, 1977.

Davidson, A. B. *Introductory Hebrew Grammar: Hebrew Syntax*. Edinburgh: T&T Clark, 1912.

Davies, J. A. *A Royal Priesthood: Literary and Intertextual Perspectives on an Image of Israel in Exodus 19:6*. Journal for the Study of the Old Testament, Supplement 395. London: T&T Clark, 2004.

Davis, J. J. *Moses and The God's of Egypt: Studies in Exodus*. 2nd ed. Grand Rapids: Baker, 1986.

Delcor, M. "מָלֵא." Pages 664–66 in vol. 2 of *Theological Lexicon of the Old Testament*. Edited by E. Jenni and C. Westermann. 3 vols. Peabody: Hendrickson, 1997.

Delitzsch, F. *A New Commentary on Genesis*. Vol. 1. Translated by S. Taylor. Edinburgh: T&T Clark, 1888. Repr., Eugene: Wipf and Stock, 2001.

Deurloo, K. A. "Narrative Geography in the Abraham Cycle." Pages 48–62 in *In Quest of the Past: Studies on Israelite Religion, Literature and Prophetism*. Edited by A. S. Van der Woude. The Netherlands: Brill, 1990.

de Vaux, R. "Reflections on the Present State of Pentateuchal Criticism." Pages 31–48 in *The Bible and the Ancient Near East*. New York: Doubleday, 1966.

Dickson, J. P. and B. S. Rosner. "Humility as a Social Virtue in the Hebrew Bible?" *Vetus Testamentum* 54 (2004): 459–79.

Dillard, R., and T. Longman. "Genesis." Pages 37–56 in *An Introduction to the Old Testament*. Grand Rapids: Zondervan, 1994.

Dillmann, A. *Genesis: Critically and Exegetically Expounded*. Translated by W. B. Stevenson. Edinburgh: T&T Clark, 1897.

Dorsey, David A. *The Literary Structure of the Old Testament: A Commentary on Genesis-Malachi*. Grand Rapids: Baker, 1999.

Douglas, M. *Purity and Danger*. London: Routledge & Kegan Paul, 1966.

Dozeman, T. B. "Rhetoric and Rhetorical Criticism." Pages 711–15 in vol. 5 of *The Anchor Bible Dictionary*. Edited by D. N. Freedman. 6 vols. New York: Doubleday, 1992.

Driver, S. R. *A Treatise on the Use of the Tenses in Hebrew and Some Other Syntactical Questions*. 3rd ed. Oxford: Clarendon Press, 1892.

Dumbrell, W. J. *Covenant and Creation: A Theology of Old Testament Covenants*. Nashville: Thomas Nelson, 1984.

———. "Creation, Covenant and Work." Pages 151–70 in *With Heart, Mind and Strength: The Best of Crux 1979–1989*. Edited by D. M. Lewis. Langley: Credo, 1990.

———. *The Faith of Israel: A Theological Survey of the Old Testament*. 2nd ed. Grand Rapids: Baker, 2002.

Bibliography

———. "Genesis 2:1–3: Biblical Theology of Creation Covenant." *Evangelical Review of Theology* 25 (2001): 219–230.

———. *The Search for Order: Biblical Eschatology in Focus*. Grand Rapids: Baker, 1994.

Durham, J. I. *Exodus*. Word Biblical Commentary. Waco: Word, 1987.

Eichrodt, W. *Man in the Old Testament*. Studies in Biblical Theology 4. Chicago: Henry Regnery Co., 1951.

———. *Theology of the Old Testament*. 2 vols. Translation by J. Baker. Philadephia: Westminster, 1961.

Eldredge, L., and J. Sandys-Wunsch. *De justo discrimine theologiae biblicae et dogmaticae regundisque recte utriusque finibus* ("On the Proper Distinction Between Biblical and Dogmatic Theology and the Specific Objectives of Each"). From "J. P. Gabler and the Distinction between Biblical and Dogmatic Theology: Translation, Commentary, and Discussion of His Originality." *Scottish Journal of Theology* 33 (1980): 133–58.

Eliade, M. *The Sacred and the Profane: The Nature of Religion*. Translated by W. R. Trask. San Diego: Harcourt Brace Jovanovich.

Ellis, E. E. "The Old Testament Canon in the Early Church." Pages 653–90 in *Mikra: Text, Translation, Reading and Interpretation of the Hebrew Bible in Ancient Judaism and Early Christianity*. Edited by M. J. Mulder. Van Gorcum: Assen/Maastricht, 1990.

Ellull, J. *The New Demons*. Translated by C. E. Hopkins. New York: Seabury, 1975.

Emery, A. C. "Warfare." Pages 877–81 in *Dictionary of the Old Testament: Pentateuch*.

Enns, P. *Exodus*. New International Version Application Commentary. Grand Rapids: Zondervan, 2000.

———, and D. McCartney. "Matthew and Hosea: A Response to John Sailhamer." *Westminster Theological Journal* 63 (2001): 97–105.

Erickson, M. J. *Christian Theology*. Grand Rapids: Baker, 1990.

Evans, C. A. *Noncanonical Writings and New Testament Interpretation*. Grand Rapids: Hendrickson, 1992.

Evans, M. "Blessing/Curse." Pages 397–401 in *New Dictionary of Biblical Theology*. Edited by T. D. Alexander and B. S. Rosner. Downers Grove: InterVarsity, 2000.

Exum, J. C. and D. J. A. Clines, eds. *The New Literary Criticism and the Hebrew Bible*. Journal for the Study of the Old Testament, Supplement 143. Sheffield: Sheffield Academic Press, 1993.

Feinberg, J. S. "Literary Forms and Inspiration." Pages 45–67 in *Cracking Old Testament Codes: A Guide to Interpreting Literary Genres of the Old Testament*. Edited by D. B. Sandy and R. L. Giese. Nashville: Broadman and Holman, 1995.

Felder, C. H., ed., *Stony the Road We Trod: African American Biblical Interpretation*. Minneapolis: Fortress, 1991.

Fewell, Danna Nowell. "Reading the Bible Ideologically: Feminist Criticism." Pages 268–82 in *To Each Its Own Meaning: An Introduction to Biblical Criticisms and Their Application*. Edited by Stephen Haynes and Steven McKenzie. Louisville: Westminster/John Knox, 1993.

Firmage, E. "Zoology." Pages 1109–51 in vol. 6 of *The Anchor Bible Dictionary*. Edited by D. N. Freedman. 6 vols. New York: Doubleday, 1992.

Fishbane, M. *Biblical Interpretation in Ancient Israel*. Oxford: Clarendon, 1985.

———. "Inner Biblical Exegesis: Types and Strategies of Interpretation in Ancient Israel." Pages 19–37 in *Midrash and Literature*. Edited by G. H. Hartman and S. Budick. New Haven: Yale University Press, 1986.

Bibliography

———. *Text and Texture: Close Readings of Selected Biblical Texts*. New York: Schocken, 1979.

Fitch, W. O. "Dr. R. H. Kennett and the Sources of the Pentateuch." Pages 145–48 in *Studia Biblica 1978*. Edited by E. A. Livingston. Sheffield: JSOT Press, 1979.

Fohrer, G. *History of Israelite Religion*. Nashville: Abingdon, 1972.

Fokkelman, J. P. *Narrative Art in Genesis*. Amsterdam: van Gorcum, 1975.

———. *Reading Biblical Poetry: An Introductory Guide*. Translation by I. Smit. Louisville: Westminster/John Knox, 2001.

Forrest, R. W. E. "Paradise Lost Again: Violence and Obedience in the Flood Narrative." *Journal for the Study of the Old Testament* 62 (1994): 3–18.

Fouts, D. M. "Selected Lexical and Grammatical Studies in Genesis 1." *Andrews University Seminary Studies* 42 (2004): 79–90.

Fox, M. J. "The Sign of the Covenant: Circumcision in the Light of Priestly 'ôT Etiologies." *Revue Biblique* 81 (1974): 568–73.

Fretheim, T. E. "The Book of Genesis: Introduction, Commentary, and Reflections." Pages 321–674 in *The New Interpreter's Bible*. Vol. 1. Nashville: Abingdon, 1994.

———. *Creation, Fall and Flood: Studies in Genesis 1–11*. Minneapolis: Augsburg, 1969.

———. *The Pentateuch*. Interpreting Biblical Texts. Nashville: Abingdon, 1996.

———. "Which Blessing Does Isaac Give Jacob?" Pages 279–91 in *Jews, Christian, and the Theology of the Hebrew Scriptures*. Society of Biblical Literature Symposium Series 8. Edited by A. O. Bellis and J. S. Kaminsky. Atlanta: SBL, 2000.

Friedman, R. E. "Torah (Pentateuch)." Pages 605–22 in vol. 6 of *The Anchor Bible Dictionary*. Edited by D. N. Freedman. 6 vols. New York: Doubleday, 1992.

Frymer-Kensky, T. "The Atrahasis Epic and Its Significance for Our Understanding of Gen. 1–9." *Biblical Archaeologist* 40 (1977): 147–55.

———. "The Sage in the Pentateuch: Soundings." Pages 275–88 in *The Sage in Israel and the Ancient Near East*. Edited by L. G. Perdue. Winona Lake: Eisenbrauns, 1990.

———. "Sex and Sexuality." Pages 1144–46 in vol. 5 of *The Anchor Bible Dictionary*. Edited by D. N. Freedman. 6 vols. New York: Doubleday, 1992.

Futato, M. *Beginning Biblical Hebrew*. Winona Lake: Eisenbrauns, 2003.

Gadamer, Hans-Georg. *Truth and Method*. 2nd ed. New York: Crossroad, 2000.

Gage, W. *The Gospel of Genesis: Studies in Protology and Eschatology*. Winona Lake: Carpenter, 1984.

Gardner, B. K. *The Genesis Calendar: The Synchronistic Tradition in Genesis 1–11*. New York/Oxford: University Press of America, 2001.

Gelander, Shamai. *The Good Creator: Literature and Theology in Genesis 1–11*. South Florida Studies in the History of Judaism 147. Atlanta: Scholars Press, 1997.

Geoghegan, J. C. "'Until This Day' and the Preexilic Redaction of the Deuteronomistic History." *Journal of Biblical Literature* 122 (2003): 201–27.

Gerleman, G. "בָּשָׂר." Pages 283–85 in vol. 1 of *Theological Lexicon of the Old Testament*. Edited by E. Jenni and C. Westermann. 3 vols. Peabody, Hendrickson, 1997.

Gerstenberger, E. "Psalms." Pages 198–207 in *Old Testament Form Criticism*. San Antonio: Trinity University Press, 1977.

Gibson, J. C. L. *Davidson's Introductory Hebrew Grammar: Syntax*. Edinburgh: T&T Clark, 1994.

———. *Language and Imagery in the Old Testament*. Peabody: Hendrickson, 1998.

Bibliography

Gitay, Y. "Rhetorical Criticism." Pages 135–49 in *To Each Its Own Meaning: An Introduction to Biblical Criticisms and Their Application*. Edited by S. L. McKenzie and S. R. Haynes. Louisville: Westminster/John Knox, 1993.

Goldingay, J. "Hermeneutics." Pages 387–401 in *Dictionary of the Old Testament: Pentateuch*. Edited by T. D. Alexander. Downers Grove: InterVarsity, 2003.

———. *Old Testament Theology: Israel's Gospel*. Vol. 1. Downers Grove: Intervarsity, 2003.

Goldsworthy, G. *According to Plan: The Unfolding Revelation of God in the Bible. An Introductory Biblical Theology*. Downers Grove: InterVarsity, 2002.

Gooder, P. *The Pentateuch: A Story of Beginnings*. Continuum Biblical Studies Series. London: Continuum, 2000.

Greenberg, M. "Exegesis." *Studies in The Bible and Jewish Thought*. JPS Scholar of Distinction Series. Philadelphia: JPS, 1995, 361–68.

Greene-McCreight, K. "Feminist Theology and a Generous Orthodoxy." *Scottish Journal of Theology* 57 (2004): 95–108.

Greenstein, E. L. "God's Golem: The Creation of the Human in Genesis 2." Pages 219–39 in *Creation in Jewish and Christian Tradition*. Edited by H. G. Reventlow and Y. Hoffman. Journal for the Study of the Old Testament, Supplement 319. Sheffield: Sheffield Academic Press, 2002.

Grenz, S. J. "Jesus as the *Imago Dei*: Image-of-God Christology and the Non-Linear Linearity of Theology." *Journal of the Evangelical Theological Society* 47 (2004): 617–28.

Groß, W. "Gen 1.26.27; 9,6: Statue oder Ebenbild Gottes? Aufgabe und Würde des Menschen nach dem hebräischen und griechischen Wortlaut." *Jahrbuch für Biblische Theologie* 15 (2000): 11–38.

Gunkel, H. *Genesis: The Legends of Genesis*. New York, 1964.

Gunn, D. M., and D. N. Fewell. *Narrative in the Hebrew Bible*. New York: Oxford University Press, 1993.

Haag, H. "חָמָס." Pages 478–87 in vol. 4 of *Theological Dictionary of the Old Testament*. Edited by G. J. Botterweck and H. Ringgren. 14 vols. Grand Rapids: Eerdmans, 1980.

Habel, N. C., and S. Wurst, eds. *The Earth Story in Genesis*. The Earth Bible 2. Sheffield: Sheffield Academic Press, 2001.

Hafemann, S. "Biblical Theology: Retrospect and Prospect." Pages 15–21 in *Biblical Theology: Retrospect and Prospect*. Edited by S. Hafemann. Downers Grove: InterVarsity, 2002.

Hallo, W. W. "Compare and Contrast: The Contextual Approach to Biblical Literature," in *The Bible in the Light of Cuneiform Literature: Scripture in Context, III*. Ancient Near Eastern Texts and Studies. Edited by W. W. Hallo, B. W. Jones, and G. L. Mattingly. Lewiston: The Edward Mellen Press, 1990, 1–30.

———. "Texts, Statues and the Cult of the Divine King." Pages 55–66 in *Congress Volume: Jerusalem 1986*. Edited by J. A. Emerton. Supplements to Vetus Testamentum 40. Leiden: Brill, 1988.

Hamilton, V. P. "אָדָם." Pages 262–66 in vol. 1 of *New International Dictionary of Old Testament Theology and Exegesis*. Edited by W. A. VanGemeren. 5 vols. Grand Rapids, Zondervan, 1997.

———. "אָרַר." Pages 75–76 in vol. 1 of *Theological Wordbook of the Old Testament*. Edited by R. L. Harris, et al., 2 vols. Chicago: Moody, 1980.

Bibliography

———. *The Book of Genesis: 1-17*. New International Commentary on the Old Testament. Grand Rapids: Eerdmans, 1990.

Harland, P. J. *The Value of Human Life: A Study of the Story of the Flood (Genesis 6-9)*. Leiden: Brill, 1996.

Hartley, J. E. *Genesis*. New International Biblical Commentary on the Old Testament. Edited by R. L. Hubbard, Jr. and R. K. Johnston. Peabody: Hendrickson, 2000.

Hartman, Th. "רב." Pages 1194-1201 in vol. 3 of *Theological Lexicon of the Old Testament*. Edited by E. Jenni and C. Westermann. 3 vols. Peabody, Hendrickson, 1997.

Hasel, G. "The Polemic Nature of the Genesis Cosmology." *Evangelical Quarterly* 46 (1974): 81-102.

Hawk, D. L. "Literary/Narrative Criticism." Pages 536-44 in *Dictionary of the Old Testament: Pentateuch*. Edited by T. D. Alexander and D. W. Baker. Downers Grove: InterVarsity, 2003.

Haynes, S. R., and S. L. McKenzie eds. *To Each Its Own Meaning: An Introduction to Biblical Criticisms and Their Application*. Rev ed. Louisville: Westminster/John Knox, 1999.

Hayes, J. H., and F. Prussner. *Old Testament Theology: Its History and Development*. Atlanta: John Knox, 1985.

Hendel, R. "Genesis, Book of." Pages 933-41 in vol. 2 of *The Anchor Bible Dictionary*. Edited by D. N. Freedman. 6 vols. New York: Doubleday, 1992.

———. "Of Demigods and the Deluge: Toward an Interpretation of Genesis 6:1-4." *Journal of Biblical Literature* 106 (1987): 13-26.

———. "Tangled Plots in Genesis." Pages 35-51 in *Fortunate the Eyes that See: Essays in Honor of David Noel Freedman in Celebration of His Seventieth Birthday*. Edited by A. B. Beck, A. H. Bartlet, P. R. Raabe, and C. A. Franke. Grand Rapids: Eerdmans, 1995.

Hengel, M. *The Septuagint as Christian Scripture: Its Prehistory and the Problem of Its Canon*. Translated by M. E. Biddle. Grand Rapids: Baker, 2002.

Hess, R. S. "Adam." Pages 18-21 in *Dictionary of the Old Testament: Pentateuch*. Edited by T. D. Alexander and D. W. Baker. Downers Grove: InterVarsity, 2003.

———. "The Genealogies of Genesis 1-11 and Comparative Literature." *Biblica* 70 (1989): 241-54.

———, and D. T. Tsumura, eds. *"I Studied Inscriptions from Before the Flood": Ancient Near Eastern, Literary, and Linguistic Approaches to Genesis 1-11*. Sources for Biblical and Theological Study 4. Winona Lake: Eisenbrauns, 1994.

———. "One Hundred Fifty Years of Comparative Studies on Genesis 1-11." Pages 3-26 in *"I Studied Inscriptions from Before the Flood": Ancient Near Eastern, Literary, and Linguistic Approaches to Genesis 1-11*. Sources for Biblical and Theological Study 4. Winona Lake: Eisenbrauns, 1994.

———. "The Roles of the Woman and the Man in Genesis 3." *Themelios* 18 (1993): 15-19.

Hiebert, T. "Warrior, Divine." Pages 876-80 in vol. 6 of *The Anchor Bible Dictionary*. Edited by D. N. Freedman. 6 vols. New York: Doubleday, 1992.

———. *The Yahwist's Landscape: Nature and Religion in Early Israel*. New York/Oxford: Oxford University Press, 1996.

Hill, A. "רָבָה." Pages 1037-41 in vol. 3 of *New International Dictionary of Old Testament Theology and Exegesis*. Edited by W. A. VanGemeren. 5 vols. Grand Rapids: Zondervan, 1997.

Bibliography

———. "רָמַשׂ." Pages 1127–28 in vol. 3 of *New International Dictionary of Old Testament Theology and Exegesis*. Edited by W. A. VanGemeren. 5 vols. Grand Rapids: Zondervan, 1997.

———. "שָׁרַץ." Pages 251–52 in vol. 4 of *New International Dictionary of Old Testament Theology and Exegesis*. Edited by W. A. VanGemeren. 5 vols. Grand Rapids: Zondervan, 1997.

Hoffman, J. M. *In the Beginning: A Short History of the Hebrew Language*. New York: New York University Press, 2004.

Hoffmeier, J. K. *Israel In Egypt: The Evidence for the Authenticity of the Exodus Tradition*. New York: Oxford, 1996.

———. "Some Thoughts on Genesis 1 and 2 and Egyptian Cosmology." *Journal of Ancient Near Eastern Society* 15 (1983): 39–49.

Holloway, J. "'From the Beginning,' The Moral Vision of Genesis 1–11." *Scottish Journal of Theology* 44 (2001): 76–92.

House, P. R. "The Rise and Current Status of Literary Criticism of the Old Testament." Pages 3–22 in *Beyond Form Criticism: Essays in Old Testament Literary Criticism*. Edited by P. R. House. Vol. 2 of Sources for Biblical and Theological Study. Winona Lake: Eisenbrauns, 1992.

Houtman, C. *Exodus*. Historical Commentary on the Old Testament. Tranlation by J. Rebel and S. Woudstra. Kampen: Kok Publishing House, 1993.

Howard, D. M. Jr., and M. A. Grisanti, eds. *Giving the Sense: Understanding and Using Old Testament Historical Texts*. Grand Rapids: Kregel, 2003.

Humphrey, W. L. *The Character of God in the Book of Genesis*. Louisville: Westminster/John Knox, 2001.

Husser, J. M. "Entre Mythe et Philosophie La Relecture Sapientielle de Genúse 2–3." *Revue Biblique* 107–2 (2000): 232–59.

Jacobsen, T. "The Graven Image." Pages 15–32 in *Ancient Israelite Religion: Essays in Honor of F. M. Cross*. Edited by P. D. Miller, Jr., P. D. Hanson, and S. D. McBride. Philadelphia: Fortress, 1987.

Jaroš, K. "Die Motive der Heiligen Bäum und der Schlang in Gen 2–3." *Zeitschrift für die Alttestamentliche Wissenschaft* 92 (1980): 204–15.

Jastrow, M. *Dictionary of the Targumim, Talmud Bauli, Talmud Yerushalmi and Midrashic Literature*. NP: Judaica Treasury, 2004.

Jenni, E. "Linguistics and Biblical Hebrew Section." Paper presented at the annual meeting of the SBL. Boston, Mass., Nov. 22, 1999.

———. "דָּמָה." Pages 339–42 in vol. 1 of *Theological Lexicon of the Old Testament*. Edited by E. Jenni and C. Westermann. 3 vols. Peabody, Hendrickson, 1997.

Jobes, K. H., and M. Silva. *Invitation to the Septuagint*. Grand Rapids: Baker, 2000.

Johnson, E. A., S. A. Ross, and M. C. Hilkert. "Current Theology. Feminist Theology: A Review of Literature." *Theological Studies* 56 (1995): 327–51.

Kaiser, W. C., et al. *Hard Sayings of the Bible*. Downers Grove, InterVarsity, 1996.

Kaiser, W. C., Jr., and M. V. Van Pelt. "מָלֵא." Pages 939–41 in vol. 2 of *New International Dictionary of Old Testament Theology and Exegesis*. Edited by W. A. VanGemeren. 5 vols. Grand Rapids: Zondervan, 1997.

Kaminski, C. M. *From Noah to Israel: Realization of the Primeval Blessing After the Flood*. JSOTSup 413. London: T&T Clark, 2004.

Bibliography

Kedar-Kopfstin. "פָּרָה." Pages 81–91 in vol. 12 of *Theological Dictionary of the Old Testament*. Edited by G. J. Botterweck, H. Ringgren, and H. J. Fabry. 14 vols. Grand Rapids: Zondervan, 2003.

Keel, O., and C. Uehlinger. *God, Goddesses, and Images of God in Ancient Israel*. Translated by T. S. Trapp. Minneapolis: Fortress, 1998.

———. *The Symbolism of the Biblical World: Ancient Near Eastern Iconography and the Book of Psalms*. Translated by T. J. Hallett. Winona Lake: Eisenbrauns, 1997.

Keller, C. A. and G. Wehmeir. "בּרך." Pages 266–82 in vol. 1 of *Theological Lexicon of the Old Testament*. Edited by E. Jenni and C. Westermann. 3 vols. Peabody: Hendrickson, 1997.

Kempf, S. "Genesis 3:14–19: Climax of the Discourse?" *Journal of Translation and Text Linguistics* 6 (1995): 354–77.

Kennedy, J. M. "Peasants in Revolt: Political Allegory in Genesis 2–3." *Journal for the Study of the Old Testament* 47 (1990): 3–14.

Kessler, M. "Rhetorical Criticism of Genesis 7." Pages 1–17 in *Rhetorical Criticism: Essays in Honor of James Muilenberg*. Edited by J. J. Jackson and M. Kessler. Pittsburg: Pickwick, 1974.

Kikawada, I. M. "Noah and the Ark." Pages 1122–31 in vol. 4 of *The Anchor Bible Dictionary*. Edited by D. N. Freedman. 6 vols. New York: Doubleday, 1992.

Kikawada, I. M., and A. Quinn. *Before Abraham Was: The Unity of Genesis 1–11*. Nashville: Abingdon, 1985.

Kitchen, K. A. "The Old Testament in its Context 1." *Theological Student's Fellowship Buletin* 59 (1971): 2–10.

Klein, M. L. *The Fragment-Targums of the Pentateuch According to Their Extant Sources*. 2 vols. Rome: Biblical Institute Press, 1980.

Klein, W., C. Blomberg, and R. Hubbard, Jr. *Introduction to Biblical Interpretation*. Dallas: Word, 1993.

Kline, M. G. *Kingdom Prologue*. Hamilton: Meridith Kline, 1993.

Klingbeil, G. A. "Historical Criticism." Pages 401–20 in *Dictionary of the Old Testament: Pentateuch*. Edited by T. D. Alexander and D. W. Baker. Downers Grove, InterVarsity, 2003.

Köstenberger, A. J. *God, Marriage and Family: Rebuilding the Biblical Foundation*. Wheaton: Crossway, 2004.

Knierim, R. *The Task of Old Testament Theology: Method and Cases*. Grand Rapids: Eerdmans, 1995.

Knight, D. A. "The Pentateuch." Pages 263–96 in *The Old Testament and Modern Study*. Edited by D. A. Knight and G. M. Tucker. Chicago: Scholars, 1985.

Knoppers, G. N. *1 Chronicles 10–29: A New Translation with Introduction and Commentary*. Anchor Bible Commentary. New York: Doubleday, 2004.

———. "Jerusalem at War in Chronicles." Pages 57–76 in *Zion: City of Our God*. Edited by R. S. Hess and G. J. Wenham. Grand Rapids: Eerdmans, 1999.

Knut, H. "The Serpent in Eden As a Symbol of Israel's Political Enemies: A Yahwistic Criticism of the Solomonic Foreign Policy?" *Scandinavian Journal of the Old Testament* 1 (1990): 106–12.

Korpel, M. "Introduction to the Series Pericope." Pages 1–50 in *Delimitation Criticism: Scripture as Written and Read in Antiquity*. Vol. 1. Edited by M. Korpel and J. Oesch. The Netherlands: Van Gorcum, 2000.

Bibliography

Kraus, H-J. *Psalms 1–59*. Translated by H. C. Oswald. Vol. 1. Minneapolis: Fortress Press, 1993.

Kroeze, J. H., J. A. Naudé, and C. H. J. van der Merwe. *A Biblical Hebrew Reference Grammar*. Hebrew 3. Sheffield: Sheffield Academic Press, 1999.

Kruger, H. A. J. "Subscripts to Creation: A Few Exegetical Comments on the Literary Device of Repetition in Genesis 1–11." Pages 429–45 in *Studies in the book of Genesis: Literature, Redaction and History*. Edited by A. Wénin. Paris: Peters, 2001.

Kselman, J. S. "The Book of Genesis: A Decade of Scholarly Research." *Interpretation* 45 (1991): 380–92.

Lambdin, T. O. *Introduction to Biblical* Hebrew. New York: Charles Scribner's Sons, 1971.

Landy, F. "On Metaphor, Play and Nonsense." Pages 219–37 in *Semeia* 61. Women, War, and Metaphor: Language and Society in the Study of the Hebrew Bible. Edited by C. V. Camp and C. R. Fontaine. Atlanta: Scholars, 1993.

LaSor, W. S. "War." Pages 791–92 in *The Oxford Companion to the Bible*. Edited by B. M. Metzger and M. D. Coogan. Oxford: Oxford, 1993.

Lemche, N. P. Prelude to Israel's Past: Background and Beginnings of Israelite History and Identity. Translated by E. F. Maniscalco. Peabody: Hendrickson, 1998.

Lemmelijn, B. "Genesis' Creation Narrative: The Literary Model for the So-Called Plague Tradition?" Pages 407–19 in *Studies in the book of Genesis: Literature, Redaction and History*. Edited by A. Wénin. Paris: Peters, 2001.

Leupold, H. C. *Exposition of Genesis*. Vol. 1. Grand Rapids: Baker, 1942.

Levenson, J. D. *Creation and the Persistence of Evil: The Jewish Drama of Divine Omnipotence*. San Francisco: Harper & Row, 1988.

Levinas, E. "On the Jewish Reading of Scriptures." Pages 17–31 in *Levinas and Biblical Studies*. Edited by T. C. Eskenazi, G. A. Phillips, and D. Jobling. *Semeia Studies* 43. Atlanta: SBL, 2003.

Levine, N. "The Curse and the Blessing: Narrative Discourse Syntax and Literary Form." *Journal for the Study of the Old Testament* 27 (2002): 189–99.

Levison, John R. and P. Pope-Levison, eds. *Return to Babel: Global Perspectives on the Bible*. Louisville: Westminster/John Knox, 1999.

Licht, J. *Storytelling in the Bible*. Jerusalem: Magnus Press, 1978.

Lim, J. T. K. *Grace in the Midst of Judgment: Grappling with Genesis 1–11*. Berlin: de Gruyter, 2002.

Ljungberg, Bo-Krister. "Genre and Form Criticism in Old Testament Exegesis." Pages 415–33 in *Biblical Hebrew and Discourse Linguistics*. Edited by R. D. Bergan. Summer Institute of Linguistics. Winona Lake: Eisenbrauns, 1994.

Loader, W. *The Septuagint, Sexuality, and the New Testament: Case Studies on the Impact of the LXX in Philo and the New Testament*. Grand Rapids: Eerdmans, 2004.

Lohfink, N. "Die Schichten des Pentateuch und der Krieg." In *Gewalt und Gewaltlosigkeit im Alten Testament*. Edited by N. Lohfink. Quaestiones Disputatae 96. Freiburg im Breisgau: Herder, 1983. Repr. "The Strata of the Pentateuch and the Question of War." Pages 173–226 in *Theology of the Pentateuch: Themes of the Priestly Narrative and Deuteronomy*. Minneapolis: Fortress, 1994.

———. *Great Themes from the Old Testament*. Chicago: Franciscan Herald, 1982.

———. "Macht euch die Erde untertan?" *Orientierung* 38 (1974): 137–42. Repr., "'Subdue the Earth?' (Genesis 1:28)." Pages 1–17 in *Theology of the Pentateuch: Themes of the Priestly Narrative and Deuteronomy*. Minneapolis: Fortress, 1994.

Bibliography

———. "The Priestly Narrative and History." Pages 136-72 in *Theology of the Pentateuch: Themes of the Priestly Narrative and Deuteronomy*. Minneapolis: Fortress, 1994.

———. *The Theology of the Pentateuch: Themes of the Priestly Narrative and Deuteronomy*. Minneapolis: Fortress, 1994.

Long, G. A. *Grammatical Concepts 101 for Biblical Hebrew: Learning Biblical Hebrew Grammatical Concepts through English Grammar*. Peabody: Hendrickson, 2002.

Long, V. P. *Art of Biblical History*. Grand Rapids: Zondervan, 1994.

Longacre, R. E. "Discourse Perspective on the Hebrew Verb: Affirmation and Restatement." Pages 77-89 in *Linguistics and Biblical Hebrew*. Edited by W. R. Bodine. Winona Lake: Eisenbrauns, 1992.

———. "The Discourse Structure of the Flood Narrative." *Journal of the American Academy of Religion, Supplement* 47 (1997): 89-133.

Longman III, Tremper. "Divine Warrior." Pages 545-49 in vol. 4 of *New International Dictionary of Old Testament Theology and Exegesis*. Edited by W. A. VanGemeren. 5 vols. Grand Rapids: Zondervan, 1997.

Luc, A. "חָטָא." Pages 87-93 in vol. 2 of *New International Dictionary of Old Testament Theology and Exegesis*. Edited by W. A. VanGemeren. 5 vols. Grand Rapids: Zondervan, 1997.

Lucas, E. C. "Cosmology." Pages 130-39 in *Dictionary of the Old Testament: Pentateuch*. Edited by T. D. Alexander. Downers Grove: InterVarsity, 2003.

Maass, F. "אָדָם." Pages 75-87 in vol. 1 of *Theological Dictionary of the Old Testament*. Edited by G. J. Botterweck and H. Ringgren. 14 vols. Grand Rapids: Eerdmans, 1997.

Machinist, P. "Literature as Politics: The Tukulti-Ninurta Epic and the Bible." *Catholic Biblical Quarterly* 38 (1976): 455-82.

———. "The Voice of the Historian in the Ancient Near Eastern and Mediterranean World." *Interpretation* (2003): 117-37.

Magdalene, F. R. "Bless, Blessing." Page 192 in *Eerdmans Dictionary of the Bible*. Edited by D. N. Freedman. Grand Rapids: Eerdmans, 2000.

Maher, M. *Targum Pseudo-Jonathan: Genesis. Translated, with Introduction and Notes*. Vol. 1B. Collegeville: The Liturgical Press, 1992.

Major, W. and J. O'Brien. *In the Beginning: Creation Myths from Ancient Mesopotamia, Israel and Greece*. Edited by C. Hardwick. Chico: Scholars Press, 1982.

Mann, T. W. *The Book of the Torah: The Narrative Integrity of the Pentateuch*. Atlanta: John Knox, 1988.

Marcos, N. F. *The Septuagint in Context: Introduction to the Greek Versions of the Bible*. Translated by W. G. E. Watson. Leiden: Brill, 2000.

Martens, E. A. "The History of Religion, Biblical Theology, and Exegesis." Pages 177-99 in *Interpreting the Old Testament: A Guide for Exegesis*. Edited by C. C. Broyles. Grand Rapids: Baker, 2001.

Mathews, K. A. "Genesis." Pages 140-46 in *New Dictionary of Biblical Theology*. Edited by T. D. Alexander and Brian S. Rosner. Downers Grove: InterVarsity, 2000.

———. *Genesis 1—11:26*. New American Commentary. Nashville: Broadman and Holman, 1996.

Matthews, R. "Kings and Kingship." Pages 170-71 in *Dictionary of the Ancient Near East*. Edited by Bienkowski, P., and A. Millard. Philadelphia: University of Pennsylvania Press, 2000.

Matthews, V. H., and J. H. Walton. *The IVP Bible Background Commentary: Genesis—Deuteronomy*. Downers Grove: InterVarsity, 1997.

Bibliography

Mathewson, D. B. "A Critical Binarism: Source Criticism and Deconstructive Criticism." *Journal for the Study of the Old Testament* 98 (2002): 3–28.

Mays, J. L. "'Maker of Heaven and Earth': Creation in the Psalms." Pages 75–86 in *God Who Creates: Essays in Honor of W. Sibley Towner*. Edited by W. P. Brown and S. D. McBride, Jr. Grand Rapids: Eerdmans, 2000.

McBride, S. D., Jr. "Divine Protocol: Genesis 1:1—2:3 as Prologue to the Pentateuch." Pages 3–41 in *God Who Creates: Essays in Honor of W. Sibley Towner*. Edited by W. P. Brown and S. D. McBride, Jr. Grand Rapids: Eerdmans, 2000.

McCarthy, D. "Twenty-five Years of Pentateuch Study." Pages 34–57 in *The Biblical Heritage in Modern Catholic Scholarship*. Edited by J. J. Collins and J. D. Crossan. Wilmington: Michael Glazier, 1986.

McConville, J. G. "The Judgment of God in the Old Testament." *Ex auditu* 20 (2004): 25–42.

McFague, S. *Models of God: Theology for an Ecological, Nuclear Age*. Philadelphia: Fortress, 1987.

McKeon, R. *Thought, Action and Passion*. Chicago: University of Chicago, 1954.

McNamara, M., et al. *Targum Neofiti 1: Genesis. Translated, with Apparatus and Notes*. Vol 1A. Collegeville: The Liturgical Press, 1992.

Meek, T. J. "Result and Purpose Clauses in Hebrew." *Jewish Quarterly Review* 46 (1956): 40–43.

Merrill, E. H. "Image of God." Pages 441–45 in *Dictionary of the Old Testament: Pentateuch*. Edited by T. D. Alexander. Downers Grove: InterVarsity, 2003.

Meyers, C. *Discovering Eve: Ancient Israelite Women in Context*. New York: Oxford University Press, 1988.

———. "Eve." Pages 79–82 in *Women in Scripture: A Dictionary of Named and Unnamed Women in the Hebrew Bible, the Apocryphal / Deuterocanonical Books, and the New Testament*. Edited by C. Meyers, T. Craven, and R. S. Kramer. Grand Rapids: Eerdmans, 2000.

———. "Gender Roles and Genesis 3:16 Revisited." In *The Word of the Lord Shall Go Forth: Essays in Honor of David Noel Freedman in Celebration of His Sixtieth Birthday*. Edited by C. Meyers and M. O'Connor. Winona Lake: Eisenbrauns, 1983. Repr. Pages 118–141 in *A Feminist Guide to Genesis*. Edited by A. Brenner. Feminist Companion to the Bible 2. Sheffield: Sheffield Academic Press, 1993.

Midrash Tanhuma-Yelammedenu Genesis. Hoboken: KTAV, 1998.

Milgrom, J. *Leviticus 23–27: A New Translation with Introduction and Commentary*. Anchor Bible 3B. New York: Doubleday, 2001.

Miller, P. D. *Genesis 1–11: Studies in Structure and Theme*. Journal for the Study of the Old Testament, Supplement 8. Sheffield: Sheffield Academic Press, 1978.

———. "The Gift of God: The Deuteronomic Theology of the Land." *Interpretation* 23 (1969): 451–65.

———. *The Religion of Ancient Israel*. Library of Ancient Israel. Louisville: Westminster/John Knox, 2000.

Miller, S. "Discourse Functions of Quotative Frames in Biblical Hebrew Narrative." Pages 155–82 in *Discourse Analysis of Biblical Literature: What It Is and What It Offers*. Edited by W. R. Bodine. Semeia Studies. Atlanta: Scholars, 1995.

Mintz, A. "On the Tel Aviv School of Poetics." *Prooftexts: A Journal of Jewish Literary History* 4 (1984): 215–35.

Bibliography

Mitchell, C. W. *The Meaning of BRK "To Bless" in the Old Testament.* Society of Biblical Literature Dissertation Series 95. Atlanta: Scholars Press, 1987.

Moberly, R. W. L. "Lament." Pages 866–84 in vol. 4 of *New International Dictionary of Old Testament Theology and Exegesis.* Edited by W. A. VanGemeren. 5 vols. Grand Rapids: Zondervan, 1997.

Moo, Douglas. "The Problem of Sensus Plenior." Pages 175–212 in *Hermeneutics, Authority, and Canon.* Edited by D. A. Carson and J. Woodbridge. Grand Rapids: Zondervan, 1986.

Moskala, J. *The Laws of Clean and Unclean Animals of Leviticus 11: Their Nature, Theology, and Rationale (An Intertextual Study).* Adventist Theological Society Dissertation Series 4. Berrien Springs: Adventist Theological Society, 2000.

Mowinckel, S. *The Psalms in Israel's Worship.* Oxford: Basil Blackwell, 1962. Repr., Grand Rapids: Eerdmans, 2004.

Muilenburg, J. "Form Criticism and Beyond." *Journal of Biblical Literature* 88 (1969): 1–18.

———. *The Way of Israel: Biblical Faith and Ethics.* Vol. 5. Edited by R. N. Anshen. New York: Harper & Brothers Publishers, 1961.

Mullen, E. T., Jr. *Ethnic Myths and Pentateuchal Foundations: A New Approach to the Formation of the Pentateuch.* Atlanta: Scholars, 1997.

Müller, H.-P. "פָּחַד." Pages 517–26 in vol. 11 of *Theological Dictionary of the Old Testament.* Edited by G. J. Botterweck, H. Ringgren, and H.-J. Fabry. 14 vols. Grand Rapids: Eerdmans, 2003.

Mulzac, K. "Genesis 9:1–7: Its Theological Connections with the Creation Motif." *Journal of the Adventist Theological Society* 12 (2001): 65–77.

Muraoka, T. *Hebrew/Aramaic Index to the Septuagint.* Grand Rapids: Baker, 1998.

Murphy, J. G. *A Critical and Exegetical Commentary on The Book of Genesis with a New Translation.* Draper, 1868. Repr., Eugene: Wipf and Stock, 1998.

Murphy, T. J. *Pocket Dictionary: For the Study of Biblical Hebrew.* Grand Rapids: InterVarsity, 2003.

Murtonen, A. *Hebrew in Its West Semitic Setting: A Comparative Survey of Non-Masoretic Hebrew Dialects and Traditions*, Part One: A Comparative Lexicon (Leiden: Brill, 1989), 111.

Nahmanides. *The Commentary of Nahmanides on Genesis Chapters 1—6:8.* Pretoria Oriental Series. Translated by J. Newman. Edited by A. Van Selms. Leiden: Brill, 1960.

Nel, P. J. "רָדָה." Pages 1055–56 in vol. 3 of *The New International Dictionary of Old Testament Theology and Exegesis.* Edited by W. A. VanGemeren. 5 vols. Grand Rapids: Zondervan, 1997.

Neusner, J. *Genesis Rabbah: The Judaic Commentary to the Book of Genesis. A New American Translation.* Vol. 1. Atlanta: Scholars, 1985.

Niccacci, A. "Analysis of Biblical Narrative." Pages 175–98 in *Biblical Hebrew and Discourse Linguistics.* Edited by R. D. Bergan. Summer Institute of Linguistics. Winona Lake: Eisenbrauns, 1994.

———. "On the Hebrew Verbal System." Pages 117–37 in *Biblical Hebrew and Discourse Linguistics.* Edited by R. D. Bergan. Summer Institute of Linguistics. Winona Lake: Eisenbrauns, 1994.

Bibliography

Nicholson, E. W. "The Pentateuch in Recent Research: A Time for Caution." Pages 10-21 in *Congress Volume Leuven 1989*. Edited by J. A. Emerton. Supplement to Vetus Testamentum 43. Netherlands: E. J. Brill, 1991.

———. *The Pentateuch in the Twentieth Century: The Legacy of Julius Wellhausen*. Oxford: Clarendon, 1998.

Niditch, S. *Ancient Israelite Religion*. Oxford/New York: Oxford University Press, 1997.

———. *Chaos to Cosmos: Studies in Biblical Patterns of Creation*. Atlanta: Scholars, 1985.

Niehaus, J. J. *God at Sinai: Covenant and Theophany in the Bible and Ancient Near East*. Grand Rapids: Zondervan, 1995.

O'Brien, P. T. "Was Paul Converted?" Pages 361-91 in volume 2 of *Justification and Variegated Nomism: A Fresh Appraisal of Paul and Second Temple Judaism*. 2 vols. Edited by D. A. Carson, P. T. O'Brien, and M. A. Seifrid. Grand Rapids: Baker, 2004.

Osborne, G. *The Hermeneutical Spiral: A Comprehensive Introduction to Biblical Interpretation*. Downers Grove: InterVarsity, 1991.

Oswalt, J. "כָּבֵד." *TWOT*. Page 430 in vol. 1 of *Theological Wordbook of the Old Testament*. Edited by R. L. Harris, et al. 2 vols. Chicago: Moody, 1980.

———. "Theology of the Pentateuch." Pages 845-49 in *Dictionary of the Old Testament: Pentateuch*. Edited by T. D. Alexander and D. W. Baker. Downers Grove: InterVarsity, 2003.

Park, C. *Caring for Creation: A Christian Way Forward*. Hammersmith, London: Marshall Pickering, 1992.

Pate, C. M. et al. *The Story of Israel: A Biblical Theology*. Downers Grove: InterVarsity, 2005.

Paul, M. J. "Adam and Eve." Pages 359-62 in vol. 4 of *New International Dictionary of Old Testament Theology and Exegesis*. Edited by W. A. VanGemeren. 5 vols. Grand Rapids: Zondervan, 1997.

Peckham, B. "Writing and Editing." Pages 364-86 in *Fortunate the Eyes That See: Essays in Honor of David Noel Freedman in Celebration of His Seventieth Birthday*. Edited by A. B. Beck, A. H. Bartlet, P. R. Raabe, and C. A. Franke. Grand Rapids: Eerdmans, 1995.

Penchansky, D. "God the Monster: Fantasy in the Garden of Eden." Pages 43-60 in *The Monstrous and the Unspeakable: The Bible as Fantastic Literature*. Edited by A. George and T. Pippin. Playing the Texts 1. Sheffield: Sheffield Academic Press, 1998.

Perdue, Leo G. *The Collapse of History: Reconstructing Old Testament Theology*. Minneapolis: Fortress, 1994.

Petersen, D. L. "The Formation of the Pentateuch." Pages 31-45 in *Old Testament Interpretation: Past, Present, and Future: Essays in Honor of Gene M. Tucker*. Edited by J. L. Mays, D. L. Peterson, and K. H. Richards. Nashville: Abingdon, 1995.

Pfeiffer, R. H. *Introduction to the Old Testament*. New York: Harper and Brothers, 1941.

Philips, A. "Animals and Torah." Pages 127-38 in *Essays on Biblical Law*. Edited by D. J. A. Clines and P. R. Davies. Sheffield: Sheffield Academic Press, 2002.

Pietersma, A. *A New English Translation of the Septuagint: And Other Greek Translations Traditionally Included Under That Title: The Psalms*. Oxford: Oxford University Press, 2000.

Pixley, J. *Biblical Israel: A People's History*. Minneapolis: Fortress, 1992.

Plantiga, C., Jr. *Not the Way It's Supposed to Be: A Breviary of Sin*. Grand Rapids: Eerdmans, 1995.

Polak, F. H. "Poetic Style and Parallelism in the Creation Account (Genesis 1:1—2:3)." Pages 2-31 in *Creation in Jewish and Christian Tradition*. Edited by H. G. Reventlow and

Bibliography

Y. Hoffman. Journal for the Study of the Old Testament, Supplement 319. Sheffield: Sheffield Academic Press, 2002.

Polzin, R. "'The Ancestress of Israel in Danger' in Danger." *Semeia* 3 (1975): 82–83.

Poole, S. C. *An Introduction to Linguistics*. New York: St. Martin's Press, 1999.

Preuss, H. D. "יָצָא." Pages 225–50 in vol. 6 of *Theological Dictionary of the Old Testament*. Edited by G. J. Botterweck and H. Ringgren. 14 vols. Grand Rapids: Eerdmans, 1990.

———. "נוּחַ." Pages 277–86 in vol. 9 of *Theological Dictionary of the Old Testament*. Edited by G. J. Botterweck, H. Ringgren, and H.-J. Fabry. 14 vols. Grand Rapids: Eerdmans, 1998.

Propp, W. H. C. *Exodus 1–18*. Anchor Bible 2A. New York: Doubleday, 1998.

———. *Water in the Wilderness: A Biblical Motif and Its Mythological Background*. Harvard Semitic Monographs 40. Atlanta: Scholars, 1987.

Radday, Y. T. et al. *Genesis: An Authorship Study in Computer Assisted Statistical Linguistics*. Analecta Biblica 103. Rome: Biblical Institute Press, 1985.

Räisänen, H., E. Schüssler Fiorenza, R. S. Sugirtharajah, K. Stendahl, and J. Barr. *Reading the Bible in the Global Village: Helsinki*. Atlanta: SBL, 2000.

Ramsey, G. "Is Name-Giving an Act of Domination in Genesis 2:23 and Elsewhere?" *Catholic Biblical Quarterly* 50 (1988): 24–35.

Reed, S. A. "Human Dominion Over Animals." Pages 328–48 in *Reading the Hebrew Bible for a New Millennium: Form Concept, and Theological Perspective*. Vol 1 of Theological and Hermeneutical Studies. Edited by W. Kim, D. Ellens, M. Floyd, and M. A. Sweeney. Harrisburg, PA: Trinity Press, 2000.

Reichenbach, B. R. "Genesis 1 as a Theological-Political Narrative of Kingdom Establishment." *Bulletin for Biblical Research* 13 (2003): 47–69.

Rendsburg, G. *The Redaction of Genesis*. Winona Lake: Eisenbrauns, 1986.

Rendtorff, R. "Covenant as a Structuring Concept in Genesis and Exodus." *Journal of Biblical Literature* 108 (1989): 385–93.

———. "Creation and Redemption in the Torah." Pages 311–20 in *The Blackwell Companion to the Hebrew Bible*. Edited by L. G. Perdue. Oxford: Blackwell, 2005.

———. "The Paradigm is Changing: Hopes and Fears." *Biblical Interpretation* 1 (1993), 34–53.

———. *The Problem of the Process of Transmission in the Pentateuch*. Translated by J. J. Scullion. Journal for the Study of the Old Testament, Supplement 89. Sheffield: Sheffield Academic Press, 1990.

———. "The 'Yahwist' as Theologian? The Dilemma of Pentateuchal Criticism." Pages 15–23 in *The Pentateuch*. Edited by J. W. Rogerson, Today's Biblical Studies 39. Sheffield: Sheffield Academic Press, 1996.

Reventlow, H. G. "Creation as a Topic in Biblical Theology." Pages 153–71 in *Creation in Jewish and Christian Tradition*. Edited by H. G. Reventlow and Y. Hoffman. Journal for the Study of the Old Testament, Supplement 319. Sheffield: Sheffield Academic Press, 2002.

Richards, A. *The Philosophy of Rhetoric*. New York: Oxford University Press, 1936.

Richards, K. H. "Bless/Blessing." Pages 753–55 in vol. 1 of *The Anchor Bible Dictionary*. Edited by D. N. Freedman. 6 vols. New York: Doubleday, 1992.

Richardson, A. "Work." Pages 285–87 in *A Theological Word Book of the Bible*. Edited by A. Richardson. New York: Macmillan, 1962.

Ricoeur, P. *Interpretation Theory: Discourse and the Surplus of Meaning*. Fort Worth: Texas Christian University Press, 1976.

Bibliography

Ringgren, H. "עָבַד." Pages 376–90 in vol. 10 of *Theological Dictionary of the Old Testament*. Edited by G. J. Botterweck, H. Ringgren, and H.-J. Fabry. 14 vols. Grand Rapids: Eerdmans, 1986.

Roberts, J. J. "In Defense of the Monarchy: The Contribution of Israelite Kingship to Biblical Theology." Pages 377–96 in *Ancient Israelite Religion: Essays in Honor of Frank M. Cross*. Edited by P. D. Miller. Philadelphia: Fortress, 1987.

Rodriguez, M. "Ancient Near Eastern Parallels to the Bible and the Question of Revelation and Inspiration." *Journal of the Adventist Theological Society* 12 (2001): 43–64.

Rofé, A. *Introduction to the Composition of the Pentateuch*. Sheffield: Sheffield Academic Press, 1999.

Rogerson, J. W. *Genesis 1–11*. Old Testament Guides. Edited by N. R. Whybray. Sheffield: Sheffield Academic Press, 1991.

Rogerson, J. W. "Old Testament Ethics." Pages 116–37 in *Text in Context: Essays by Members of the Society for Old Testament Study*. Edited by A. D. H. Mayes. Oxford: Oxford University Press, 2000.

Rose, W. H. "Messiah." Pages 565–68 in *Dictionary of the Old Testament: Pentateuch*. Edited by T. D. Alexander and D. W. Baker. Downers Grove: InterVarsity, 2003.

Ross, A. *Creation and Blessing: A Guide to the Study and Exposition of Genesis*. Grand Rapids: Baker, 1988.

Rosten, L. *The Joys of Yiddish*. New York: McGraw-Hill, 1968.

Sailhamer, J. H. "Biblical Theology and the Composition of the Hebrew Bible." Pages 25–37 in *Biblical Theology: Retrospect and Prospect*. Edited by S. Hafemann. Downers Grove: InterVarsity, 2002.

―――. "The Canonical Approach to the Old Testament: Its Effect on Understanding Prophecy." *Journal of the Evangelical Theological Society* 30 (1987): 307–15.

―――. "Creation, Genesis 1–11, and the Canon." *Bulletin for Biblical Research* 10 (2000): 89–106.

―――. *Genesis*. The Expositor's Bible Commentary. Edited by F. E. Gaebelein. Grand Rapids: Zondervan, 1990.

―――. "Genesis 1 as a Theological-Political Narrative of the Kingdom Establishment." *Bulletin for Biblical Research* (2003): 47–69.

―――. "Hosea 11:1 and Matthew 2:15." *Westminster Theological Journal* 63 (2001): 87–96.

―――. *An Introduction to Old Testament Theology: A Canonical Approach*. Grand Rapids: Zondervan, 1995.

―――. "The Land and the Blessing." Pages 87–96 in *Genesis Unbound: A Provocative New Look at the Creation Account*. Sisters: Multnomah Books, 1996.

―――. "The Messiah and the Hebrew Bible." *Journal of the Evangelical Theological Society* 44 (2001): 5–23.

―――. *The Pentateuch as Narrative*. Grand Rapids: Zondervan, 1992.

Sanders, J. A. *Canon and Community*. Philadelphia: Fortress, 1984.

Sanders, S. L. "Performative Utterances and Divine Language in Ugaritic." *Journal of Near Eastern Studies* 63 (2004): 161–81.

Sarna, N. M. "The Anticipatory Use of Information as a Literary Feature of the Genesis Narratives." Pages 211–20 in *Studies in Biblical Interpretation*. Philadelphia: JPS, 2000.

―――. *Genesis*. JPS Torah Commentary. 1. Philadelphia: JPS, 1989.

Bibliography

Scharbert, J. "בָּרַךְ." Pages 279–308 in vol. 2 of *Theological Dictionary of the Old Testament*. Edited by G. J. Botterweck and H. Ringgren. 14 vols. Grand Rapids: Eerdmans, 1999.

Scherman, N. *The Chumash: Bereishis*. Brooklyn: Mesorah Publications, 2002.

Scherman, N., and M. Zlotoqitz, eds. *Bereishis/Genesis: A New Translation with a Commentary Anthologized from Talmudic, Midrashic and Rabbinic Sources*. Vol. 1. New York: Mesorah Publishers, 2002.

Schmid, H. H. "In Search of New Approaches in Pentateuchal Research." Pages 24–32 in *The Pentateuch*. Edited by J. W. Rogerson. Today's Biblical Studies 39. Sheffield: Sheffield Academic Press, 1996.

Schmitt, J. J. "Like Eve, Like Adam: *mšl* in Gen 3,16." *Biblica* 72 (1991): 1–22.

Schöckel, L. S. *A Manual of Hebrew Poetics*. Subsidia biblica 11. Rome: Pontifical Institute, 1988.

Schüle, A. "Made in the 'Image of God': The Concepts of Divine Images in Gen 1–3." *Zeitschrift für die Alttestamentliche Wissenschaft* 117 (2005): 1–20.

Schultz, R. L. "What Is 'Canonical' About a Canonical Biblical Theology." Pages 83–99 in *Biblical Theology: Retrospect and Prospect*. Edited by S. Hafemann. Downers Grove: InterVarsity, 2002.

Schultz, S. J. "Interpreting the Pentateuch." Pages 21–38 in *The Literature and Meaning of Scripture*. Edited by M. A. Inch and C. H. Bullock. Grand Rapids: Baker, 1981.

Seitz, C. R. "Biblical Authority in the Late Twentieth Century." Pages 83–101 in *Word Without End: The Old Testament as Abiding Theological Witness*. Grand Rapids: Eerdmans, 1998.

Shapiro, S. E. "'And God Created Woman': Reading the Bible Otherwise," in T. C. Eskenazi, G. A. Phillips, and D. Jobling, eds., *Levinas and Biblical Studies*, Semeia Studies 43. Atlanta: SBL, 2003. 159–95.

Sheppard, G. T. "Theology and the Book of Psalms." *Interpretation* 46 (1992): 143–55.

Sheriffs, D. "'Personhood' in the Old Testament? Who's Asking?" *Evangelical Quarterly* 77 (2005): 13–34.

Silva, M. *Has the Church Misread the Bible? Foundations of Contemporary Interpretation*. Grand Rapids: Zondervan, 1987.

———. "The New Testament Use of the Old Testament: Text, Form, and Authority." Pages 147–72 in *Scripture and Truth*. Edited by D. Carson and J. Woodbridge. Grand Rapids: Zondervan, 1992.

Simkins, R. A. "Worldview," in *Eerdmans Dictionary of the Bible*. Edited by D. N. Freedman. Grand Rapids: Eerdmans, 2000, 1387–89.

Sinclair, D. "Procreation." In *The Oxford Dictionary of the Jewish Religion*. Edited by R. J. Z. Werblowsky and G. Wigoder. Oxford: Oxford University Press, 1997.

Singer, M. A. "How the Bible Has Been Interpreted in Jewish Tradition." Pages 65–82 in *The New Interpreter's Bible*. Vol. 1. Nashville: Abingdon, 1994.

Skinner, J. *Genesis: A Critical Commentary*. International Critical Commentary. Edited by S. R. Driver, A. Plummer, and C. A. Briggs. Edinburgh: T&T Clark, 2000.

Smith, G. V. "Structure and Purpose in Genesis 1–11." *Journal of the Evangelical Theological Society* 20 (1977): 307–19.

Snijders, A. "מָלֵא." Pages 297–308 in vol. 8 of *Theological Dictionary of the Old Testament*. Edited by G. J. Botterweck, H. Ringgren, and H.-J. Fabry. 14 vols. Grand Rapids: Eerdmans, 1997.

Bibliography

Soggin, J. A. "The Equality of Humankind from the Perspective of the Creation Stories in Genesis 1:26–30 and 2:9, 15,18–24." *Journal of Northwest Semitic Languages* 23 (1997): 21–33.

Soulen, R. N. "Rhetorical Criticism." Pages 169–170 in *Handbook of Biblical Criticism*. 2nd ed. Atlanta: John Knox, 1981.

Speiser, E. A. *Genesis*. Anchor Bible 1. Garden City: Doubleday, 1980.

Stadelmann, L. I. J. *The Hebrew Conception of the World*. Rome: Pontifical Biblical Institute Press, 1970.

Stahl, N. *Law and Liminality in the Bible*. Journal for the Study of the Old Testament, Supplement 202. Sheffield: Sheffield Academic Press, 1995.

Stassen, G. H., and D. P. Gushee. *Kingdom Ethics: Following Jesus in Contemporary Context*. Downers Grove: InterVarsity, 2003.

Steiner, V. J. "Literary Structure of the Pentateuch." Pages 544–56 in *Dictionary of the Old Testament: Pentateuch*. Edited by T. D. Alexander and D. W. Baker. Downers Grove: InterVarsity, 2003.

Stendebach, F. J. "צֶלֶם." Pages 386–96 in vol. 12 of *Theological Dictionary of the Old Testament*. Edited by G. J. Botterweck, H. Ringgren, and H.-J. Fabry. 14 vols. Grand Rapids: Eerdmans, 2003.

Stern, P. "Torah." Pages 747–48 in *The Oxford Companion to the Bible*. Edited by B. M. Metzger and M. D. Coogan. Oxford: Oxford, 1993.

Sternberg, M. *The Poetics of Biblical Narrative: Ideological Literature and the Drama of Reading*. Bloomington: Indiana University Press, 1985.

Stiver, D. R. *Theology After Ricoeur: New Directions in Hermeneutical Theology*. Louisville: Westminster/John Knox, 2002.

Stratton, B. J. *Out of Eden: A Feminist, Theological Study of Reading, Rhetoric, and Ideology in Genesis 2–3*. Journal for the Study of the Old Testament, Supplement 208. Sheffield: Sheffield Academic Press, 1995.

Stuart, D. *Old Testament Exegesis: A Handbook for Students and Pastors*. 3rd ed. Louisville: Westminster/John Knox, 2001.

Sugirtharajah, R. S. ed., *Voices from the Margin: Interpreting the Bible in the Third World*. 2nd ed. Maryknoll: Orbis/SPCK, 1995.

The Talmud of the Land of Israel: A Preliminary Translation and Explanation. Vol. 21. Translated by N. Neusner. Chicago: University of Chicago Press, 1987.

Tate, M. E. "An Exposition of Psalm 8." *Perspectives in Religious Studies* 28 (2001): 343–59.

Taylor, R. A. "Form Criticism." Pages 336–43 in *Dictionary of the Old Testament: Pentateuch*. Edited by T. D. Alexander and D. W. Baker. Downers Grove: InterVarsity, 2003.

Thiselton, Anthony C. *New Horizons in Hermeneutics*. Grand Rapids: Zondervan, 1997.

Thomas, R. "The New Testament Use of the Old Testament." *The Master's Seminary Journal* (2002): 79–98.

Thompson, T. L. "How Yahweh Became God: Exodus 3 and 6 and the Heart of the Pentateuch." Journal for the Study of the Old Testament, Supplement 68 (1995): 57–74.

———. "Kingship and the Wrath of God: Or Teaching Humility." *Revue Biblique* 109 (2002): 161–196.

Tigay, J. H. "The Evolution of the Pentateuchal Narratives in the Light of the Evolution of the *Gilgamesh Epic*." Pages 21–52 in *Empirical Models for Biblical Criticism*. Philadelphia: University of Pennsylvania Press, 1985.

Bibliography

───. "What Is Man That You Have Been Mindful of Him" (On Psalm 8:4-5)." Pages 170-71 in *Love and Death in the Ancient Near East: Essays in Honor of Marvin H. Pope*. Edited by J. H. Marks and R. M. Good. Guilford: Four Quarters, 1987.

Tomasino, A. J. "History Repeats Itself: The 'Fall' and Noah's Drunkenness." *Vetus Testamentum* 62 (1992): 128-30.

Tov, Emanuel. *The Greek and Hebrew Bible: Collected Essays on the Septuagint*. Leiden: Brill, 1999.

───. "The Septuagint." Pages 161-88 in *Mikra: Text, Translation, Reading and Interpretation of the Hebrew Bible in Ancient Judaism and Early Christianity*. Edited by M. J. Mulder. Van Gorcum: Assen/Maastricht, 1990.

───. *Textual Criticism of the Hebrew Bible*. Minneapolis: Fortress, 2001.

Towner, W. S. *Genesis*. Louisville: Westminster John Knox, 2001.

Trible, P. *God and The Rhetoric of Sexuality*. Philadelphia: Fortress, 1978.

───. *Method, and the Book of Jonah*. Edited by G. M. Tucker. Guides to Biblical Scholarship. Minneapolis: Fortress, 1994.

───. *Texts of Terror: Literary-Feminist Readings of Biblical Narratives*. Overtures to Biblical Theology. Minneapolis: Fortress, 1984.

Tsumura, D. T. "Genesis and Ancient Near Eastern Stories of Creation and Flood: An Introduction." Pages 27-57 in *"I Studied Inscriptions from Before the Flood:" Ancient Near Eastern, Literary, and Linguistic Approaches to Genesis 1-11*. Edited by R. S. Hess and D. T. Tsumura. Winona Lake: Eisenbrauns, 1994.

Tuell, S. "The Rivers of Paradise: Ezekiel 47:1-12 and Genesis 2:10-14." Pages 171-89 in *God Who Creates: Essays in Honor of W. Sibley Towner*. Edited by W. P. Brown and S. D. McBride, Jr. Grand Rapids: Eerdmans, 2000.

Tull, P. K. "Rhetorical Criticism and Intertextuality." Pages 156-80 in *To Each Its Own Meaning: Biblical Criticisms and Their Application*. Edited by S. L. McKenzie and S. R. Haynes. Rev. ed. Louisville: Westminster/John Knox, 1999.

Turner, L. A. *Genesis*. Sheffield: Sheffield Academic Press, 2000.

Urbrock, W. J. "Blessings and Curses." Pages 755-61 in vol. 1 of *The Anchor Bible Dictionary*. Edited by D. N. Freedman. 6 vols. New York: Doubleday, 1992.

Vaage, L. E., ed. *Subversive Scriptures: Revolutionary Readings of the Christian Bible in Latin America*. Valley Forge: Trinity Press, 1997.

Van Hecke, P. "Shepherds and Linguists: A Cognitive-Linguistic Approach to the Metaphor 'God is Shepherd' in Gen 48:15 and Context." Pages 478-493 in *Studies in the Book of Genesis: Literature, Redaction and History*. Edited by A. Wénin. Paris: Peeters, 2001.

Vanhoozer, K. *First Theology: God, Scripture, and Hermeneutics*. Downers Grove: InterVarsity, 2002.

───. *Is There Meaning in This Text? The Bible, the Reader, and the Morality of Literary Knowledge*. Grand Rapids: Zondervan, 1998.

───. "Language, Literature, Hermeneutics and Biblical Theology." Pages 11-47 in *A Guide to Old Testament Theology and Exegesis*. Edited by W. A. VanGemeren. Downers Grove: InterVarsity, 2002.

Van Leeuwen. "Form, Image." Pages 643-44 in vol. 4 of *New International Dictionary of Old Testament Theology and Exegesis*. Edited by W. A. VanGemeren. 5 vols. Grand Rapids: Zondervan, 1997.

Van Seters, J. *Abraham in History and Tradition*. New Haven: Yale University Press, 1990.

───. "The Creation of Man and the Creation of the King." *Zeitschrift für die Alttestamentliche Wissenschaft* 101 (1989): 333-42.

Bibliography

Vanoni, M. "שִׂים." Pages 89–112 in vol. 14 of *Theological Dictionary of the Old Testament*. Edited by G. H. Botterweck, H. Ringgren, and H.-J. Fabry. 14 vols. Grand Rapids: Eerdmans, 2004.

van Seters, J. *The Pentateuch: A Social Science Commentary*. Trajectories 1. Sheffield: Sheffield Academic Press, 1999.

van Wolde, E. J. "Man and Woman in the Garden of Eden." Pages 13–31 in *Words Become Worlds: Semantic Studies of Genesis 1–11*. Leiden: Brill, 1994.

———. "Rhetorical, Linguistic and Literary Features in Genesis 1." Pages 134–51 in *Literary Structure and Rhetorical Strategies in the Hebrew Bible*. Edited by L. J. de Regt, J. de Waard, and J. P. Fokkelman. Winona Lake: Eisenbrauns, 1996.

Vawter, B. *On Genesis: A New Reading*. Garden City: Doubleday, 1977.

Vervenne, M. "Genesis 1:1—2:4: The Compositional Texture of the Priestly Overture to the Pentateuch." Pages 35–79 in *Studies in the Book of Genesis: Literature, Redaction and History*. Edited by A. Wénin. Paris: Peeters, 2001.

Visotzky, B. L. "Hermeneutics, Early Rabbinic." Pages 154–55 in vol. 3 of *The Anchor Bible Dictionary*. Edited by D. N. Freedman. 6 vols. New York: Doubleday, 1992.

Viviano, P. A. "Source Criticism." Pages 29–51 in *To Each Its Own Meaning: Biblical Criticisms and Their Application*. Edited by S. L. McKenzie and S. R. Haynes. Rev. ed. Louisville: Westminster/John Knox, 1999.

Voelz, J. W. *What Does This Mean? Principles of Biblical Interpretation in the Post-Modern World*. 2nd ed. Saint Louis: Concordia, 1997.

von Rad, Gerhard. *Genesis*. Old Testament Library. Rev. ed. Philadelphia: Westminster, 1972.

———. *Holy War in Ancient Israel*. Translated by M. J. Dawn. Eugene, OR: Wipf and Stock, 2000.

———. *The Problem of the Hexateuch and Other Essays*. Translated by E. W. Trueman Dicken. New York: McGraw and Hill, 1966.

Waaler, Erik. "A Revised Date for Pentateuchal Texts? Evidence from Ketef Hinnom." *Tyndale Bulletin* 53 (2002): 29–55.

Wagner, M. "כָּבַשׁ." Pages 52–57 in vol. 7 of *Theological Dictionary of the Old Testament*. Edited by G. H. Botterweck, H. Ringgren, and H.-J. Fabry. 14 vols. Grand Rapids: Eerdmans, 1995.

Wallace, H. N. "Adam." Pages 62–64 in vol. 1 of *The Anchor Bible Dictionary*. Edited by D. N. Freedman. 6 vols. New York: Doubleday, 1992.

Walsh, J. T. "Genesis 2:4b—3:24: A Synchronic Approach." Pages 362–82 in *"I Studied Inscriptions from Before the Flood": Ancient Near Eastern, Literary, and Linguistic Approaches to Genesis 1–11*. Sources for Biblical and Theological Study 4. Winona Lake: Eisenbrauns, 1994.

———. *Style and Structure in Biblical Hebrew Narrative*. Collegeville: Liturgical, 2001.

Waltke, B. K. "A Canonical Approach to the Psalms." Pages 3–18 in *Tradition and Testament: Essays in Honor of Charles Lee Feinberg*. Edited by J. S. Feinberg and P. D. Feinberg. Chicago: Moody, 1981.

———. *Genesis: A Commentary*. Grand Rapids: Zondervan, 2001.

Walton, J. H. *Ancient Israelite Literature in Its Cultural Context: A Survey of Parallels Between Biblical and Ancient Near Eastern Texts*. Library of Biblical Interpretation. Grand Rapids: Zondervan, 1990.

———. *Genesis*. New International Version Application Commentary. Grand Rapids: Zondervan, 2001.

Bibliography

———. "Inspired Subjectivity and Hermeneutical Objectivity." *The Master's Seminary Journal* (2002): 65–77.

Warning, Wilfried. "Terminological Patterns and the First Word of the Bible: ‏(ב)ראשית‎ '(In The) Beginning.'" *Tyndale Bulletin* 52 (2001): 267–74.

Webster's 3rd New International Dictionary. Springfield: Merriam-Webster, 1993.

Weinfeld, M. *Deuteronomy and the Deuteronomic School*. Winona Lake: Eisenbrauns, 1992.

———. "Deuteronomy, Book of." Pages 168–83 in vol. 2 of *The Anchor Bible Dictionary*. Edited by D. N. Freedman. 6 vols. New York: Doubleday, 1992.

Wellhausen, Julius. *The Composition of the Hexateuch and the Historical Books of the Old Testament*. 3rd ed. Berlin: Georg Reimer, 1899.

———. *Introduction to the History of Israel*. Edinburgh: Adam & Charles Black, 1878; reprinted *Prolegomena to the History of Ancient Israel* (Eugene, OR: Wipf & Stock, 2003).

———. *Prolegomena to the History of Ancient Israel*. Eugene, OR: Wipf & Stock, 2003.

Wells, M. J. "Figural Representation and Canonical Unity." Pages 111–25 in *Biblical Theology: Retrospect and Prospect*. Edited by S. Hafemann. Downers Grove: InterVarsity, 2002.

Wenham, G. "The Coherence of the Flood Narrative." *Vetus Testamentum* 28 (1978): 336–48.

———. "Composition of the Pentateuch." Pages 159–85 in *Exploring the Old Testament: A Guide to the Pentateuch*. Vol. 1. Downers Grove: InterVarsity, 2003.

———. "The Face at the Bottom of the Well: Hidden Agendas of the Pentateuchal Commentator." Pages 185–209 in *He Swore an Oath: Biblical Themes from Genesis 12–50*. Edited by R. S. Hess, P. E. Satterthwaite, and G. J. Wenham. Cambridge: Cambridge University Press, 1993.

———. *Genesis 1–15*. Word Biblical Commentary. Waco: Word Books, 1987.

———. *Genesis 16–50*. Word Biblical Commentary. Waco: Word Books, 1994.

———. "Genesis: An Authorship Study and Current Pentateuchal Criticism." *Journal for the Study of the Old Testament* 42 (1988): 3–18.

———, et al, ed. *New Bible Commentary: 21st Century Edition*. Downers Grove: InterVarsity, 1994.

———. "Pentateuchal Studies Today." *Themelios* 22 (1996): 3–13.

———. "Pondering the Pentateuch: The Search for a New Paradigm." Pages 16–44 in *The Face of Old Testament Studies: A Survey of Contemporary Approaches*. Grand Rapids: Baker, 1999.

———. "Sanctuary Symbolism in the Garden of Eden Story." *Proceedings of the Ninth World Congress of Jewish Studies* 9 (1986): 19–25.

———. *Story as Torah: Reading Old Testament Narrative Ethically*. Grand Rapids: Baker, 2004.

West, G. O. and M. W. Dube, eds. *The Bible in Africa: Transactions, Trajectories and Trends*. Leiden: Brill, 2001.

Westcott, B. F. *The Gospel According to St. John: The Authorized Version with Introduction and Notes*. Cambridge: Cambridge, 1881. Repr., Grand Rapids: Eerdmans, 1971.

Westermann, C. "אָדָם." Pages 31–42 in vol. 1 of *Theological Lexicon of the Old Testament*. Edited by E. Jenni and C. Westermann. 3 vols. Peabody: Hendrickson.

———. "Genealogies." Pages 243–45 in *The Oxford Companion to the Bible*. Edited by B. M. Metzger and M. D. Coogan. Oxford: Oxford, 1993.

Bibliography

———. Neukirchener Verlag, 1974. Repr., *Genesis 1–11: A Commentary*. Translated by J. J. Scullion. Minneapolis: Augsburg, 1984.

Wevers, J. *Notes on the Greek Text of Genesis*. Atlanta: Scholars, 1993.

———. *Notes on the Greek Text of Numbers*. Atlanta: Scholars, 1998.

White, H. C. *Narration and Discourse in the Book of Genesis*. Cambridge: Cambridge University Press, 1991.

Whitekettle, R. "Rats are Like Snakes, and Hares Are Like Goats: A Study in Israelite Land Animal Taxonomy." *Biblica* 82 (2001): 345–62.

———. "Where the Wild Things Are: Primary Level Taxa in Israelite Zoological Thought." *Journal for the Study of the Old Testament* 93 (2001): 17–37.

Whitelam. "King." Pages 40–48 in vol. 4 of *The Anchor Bible Dictionary*. Edited by D. N. Freedman. 6 vols. New York: Doubleday, 1992.

Whybray, R. N. *The Good Life in the Old Testament*. London: T&T Clark, 2002.

———. *Introduction to the Pentateuch*. Grand Rapids: Eerdmans, 1995.

———. *The Making of the Pentateuch: A Methodological Study*. Journal for the Study of the Old Testament, Supplement 53. Sheffield: Sheffield Academic Press, 1987.

Wildberger, H. "צֶלֶם." Pages 1080–85 in vol. 3 of *Theological Lexicon of the Old Testament*. Edited by E. Jenni and C. Westermann. 3 vols. Peabody: Hendrickson.

Wilfong, M. M. "Human Creation in Canonical Context: Genesis 1:26–31 and Beyond." Pages 42–52 in *God Who Creates: Essays in Honor of W. Sibley Towner*. Edited by W. P. Brown and S. D. McBride, Jr. Grand Rapids: Eerdmans, 2000.

Williamson, P. R. "Covenant." Pages 139–55 in *Dictionary of the Old Testament: Pentateuch*. Edited by T. D. Alexander and D. W. Baker. Downers Grove: InterVarsity, 2003.

Wilson, G. H. *Psalms*. Vol. 1. *New International Version Application Commentary*. Grand Rapids: Zondervan, 2002.

———. "Psalms and Psalter: Paradigm for Biblical Theology." Pages 100–110 in *Biblical Theology: Retrospect and Prospect*. Edited by S. Hafemann. Downers Grove: InterVarsity Press, 2002.

Wilson, V. M. *Divine Symmetries: The Art of Biblical Rhetoric*. New York: University Press of America, 1997.

Wold, D. *Out of Order*. Grand Rapids: Baker, 1998.

Wolff, H. W. "The Interpretation of the Old Testament." *Interpretation* 25 (1957): 439–472.

Wright, N. T. *The Climax of the Covenant: Christ and the Law in Pauline Theology*. Minneapolis: Fortress, 1992.

———. *The Resurrection of the Son of God*. Vol. 3. Minneapolis: Fortress, 2003.

Wynn-Williams, D. J. *The State of the Pentateuch: A Comparison of the Approaches of M. Noth and E. Blum*. Beihefte zur Zeitschrift für die alttestamentliche Wissenschaft 249. Berlin/New York: de Gruyter, 1997.

Yee, G. A. "Gender, Class, and the Social-Scientific Study of Genesis 2–3." Pages 177–92 in *The Social World of the Hebrew Bible: Twenty-Five Years of the Social Sciences in the Academy*. Edited by R. A. Simkins and S. L. Cook. Semeia 87. Atlanta: SBL, 1999.

Yehuda, E. B. "ברך." Pages 330–32 in vol. 1 of *A Dictionary & Thesaurus of the Hebrew Language*. New York: Sagamore Press, 1960.

Yon, M. "Ugarit." Pages 695–21 in vol. 6 of *The Anchor Bible Dictionary*. Translation by S. Rosoff, D. Pardee and P. Bordreuil. Edited by D. N. Freedman. 6 vols. New York: Doubleday, 1992.

Zobel, H.-J. "רָדָה." Pages 330–36 in vol. 13 of *Theological Dictionary of the Old Testament*. Edited by G. H. Botterweck, H. Ringgren, and H.-J. Fabry. 14 vols. Grand Rapids: Eerdmans, 2004.

www.ingramcontent.com/pod-product-compliance
Lightning Source LLC
Chambersburg PA
CBHW050435240426
43661CB00055B/2385